Global Studies

A Review Text

Authors:

John Osborne
North Salem High School
North Salem, New York

Sue Ann Kime
Arlington High School
LaGrangeville, New York

Regina O'Donnell
New York Archdiocesan Schools
Cardinal Spellman High School, Bronx, NY

Editors:

Wayne Garnsey and Paul Stich
Wappingers Central Schools
Wappingers Falls, New York

Cover Design, Illustrations, and Artwork:

Eugene B. Fairbanks
John Jay High School
Hopewell Junction, New York

N & N Publishing Company, Inc.
18 Montgomery Street   Middletown, New York 10940
(914) 342 - 1677

Dedicated to our students, with the sincere hope that

Global Studies — A Review Text

will further enhance their education and better prepare them
with an appreciation and understanding of the people
and historical events that have shaped our world.

Special Credits

Thanks to the many teachers who have contributed their knowledge, skills,
and years of experience to the making of our Review Text.

To these educators, our sincere thanks
for their assistance in the preparation of this manuscript:

Cindy Fairbanks
Kenneth Garnsey
Bonnie Kieffer
Virginia Page
Patrick Ryan
Victor Salamone
Gloria Tonkinson

Special thanks to our understanding families.

Global Studies — A Review Text has been produced on the Macintosh II and LaserMax 1000.

MacWrite II by Claris and *Canvas* by Deneba were used to produce text, graphics, and illustrations. Original line drawings were reproduced with *VersaScan* on a Microtek MSF-300ZS scanner and modified with *DeskPaint* by Zedcor. The format, special designs, graphic incorporation, and page layout were accomplished with *Ready set Go!* by Manhattan Graphics.

Special technical assistance was provided by Frank Valenza and Len Genesee of *Computer Productions*, Newburgh, New York.

To all, thank you for your excellent software, hardware, and technical support.

Printed in the United States of America

Revised
3/1/94

SAN # 216-4221   **ISBN # 0935487-35-2**
7 8 9 0 BMP 0 9 8 7 6 5 4

Table of Contents

Introductory Unit .... Page 7

Unit One: Africa .... Page 12

I.   The Physical/Historic Setting 14
II.   The Dynamics of Change 24
III.   Contemporary African Nations 30
IV.   Economic Development 42
V.   Africa in the Global Context.. 49

Unit Two: South & Southeast Asia .... Page 54

I.   The Physical/Historic Setting 56
II.   The Dynamics of Change 64
III.   Contemporary South and Southeast Asian Nations 70
IV.   Economic Development 81
V.   South and Southeast Asia in the Global Context 88

Unit Three: East Asia .... Page 92

I.   China: The Physical/Historic Setting 94
II.   China: The Dynamics of Change 102
III.   Contemporary China 109
IV.   China's Economic Development 114
V.   China in the Global Context... 119
VI.   Japan: The Physical/Historic Setting 125
VII.   Japan: The Dynamics of Change 133
VIII. Contemporary Japan 141
IX.   Japan's Economic Development 144
X.   Japan in the Context 148

Unit Four: Latin America .... Page 152

I.   The Physical/Historic Setting 154
II.   The Dynamics of Change 163
III.   Contemporary Latin American Nations 169
IV.   Economic Development 176
V.   Latin America in the Global Context 181

Unit Five: The Middle East .... Page 186

I.   The Physical/Historic Setting 188
II.   The Dynamics of Change 199
III.   Contemporary Middle Eastern Nations 209
IV.   Economic Development 218
V.   The Middle East in the Global Context 222

Unit Six: **Western Europe** ....Page 228
   I.   The Physical /Historic Setting 230
   II.   The Dynamics of Change 243
   III.   Contemporary Western European Nations 269
   IV.   Economic Development 282
   V.   Western Europe in the Global Context 288

Unit Seven: **Russia, Eastern Europe,**
              and Central Asia ....Page 296
   I.   The Physical /Historic Setting 298
   II.   The Dynamics of Change 306
   III.   Contemporary Russia, Eastern European and
        Central Asian Nations 320
   IV.   Economic Development 335
   V.   Russia, Eastern European and
        Central Asian Nations in the Global Context 340

Unit Eight: **The World Today** ....Page 347
   I.   Population Pressures 348
   II.   Economic Development 350
   III.   Political Power Structures 351
   IV.   Environmental Issues 353
   V.   Human Rights 356
   VI.   Technology 357
   VII. Interaction of Cultures 360

Appendices..Page 366
   I.   Global Concepts Chart 366
   II.   World Issues Chart 369
   III.   Glossary and Index 370
   IV.   Examination Strategies 406
   V.   Practice Exams with Answers and Explanations 417

How To Use This Book

Global Studies - A Review Text has been designed to assist you in understanding the events of the past and present. It provides basic information about the topics found in Global Studies.

The Global Studies course emphasizes fifteen (15) key *Global Concepts* and eleven (11) *World Issues*. Since these items are central to the course and examination, you should focus your attention on them.

To help you in your study, this review book uses special icons to indicate when the concepts and issues are being discussed.

The Fifteen Key Concepts Are:

Change   Environment   Interdependence
Choice   Justice
Citizenship      Political Systems
Culture   **Human Rights**   Power
Diversity   Scarcity
Empathy   Technology
                    Identity

The Eleven World Issues Are:

Terrorism
Population
War and Peace
Human Rights
Hunger and Poverty
World Trade and Finance
Environmental Concerns
Political and Economic Refugees
Economic Growth and Development
Determination of Political and Economic Systems

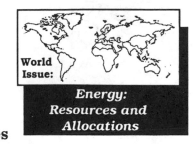

World Issue: Energy: Resources and Allocations

Explanations and selected examples of these concepts and issues, along with suggested procedures for a year-end review, are contained in appendices at the end of the book.

Success In Review

It is suggested that you use the following procedures to prepare for the Global Studies examination:

1.   _**Look**_ at each Unit divider. Review your understanding of how the illustrations, the list of terms, and the events on the time-line are related.

2.   _**Read**_ each section of the Unit material. _Answer_ all the drill questions that follow. Obtain the correct answers from your teacher.

3.   _**Re-read**_ the section and _re-answer_ the questions missed the first time. (All questions are based on the style and format of recent state examinations.)

4.   _**Use the glossary**_ to check the terms and concepts used on state examinations. List the terms of which you're unsure. Look them up in the appropriate section and _write out_ a definition and example.

5.   _**Review**_ the "Test Strategies" section, then take the practice examination at the end of the book. Check the answers with your teacher. Concentrate your efforts on re-reading the text sections and glossary terms on which you did not do well.

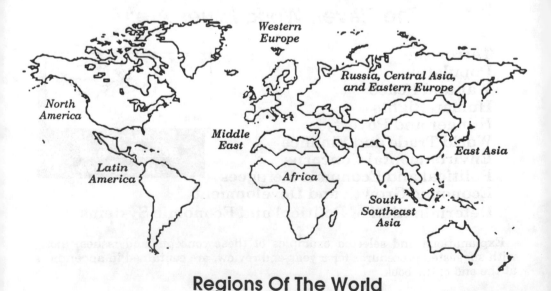

Regions Of The World

Introduction To Global Studies

Our Interdependent World

Most students (or adults, for that matter) that live in the United States know very little about the people and countries of other regions on this Earth. Because Americans have close business, educational, diplomatic, and tourist ties throughout the world, it is imperative that we should know these people better, and learn to appreciate their achievements, concerns, and needs. There is a definite need to establish cross-cultural connections.

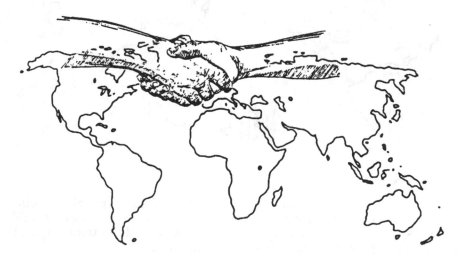

The Physical World

By examining a global regions' historic, political, social, and economic development, we observe that human needs are similar but that differences in **environment** (the setting in which people live) contribute to unique cultural identities.

The study of global regions should help the student understand that all peoples have made contributions to world cultures. Our course will study the following regions: *Africa, South Southeast Asia, East Asia, Latin America, Middle East, Western Europe,* and *Russia, Eastern Europe, and Central Asia.*

Maps And Their Uses

Maps are critical in understanding our global environment. They portray some of the reasons for the differences among people. It would be wise to review the maps on the pages of this section to note the regions, their respective sizes, and major features. Throughout the book, regional maps will provide a closer look at each of the regions.

It is important to note that maps have many uses, and provide a wide variety of information: landscape and water-forms (**topographical maps**), climate, vegetation, population distribution (**demographic maps**), and political boundaries. Also, it is wise to note that maps have limitations, and one should always be on the alert for distortions.

Relative distances on our globe have begun to shrink through numerous transportation and communication advances in modern technology. This has produced more interaction of the world's people, and caused a more **interdependent** world. People's lives depend on their knowledge of resources of other regions.

Regions

A **region** is defined as an area with some common physical, political, economic, and/or cultural features. A region could be as small as a neighborhood or as large as a subcontinent. Regions provide definitions for units of study which help us build our knowledge of the world.

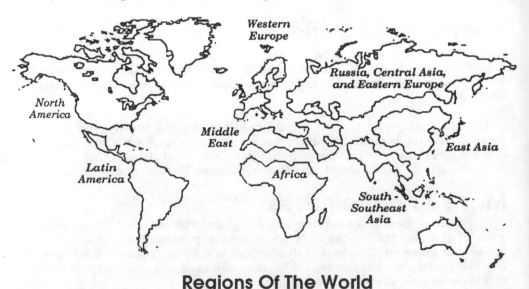

Regions Of The World

Each of the seven global regions used in this course has a variety of characteristics, and can be further divided into sub-regions. For each regional study, many factors have influenced its current status. Throughout this review book, the emphasis has been placed on the impact of **environment** on the culture, distribution, and movements of people.

Climate is a much more important environmental factor than most Americans realize. In each of the world regions, climate is a key factor in shaping the culture and progress people have made throughout history. Geographers know that climate is a complex area of study. We will use an adaptation of the standard climate classification system by Wladimir Koeppen.

Climate Classifications*

A - Tropical Rainy Climates:

Af - Highland, wet all year

Aw - even amount of wet and dry

Am - tropical and humid

B - Dry Climates:

Bs - steppe (or savanna), low, but even rainfall (Continental Steppe)

Bw - hot with low rainfall (Continental Desert)

C - Mid - Latitude Rainy Climates:
(cold winter)

Cs - Mediterranean, even wet and dry

Cw - wet and dry, mild winter

Cf - rainy, mild winter

D - Mid - Latitude Wet And Dry Climates:
(cold winter)

Dw - wet and dry, cold winter (Humid Subtropical)

Df - rainy, cold winter (Humid)

E - Polar Climates

ET - Tundra

EF - Ice Cap

* based on the system devised by:
Austrian geographer Wladimir Koeppen

Culture And Regions

The Meaning Of Culture

It is also extremely important to realize the impact on a region of past events as well as its resources. As we study each of the seven global regions, one will survey a number of cultures. **Culture** is a term that refers to a people's whole way of living.

The Elements Of Culture

A culture is a way of life. Culture is made up of a number of elements: religion and values, language, history, social organization, customs and traditions, literary and artistic expression, and economic organization.

By observing these elements, we realize that culture is learned rather than inherited, and that every person learns the accepted cultural characteristics from their relatives, peers, and neighbors. Although humans are born into racial groupings, their behavioral habits are practiced according to the ways of their regional culture.

Cultural Diffusion

The movements of people throughout history has caused **cultural diffusion**, an action that occurs when the cultural patterns spread from one group to another.

In our modern world, **technology** and **global interdependence** have increased the speed and extent of cultural diffusion. Often, a new culture is adapted or changed to meet the needs of that group. However, no single culture exists today that has not been affected by cultural diffusion, and the world has increasingly moved toward a global culture.

Studying World Issues

Throughout this global studies program, the following major world issues will be used to illustrate connections among the regions: *War and Peace; Population; Hunger and Poverty; Political and Economic Refugees; Environmental Concerns; Economic Growth and Development; Human Rights; World Trade and Finance; Determination of Political and Economic Systems; Energy Resources and Allocations;* and *Terrorism.*

Any of these issues can be used to illustrate that people live in a world of global interdependence. We cannot view global regions as separate from each other or the rest of the world. A global perspective provides us with a better understanding of our world and its wide variety of peoples and cultures.

Questions

1 Environment refers to the
   1   setting where humans live.
   2   climates of the Earth.
   3   waterways around the globe.
   4   natural resources of a region.

2 A people's way of life is called
   1   values.
   2   survival.
   3   culture.
   4   density.

3 A world political map will show
   1   the Earth's climate.
   2   vegetation regions.
   3   land-forms on the Earth.
   4   national boundaries.

4 One factor that underdeveloped regions of the world have in common is
   1   highly educated populations.
   2   high standards of living.
   3   lack of important resources.
   4   smooth transportation and communications networks.

5 Which might a topographical map of South America reveal?
   1   where the majority of people live
   2   temperatures near the Equator
   3   location of major mountain ranges
   4   patterns of cultural diffusion

Essay

The 20th century has witnessed numerous technological changes which have created greater global interdependence.

Areas of Interdependence

   • Trade   • Defense
   • Health   • Education
   • Economic Development

Choose *three* of the areas listed above and for each one chosen discuss how a recent technological advance has had a positive or negative effect on global interdependence. [5,5,5]

Unit One

Africa

Apartheid
Slave Trade
Imperialism
Subsistence
Exploitation
Pan-Africanism
Cultural Diversity
"Scramble for Africa"

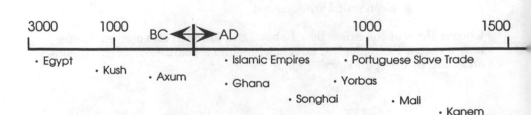

3000	1000	BC ⟷ AD		1000	1500

• Egypt
  • Kush
    • Axum
        • Islamic Empires   • Portuguese Slave Trade
        • Ghana   • Yorbas
            • Songhai   • Mali
                        • Kanem

| 1700 | | 1900 | 1950 | | 1980 | 2000 |

• British in South Africa   • Apartheid Begins   • Nigerian Civil War

• Independence Movements

• European Colonial Scramble

Anti-apartheid •
Movement

Unit One: Africa

I. The Physical/Historical Setting

A close relationship exists between the climate and physical features of Africa and the cultures and economies which developed there.

A. Size And Location Have Made Africa Important In World Affairs

Africa, the second largest continent in land mass, is three times the size of the continental United States. Bisected at the Equator, Africa is bordered on the west by the Atlantic Ocean and on the east by the Indian Ocean. Major waterways to the north and the northeast are the Mediterranean Sea, Suez Canal, and Red Sea. Africa's southernmost land tip is the Cape of Good Hope. Africa's natural resources and exports are most important to the world's economy. Some of these are: petroleum, gold, copper, diamonds, cobalt, cotton, peanuts, coffee, and lumber. From early antiquity, Africa's waterways have been avenues of cultural exchange among civilizations. Merchants from India and Southeast Asia reached East Africa long before the Europeans.

B. Physical And Topographical Features

Environment

Africa was once known as the "Dark Continent" because its interior was unknown and mysterious. Geographic features and the climate worked together to keep Africa an enigma. These factors have limited African development, isolated its interior peoples, and contributed to the development of a vast number of cultures.

Africa possesses sharp delineations between its basins and plateaus. Africa's elevation is higher than that of other continents, nearly 90% of its land is at least 500 feet above sea level. This plateau structure is broken by mountains: the **Atlas Mountains** in the northwest and the **Drakensberg Mountains** in the southeast.

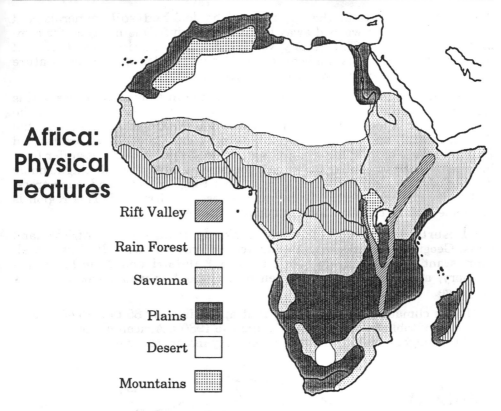

Africa: Physical Features

- Rift Valley
- Rain Forest
- Savanna
- Plains
- Desert
- Mountains

Five basins also interrupt the plateau structure. The largest, the **Zaire** River basin (once called the Congo), is in the center of the continent. North of the Zaire basin are the **Nile, Chad,** and **Niger** river basins. To the south lies the **Kalahari** basin, a huge desert wasteland. The Nile, Niger, and Zaire Rivers drain into the seas.

Also breaking the African plateau is the **Great Rift Valley,** a 3,000 mile long crack in the Earth's surface running along the east coast south from Ethiopia. This great valley has channeled human migration in north-south patterns in East Africa.

The world's largest desert, the **Sahara** (3.2 million square miles), lies across North Africa. Today, it is still mostly uninhabitable. Some tribes continue to survive in a **nomadic** (life-style of constant moving about, seeking food) existence as their wanderings reflect the search for **oases** (small fertile spots with water) for their herds. (One such people are the **Tuareg.**) Beginning in the early centuries A.D., Arab traders crossed this great barrier of desert in search of the products of sub-Saharan Africa.

Geographers determine the type of **climate** of an area by the amount of annual rainfall it receives and by its latitude (distance north or south of the equator). Since most of Africa lies in the tropics, Koeppen's Type A and B climates prevail.

• **Tropical Rainy (Aw),** *"rain-forest,"* climate dominates West Africa and Equatorial Africa. A small amount of rain falls each day, and the average daily temperature is in the 80° range. The **leached soil** (minerals and nutrients have been washed away by constant rainfall) is not good for commercial agriculture. This thickly vegetated area comprises about 15% of Africa's land mass. It is the home of the Pygmy people, whose small stature is indicative of the nutrition this climate provides.

• **Savanna (Bs)** is another climate type found in tropical latitudes and is sometimes called *"Tropical Grassland."* In Africa, it covers about 40% of the continent and is found in the regions bordering the tropical rainy areas: the Sudan, central, and southern regions. Many tribal groups here are labeled **Bantu** because of their linguistic classification. Savanna climates suffer from high temperatures similar to the rain-forest, but have more distinguishable dry periods. Rainfall is sufficient to support rough grasses and some trees. Soil is dry and too infertile for farming unless it is irrigated. This region is big-game "safari" country, home to nomadic hunters.

• **Deserts, semi-deserts (steppes)** make up another 40% of Africa's land mass. Geographers classify their climates as **Tropical Dry (Bw)** (warm all year, scant rainfall only in summer). The **Kalahari** and **Namib**, in this category, are home to the Bushmen and Hottentots who speak the Click language.

Africa's climatic picture indicates that approximately 85 to 90% of its surface is unsuitable for agriculture. During the 1980's, African nations suffered terrible droughts, making hunger and poverty major concerns.

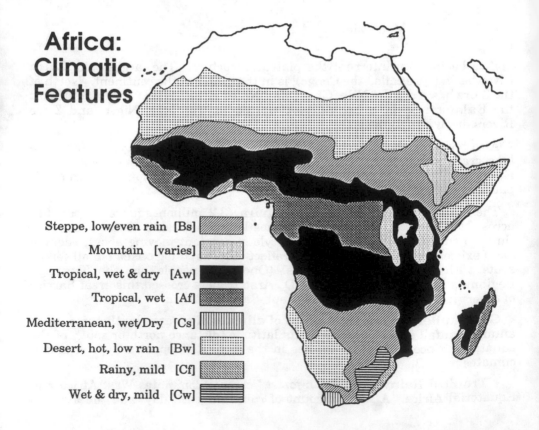

Africa: Climatic Features

Steppe, low/even rain [Bs]

Mountain [varies]

Tropical, wet & dry [Aw]

Tropical, wet [Af]

Mediterranean, wet/Dry [Cs]

Desert, hot, low rain [Bw]

Rainy, mild [Cf]

Wet & dry, mild [Cw]

C. Early Cultural Development And Civilization Of Africa

The history of human existence in Africa seems to go back farther than that of people elsewhere. Until recently, western civilization's awareness of Africa's past was blinded by its definition of history being confined to literate society.

A number of modern historical tools have opened the African past:

- **Archeology.** The study of human existence by means of its physical remains, has given us information as archeologists have studied the pyramids of Egypt and the stone structures of Zimbabwe.

- **Radio-Carbon Dating** is a scientific method of determining the age of dead organic matter by measuring its **Carbon 14** emissions.

- **Oral Traditions** are myths, legends, anecdotes that provided entertainment and education for the young, and preserved traditions.

- **Written Records.** Muslim traders and settlers began to keep records of African civilization in the 9th century A.D.

Anthropology is the study of the origins and development of human culture. Anthropologists have made discoveries in Ethiopia, Kenya, and Tanzania that seem to prove that modern human beings first emerged in Africa. In 1959, in Olduvai Gorge, Tanzania, one of the most famous finds in modern anthropology was made. **Mary Leakey** discovered the 1.75 million-year-old remains of **"Homo Habilis"** (able man). In 1972, **Richard Leakey** found an older skull with a larger brain capacity than Homo Habilis in Kenya. Four human bones, estimated to be over 3 million-years-old were discovered in the region in 1974.

History. African history opens with oral history, tales, and genealogies of tribal chiefs. One important event of pre-literate Africa tells of the fall of the **Hittite Empire** of North Africa in 1200 B.C. and the migrations of its skilled iron-smiths bringing plows, hammers, and swords to peoples to the south.

Myths and legends provide identity and continuity to Africa's past. Much of this literature has now been recorded because it is an important source of information for scholars. It reconstructs **Identity** segments of African history and pictures the African perception of the forces of the world which play upon them. Included are animal tales, myths, legends, proverbs, and episodes from the lives of the people.

Geography and climate have been obstacles to cross-cultural contact. Geographic features have led to the creation of over 800 culturally distinct societies and languages. African geography pro- **Diversity** moted cultural diversity, and this gave rise to distinct early civilizations of importance. **(See Ancient Civilization Chart on the next page.)**

Cultural Patterns of

Civilization	Products	Technology	Region
		Trade	
Kush 2000 BC	iron products, gold, ivory, spices	iron-working center of the ancient world	Egypt, Red Sea, Mediterranean
Axum 300 AD	iron products, gold, ivory, spices	iron-working center of the ancient world	Egypt, Greece, Rome, Semites of Arabia
Ghana 300 AD	salt, gold, slaves	metal weapons, tools, jewelry	across Sahara to North Africa
Zimbabwe 1100 AD	cattle, grains, gold, ivory	metalworking, dry stone building techniques	India and Indonesia
Mali 1200 AD	cattle, grains, gold, ivory, slaves	cloth, Jewelry, metal tools	North Africa, Mediterranean, Arabia
Kongo 1300 AD	slaves	metalwork, pottery, coppersmiths	slave trade with Portugal
Songhai 1400 AD	salt, cattle, gold, slaves	cloth, Jewelry, metal tools	North Africa, Mediterranean, Arabia

D. Barriers To Development: Geography, Vegetation, Absence Of Technology

Although Africans have shown skill and success in adapting crops and animals to their environment, serious limitations still remain:

Scarcity

Scarcity of water resources. Much of Africa's infertile land is due to its climate and lack of capital to expand irrigation efforts.

Limited use of available natural resources. Africans lack technological training, equipment, and surplus capital to develop their various natural resources.

Pervasiveness of insect pests like the **tsetse fly** which carry the "sleeping sickness" and destroys the effectiveness of the horse, oxen, and manpower in sub-Saharan Africa.

Lack of access to markets. Because of falls and rapids, rivers are unfavorable to transportation and communication. Mountains, deserts, and rain-forests are also barriers. In addition, there is a shortage of wheeled vehicles.

Africans rely too heavily on traditional methods of production. Again, technology, equipment, and training compound their problems.

Ancient African Civilizations

Social Units	Religion	Governemnt	Decline
family (reflects Egyptian influence)	blend: Kushite – Egyptian gods	kingdom under devine pharaoh	succeeded by Axum (c. 350 AD)
family (reflects Greek influence)	Coptic rite Christian c. 100 AD	kingdom	evolved into Ethiopia
matrilinial clans & tribes	tribal religions	devine king	Muslim conquest
clans: Bantu people	tribal religions	devine king	European conquest 1660 AD
matrilinial clans & tribes	Muslim	empire divided into provinces	Muslim conquest 1300 AD
clans: Bantu people	Christianity introduced by Portuguese (1480)	elected king, empire divided into provinces	civil wars over slave trace
matrilinial clans & tribes	Muslim	empire divided into provinces	European conquest 1550 AD

E. In Traditional African Tribal Cultures, Religion Was Important In Everyday Life.
Common Traits

African religions are essentially tribal religions, inseparable from traditional social and political order. They vary widely, but have certain basic characteristics:

Ancestor worship. Forebearers are considered a living part of the tribal community.

Reinforcement of family group associations. One's lineage and membership in a clan is important. **Lineage** is the tracing of one's ancestry to a common ancestor. A **clan** is an association of lineages. In traditional African culture, one belongs to a family, the family to a clan, the clan to a tribe, the tribe to a nation. Lineage is important as individuals then associate with others worshiping common ancestors.

Divine Rulers. Chiefs were not merely political rulers, but they were considered lesser gods or priests in charge of ceremonies worshiping ancestral deities. People identified with the special connections their chiefs had to ancestors. This enhanced the powers of the chieftains in social and political matters.

Culture

Early religions shared common divinities. There was a belief in a supreme being who created life and was associated with concepts of good and evil, and had great healing powers. Lesser deities and invisible forces held powers of life and death over mortals.

Ritual ceremonies at birth, puberty, and death were important. The local witch doctor or diviner was thought to control certain supernatural powers. **Charms** and **amulets** offered protection to the individual. Evil acts were to be avoided because they dishonored the lineage.

Rise Of Islam

In the 7th century A.D., **Islam** overcame Christianity (which had been slowly spreading throughout northern Africa), and began to spread across the Sahara with Muslim traders. By the 11th century, the larger West African empires, like **Ghana,** were converted to Islam for the following reasons:

- **Islam's diversity of structure** accommodated many of the practices of traditional African religions allowing it to spread rapidly.

- **Islam influenced the authority structure** of tribal life because it undermined some of the divine power of chiefs and witch doctors.

- **Islam brought increased trade and knowledge** to West Africa. The **Hausa** city-states of the 14th century **Political Systems** and West African Islamic kingdoms like **Mali** became **theocratic.** In a theocracy, religious leaders run the government. The most famous of the Muslim rulers of Mali, **Mansa Musa** (1312-1332), made the fabled city of **Timbuktu** a leading center of Islamic learning and wealth. In the 19th century, the Muslim Fulani tribe of northern Nigeria began a **jihad** (holy war) which ended in their domination of the area. Islam became a powerful force along the southern reaches of the Sahara, but never entered the central or southern areas, except for traders along the east coast.

- In the modern era, there has been a **resurgence of aggressive Islamic missionary activity** which played an important role in the drive of certain African nations for their independence from colonial rule.

Christian Influences

Christianity has also had an ongoing impact on many areas of Africa. In the early Christian era, Greek-influenced **Coptic Christianity** spread rapidly into the upper Nile area of Nubia and gradually into Ethiopia. This area later resisted Islamic conversion while the predominance of the **Roman Christian** church along the Mediterranean coast of Africa was overwhelmed by the Muslims' jihad.

Except for some Portuguese missionary work along the Sub-Saharan coastal regions in the 16th and 17th centuries, southern Africa was not the focus of Christian missionary work until the 19th century. The Christian influence is greatest today in South Africa, Zimbabwe, and Tanzania.

Independent African churches emerged in opposition to European colonial rule. Black churches incorporated Christian missionary teachings with native religious concepts - the movements are sometimes referred to as "Ethiopianism" or " Zionism." (This Christian "Zionism" is not to be confused with the 19th and 20th century nationalistic movement for a Jewish homeland discussed in Unit Five.)

F. Traditional African Art
Forms Of African Art

The forms of African art were strongly influenced by the traditional social structure and tribal religions. The arts were often functional as instruments of social control. Gods were called on to punish wrong-doers and to protect humans, animals, and the environment.

The arts also gave identity to clans, tribes, and families through the medium of body painting and tattooing. Not one African society has been found to be without some form of art. There are three major art forms of sub-Saharan Africa:

• **Visual Arts** include woodcarving, terra cotta figures, metalworking, stone, ivory, and bone carving. Use of gold was limited to leaders. Masks were used in ritual ceremonies. Figurines, sometimes symbolizing ancestors, were used at funeral, fertility, and healing rites. The Benin and Ife bronzes are examples.

• **Music and Dance.** Early paintings from 6000-4000 B.C. depict dancers and men playing instruments. This indicates these art forms have always been a vital part of traditional activities. Instruments included drums, marimba gourds, stringed bows, harps lutes, and whistles. African music is **polyrhythmic,** employing two or more rhythms at once. Hand-clapping supports the dancers. Important events in family and tribal life were usually accompanied by ritual dancing.

• **Architectural Forms** reflected an interplay of natural environment, available technology, and prevailing religious, social, and political institutions. Examples ranged from round mud-huts with cone-shaped thatch roofs to the famous stone fortress-temples of Zimbabwe. Typical tribal homes were built from local materials and reflect the traditional life of the village.

Questions

1 Which problem is common to emerging nations in Africa?
 1 exhaustion of natural resources
 2 interference by the United Nations in internal affairs
 3 continuing oppression by European colonial powers
 4 insufficient numbers of technically trained persons

2 An *archeologist* is a scientist who
 1 studies the physical remains of ancient civilizations.
 2 paints and sculpts ancient humans.
 3 builds stone bridges.
 4 studies the habits of migratory animals.

3 In comparison to the size of the United States, Africa is
 1 smaller.   3 much larger.
 2 about the same size.   4 only slightly larger.

4 In discussing the relationship between humans and their environment, which of the following statements would be valid? The *environment*
 1 limits human actions.
 2 is unimportant in urban areas.
 3 controls humans in rural areas.
 4 can be fully controlled by humans.

5 In which area would nomadic tribes be found?
 1 large cities and suburbs
 2 lands facing water shortages
 3 large tracts of fertile land
 4 major seaports and canals

6 *Heavy rainfall and high temperatures are constant throughout the year in the Zaire Basin.* Which climate does this describe?
 1 Tropical Rainy   3 Tropical Desert
 2 Mediterranean   4 Savanna

7 *Long periods of drought, high temperatures, and grassy vegetation are found in the Sudan.* Which climate does this describe?
 1 Tropical Rainy   3 Tropical Desert
 2 Mediterranean   4 Savanna

8 The soil of Africa may be generally described as
 1 highly productive.
 2 similar to the "Great Plains" of the USA.
 3 too rocky for agriculture.
 4 largely infertile.

9 Africa's tribal cultures are
 1 in close contact with the outside world.
 2 closely related to religion and tradition.
 3 forerunners of capitalistic economies.
 4 forerunners of the Islamic religion.

10 Early African religions resembled modern world religions in the belief in
1 ancestor worship.   3 charms to drive off evil spirits.
2 a creator of the universe.   4 the divinity of the ruler.

11 The absence of which of these presents the greatest barrier to Africa's development?
1 dangerous animals   3 lineage
2 technological knowledge   4 zionism

12 In Sub-Saharan Africa, the introduction of Islam eventually
1 provided uniformity of laws.
2 destroyed tribal religions.
3 isolated cultural growth.
4 stopped communications among tribes and clans.

13 Which aspect of a society would an anthropologist study in depth?
1 development of self-image, causes of insanity
2 family patterns, legends, festivals
3 problems of scarcity, production of goods
4 results of opinion polls

14 Which of these newspaper reports best illustrates a major problem of Africa?
1 *Africa Lacks Deep Water Ports*
2 *African Economy Dependent on Foreign Technology*
3 *Chinese Experience Difficulty with African Transport System*
4 *Rail Travel More Dependable in Africa Than in Asian Countries*

Essays

1 Until recently, Western Civilization was basically unaware of African cultural achievements.

a Identify *two* historical tools which have revealed African history. [4]

b Discuss *three* proofs that Africa enjoyed a varied cultural history before the age of European exploration. [12]

2 Africa suffers from several barriers to development. Select *three* different African nations and discuss how geographic factors and the absence of technology have affected their development. [5,5,5]

II. The Dynamics Of Change

A. Ancient African Kingdoms

- **Kanem - Bornu,** an Islamic state northeast of Lake Chad, was overthrown by the French by the end of the 19th century.
- **Hausaland** (Hausa city-states) was a Saharan Islamic state west of Bornu which was conquered by the Fulani and eventually fell to the British.

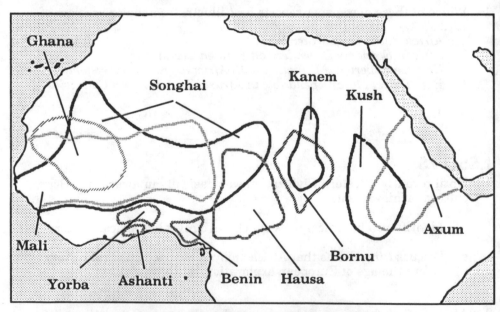
Political Systems

- **Benin, Yorba,** and **Ashanti** disintegrated because of the slave trade and were incorporated into the British colonies of Gold Coast, Togo, and Nigeria.
- **Kongo** (modern Angola) was also destroyed because of the slave trade and fell to the Portuguese.
- **Zimbabwe** was conquered in the 19th century and named Rhodesia after **Cecil Rhodes,** the great "Empire Builder" of British East Africa. Upon independence, the country was renamed Zimbabwe.

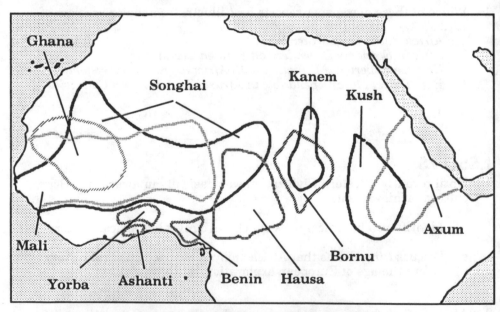

Ghana

Songhai   Kanem   Kush

Mali

Axum

Yorba   Ashanti   Benin   Hausa   Bornu

Ancient African Kingdoms

B. Slavery And The Slave Trade

Slavery has existed since the dawn of humankind. It has been traced from the Roman Empire to ancient China. During the 12th century, Muslim traders began to take captive Africans back to sell in Arab lands. Later traders, whether black, white, or of mixed race, became intensely motivated by monetary rewards.

Slave Trade With The Americas

The trade in slaves increased tremendously by the mid-16th century due to the demands of the agricultural economies of the New World. Slaves were used on the large-scale sugar and tobacco plantations of the Western Hemisphere.

Europeans became highly involved in buying slaves ("black ivory") from the 1500's to the early 1800's. In return for guns, whiskey, and utensils, African chiefs sold prisoners captured in battles with rival tribes. The transactions took place in fortresses along the coast constructed by slavers. The Dutch, Portuguese, Spanish, and English became the major transporters. Their ships dropped survivors for plantation owners in South and Central America, the Caribbean, and the southern colonies of North America.

Traditional African Society Suffered

Social Upheaval. It became the largest and longest forced migration of people in history. Uncounted millions were sold into slavery over three centuries.

Violence. It led to an escalation of violence as once proud kingdoms deteriorated into civil warfare to capture prisoners to be sold to the coastal slavers. Slavers themselves recruited natives to go on raiding parties.

Social Collapse. The intensity of the slave trade caused a collapse of traditional African social and political order. African art, culture, and prosperity were sacrificed as millions of young, healthy individuals were forcibly exiled to other parts of the world. This weakness later encouraged European governments to enter and colonize the region.

Prejudice. The legacy of racial prejudice resulted from slavery as those engaged in the trade searched for justification by instilling a sense of inferiority in their victims. This left a heritage of bitterness in the relationship between the West and Africa.

Political Adjustment. Many African kingdoms fell victim to the political realignments as new sources of wealth and power emerged from the slave trade. As the Hausa Kingdoms fell to the Fulani, old trans-Saharan trade routes deteriorated. West coast states like **Benin, Yorba,** and **Ashanti** rose in the 18th and 19th centuries.

Abolition Of The African Slave Trade

Gradually, the evils of slavery gave rise to an **abolitionist movement** in Western Europe and the United States. Among the forces that produced the anti-slavery drive were an emphasis on the doctrine of the **Natural Rights of Man** and the movement known as **Humanitarianism.** Both grew out of the 18th century **Age of Enlightenment.** Also, a large wave of missionary zeal among Catholics and Protestants at beginning of the 19th century added moral commitment to the movement.

In 1808, the *U.S. Constitution* ended importation of slaves, and in 1833, slavery was abolished in the British Empire. (It would not be abolished in the United States until the 13th Amendment to the Constitution was passed in 1865.) While the slave trade ended officially in West Africa in the early 19th century, an illegal trade continued for a long time.

The abolition of the slave trade seriously disrupted the African economic structure once more. Many tribes and states had become dependent on this source of revenue while neglecting other industries. The economic dislocations of the early 19th century provided an excuse for European nations, needing raw materials for industrialization, to begin the imperialistic development of Africa.

C. Era Of Discovery And Charter Companies

Europe was able to dominate sub-Saharan Africa because of trade and technological superiority.

Trade Rivalries

In the late 15th century, trade rivalries among European states led to a period of exploration followed by the setting up of commercial colonial development by the Dutch, Spanish, Portuguese, English, and French. Political colonies eventually emerged from way stations established by **private charter companies** along sea routes to the Orient. One example was Britain's **Royal Niger Company**.

Imperialism

A second factor in the evolution of the 19th and 20th century wave of European imperialism was the emergence of industrial capitalism. As the 19th century progressed, the factory systems and technical breakthroughs, like the application of steam power, were beginning to create great demand for raw material and markets. Limited resources on the European continent made conquest and exploitation of overseas territories more urgent.

Power

However, movement into interior sections was slow. As late as 1880, Europeans controlled a relatively small area of Africa. The announcement that **Belgium** was officially claiming the vast equatorial region known as the **Congo** (today's Zaire), set off an intense "**Scramble for Africa.**" The Berlin Conference in 1884-85 divided the continent into colonial regions. By 1914, only the nations of **Liberia** and **Ethiopia** remained independent.

Opposition

The "Scramble" for African colonies produced a varied response on the part of Africans themselves.

Violent opposition took place in some areas: Dutch "**Boer**" settlers met fierce resistance from the **Zulu** people in their "**Great Trek**" into the interior of South Africa in 1836, and it took decades before the British broke the power of the **Ashanti** in 1896.

Passive movements were also employed: Indian independence leader Mohandas Gandhi led non-violent protests in South Africa in the 1890's and founded a passive resistance movement which became a model for 20th century nationalist movements.

Cooperation did occur in some areas. Many tribal leaders agreed to become mercenaries in the pay of European conquerors. Also, the British followed an "indirect rule" approach wherein the power of traditional African chiefs was preserved as long as they followed English imperial policies.

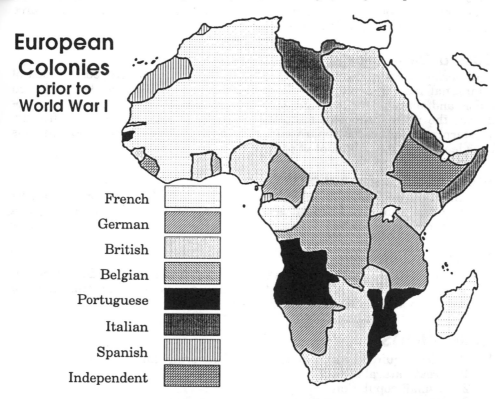

European Colonies
prior to
World War I

French
German
British
Belgian
Portuguese
Italian
Spanish
Independent

D. Effects Of European Rule

The period of European imperialistic dominance caused both a positive and a negative effect on the African continent.

Unifying Influences
The colonial powers altered African political, economic, and linguistic structures by unifying diverse groups into larger entities. Yet, in their partition of the continent, they created new national boundaries, cutting across traditional tribal and clan lines which remain a source of disputes.

Physical Improvements
While Western developments in medical care and nutrition lowered infant mortality rates, they also led to a **population explosion**, which places a strain on African resources today.

Agricultural Changes

Changes in agricultural practices increased production of cash crops need ed in Europe, but eclipsed domestic staple crops, making Africans more dependent on importing food.

Rampant Exploitation

Exploiting natural resources, such as minerals, lumber, and rubber did serious damage to the African economy and ecology. At the same time, improved transportation and communication in the zones of natural resource development opened previously remote areas.

Cultural Destruction

Imperial rule was destructive to African culture. It destroyed the idea of communal land ownership, weakened family and tribal ties, led to forced labor, and abused Africans' rights. While Western political ideas were intro-duced, the white European minorities refused to extend them to Africans. Westernized legal codes separated older combinations of civil and religious laws leading to abandonment of previous legal customs.

Economic Transformations

While the transformation of economic transactions from a barter to a cur-rency system stimulated capital accumulation and trade, it created gaps in wealth and social tensions.

Educational Improvement

Expansion of educational opportunity gave Africans a wider choice of career opportunities, but some of the training was in areas unrelated to African needs and it often downgraded tribal culture.

Questions

1　Colonies acquired by imperialists would generally have
　　1　great natural beauty.
　　2　a small population.
　　3　surplus investment capital.
　　4　good natural resources.

2　Which colonial power controlled the largest area in Africa by 1914?
　　1　France　　　　　　　　　3　Netherlands
　　2　Germany　　　　　　　　4　Spain

3　In the 19th century, which two powers were least concerned with the acquisition of colonial possessions in Africa?
　　1　United States and Russia　　3　England and France
　　2　Belgium and Portugal　　　4　Germany and Italy

4　European colonialism in Africa reached its height during the period just
　　1　prior to the Franco-Prussian War.
　　2　before World War II.
　　3　prior to World War I.
　　4　after World War II.

5 The fundamental cause for the revival of imperialism in the late 19th century was the
1 increase in merchant guilds.
2 outbreak of the French Revolution.
3 expansion of the Industrial Revolution.
4 desire for collective security.

6 In 1914, which two nations controlled the greatest amount of African territory?
1 Germany and Italy   3 Belgium and the Netherlands
2 Portugal and Spain   4 France and Britain

7 Which cause for imperialism has also contributed to its decline?
1 nationalism   3 surplus capital for investment
2 search for markets   4 missionary activity

8 Which two countries expanded their colonial empires as a result of treaty provisions at the end of World War I?
1 Germany and Turkey   3 Austria and Italy
2 England and France   4 Russia and Germany

9 Historians writing about slavery could accurately state that it
1 was first introduced in Europe.
2 was limited to areas of the Western Hemisphere.
3 seems to have existed in some form since earlier times.
4 has been abolished for many centuries in all nations.

10 *We shall not ask England, France, Italy, or Belgium, "Why are you here?" We shall only command them to "Get out!"* The speaker reflects African
1 nationalism.   3 cooperation.
2 imperialism.   4 neutrality.

11 *We must bring the benefits of Western Civilization and Christianity to the less fortunate.* This idea has been used to justify
1 imperialism.   3 socialism.
2 nationalism.   4 feudalism.

12 Which was a major result of European imperialism in sub-Saharan Africa during the late 19th and early 20th centuries?
1 adoption of Islam as the dominant African religion
2 decline of traditional African cultures
3 strengthening of tribal organization
4 beginning of slavery

Essays

1 By 1914, only Liberia and Ethiopia remained independent of European control. Briefly discuss *three* reasons why European nations of the late 19th century became interested in the continent of Africa. [5,5,5]

2 Europe was able to dominate Sub-Saharan Africa due to its technlogical superiority.
  a Discuss *two* ways in which colonies benefited from European imperialism. [6]
  b Discuss *three* ways colonies were harmed by imperialism. [9]

III. Contemporary Nations

In examining contemporary African Nations and their cultures, it is im
portant to understand the effect that European rule had on Africans and
their institutions. It is also important to comprehend the origins, development, and outcome of African nationalism and **Pan-Africanism** (an effort to
promote African unity). We should also see the relationship between free and
non-free persons and societies. Furthermore, there is a mixture today of
traditional and contemporary elements in Africa since a majority of Africans
are still dependent upon a rural-agrarian lifestyle.

African
Nations

Mediterannean
Sea

Algeria   Libya   Egypt

Senegal
Gambia
Mauritania Mali   Niger
Guinea
Bissau
Guinea
Sierra Leone
Liberia
Ivory Coast Ghana
Burkina
Togo
Benin
Cameroon
Equatorial Guinea
Gabon
Congo
Cabinda

Djibouti

Sudan

Chad

Nigeria

Cen. Afr. Rep.

Uganda   Ethiopia

Somalia

Rwanda   Kenya
Burundi   Indian
Tanzania   Ocean
Zaire   Malawi

Angola
Zambia
Zimbabwe
Namibia   Madagasgar
Botswana

Mozambique
Atlantic
Ocean
South   Swaziland
Africa
Lesotho

A. African Nationalism And Pan-Africanism

Full scale colonial rule lasted for less than a century, most of the continent
achieved independence by the mid-1960's.

Initially, African nationalist movements were non-violent, non-racial, and
non-ideological. They placed strong emphasis on human rights and dignity.
The roots of these self-government movements reflected American influences.

Nationalism *is a strong feeling of unity for people who desire to control their own destinies.* In Africa, it had a distinct **anti-imperialist** character (a strong desire for freedom from foreign control). The main demand by early African nationalists was a greater voice in running their own governments.

Nationalist movements were led by an educated elite that had studied in Europe and America. There, they had seen societies where people had human rights unknown in their homelands: the right to vote and hold political office, trial by jury, and freedoms of speech, press, and assembly.

Returning to their homelands, these educated Africans felt humiliated when their European colonial rulers would not accept them as equals. They felt that their only recourse was political action to achieve self government. With slogans like  **Political Systems**

"**Uhuru**" (freedom) and "**Self-government Now**," Africans pushed for their independence. They wished to restore their rights and dignity, and to break down the economic and social discrimination.

The transition from foreign to African leadership varied, but a pattern soon developed whereby nationalist politicians organized political parties. They became looked upon as the emancipators and fathers of their nations. They received great encouragement for their efforts from hundreds of thousands of Africans who had been affected by World War I and World War II.

During World War I, many African villagers were recruited by colonial governments to work the mining and industrial centers. There they were to learn of Western constitutional and electoral policies. By World War II, Africans were serving as troops for the colonial governments and providing necessary raw materials for the Allied Powers. Many Africans were sent overseas and saw what freedom meant to the others. The **Atlantic Charter** (proclaimed by the United States' President Franklin Roosevelt and Great Britain's Prime Minister Winston Churchill in 1941) stated that all people had the right to choose their own form of government.

Haile Salasse
(Ethiopia)

Kwame
Nkrumah
(Ghana)

Mobutu
Sesu Seko
(Zaire)

Jomo Kenyatta
(Kenya)

Julias Nyerere
(Tanzania)

After the war, these ideals were the basis for the **United Nations Charter**. Together, these two documents promoted human rights and self-determination. Many of the Asian nations were given their independence following World War II, but the Africans waited to achieve their independence until the 1950's and 1960's.

In 1957, Britain's Gold Coast colony in West Africa became the first Sub-Saharan colony to be released from European rule. Under its charismatic nationalistic leader **Kwame Nkrumah**, it changed its name to honor the ancient empire of Ghana.

In the next decade, more than 35 African colonies achieved independent nationhood. Most of the independence movements were accomplished without violence, and many followed Ghana's example taking names associated with great African kingdoms of the past.

Political problems in the new nations have occurred because of an erosion in participatory democracy and conflicts between tribal groups within the new nations. For cultural reasons, many villagers have a difficulty shifting allegiance from their traditional tribal units to national governments. At times, this has led to civil war.

New African leaders had difficulty balancing their own nationalistic loyalties with **Pan-Africanism**. Often, conflicts among neighboring countries (such as Kenya and Tanzania in the 1960's and Nigeria and Ghana in the 1980's) created intense national pride, and have made regional and continental unity difficult.

World War II signaled the beginning of the end of colonial rule in Africa. African nationalism brought a shift in political power from the Europeans to a group of Western educated, urban-oriented African leaders. Many of the newly independent African nations were poorly prepared for governing themselves, and many of the leaders failed to maintain the support of their citizens. Numerous **coups d'etat** (military overthrows of the governments) occurred as authoritarian military groups seized power when leaders failed.

Today, most African nations belong to the **Organization for African Unity (OAU)**. It was created in 1963 to help settle disputes and to promote common causes and a common defense of members' independence.

B. Case Studies

In this section, information about four Sub-Saharan African nations will be examined. South Africa, Zaire, Nigeria, and Kenya provide diverse examples of the problems and promises facing the many nations on the African Continent.

The Republic Of South Africa
History Of South Africa

The Dutch established a naval outpost at the Cape of Good Hope in 1652 and their settlers, called **Afrikaners or Boers**, expanded it into the **Cape Colony**. It was captured in 1806, during the Napoleonic Wars, by the British. Wishing to preserve their Dutch culture, thousands of Boers migrated to the interior in the "**Great Trek**" of 1836. The Zulu people were subjugated by the Boers after years of fierce resistance. The Boers set up two independent republics: **Transvaal** and **Orange Free State**.

After the discovery of gold and diamonds in the late-1800's, British settlers began to migrate into the Boer territories, touching off skirmishes. They were encouraged by **Cecil Rhodes**, a British imperialist who wished to see a **Cape-to-Cairo Railroad** linking British territories along Africa's east coast. The result was the **Boer War**, lasting from 1899 to 1902. Following the British victory, the **Union of South Africa** was formed in 1910, and remained a self-governing British Commonwealth until severing ties with England and becoming the independent **Republic of South Africa** in 1961.

Government And Economy Of South Africa

South Africa is a parliamentary republic. It has an administrative capital in **Pretoria** and a legislative capital in **Capetown**. Its economy is one of the most prosperous on the continent. Its principal agricultural products are corn, wheat, citrus fruits, and wool. Its most important natural resources are gold, diamonds, uranium, asbestos, iron ore, and coal.

Racial Problems Of South Africa

One of the nation's key problems is "**apartheid**" (the government policy of total racial separation). When Britain took control of South Africa, it allowed those provisions of the Boer Constitution which permitted segregation to continue. Additional restrictions on the Bantu people were instituted.

World Issues: *Human Rights*

The **Native Land Act** of 1913 forbade them to own land outside reservations. In 1950, the **Groups Area Act** divided 13% of South Africa among ten homelands for the peoples, while the rest of the country was reserved for whites. Up to 1985, the government pursued a policy of forcibly relocating people to these reservations or "homelands."

As far back as 1913, the **African National Congress (ANC)** has fought against racial segregation. Well known leaders against apartheid include Episcopal **Bishop Desmond Tutu** and **Nelson and Winnie Mandela**.

Nelson Mandela became a symbol of defiance while serving a life prison term for leading anti-apartheid demonstrations in 1961. In mid-1989, a new reform government under Prime Minister F. W. de Klerk announced a more conciliatory policy. Early in 1990, de Klerk freed Mandela and legalized the ANC once again.

The Imbalance between "white" and "black" representation in South Africa

World Issues:
World Trade and Finance

Worldwide pressures have been placed on the government as sympathy for the anti-apartheid movement has grown. International corporations doing business in South Africa have received pressure to pull out of the country. A movement of universities and other institutions to **divest** themselves of stocks in these corporations has grown more intense.

The 1990's began on a note of optimism with the lifting of restrictive **Pass Laws**, allowing peaceful protests, the legal recognition of numerous outlawed opposition groups, and the releasing of many black leaders. Under the constitution, 73% of the population are denied voting rights. Blacks could only vote for local leaders of their segregated **Bantustan** homelands. In a 1992 referendum, 68% percent of the white voters agreed to abolish apartheid. In 1994 a new constitution guaranteeing political equality became effective.

Bantustan "Homelands"

Issue Of Namibia

After World War I, administration of the former German colony of South-West Africa was given to the Republic of South Africa. In 1966, the **South-West Africa People's Organization** (**SWAPO**), a communist-influenced group, began a guerrilla war against the South African backed white minority government. In 1968, **United Nations Resolution 435** named the area Namibia and condemned South African efforts to block independence. Steady pressure from the United Nations, the United States, and SWAPO as well as the internal upheaval within South Africa resulted in the formal withdrawal of the South African colonial government in 1990. Namibia became independent after a United Nations supervised election in 1990.

The Republic Of Zaire
History Of Zaire

European conquest began after the mid-1800's. American news correspondent **Henry Stanley** discovered the mouth of the Congo River in 1877, and opened the interior to conquest. Later, acting in service to an independent company headed by **King Leopold II of Belgium**, Stanley returned to make a series of treaties with tribal chiefs which enabled Leopold to announce a **Congo Free State** claiming a vast central African area at the Berlin Conference in 1885. It was this claim that set off the European "**Scramble for Africa**."

King Leopold was ruthless in his exploitation of the Congo. The lands were stripped of their raw materials. He levied a "labor tax" on the chiefs. Under it, they had to turn over a set number of workers every year for forced labor to private companies. The system was known for its excessive cruelty.

Growing criticism of these practices prompted Belgium to take over control of the colony before World War I. With authoritarian rule, there was little preparation of the colony for self-government. After World War II, a nationalist movement gained strength. Violent demonstrations began in the capital which caused many European settlers to leave. Fearing a prolonged and costly struggle, Belgium moved rapidly to grant independence in 1960.

The republic's first democratic election was a shamble. Civil war broke out and U.N. troops were brought in to keep order. A three-way power struggle began among **Moise Tshombe, Joseph Kasavubu,** and **Patrice Lumumba.** Lumumba was removed as Premier and began an opposition movement in the southern provinces. Lumumba was killed in 1961.

Three years later, U.N. troops were withdrawn and Tshombe was elected President. Communist rebels began a slaughter in the South that caused the U.N. to enter the  **Political Systems** country again in 1965. **General Joseph Mobutu** seized control as the rebellion was ended. Mobutu ordered "Africanization" of the country, taking over European-held industries and forcing people to adopt traditional African names. He changed his own name to **Mobutu Sese Seko** and renamed the country Zaire. Since that time, he has ruled as a virtual dictator.

The country has not prospered, and in 1977, the government invited former industrialists to return, but two rather serious invasions by leftist rebels backed by Angola have discouraged resettlement by European businesses.

Government And Economy Of Zaire

Zaire's capital is **Kinshasa**. The country has a one-party republican form of government dominated by a strong executive. Its principal agricultural products are coffee, palm oil, manioc, sugar, cotton, cocoa, and bananas. Zaire is a land rich in mineral resources and its major economic activities revolve around mining and processing them. Chief among these minerals are: cobalt (60% of the world's known supply), copper, zinc, industrial diamonds, tin, gold, silver, iron, and coal.

The Federal Republic Of Nigeria

History Of Nigeria

Nigeria has a rich history which dates back to the **Nok** culture (c. 700 B.C.), and included the advanced Mali and Songhai Empires from the 12th to the 14th centuries when Muslim influence prevailed throughout its northern region. Portuguese and British slaves worked the coastal areas in the 15th and 16th centuries.

By the 18th century, the British controlled the slave trade in Nigeria, and seized Lagos in 1861. Most of Nigeria came under firm British colonial rule by the early 1900's as the former Muslim regions in the north were consolidated into an artificial administrative unit. Nigeria was carefully prepared for independence as the British acknowledged local self-rule after World War I, and a central government was created at Lagos to administer a federated nation. In 1960, Nigeria was granted independence and it became a member of the **British Commonwealth of Nations**.

The Nigerian Constitution guarantees respect for political, religious, and cultural differences among its many ethnic (tribal) groups. However, open hostility developed in the mid-1960's. Two coups and a series of political assassinations brought Nigeria to the brink of civil war.

 Power In May 1967, the Eastern region dominated by the **Ibo** people seceded from the federation and declared itself the **Republic of Biafra**. A civil war erupted which lasted 2½ years with hundreds of thousands of the Ibos losing their lives from fighting and famine. The Ibo people finally surrendered in January 1970. The national government promised protection and restoration of political rights for all people.

In the 1970's, Nigeria developed an economic policy geared to controlling its industrial, banking, and commercial interests, as well as to make the nation agriculturally self-sufficient. In 1979, the nation peacefully returned to civilian rule with a new constitution and competing political parties.

In 1983, another military coup d'etat took place; however, the nation has continued the policy of modified socialism.

Nigeria has the largest population in Africa with over 100 million. It continues to rely on its oil revenues for its economic and social improvements. Much of its overseas business is with the United States. Nigeria is one of the few African nations to protest the communist nations' military advisors present in Africa. Today, Nigeria seeks to promote African unity and opposition to South Africa's apartheid policy.

Economy Of Nigeria

While Nigeria produces a variety of agricultural products from cacao to cotton and palm oil, petroleum has become the mainstay of its economy. (Most of the petroleum is traded to the United States and Britain.) Nigeria's major problem is its rapid population growth. (Current projections indicate it will reach 500 million by 2030.) Soil erosion, lack of productivity, desertification in the north, and a foreign trade tied to a questionable oil commodity all make the economic future look bleak for Nigeria.

The Republic Of Kenya
History Of Kenya

Maritime city-states existed as early as the eighth century in Kenya at **Faza** and **Mombasa** on the Indian Ocean and conducted a spice and slave trade with the Arab world. In the colonial movement that occurred in the late 19th century in Africa, Kenya came under the rule of Great Britain. The British were very interested in developing the highland region with its rich agricultural farmland and pleasant climate, and by the end of World War II, there were over 30,000 British settlers in this region.

Kenya's largest tribal group, the **Kikuyu**, resented this intrusion and organized a secret society to spread terrorism against the white farmers. Known to British settlers as the **Mau Mau**, the society's tactics were bloody and brutal in their attempt to regain their lost lands. This became the core of a strong nationalist independence movement. In over a decade, more than 12,000 people were killed before resistance was broken in 1956.

The leader and hero of this nationalist movement among the Kikuyu was **Jomo Kenyatta**. He was jailed by the British for allegedly organizing the Mau Mau. Kenyatta denied these charges to the day he died.

By 1961, Kenyatta had been released from prison, and Britain agreed to majority rule by black Kenyans.

In 1963, Kenya was granted its independence and Kenyatta became the nation's first President. Under his leadership, European ownership of land and Indian control of commerce was phased out, and black Kenyans filled these positions. Kenyatta's power declined before his death in 1978. At first, President Daniel Moi's regime allowed political freedom, but then began to use the military to silence opposition.

Economy Of Kenya

Kenya's capital is **Nairobi,** a city of over one million people in the cooler western highland region of the nation. Kenya's economy is primarily agricultural. Coffee, tea, cotton, and sisal are exported to the rest of the world. There are limited amounts of natural resource: gold, limestone, sapphires, garnets, salt, and feldspar. Other economic resources include: timber, hides, beef and lamb production, fishing, light industry, and tourism. Kenya has close economic ties to Western nations through its membership in the Commonwealth.

C. Western Impact On Cultural And Social Institutions

The cultural impact of the Western World on Africa has been significant in the latter half of the twentieth century as witnessed in the numerous changes in African lifestyles and world views. Also, European and American ethnocentrism (proclaiming one's own race or culture as superior) alienated many Africans and caused them to search for their own heritage and to develop their own unique cultural identity.

The development of large towns and urban centers has lured Africans away from their tribal villages, and has weakened traditional **lineage** and **kinship** bonds. As Africans change and adapt to new ways, a transitional period occurs when people question the usefulness of the new ideas and institutions. The new ideas of nationalism and politics, technology, medicine and religion pressure today's urban African to relinquish his former tribal ways. This has often created conflicts between the generations as these new attitudes cause the young to re-examine and often discard former tribal traditions. **Extended families** (three or more generations under one roof) are no longer the norm in the towns and cities as the **nuclear family** (mother, father, and children) has replaced this traditional clan structure.

When an African couple practices family planning and limits themselves to only one or two children, the lineage bond is weakened and the power of tribal chiefs is diminished. Also, the traditional practice of **polygamy** (having two or more wives) has declined in popularity since World War I, and **monogamy** is more widely practiced in the urban areas.

The changing role of women in today's African urban centers is very evident in their social and economic lives. About 25% of modern African women, predominantly in urban areas are involved politically while continuing to raise families and manage households.

African women often pursue careers in medicine, education, law, and technology. Even though some of the rural village women, especially among the Muslims, lead lives that are still centered at home, many African women are assuming roles of equality in modern Africa.

The urban centers are the hubs of government and industry. **Technology** They are also the centers of significant change in Africa. People in these cities are continually influenced by world views through trade and telecommunications. As new generations of Africans are born and grow up in urban centers, their education and experiences pull them further from the traditional tribal ways. The modern-day urban African is more interested in personal career, national, and international events than the lifestyles of his ancestors in the tribal villages.

D. African Life In Transition

African life is in transition, yet the rural areas continue to retain their traditional values with fierce loyalty to the council of elders and their chief. These are the areas where subsistence agriculture is still widely practiced and where family members learn to work together for the good of the whole group. If the harvest is good or bad, the food is shared equally within the tribal group.

Children are taught the importance of the family by sharing in the care of younger children, or the elderly, and are taught farming, fishing, herding, or trade skills. Initiation ceremonies with elaborate rituals signal the end of childhood and the beginning of their adulthood. This has strengthened the tribal bond.

Women have an important role in the tribal tradition, and young girls have marriages that are pre-arranged by their families. Women work in the fields besides sharing motherhood and household chores, and generally have assumed the roles of perpetuating the next generation in the lineage system.

But new attitudes and values are clashing with traditional tribal practices and modern technology has found its way to the rural areas. With increased education, better communication (TV, radio, movies, and news media), and continual influence from the outside world, traditional practices will come under closer scrutiny.

World Issues:
Economic Growth and Development

How rapidly these new attitudes and values will be accepted, or which ones will be assimilated and/or culturally diffused into a new African lifestyle remains to be seen.

Questions

1   Which individual is correctly paired with the colonial area with which he was associated?
  1   Joseph Mobutu — Nigeria   3   Cecil Rhodes — Zaire
  2   King Leopold — Transvaal   4   Henry Stanley — Congo

2   The policy of apartheid in South Africa was
  1   imposed by the British after World War II.
  2   advocated by the descendents of the Dutch.
  3   proposed by Bantu leaders.
  4   introduced by communists.

3   A nuclear family consists of
  1   the bride, groom, and in-laws.
  2   father, mother, and children.
  3   several generations living under one roof.
  4   all the people of the tribe.

4   Once the scene of a brutal war between the British and Boer settlers, which country now suffers from violent civil strife over racial inequality?
  1   Zimbabwe   3   Republic of South Africa
  2   Nigeria   4   Zaire

5   The custom of African men having two or more wives is called
  1   monogamy.   3   polygamy.
  2   nepotism.   4   ethnocentrism.

6   The Commonwealth of Nations is best defined as an association
  1   strictly for defense.
  2   strictly for free trade.
  3   of possessions owing allegiance to the crown.
  4   of sovereign nations.

7   Early African nationalist leaders were looked upon by their peoples as
  1   terrorists.   3   social discriminators.
  2   emancipators.   4   traditionalists.

8   The United Nations Charter helped promote nationhood for the former African colonies because it supported
  1   self-determination.   3   colonialism.
  2   tribal religion.   4   imperialism.

9   The first Sub-Saharan African colony to achieve independence after World War II was
  1   Nigeria.   3   Zaire.
  2   Kenya.   4   Ghana.

10   The most heavily populated nation in Africa today is
  1   South Africa.   3   Nigeria.
  2   Zaire.   4   Kenya.

11 Tribal initiation ceremonies commonly occur
   1   at marriage.
   2   between childhood and adulthood.
   3   when a child is born.
   4   when an elder makes a major decision.

12 In the 1960's, U.N. forces were twice brought into this nation suffering from a violent civil war.
   1   Zaire
   2   Kenya
   3   Republic of South Africa
   4   Orange Free State

13 Which situation is most similar to the practice of apartheid in the Republic of South Africa?
   1   establishment of official state religions in Europe
   2   economic oppression bringing about the American Revolution
   3   government censorship of the press in communist nations
   4   segregation laws in southern states in the U.S. (1860's -1960's)

Essays

1   Imperialism of the 19th century set the stage for continuing conflict in the 20th century. Describe how *three* of the following have affected African nations after European colonial rule ended. [5,5,5]

   - tribal ties
   - nationalism
   - race relations
   - Pan-Africanism
   - the (British) Commonwealth of Nations
   - coups d'etat
   - urbanization
   - technology
   - the United Nations

2   The dramatic pace of urbanization in Africa in the last half of the 20th century has caused African life to change significantly.

Aspects of African Life

   - status of women
   - agriculture
   - religion
   - tribalism
   - education

Choose *three* of the aspects of African life listed above. For *each* one chosen describe how it has been affected by urbanization. [5,5,5]

IV. Economic Development

Though most African nations have achieved political independence, many obstacles remain for the countries in their search for national unity and economic self-determination. Economic and social development has been hampered by rapid population growth and its accompanying poverty cycle. Also, there remain political and social forces outside and within the new African nations that would undermine freedom.

It is important to identify the causes of rapid growth in the urban areas of Africa and the problems that have emerged from this growth. Studying the underlying reasons, it becomes evident that the new nations remain largely dependent on the Western World for trade, foreign aid, and food supplements. This dependency has fostered demoralization and bitterness and continued the tension between African nations and the industrialized nations of the world.

A. Establishing Economic Independence

When the nations were freed from colonial domination, most of the trained people in technical, business, and management positions were non-African and they returned to their European homelands. Africa's new leaders realized that their nations' economies remained dependent on European markets. They had to create new markets and new industries. This required extensive capital investment. The prospect of going into debt to foreign lending institutions renewed fear of **neocolonialism** (a new outside control of African life).

Interdependence

This is the reason much of the economic aid that has been lent to the newly developing nations is from international monetary agencies like the World Bank and the European Common Market. In this way, one nation does not overly influence the new nation's affairs. Banks and export companies of former colonial countries still remain firmly entrenched in many African nations.

Many African nations have offered favorable incentives (cheap labor, tax breaks, and plentiful raw materials) to **multinational corporations** (major businesses that are involved in many nations) in an attempt to attract their investment and business.

Urban Industrial Development

African nations have quickly learned that **subsistence agriculture** (producing for one's own basic needs) is not the answer for annual economic growth, and have placed their emphasis upon industrial development in urban areas. The result has been state-run corporations. Often, the rural sector suffers as populations shift from the countryside to the urban industrial centers. The result is a labor force of skilled and semi-skilled workers developing into a growing middle class in cities, but many of these people have difficulty in finding adequate housing.

Recent Drought Conditions

The last two decades have seen agricultural supplies and severe water shortages in nations of the **Sahel Region** (a drought-stricken area of West Central Africa). Many nations that had sufficient food supplies are now becoming dependent on food imports. This further drained their limited investment capital, preventing significant development.

Socialist And Mixed Economic Models

Since independence, conflicting ideological and economic goals have created mixed economic systems. In Tanzania and Ethiopia, socialist economies have been instituted in an attempt to promote cooperation in the work force and sharing of profits. Authoritarian socialism (strict government command) had strong backing from major communist nations in the 1970's and 1980's.

In both nations, a system of government-controlled agricultural cooperatives and state controlled industries and marketing has caused severe economic problems. Widespread shortages of vital goods and services have occurred.

Other African nations, such as Kenya and Nigeria, have reluctantly accepted programs of assistance from their former colonial masters, and have developed **mixed socialist-capitalist economies.**

More recently, the United States has assumed a greater role as a trading partner, and in the case of Nigeria, imports almost 60% of Nigerian oil production. In most instances, efforts at regional economic cooperation within Africa or even a strong Pan-African cooperation have been limited because of cultural and ethnic diversity and nationalism.

The strongest and most diversified economy in Africa still remains the white-ruled nation of the Republic of South Africa. South Africa has a long history of racial and ethnic conflict, and the lack of empathy of whites towards Africans and Cape Coloureds serves as a major roadblock to the achievement of a popularly elected multi-racial democracy.

Many world governments and economic corporations have debated **boycotting** South African goods and **divesting** their financial interests in South Africa as a pressure tactic against South Africa's policy of apartheid.

B. Population Problems

Another serious economic condition revolves around the problem of overpopulation which contributes to widespread poverty. Nations such as Nigeria and Kenya have extremely high population growth rates. This may be attributed

to traditional beliefs and pressures for large families in agricultural areas where many children are needed to work in the fields or tend the herds. Many parents also look upon their children as "social security," a support system in their old age.

Many areas still lack access to proper educational and health services. Africans have migrated to urban areas in search of employment opportunities, but demand has far exceeded the number of jobs, and this puts an additional burden on the cities.

As population continues to grow, agricultural production has not kept pace, and the problem of hunger adds to the woes of the developing nations. As life expectancy increases, the population rates in Africa have continued to be among the highest in the world.

Rapid Urbanization

A prime example of the ill-effects of severe population growth can be witnessed in the urbanization process in Africa. Massive unemployment has created shanty towns and poverty, and a wide gulf of inequality between the wealthy and the poor. In the early 19th century, about three percent of the world's population lived in metropolitan regions.

By the 21st century, experts predict that more than fifty percent will live in cities. African cities are experiencing a staggering growth rate. Growth can be attributed to the industrial economic development of the colonial era, and modern buildings and services created by today's nationalist leaders who wish to showcase their achievements. Waves of migrants from rural areas flood the cities searching for jobs, and create severe urban congestion, and strain essential services (transportation, housing, sewage, etc.).

Another problem occurs when the unskilled rural worker is unable to perform the skilled labor associated with modern industrial technology. This has caused high unemployment, and forced many of the recent migrants to live in slum areas. Within sight of these depressing shanty towns are the thriving business districts and wealthy neighborhoods. This causes a bitterness between the rich and poor.

As long as cities continue to be the industrial hubs and the government centers for new nations, and the centers of modernity and change, it will be very difficult to control population shifts from rural to urban areas.

African youth, once content to live the traditional life of the rural regions, now face the decision of moving to the city and gambling their futures on the opportunities (education, economic, and social mobility). With this new mobility and rapid urbanization has come a breakdown in ethnicity (tribal values). The new urban dwellers face cultural patterns that are very cosmopolitan (a wide mixture of cultural traits), and this has often resulted in a crises of personal identity, alienation, and frustration.

Agriculture And Food Supply

All nations must manage the problem of maintaining an adequate balance between population and food supplies, but the African nations are faced with the dilemma of scarce food resources and high prices. This has forced the African governments to devote much of their time coping with this serious problem.

In many African nations, the tremendous population growth has surpassed the growth in food production, and nations which once exported agricultural products are now forced to import food to feed their people.

Major Food Crops - Imported And Domestic

In the past, African nations witnessed three distinctly different types of farming: subsistence farming, cash crop farming (agricultural products sold to the urban areas and exported), and mixed farming (combination of subsistence and herding). The dominant exports have been palm oil, coffee, tea, cacao, cotton, peanuts, and sisal (used for rope and cord).

Many African countries have relied on only one or two cash crops. This can be a dangerous gamble for a nation. Poor weather, a bad harvest, or falling prices in the world market, can quickly bankrupt a nation's economy.

Africans must learn to make their land more productive if they are to return to selling their surplus in the world market place. The **Green Revolution** of the 1960's (scientific breakthroughs in agriculture) encouraged new African nations to use improved seeds, fertilizers, and modern farm machinery to increase crop production.

Many African farmers are traditionalists and are reluctant to change, especially when the new methods will require an additional expense. Without change, the land will not yield the export surplus needed to provide African nations the money needed for further development.

Most of the African nations have become dependent on food subsidies from grain surpluses of the Western world. African diets have often been altered by this recent trend of food imports. African nations are forced to take what is provided as foreign aid or purchase the least expensive foodstuffs. This often causes a lack of proper nutrition in many of the peoples' daily food supply.

Desertification

In an area called the "Sahel" in West Africa, the process of **"desertification"** (loss of available land to the desert) has occurred because of soil erosion. This, combined with the severe drought in Mauritania, Mali, Niger, and Chad, brought widespread starvation and death to the regions' people and herds.

The disaster was not entirely created by nature. The region's farmers and nomads had traditionally over-cut trees for firewood, maintained large camel, goat, sheep, and cattle herds which over-grazed the limited grasslands, and over-cultivated the land. The local ecological balance had been pushed to its limits. The resulting desertification has created a land not suitable for human life.

Additional Problems Facing African Agriculture

African governments have failed to provide enough financial incentives to their agricultural producers and in many cases have created state-run monopolies which have fostered an ever-growing bureaucracy. Any profits realized through agricultural production are very often absorbed by these government officials and rarely filter down to the farmers.

World Issues:
Environmental Concerns

Also, in many areas there is a scarcity of water resources, and the costs are prohibitive for irrigation projects and well drilling. In summary, a major problem concerns the transferring of agricultural technology from the western industrialized countries to a tradition-based agricultural system in the nations of Africa.

Before the newly independent African nations can achieve economic self-sufficiency, they must overcome many barriers. Continued over-population, coupled with scarce food resources, is a major concern. Technical training and financial assistance must be brought in from the outside world to develop and exploit its vast natural resources.

Urban growth must be controlled, or there will be a continual breakdown of services and alienation of the masses. African nations will attempt to find solutions to these problems in their own way in their search for national unity and economic self-determination.

Questions

1 The new African nations often need foreign aid to develop
1 larger military forces.
2 large mineral deposits.
3 new government buildings for the growing bureaucracy.
4 their human and natural resources.

2 Desertification is caused by
1 flooding of low lying plains.
2 overgrazing, deforestation, and over-cultivating.
3 strip mining for gold.
4 over mechanization.

3 A new middle class in modern-day Africa consists of
1 former tribal chieftains.   3 urban dwelling skilled laborers.
2 a military elite.   4 rural farmers.

4 The Sahel is a region in Africa that over the past two decades experienced
1 widespread drought.   3 devastating floods.
2 massive earthquakes.   4 extensive volcanic eruptions.

5 A major reason for widespread overpopulation in the newly developing African nations is
1 a higher life expectancy rate.
2 government's subsidizing of larger families.
3 improved birth control.
4 poor medical facilities.

6 A major cause of shanty towns has been
1 a breakdown of essential urban services.
2 increased employment in cities.
3 increased social mobility.
4 the rural to urban population shifts.

7 In new African nations, traces of colonial institutions remain most noticeably in
1 rural areas.   3 military forces.
2 banking industry.   4 government bureaucracy.

8 One form of socialism recognizable in new African nations can be seen in
1 the African Common Market.
2 the use of the American corporate form of business organization.
3 governmentally controlled economic development.
4 numerous collective farms and communes.

9 Lower birth rates have occurred among the middle class of developing nations because
1 governments offer couples financial incentives to limit families.
2 educational programs on family planning have become available.
3 tribal religions encourage modesty.
4 traditional extended family bonds are strong.

Essays

1   Africa's economic development is tied to a number of conflicts.

Conflicts

- traditional agriculture v. the Green Revolution
- traditional values v. urbanization
- independence v. close ties with former colonial powers
- overgrazing v. desertification
- socialist systems v. capitalist systems

Choose *three* of the above conflicts and discuss how *each* one affects the economic development of African nations. [5,5,5]

2   Overpopulation in many newer African nations has contributed to widespread poverty.

    a   Describe the causes of overpopulation in one specific African nation. [5]

    b   Explain how urbanization has affected the population problem. [5]

    c   Show how the problems discussed in *a* and *b* affect African agriculture. [5]

V. Global Context

The major global powers exert strong influence on African nations. It is very difficult for the newly independent African nations to maintain policies of **non-alignment** (refusing to always be on the same side in all issues). The strategic location, vast size, and unlimited resources of the African Continent continue to be of extreme importance to the communist and non-communist powers of the world. The complexity of the South African racial issue makes that region volatile in a global context.

A. Africa's Alliances And Linkages

Many African nations maintain close diplomatic ties with the western world because of their persistent economic crises. Africans have to compromise their status of non-alignment, and play a difficult balancing act with the eager industrial powers of the world. Modern African leaders realize that cooperative sharing will help insure their survival and progress.

1975 Lome (Togo) Convention

An economic trade agreement was signed between the **European Economic Community** (EEC) and over fifty African, Caribbean, and Pacific nations to provide trade among themselves, stabilize prices, and increase Western investment. Security is provided for the African nations, but they still remain the providers of raw materials, not finished products.  **Interdependence**

The Commonwealth

Many of the former British colonies (such as Nigeria) maintain close economic and cultural ties with England, and more than a dozen nations use English as their official language. Most have joined the **Commonwealth of Nations** (a worldwide organization of former British colonies) which gives them the cooperative benefits of favorable trade agreements and shared social programs.

The United Nations

More than one third of member nations of the U.N. are African. This gives African nations a powerful voice and voting bloc in the General Assembly. The United Nations goal of self-determination for all peoples and its strong position of human rights has encouraged the emerging nations of Africa.

Economic assistance to the developing nations has been provided to the African nations through the United Nations educational and social agencies. Also, the African nations have used the United Nations as a world forum to insure that their human needs are met by the wealthier nations of the world. The **World Bank** and **IMF** (International Monetary Fund) are United Nations agencies. They have provided vast amounts of loans and technical assistance for economic development in the emerging African nations.

Often encouragement has been made to developing nations to co-finance major projects with monies from the public and private sector.

Organization Of Petroleum Exporting Countries (OPEC)

Nigeria and Gabon are two sub-Saharan nations which belong to this Thirteen nation group, which has been successful in determining world oil prices and in promoting trade with the oil-dependent Western world.

B. Direct Foreign Interference In Africa

World Issues: *War and Peace*

Even after independence had been achieved in Africa in the 1950's and 1960's, peace did not always come immediately. The deep loyalties of certain nations led to direct foreign involvement in the new countries' internal affairs by the major powers. The Zaire profile in SectionIII is a good example of this. Others include:

French Military Involvement In Its Former Colonies

When France granted independence to its former West African colonies in the early 1960's, it pulled out with the assurance that it would not meddle in the new nation's domestic affairs. However, the French offered to assist their former colonies with foreign affairs, finances, and defense. When a civil war erupted in 1966 between Northern Muslim rebels with close ties to Libya and

Power

their Southern Christian and animist countryman, French troops were sent to assist the Southern forces and restore order. Libya and Chad announced their intentions to unite in 1981 but this was condemned by France and neighboring African nations. By 1983, France had sent over 3,000 troops to Chad to suppress Libyan-backed rebels. Since then, France and Libya have launched bombing raids on each other's positions in Northern Chad.

Cold War Rivalries In Africa

Europe strongly influenced Africa's development in modern times. African colonies became involved in both World Wars. After World War II, Europe involved Africa in the struggles of the Cold War between the U.S.S.R. and the western democracies. As the African colonies moved toward independence, they became sites for the Cold War power struggles. The major communist nations at the time (China, U.S.S.R.) sent aid to Communist Parties in the newly emerging nations.

World Issues: *Determination of Political and Economic Systems*

Communist regimes dominate several African nations. One example is Angola. This former Portuguese colony received its independence in 1974. A political power struggle grew into a full scale civil war. The Soviets and Cubans backed a communist "Popular Movement." South Africa, the U.S., and European democracies backed the "National Union." During the 14 year war, the National Union became the UNITA guerrilla fighters, led by Jonas Savimbi. The Reagan administration gave $15 million dollars to Savimbi's cause. The two sides worked out a truce in 1991.

Renewed American involvement occurred in 1986 when President Ronald Reagan provided **Jonas Savimbi**, leader of **UNITA** (formerly the National Union) with some 15 million dollars of military assistance.

Another Cold War battleground involved the Horn of East Africa. In the drought plagued nation of Ethiopia, the Soviet-backed communists overthrew pro-western Emperor Haile Salassie in 1974. The Soviets also backed a communist regime in neighboring Somalia. In the late 1970's, a territorial dispute erupted between Somalia and Ethiopia. Soviet and Cuban forces helped Ethiopia hold its Ogaden Province. In retaliation, Somalia expelled Cuban advisors and accepted U.S. aid. U.S. supplied arms fell into the hands of local warlords who terrorized the countryside until the government collapsed in 1991. U.N. and U.S. forces attempted to relieve the terrible famine resulting from the political chaos. By 1993, neither experienced much success.

C. United States - African Relations

In many ways, the U.S. and the newly formed African nations had similar colonial experiences, and during the 1960's, American Presidents Kennedy and Johnson openly encouraged self-determination for all African peoples with supporting financial aid and developmental assistance. Young volunteers have been sent by the **Peace Corps** for the development of educational, agricultural, and industrial programs.

American philanthropy has always been evident in Africa and is **Empathy** most noteworthy in the Food for Peace program which has helped feed many nations faced with the prospects of massive starvation. Also, many promising African scholars have been provided with tuition-free study at American universities. Most of the Americans serving in African nations are volunteers, not government officials. These volunteers serve in the spirit of humanitarian need, and it is through these people that a better understanding may be made between the U.S. and their African host nations.

In the tense years of the Cold War, the United States provided military aid to pro-western leaders throughout Africa. It built military communications bases in Kenya, Liberia, and Somalia. Pro-western forces in the Congo (Zaire), Nigeria, and Angola received American military aid.

An area that has caused the largest strain in American-African relations is the issue of racism. When photographs and stories of blacks being discriminated against in the United States are shown in the newspapers of Africa, it forces many Africans to think of the United States as a white-ruled nation. Fortunately, many African leaders have noticed the progress that has been made in American race relations and are often impressed that American democracy provides the mechanism to peacefully remedy injustice. Also, a growing number of American businesses have divested their interest in the Republic of South Africa as a protest towards that government's racial policies.

D. Africa's Role In World Affairs

African nations are strategically linked to three different world views: the West, the East, and the Third World. They are caught in the middle, yet are unable to remain truly neutral. For most of the new nations, non-alignment is the most effective policy.

National politics must stress a form of economic development which seeks full employment for Africans in agriculture and industry. It must be a policy that will bring direct benefits to the nation rather than support the corporate economics of a multi-national corporation. This is a difficult balancing act to contend with as the capital for initial investment is often provided by the foreign investor. Developing the "keep-out-but-help-me" attitude is perplexing and at times irritating to the outside corporate world.

Increased sensitivity to the impact of racial issues must be a concern for any of the world's nations when becoming involved in any form of international activity with African nations. Respect for human equality and human rights is the basic beginning to develop any relationship. These are lofty aspirations but ones which will contribute to peace and the development in the African nations.

The African Continent and its nations are strategically important to the entire world. The complex issues of non-alignment, racial policy, and economic development must be addressed through masterful diplomacy. At present, the United Nations has served as the international forum for African concerns.

Questions

1　Most African nations have foreign policies that favor non-alignment because they want to
  1　receive aid from only the communist world.
  2　avoid entangling alliances.
  3　remain loyal to their former European colonizers.
  4　maintain a policy of neutrality.

2　The Lome Convention in 1975 was a meeting of European, African, Caribbean, and Pacific nations which concentrated on
  1　education.   3　trade agreements.
  2　defense budgets.   4　medical advances.

3　The Commonwealth is a group of nations that are former British colonies which share
  1　extensive Christian missionary work.
  2　the apartheid policies in South Africa.
  3　a mutual defense alliance.
  4　social and economic programs.

4   What percent of U.N. nations are African?
    1   twenty-five percent   3   sixty-seven percent
    2   fifty percent   4   thirty-three percent

5   A sub-Saharan African OPEC nation is
    1   Republic of South Africa.   3   Angola.
    2   Somalia.   4   Nigeria.

6   African nations have needed loans from the World Bank and the
    International Monetary Fund because they want
    1   to build up military defenses.
    2   capital for economic development.
    3   to strengthen their ties with colonial powers.
    4   to attract highly skilled professionals for their bureaucracies.

7   During the Cold War, the U.S. sent aid to groups in Africa to
    1   spread Islam.   3   resist communism.
    2   promote apartheid.   4   assure neutrality.

8   The U.S. has successfully used the Peace Corps in Africa to assist
    1   anti-communists guerrillas in local civil wars.
    2   in developing native literature and art.
    3   in educational, agricultural, and industrial development.
    4   in developing a new form of military alliance.

9   A subject which has caused the greatest strain in United States and
    African relations is
    1   repayment of loans.   3   the Food for Peace Program.
    2   the Peace Corps.   4   the issue of racism.

Essay

During the past 20 years, communism has made steady inroads in Africa
as nationalist leaders have leaned favorably toward Marxism.

a   Explain what aspects of this political philosophy are attractive to the
      Africans. [5]

b   Select *two* nations below and explain why communism has had such a
      significant impact on the leadership. [5,5]

Nations

• Angola   • Ethiopia
• Somalia   • Tanzania
• Zaire

Unit Two

Gandhi
Monsoons
Buddhism
Non-alignment
Mixed Economy
Self-Government

Castes
Hinduism
Himalayas
Overpopulation
Green Revolution

3000   1000   BC ◄◆► AD   1000   1500   1700

- Indus Valley Civilization
- Hinduism
- Maurya Dynasty
- S.E. Asians to Japan
- Gupta Dynasty
- Khmer Empires (S.E. Asia)
- Arabs in Indonesia
- Mongols (India)
- Spain in Philippines
- British in India

South
and
Southeast
Asia

1800	1900	1945	1965	2000

- Dutch Take Indonesia
  - U.S. Takes Philippines
- French Take Indochina
- WW II
- India & Pakistan Independence
  - French Defeat in Indochina
- Gandhi's Independence Movement
  - Philippine Independence
  - E. Pakistan becomes Bangladesh
- U.S.–Vietnam War

Unit Two:
South And Southeast Asia

Stretching from the Persian Gulf and Arabian Sea to the Pacific Ocean, the vast southern region of the continent of Asia encompasses such wide variety of people and cultures that it will be considered in two sub-sections: **South Asia**, in which the large nation of India will be the focus, and **Southeast Asia**, with seven nations on its large peninsula and two vast island nations off its coasts.

I. The Physical/Historical Setting

A. South Asian Sub-Continent

The Indian subcontinent's geographic characteristics and general location have had enormous influence on the cultures and economies of this area.

Today, it is the site of two large nations (Pakistan and India) and four smaller ones (Bangladesh, Bhutan, Nepal, and Sri Lanka). The area is a huge peninsula, jutting into the Indian Ocean with the Arabian Sea on the west and the Bay of Bengal on the east.

The subcontinent is north of the equator, and its climate is generally of the "**C**" **Type** (Mid-Latitude Rainy). The major physical features of the region have a considerable effect on the climate.

The world's highest mountains, the **Himalayas**, stretch 1,500 miles along the northern reaches of the subcontinent in three parallel ranges. The prevailing summer winds ("**summer monsoons**"), which blow northeastward off the Indian Ocean, deposit considerable rains. The mountain barriers capture the rains, and drain into three major river systems: the **Brahmaputra, Ganges**, and **Indus**. The **winter monsoons** blow southward across the dry Asian interior and, while cooler, these winds are very dry.

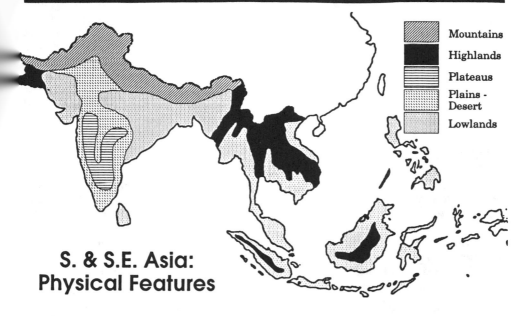

▨	Mountains
■	Highlands
☰	Plateaus
▦	Plains - Desert
░	Lowlands

S. & S.E. Asia: Physical Features

The **Indo-Gangetic Plain**, stretches from Pakistan to Bangladesh. Located at the foot of the Himalayas, it has fertile, **alluvial soil** (rich in minerals from mountains' drainage), a benefit of the steady summer monsoon.

The **Deccan Plateau** occupies most of the peninsula area and holds much of India's mineral wealth. Most of the population lives along the Deccan's edges, in the narrow coastal valleys where the rainfall is heavy.

Environment

Because India's rainfall is uneven, it has been a decisive influence on life in the region. Life in the three major river valleys revolves around the summer monsoons. An insufficient seasonal accumulation can often cause drought and famine, while too much rain can cause flooding and destruction. The Indus River irrigates northwest India and Pakistan. Major crops along its route to the sea include wheat, cotton and vegetables. The Ganges and Brahmaputra flow through northwest India, and both empty into the Bay of Bengal. Products of their valleys include wheat, rice, jute, sugar cane, and vegetables.

B. Southeast Asia

Geographic factors were also influential in shaping a variety of cultures in Southeast Asia. The term "Southeast Asia" was coined by the Allied military command in World War II, when the area, known for its diversity, was occupied by the Japanese.

Southeast Asia is bounded by the Indian Subcontinent on the west, China on the north, the Pacific on the east, and Australia to the south. It is approximately 4,000 miles east to west, and 3,000 miles north to south. It is divided into nine nations: **Myanmar** (formerly Burma, name changed in 1989), Thailand, Malaysia, Cambodia, Laos, and Vietnam on the mainland; and the island nations of Indonesia, the Philippines, and Singapore.

Diversity

Like India, the portion of the region on the Asian mainland is a vast peninsula jutting out into the Indian and Pacific oceans. It has a rugged, mountainous terrain with the population clustered around its river valleys. The north-south mountain ranges of the mainland divide the populations and are responsible for the numerous cultures of the area. The scattered islands of the south and east are another reason for cultural diversity. Of the islands, Singapore is a small island group, extending from the tip of the Malayan peninsula. Indonesia and the Philippines are **archipelagos** (chains of islands which are really the peaks of undersea mountain ranges).

The rivers and surrounding seas are the connecting tissues of life in Southeast Asia. The most important river systems of the mainland area are the **Irrawaddy** and **Salween** in Burma, the **Chao Phraya** in Thailand, and the **Red River** in Vietnam. The longest river of the area is the 2,800-mile **Mekong**. It starts in the north as the border between Laos and Thailand, then flows through the heart of Cambodia and empties into the sea at the southern tip of Vietnam. Each river system has served as an avenue of contact for the people living in their fertile valleys. They remain the main areas of agricultural production and commercial avenues.

Half of the area of Southeast Asia is composed of seas and straits. These sea lanes have provided easy access for the coastal inhabitants and island-dwellers. Examples of these traditional routes are the Gulfs of Thailand and Tonkin, the Java Sea, and the Luzon Strait.

As with India, **monsoons** dominate Southeast Asia's climate. The summer monsoon, blowing off the Indian Ocean from the south, is very wet. Unlike India, however, the Southeast Asian winter monsoon blows southwestward, off the Pacific, and carries considerably more moisture along the east coast and into the islands. Therefore, the region has more **climatic variations (A and C Types** dominate).

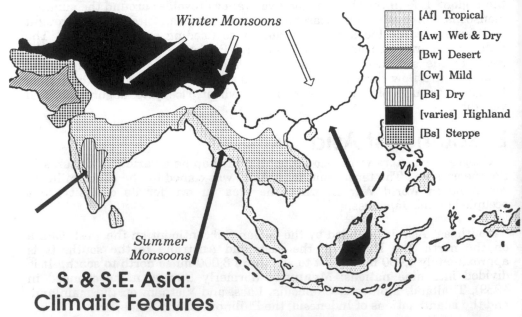

Winter Monsoons

[Af] Tropical
[Aw] Wet & Dry
[Bw] Desert
[Cw] Mild
[Bs] Dry
[varies] Highland
[Bs] Steppe

Summer Monsoons

S. & S.E. Asia:
Climatic Features

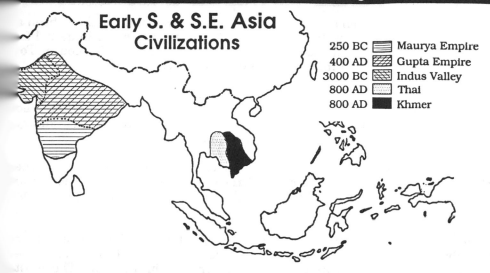

Early S. & S.E. Asia Civilizations

250 BC	Maurya Empire
400 AD	Gupta Empire
3000 BC	Indus Valley
800 AD	Thai
800 AD	Khmer

C. Early Civilizations

Geographic conditions have contributed greatly to South Asia's long history of disunity and the evolution of a variety of cultures.

The Indus Valley is the birthplace of India's civilization. Two early city-states were **Mohenjo Daro** and **Harappa**. Their inhabitants raised rice, wheat, and cattle. Pottery and dwellings excavated by archeologists at the sites of these cities date back to 3000 B.C.

The subcontinent's history alternates between waves of conquest and stable periods with the conquerors being assimilated. The most common path of conquerors was out of Central Asia through the Khyber Pass of northwestern India. From 1500 to 500 B.C., the **Aryans** brought the **Sanskrit** language, the horse, and iron products. **Alexander the Great** led an invasion in the 4th century B.C. The **Mauryas**, under their great leader, **Asoka**, established an empire in the 3rd century B.C. which unified most of the subcontinent. The Muslims established a **Mughal** (Mongol) **Empire** which lasted from 1526 to 1857 A.D.

Long before the birth of Christ, Indians had established a thriving trade with Arabia, Persia, and the east coast of Africa. The first Europeans to reach India were the Portuguese, who established trade stations and made India the gateway to the Orient.

D. Development Of Hinduism

Since its origin around 3000 B.C., Hinduism has had great influence on Indian society. While Hinduism allows for many variations, there are certain basic beliefs. Chiefly worshorped are: **Brahma**, the creator; **Vishnu**, the preserver; and **Shiva**, the destroyer. A central belief is **reincarnation** (rebirth of the soul in another form of life). Hindus believe in two key principles, Karma and Dharma. **Karma** is the idea that a person's actions carry unavoidable consequences and determine the nature of subsequent reincarnation. **Dharma** is the sacred duty one owes to family and caste.

Hinduism is more than a form of worship. It is a way of life and has been a strong, unifying element in Indian culture. It plays a major role in daily life, determining an individual's associations, occupation, and one's spouse. Today, eighty five percent of Indians consider themselves Hindus.

Two other major sects, **Buddhism** and **Sikhism**, began as movements to reform Hinduism. Buddhism emerged in the 4th century B.C. It attempted to diminish the importance of **castes**, the rigid Hindu system of hereditary social groupings dictating one's rank and occupation.

Buddhists believe that the cycle of reincarnation is broken when one achieves a perfect state of mind called **Nirvana**. Sikhism was founded in in the 15th century A.D. It totally rejects the caste system, teaching complete human equality.

The intertwining of the Hindu religion and the social class structure through castes, created a stable and ordered society for centuries. Caste assignment was accepted as one's lot in a present incarnation. The most desirable castes, or *varnas*, were: Brahmin (priests), Kashatriya (warrior), Vaishya (merchant or farmer), and Sudras (laborers). The Untouchables were the lowest caste, prohibited from contact with others and assigned the most distasteful tasks.

E. Buddhism: Outgrowth Of Hinduism

The Buddhist movement had a profound effect on the Hindu social structure. It follows the basic beliefs set forth in the 6th century B.C. by **Siddarta Gautama**, a noble of northern India known as **Buddha**, or the Enlightened One. He issued the *Eightfold Path* and the *Four Noble Truths*. Through prayerful contemplation, one seeks to follow these rules to achieve Nirvana, a state of blissful happiness.

In the 3rd century B.C., **Ashoka** unsuccessfully sought to make Buddhism the established religion of the empire. However, the faith did become popular in Asia. Through the zealous missionary work of its priests, the movement spread into Tibet, China, Japan, Korea, and most of the Southeast Asian peninsula.

F. Islam Becomes A Major Religion

Islam spread rapidly in the Middle East and North Africa after its establishment in the 7th century A.D. Waves of Muslim conquerors also moved eastward into Persia and the subcontinent from the 8th to the 16th centuries. The Hindu population resisted the Islamic faith of their rulers and this created instability for a long period. Arabian Muslim invasions in the 8th century was followed by Turkish and Mongol Muslims c. 1000 A.D.

Beginning in the 16th century A.D., the **Mughal** conquest provided the highest degree of centralization since the Asokan Empire of the 3rd century B.C. The Mughals established the Sultanate of Delhi. Under the emperor **Akbar** (1555-1605), efficient government, religious toleration, and culture flourished.

Subsequent rulers were less able to keep the empire under control and fanaticism and civil war became frequent. An exception was Emperor **Shah Jahan** (1629-58) in whose reign religious strife diminished, trade expanded, and art flourished. Shah Jahan built magnificent palaces and buildings such as the famous **Taj Mahal.**

Many of the Muslim rulers' difficulties can be traced to the fundamental differences between Islam and Hinduism. **Mohammed** (570-632) was the originator and major prophet of the faith. God's (Allah's) revelations to Mohammed appear in Islam's sacred text, the *Qur'an (Koran).* Muslims must follow the rules of the **Five Pillars** (bearing witness, giving alms, praying five times each day, fasting during the holy month of Ramadan, and making a pilgrimage to Mecca). Islam also follows the concept of spreading through the **jihad,** or holy war, against non-believers.

Islam moved into Southeast Asia beginning around the 13th century A.D. primarily as Muslim merchants spread trade along the Malay peninsula and into the islands of Indonesia and the Philippines.

Hinduism And Islam Compared

	Hinduism	Islam
Sacred Writings	*Vedas* - epics of the gods	*Qur'an (Koran)*
Social Organization	rigid castes	social equality
Dietary Laws	no beef or milk products	no pork or wine
Concept Of Duty	Dharma	*Five Pillars*
Position On Violence	Forbidden - no taking of any form of life	holy wars accepted
Pilgrimage	city of Benares	Mecca
Submission To Authority	family more important than individual	all submit to will of God
Afterlife	reincarnation as reward or punishment for actions	paradise, or punishment for evildoers

G. Other Religious Movements And Influences

Hinduism's long history has seen numerous reform movements centering on the caste system and the individual's responsibility in the scheme of reincarnation.

Ghuru Mahavira founded a sect in the 6th century A.D. called **Jainism.** It teaches that escape from the cycle of rebirth comes from correct faith, knowledge, and non-violence to any living thing.

Diversity

Ghuru Nanak founded **Sikhism** in the 15th century. It combines elements of Hindu and Islamic beliefs. It is monotheistic and holds to the total equality of all men. Martyrdom of Sikhs was influential in changing this group into a cult of military brotherhood. Today, the Sikhs are known for their military skills. They form a large group within the Indian army, and some seek independence for their home province of Punjab, in northwestern India.

Reformers failed to bridge the gap between the two major religions. By the arrival of Europeans the divisions in Indian society were deep-seated, and would remain a source of friction.

Questions

1   A person studying Hinduism would be interested in the concept of fate or destiny called
    1   Karma.   3   Qur'an (Koran).
    2   Ashoka.   4   Jihad.

2   A caste, as in the Hindu religion, is
    1   method of worshipping gods.
    2   a form of reincarnation.
    3   system of hereditary social grouping.
    4   the waging of a holy war.

3   The Deccan Plateau, which contains most of India's mineral wealth is located
    1   north of the Himalayas.
    2   in the Indus River Valley.
    3   along the coast.
    4   in the center of the peninsula.

4   Monsoons are seasonal
    1   prevailing winds.   3   hurricanes.
    2   grain harvests.   4   religious rites.

5   Which separates the Indian subcontinent from the rest of Asia?
    1   Pacific Ocean   3   Himalaya Mountains
    2   Deccan Plateau   4   Ganges Valley

6 Hinduism and Buddhism are similar in that both religions
1 practice the belief in many gods.
2 provide followers with a rigid caste system.
3 stress attainment of a better life through spiritual rebirth.
4 follow the teachings of the same person as their basic belief.

7 Which is an archipelago?
1 Singapore   3 Vietnam
2 Sri Lanka   4 Indonesia

8 Which religion is correctly paired with its major belief?
1 Hinduism: one's present status in life is a merited incarnation.
2 Buddhism: an active life is preferred to contemplation of the hereafter.
3 Islam: one must worship a vast array of gods to achieve perfection.
4 Sikism: the caste system is the key to eternal happiness.

9 Climatically, what is the major difference between South and Southeast Asia?
1 The annual rainfall in India is constant all year.
2 The lack of mountains in Southeast Asia account for its dryness.
3 The winter monsoons are wetter in Southeast Asia.
4 India is too far from the Pacific to benefit from the summer monsoons.

10 Which statement about the role of religion in Indian culture is most accurate?
1 Religious leaders have often held formal political offices.
2 Religious differences have been the cause of division and conflict.
3 Religion has historically had little influence on the secular world.
4 Religious principles have seldom provided a base for civil laws.

Essays

1 Geographic factors often have an important influence on a nation's or region's history, economy, and cultural diversity.

Geographic Factors:

- Khyber Pass
- Monsoons
- river valleys
- Himalaya Mountains
- Indo-Gangetic Plain
- Deccan Plateau

Select *three* of the above factors and discuss its influence on a South or Southeast Asian nation. [5,5,5]

2 Discuss how Hinduism, Buddhism, and Islam have contributed to the culture of Southeast Asia. [5,5,5]

II. The Dynamics Of Change

A. British Assumption Of Power

As the Commercial Revolution emerged in 16th century Europe, trade opportunities led the British and other powers to begin subjugation of South and Southeast Asia.

Role Of The British East India Company

British conquests began in 1612. The East India Company, a government chartered trading monopoly, was granted commercial rights by the Mughal emperor. As competition arrived from the Netherlands, Portugal and France, the emperors often found themselves involved in violent commercial struggles.

Success Of The British

In the 18th century, the English interests were able to win out over the commercial enterprises of other European states, because of better organization and the government's military commitment. In the mid-1700's, **Sir Robert Clive**, commanding mercenaries employed by East India Company, led a series of military expeditions in the Bengal region which ousted the French from India. Clive was made Governor by Parliament. Superior sea-power also enabled the British to move quickly to different areas on the peninsula. Clive's diplomatic skills enabled the British to make alliances with local Hindu princes who were not loyal to the Islamic Mughal rulers. Offers of financial gain caused many natives to join the British forces as mercenaries.

The British royal government gradually replaced the East India Company in dealing with India. In 1858, after the **Sepoy Rebellion**, a widespread mutiny by Hindu and Moslem mercenaries, the royal government brought the subcontinent into the British Empire.

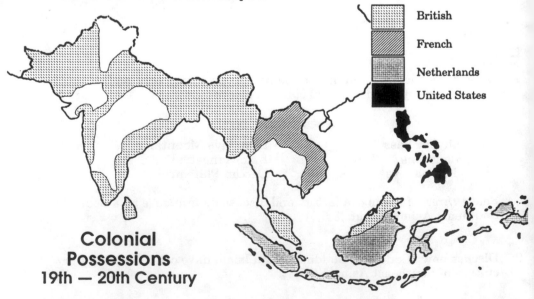

British

French

Netherlands

United States

**Colonial
Possessions**
19th — 20th Century

B. British Colonial Rule

British authority was not based on dominance of a religion and was able to unify the diverse elements of Indian society. The British minimized their role in local affairs and used a "divide and conquer" strategy to control opposition from local princes. They also employed Indians, especially Hindus, in many capacities. The Hindu acceptance of fate (karma) and loyalty (dharma), made them easier to work with than Muslims.

Changes were gradually introduced under the British imperialists more to consolidate their power than to improve conditions among the Indian populations. As in Africa, transportation and communication systems were modernized in order to exploit the human and natural wealth of the colony. The needs of the "mother country" usually superceded those of the colony.

Power

Indians joined other people of the British Empire in traveling and studying in England and other countries of Europe. The exposure they received to western political ideas often laid the groundwork for independence movements which came in the turmoil of the 20th century. Returning to India, these individuals began to organize opposition to their mistreatment and second-class status as citizens.

The British usually maintained that the people were uneducated and unfit for self-government, while the people perceived themselves and their national resources being exploited. During this period, several Asian leaders fomented bloody riots and confrontations with colonial authorities, but the British were too strong militarily, and the revolts were quickly crushed.

In 1906, out of reaction to the British division of Bengal province into Muslim and Hindu sections, an **All-India Muslim League** was founded under the Aga Kahn.

C. Evolution Of Limited Self-Government

Indian nationalist leaders, many of whom were educated in western schools were at first rebuffed by Britain when they sought democracy, but the British did make a series of small concessions as opposition became more organized.

The Morley-Minto Reforms (1908-09)

Named for the British Secretary of State and the Viceroy of India, these reforms were passed by the British Parliament to allow more natives to participate in the colony's government.

Political Systems

These actions were in response to agitation by the **National Congress Party.** The party was founded in 1885 to expand self-government. In the early 20th century, the movement's goals changed to securing total independence for India.

Mohandus Gandhi (1869-1948)

The charismatic Gandhi became the central figure in the independence movement. He was able to unite the needs of both the intellectuals and the masses by dramatizing the desire of the National Congress Party to use independence to alleviate poverty. He emphasized that the spiritual and moral strength of Indians was superior to the materialism of Western society. He advocated **passive, non-violent resistance** to British rule and championed social justice, and equal rights for untouchables. He desired Indians to think of themselves as citizens of a unified nation first, and as Hindus or Muslims second.

A brutal suppression of a 1919 demonstration in Punjab (**the Amritsar Massacre**) touched off riots and a more violent British reaction. In 1920, Gandhi seized the public's sense of outrage. "The Saintly One" urged non-violent passive resistance. Gandhi was imprisoned for his role. Famous for his hunger strikes and organizing economic boycotts of British cotton goods, he encouraged Indians to spin and weave their own cloth ("**cottage industries**").

The spinning wheel became a powerful symbol of protest. (Today, it is incorporated in the Indian flag.) In 1930, he led the **Salt March**. In a symbolic protest against the British tax system, thousands joined him in gathering salt from the sea.

The British Parliament responded with the **Government of India Act** in 1935. A federal constitution was established which gave the colony a measure of **autonomy** (self-rule).

D. Effect Of WW II: British Withdrawal

Events of the 20th century, especially the two world wars weakened European imperialism in most areas of the world. The Indian National Congress stated it would not aid Britain's war effort unless India was granted independence. In 1942, the third of Gandhi's campaigns was begun. He and other leaders were jailed until 1944. In 1947, India was finally granted independence with membership in the **British Commonwealth**. However, the British also yielded to Muslim pressure and agreed to partition the subcontinent into Hindu India and eastern and western sections of Muslim Pakistan.

Change

As independence drew closer, it was obvious that a united nation would not satisfy Hindus and Muslims. **Mohammed Ali Jinnah** (1876-1948) was the founder of a movement to create the Muslim state of Pakistan. Protesting Hindu domination, he had resigned from the All-India Congress to form the **Muslim League**. In the 1920's and 30's he and his followers agitated for the partition of India into Hindu and Muslim sectors. In 1947, Jinnah became the first Governor-General of Pakistan.

Myanmar (Burma) was another area controlled by Britain since the 1880's when it was acquired to block French imperial expansion westward from the Indochina region. Burma (Myanmar) received independence in 1947 and elected not to join the British Commonwealth.

E. Southeast Asia And Colonial Experience

Most of Southeast Asia had come under European control by the end of the 19th century. There were many similarities with the Indian experience, including the lack of political unity and rivalry between different cultures, which made European conquest easier. The pattern of casual commercial contact, missionary work, and increased political control was similar.

Several differences in the colonial pattern are important because the areas did have very different experiences after achieving independence.

India And Southeast Asia Compared		
	India	**Southeast Asia**
Colonial Power	Great Britain	France, Britain, United States, Netherlands, Portugal, Spain
Involvement In World War II	Aided in Allied efforts against Axis	Entire region conquered by Japan
Commercial Domination	British and Indian merchant groups	Chinese dominated mainland trade

World War II's end gave impetus to the independence movement throughout Southeast Asia. The psychological effects of seeing the Western colonizers defeated by an Asian power, and guerrilla resistance fighting receiving little help from the colonial powers during the war, gave strong momentum to independence movements.

Change

The Philippines had been promised independence in the early 1940's by the United States. Independence was postponed by the attack on Pearl Harbor and America's entry into the war. Independence was granted after little agitation in 1946. A United States of Indonesia was created as the Dutch left their colony in 1949.

On the mainland, a series of bloody wars broke out in the Indochina region and continued until 1954, when the French colonial empire crumbled. Laos, Cambodia, and North and South Vietnam were created as France left Southeast Asia.

Questions

1   Which statement is most consistent with the political views of Mohandus Gandhi?
1   Not until the last Englishman has left India will I put down my sword.
2   To protest injustice is to use one's time unproductively.
3   Independence is a goal we may seek but never attain.
4   Opposition to evil is as much a duty as is cooperation with good.

2   During the era of 19th century European Imperialism, the central theme of colonial economies such as India's became
1   exportation of raw materials.
2   commercial investment and banking.
3   heavy industry.
4   agricultural communes.

3   In the 18th century, Robert Clive established British rule in India by means of his
1   diplomatic skill.
2   his alliances with the Portuguese.
3   his peace treaties with the Dutch East India Company.
4   promoting religious equality.

4   After the Sepoy Mutiny, the British Government took control of India from
1   the East India Company.   3   France.
2   the Mughal Emperor.   4   the Muslim League.

5   While struggling for independence in the 20th century, Indian strategy emphasized
1   terrorism.   3   troop mutinies.
2   assassinations.   4   non-violence.

6   Which would historians consider a cause of disunity in 19th century India?
1   abolition of castes   3   high literacy rates
2   popular government   4   religious diversity

7   Despite their size and large populations, both India and Southeast Asia were easy victims of European imperialism because they
1   lacked strong, unified governments.
2   had uniform, peace-loving religions.
3   wished to obtain western technology to advance.
4   lacked sufficient food supplies.

8   A major reason the British government was able to consolidate its rule over the Indian subcontinent in the 18th and 19th centuries was that it
1   was the dominant power on the European continent.
2   used its Southeast Asian colonies as an invasion base.
3   was on friendly terms with the Islamic rulers.
4   gave strong backing to its private commercial companies.

9   Which was a major result of World War II in South and Southeast Asia?
1   France replaced England as the dominant colonial power.
2   Islam replaced Hinduism as the official religion of India.
3   The East India Company gave up control to the British Parliament.
4   The European powers could no longer control their colonies.

10 Mohammed Ali Jinnah wanted the separate state of Pakistan because of
1   language difficulties.   3   fear of Hindu domination.
2   possible economic barriers.   4   the example of Burma.

Essays

1   This century has been a time of turmoil for the subcontinent of India.

    a   While some revolutions have expressed the power of the pen, Gandhi's revolution in India has expressed the power of an idea. Explain. [5]

    b   Explain fully how India freed itself from imperialistic control in the 20th century. [5]

    c   Briefly describe one specific cause of serious disagreement in the 20th century between India and Pakistan. [5]

2   Imperialism declined in South and Southeast Asia after WW II.

    a   Why had the people of India and Southeast Asia been such easy prey for European imperialism? [6]
    b   Why did imperialism decline in Southeast Asia after 1945? [6]

    c   Name *three* European nations which lost their colonies after World War II. [3]

III. Contemporary South And Southeast Asian Nations

A. Partition Of Indian Sub-continent

Granting independence to India and Pakistan caused considerable disruption on the subcontinent. People in both areas protested having to leave their homes. The forced population exchange not only accentuated the religious hostilities, but the poverty, famine, disease and displacement of the people. As independence drew near, over 200,000 were killed in riots.

Gandhi himself was a victim of this violence. He was assassinated in January of 1948 by a Hindu fanatic incensed by the idea of religious equality. Gandhi's death ended any hope for religious calm on the subcontinent.

Diversity   The partition did not solve all the territorial disputes between the two rival nations. Two areas in the mountainous northwest are problematic even today. **Kashmir/Jammu** are two Muslim states claimed by both countries. Currently they are part of India. When **Punjab** was divided in 1947, an estimated five million Hindus and Sikhs moved into the Indian sector. **Tara Singh,** a powerful Sikh leader, demanded special status for Punjab as a semi-autonomous Sikh homeland. The Sikh military contribution during a 1960 war with Pakistan persuaded then Prime Minister Indira Gandhi to divide Punjab into three regions. The Sikhs hold a majority in one of them.

Nations Of S. & S.E. Asia

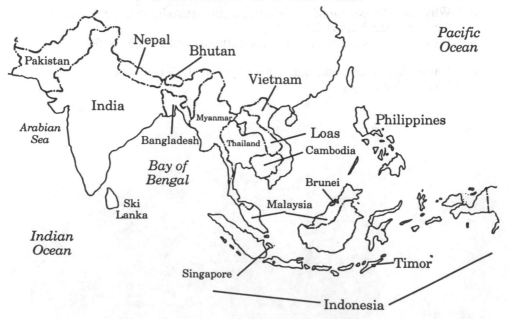

B. New Indian Government: Used A British Framework

India is an example of a newly independent country adapting its previous colonial form of government.

British And Indian Government Systems Compared		
	British System	**New Indian System**
Legislature:	*bicameral.* hereditary House of Lords, elected House of Commons	*bicameral.* Council of States (Rajya Saba); Council of People (Lok Saba) elected every 5 yrs.
Head Of State:	*monarch* (hereditary)	*president* (elected, 5 yr. term)
Executive:	prime minister & cabinet selected by majority of House of Commons	prime minister & cabinet selected by majority of both houses of legislature
Parties:	two major parties: *Conservatives* & *Labour Party*	two major parties: *Congress Party* and *Lok Dal*

C. Indian Constitution Of 1950

Like the government structure, the entire legal system of India reflects the British colonial legacy. The 1950 Constitution reflects a federal republic with a parliamentary form. It included many social and economic goals: free, universal education up to 14 years of age; prohibitions against discrimination because of race, religion, caste, sex, or place of birth; enfranchisement of citizens over 21.

D. Problems Of Indian Independence

Many difficulties faced the leaders of the new nation. The popular slogan **"Unity in Diversity"** became a guideline for the early leaders. It meant that India wished to preserve individual freedom while maintaining a strong federal union among its many different states and cultures. One difficulty has been that the constitution recognizes 15 different languages, including English. Making **Hindu** the main language has been a controversial issue for many years. Cultural diversity often leads to conflict. The reasons for clashes vary. Some revolve around religion, but **Diversity** dress, language, and even eating habits can become controversial.

Jawaharlal Nehru, a disciple of Gandhi in the Congress Party, became the first Prime Minister. Gandhi and Nehru were both committed to unifying the Indian people. Gandhi had championed rights for the untouchables and fought for religious toleration. He worked to elevate the role of women in political affairs. Nehru tried to break down traditional Hindu discrimination regarding womens' rights to own property, to obtain divorces, and for widows to remarry.

E. Social Change In Independent India

Solving India's social problems will unlock many doors to economic progress. The traditional village life remains central to India's social structure. Loyalty to local tradition has made it difficult for the central government to develop national unity. Since independence, the central government has tried to institute land reform measures, hoping to break the local power of large landholders and provide a more even distribution to citizens. The landholders' power rests in 550,000 **panchayats** (village councils) made up of tradition-bound elders.

The caste system also continues to be a problem. Despite efforts to abolish castes at the national level, traditional villages still maintain them. Local housing and selection of panchayat members still reflect castes.

Population issues plague India and Pakistan. For decades, the subcontinent has supported a population increasing at one of the highest rates in the world. The most crucial problem facing India is the ratio of diminishing food supplies to the demands of the increasing population.

In 1952, India was the first country to adopt a **nationwide family planning** program, and improved medical care has increased life expectancy. Despite efforts to control the population, however, there has been a steady increase. There are both traditional and religious reasons for this.

In labor-intensive agriculture, large families have been a necessity. Technological progress in farming has lagged and farm families continue to grow. Family loyalty is still strong. Those children who migrate to India's cities are expected to send contributions home. Hinduism teaches that having children is virtuous and that a son is needed to light a parent's funeral pyre.

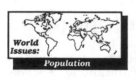

World Issues: Population

The continued population growth (over 800 million) has had widespread effects on the economy, on urban development, and on the general quality of life in India. The country does not have the natural or financial resources to provide the necessary consumer goods demanded by such a rapidly expanding population.

Unemployment is high. Annual per capita income in 1989 was only $308. Land tenure programs have given more small farmers land, but small-scale subsistence agriculture cannot supply the kinds of harvests India needs annually. More than half the farms in India today are one acre or less. Rural poverty has caused a massive migration to urban areas. Since 1960, cities have grown at three times the rate of rural areas. Crowded slums, poor sanitation, inadequate housing, disease, and crime abound.

City life has torn down some of the old caste traditions. Increased mobility and modern communication systems tend to destabilize its rigidity. Radio, television, newspapers, and cinema have a unifying effect. Economic freedom for women has broken the necessity for arranged marriages.

Identity in South Asia is still based more on cultural groupings than on national or political loyalty. For instance, the Sikhs have often been rebuffed in their demands for greater freedom in the Punjab. Tensions increased in 1984, when former Prime Minister **Indira Gandhi** ordered the army to storm the Gold Temple of Amritsar, a symbol of Sikh independence. Sikh terrorists were using the temple as a refuge. The action was viewed by India's 14 million Sikhs as a sacrilege. In October of that year, Mrs. Gandhi was assassinated by two of her Sikh bodyguards. Riots against the Sikhs broke out all over India.

Rajiv Gandhi became Prime Minister after his mother's assassination in 1984. He restored order, but Sikh uprisings brought another clash at Amritsar in 1988. Opponents forced Rajiv from office in 1989 on corruption charges. In 1991, fanatics assassinated him while trying for reelection.

Kashmir presents a similar problem. Hindu leaders dominate this area in which the population is mainly Muslim. It caused the first of a series of **Indo-Pakistani Wars in 1948.** The U.N. attempted to settle the dispute, but wars broke out again in 1965 and 1971. In 1972, another partition took place, but it has not settled the issue.

F. Pakistan As An Independent Nation

Pakistan has also experienced difficulties achieving economic and social reform through the medium of Islam. It has been plagued with both internal and international problems.

Muslims had not gained much experience in self-government in the colonial period. The British had controlled the entire subcontinent through the Hindu majority. The Muslims were poorly prepared to govern when Jinnah's request for a separate Muslim nation was honored in 1947.

Governing the two sections of Pakistan, separated by over 1,000 miles of Indian territory, presented a major obstacle. The two sections were different geographically, economically, and had different interpretations of some Islamic concepts. Prime Minister **Ayub Kahn**'s ruling group in West Pakistan wished to modernize the country and had liberal views of Islamic law.

In East Pakistan, Kahn's modernizations were resented by fundamentalist Muslims who were in the majority. When Kahn left office in 1969, East Pakistan began refusing to pay taxes to the central government. West Pakistani troops were sent into the East, setting off civil war. East Pakistan declared its independence as **Bangladesh** (the nation Bengal). Thousands were killed and millions escaped to India. India entered the war and helped Bangladesh win independence in 1972.

Political violence has disrupted Pakistan in recent times. In 1988, President **Zia ul-Haq**'s plane mysteriously exploded, with the U.S. ambassador aboard. **Benazir Bhutto** became Pakistan's first woman Prime Minister in 1988. She was forced from office in 1990 due to corruption charges against some of her cabinet ministers.

G. Southeast Asia:
Varied Responses To Independence

Amid background struggles by the major world powers after World War II, the nations of Southeast Asia took different routes to independence.

Political Systems

In **Indochina**, the area once dominated by the French, three nations eventually emerged from a long and bloody series of struggles: Vietnam, Laos, and Cambodia.

Socialist Republic Of Vietnam

The country runs along the eastern coast of the Southeast Asian mainland peninsula. It is bordered by China on the north, the South China Sea to the east, and Laos and Cambodia to the west. Communist rebel leader **Ho Chi Minh** (1890-1969) fought against the French before and after World War II. During the war, he organized guerrilla resistance fighters against the Japanese. This experience accelerated the drive for independence. As they retreated from Indochina, the Japanese proclaimed **Bao Dai** as Emperor of Vietnam, but nationalist insurgents rushed to assume power before the French could return.

Vietnam

Ho Chi Minh

Ho Chi Minh, heading the communist **Vietminh** party, called for the establishment of the Democratic Republic of Vietnam. A north Vietnamese Vietminh state was recognized as a member of the French Empire in March 1946, but within months, the French attacked it and began an eight-year war. By 1953, the United States was paying over 80% of the costs of this struggle, viewing it as necessary to contain the spread of communism as it had in Korea from 1950-53. In 1954, the French withdrew after the fall of the fortress at **Dienbienphu**.

The 1954 peace conference in Geneva created a Vietminh state (capital: Hanoi), and South Vietnam (capital: Saigon) below the 17th parallel to be governed by Bao Dai. Communist insurgents (**Viet Cong**) began infiltrating South Vietnam almost immediately. The emperor was deposed by **Ngo Dinh Diem** in 1955, who proclaimed himself President of the **Republic of South Vietnam**. Buddhist leaders began to protest in 1960. In response to the U.S. cutting aid to Diem's regime, in 1963, a military faction led a **coup d'état** (forceful overthrow) which ended in his assassination.

U.S. Troop Escalation In the Vietnam War

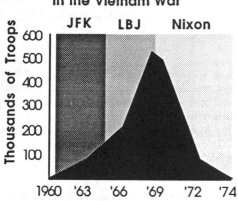

In 1964, President **Lyndon B. Johnson** ordered troops into the region and America's combat phase of the Vietnam War began. By 1968, the war had become so extremely unpopular that Johnson decided not to run for reelection. His party nominee, Vice-President **Hubert Humphrey**, lost to Republican **Richard Nixon**, who had promised to end the war. Instead, Nixon ordered increased U.S. military aid and broadened the war by bombing Viet Cong supply bases inside Cambodia. Anti-War protests in America became more widespread and violent.

In 1972, Nixon began a slow withdrawal of American troops, "Vietnamizing" the war, as South Vietnamese troops bore more and more of the fighting. Simultaneously, Nixon ordered heavy bombing of Hanoi and North Vietnamese harbors. Eventually, secret peace talks brought about a cease-fire agreement in 1973 which resulted in complete withdrawal by the U.S.

North Vietnamese troops swiftly moved into the south and captured Saigon in April 1975, unifying the country under a communist government. Today, Vietnam is engaged in sporadic border clashes with China, a traditional enemy.

Cambodia

Cambodia (also called Kampuchea) is also located in the south-central area of what was French Indochina. It is bordered by Laos and Thailand on the north, and Vietnam on the east and south. The French were pushed out of the area by the Japanese in World War II. Japan brought **Prince Norodom Sihanouk** to the throne.

Cambodia
(Kampuchea)

After the war, the French allowed Sihanouk to remain, and, in 1953, granted independence. In 1963, Sihanouk attempted to secure neutral status as the war in Vietnam intensified. While attempting to get Viet Cong bases out of Cambodian territory, he was overthrown by a coup headed by General Lon Nol.

As North Vietnamese troops further infiltrated the country, threatening its capital at Phnom Penh, President Nixon ordered a force of South Vietnamese and U.S. troops into Cambodia.

Power

The 1973 Vietnamese cease-fire included a withdrawal of foreign troops from Cambodia, but fighting between government troops and communist **Khmer Rouge** insurgents continued.   Lon Nol was overthrown in 1975. A communist government under Premier **Pol Pot** began a massive **purge** and resettlement which resulted in a terrible blood-bath of nearly 4 million.

From 1977 to 1985, a civil war raged in Cambodia, spilling into neighboring Thailand. **Heng Samrin**, a former Khmer Rouge leader backed by North Vietnam, led the pro-Soviet faction which emerged victorious and temporarily gave the country the name **Kampuchea**. In 1992, United Nations' peacekeepers entered the country to oversee national elections. **Prince Sihanouk** was elected president in May 1993.

Laos

The Lao People's Democratic Republic is the land-locked nation of Indochina, surrounded by China on the north, Vietnam on the east, Kampuchea on the south, and Thailand and Burma on the west. In 1950, France granted Laos independence within the French Union. The next year, Prince **Souphanouvong** launched a communist **Pathet Lao** movement. Aided by the Vietminh, this Pathet Lao invaded Laos in 1953 and gained two provinces in the North as a result of the 1954 Geneva settlements.

Pathet Lao influence grew and in 1957, Souphanouvong joined an uneasy **coalition** government led by a rival prince, **Souvanna Phouma**. Armed conflict broke out between the two factions which lasted until 1961. The war in Vietnam increased foreign influence in Laos, with the Vietminh running supplies south through Laos, and the U.S. and South Vietnamese moving to block them. In 1975, the Pathet Lao overthrew the weak coalition and Souphanouvong became President of a communist state.

Outside the French colonial area of Indochina, the pattern of independence was somewhat different.

Malaysia

Malaysia is found at the southern tip of the Malay peninsula. The Malay states were overrun by Japan in World War II, but were easily restored to British rule after the war. Communist insurgency began in 1948, but the nationalist resistance forged a strong sense of national unity. It created a strong base on which the British were able to move the country toward independence.

In 1957, the **Federation of Malaya** was formed with its capital at Kuala Lumpur. The country renamed itself **Malaysia** (Malaya, Singapore, North Borneo, and Sarawak) in 1963, but Singapore withdrew in 1965. The country was troubled by insurgents from Indonesia until 1965, and then anti-Chinese riots because of the economic dominance of that group. During the 1970's, the country took in most of the **Vietnamese** "**boat people**" fleeing the communist takeover in their country.

The Republic Of Singapore

Singapore, which is 75% Chinese, proclaimed itself an independent republic after leaving the Malaysian federation in 1965. It is an island nation consisting of one main island and 54 smaller ones, off the Malay peninsula between the Indian Ocean and the South China Sea. **Prime Minister Lee Kwan Yew** led the anti-British movement in the late 1950's when Singapore joined the Federation of Malaya. Despite leaving the federation because of the anti-Chinese agitation, Singapore remains closely tied to Malaysia commercially, and through military alliances.

The Republic Of The Philippines

The Philippines is an archipelago nation lying in the Pacific some 500 miles off the southeastern coast of Asia. The islands were ceded to the U.S. as a result of the Spanish-American War in 1898. In 1935, they were granted commonwealth status and were preparing for independence when World War II broke out in the Pacific. The Japanese captured the islands, but were forced out by the Allies in 1945. In July of 1946, they received their independence.

President **Ramon Magsaysay** (1953-57) directed successful military actions against the communist insurgent **Huk** guerrillas who constantly stirred up landless peasants.

Subsequent presidents were relatively weak until **Ferdinand Marcos** emerged in 1965. Marcos ruled as a dictator for over 20 years. During most of this time the country was under martial law partially due to a Muslim secessionist rebellion in the south. In 1981, after martial law was lifted and parliamentary rule restored, massive demonstrations began against the Marcos regime. They intensified after the assassination of opposition leader Benigno Aquino.

By 1986, most of the military joined the opposition backing the widowed **Corazon Aquino**. Marcos was forced into exile. Two major problems remain: communist insurgency, and pockets of discontented troops who attempted a coup in December 1989. Aquino stepped down in 1992, and her ally, **Fidel Ramos**, became president.

The Republic Of Indonesia

Indonesia is also an archipelago nation of over 13,000 islands (half are inhabited). Until the Japanese invasion in 1941, it was an integral part of the Kingdom of the Netherlands. After a four year struggle, independence was won in 1949. It became a "guided democracy" under the dictatorial rule of **President Sukarno**. Sukarno's troops, fearing too many concessions to communist opponents, helped to remove him in 1965. Violent anti-communist riots swept the country.

Indonesia

Since 1967, Army **General Suharto** has ruled as President. Oil-rich Indonesia remains a strong anti-communist state. In 1975, Indonesia attacked and annexed the Portuguese colony of Timor, but the mistreatment of the native population has caused considerable criticism of the government.

Questions

1 Which is viewed as India's most serious problem?
   1 protection of its oil resources
   2 communist insurgency
   3 Sikh terrorism
   4 overpopulation

2 Why would the new nations of Asia distrust Western powers?
   1 Western nations have opposed their entry into the United Nations.
   2 Russia has sent troops to block their independence movements.
   3 Most Western nations have sponsored communist insurgencies.
   4 Western nations formerly controlled them as colonies.

3 After independence from the Netherlands, President Sukarno ruled the Republic of Indonesia as a "Guided Democracy," actually it was a
   1 colony.   3 religious state.
   2 dictatorship.   4 communist government.

4 Language diversity is a major problem for
   1 Singapore.   3 Laos.
   2 India.   4 Vietnam.

5 A major problem in the agricultural development of India is
   1 small land holdings.
   2 British trade boycotts.
   3 huge food surpluses.
   4 summer monsoon floods.

6   As the first prime minister of India, Jawaharlal Nehru sought to
   1   break down traditional discrimination regarding womens' rights.
   2   end the communist rebellions in his country.
   3   institute a caste system.
   4   have all Indians accept the Hindu religion.

7   Communism has been successful in Asia because
   1   Asians feel indebted to former colonial powers.
   2   coalition governments are common.
   3   poverty and inequality are widespread.
   4   most nations are archipelagos.

8   The first President of South Vietnam, Ngo Dinh Diem, lost popular support because of his administration's
   1   collaboration with the communists of North Vietnam.
   2   corruption and reliance on United States' aid.
   3   attempt to make Buddhism the national religion.
   4   desire to unite all former French colonies under his leadership.

9   Punjab and Kashmir have been problems since India's early nationhood because
   1   widowed women cannot own property.
   2   the people want a separate communist government.
   3   they remained under British colonial rule.
   4   of religious struggles.

10 Which was a problem of Pakistan in its early nationhood?
   1   domination by Christians
   2   communist revolutionary activities
   3   control of sea lanes
   4   territorial division

11 Which contributes to South Asia's population problem?
   1   over production of staple crops
   2   the rapid pace of industrialization
   3   urbanization changing womens' roles
   4   medical technology decreasing death rates

12 A beneficial change that has taken place since India's independence is
   1   development of urban technology.
   2   banning of ritual suicide for widows.
   3   abolition of castes.
   4   adoption of Hindu as the official language.

13 The rivalry between India and Pakistan led to India's military intervention in the
   1   Buddhist-Muslim War.
   2   Bangladesh independence movement.
   3   Vietnam Conflict.
   4   Sikh Rebellion.

14 The economy of Singapore is dominated by
   1   Chinese merchants.   3   British imperialists.
   2   Buddhist priests.   4   communist insurgents.

15 India is considered an underdeveloped nation because it
   1   is divided into two separate regions.
   2   is dominated by Sikhs.
   3   has a low standard of living.
   4   follows communist doctrines.

16 Which European nation was involved in independence struggles in Indochina from 1946-1954?
   1   Netherlands   3   Spain
   2   France   4   Britain

17 The Vietnamese communist leader who fought both the French and Japanese was
   1   Sukarno.   3   Bao Dai.
   2   Aquino.   4   Ho Chi Minh.

18 Which is a problem to India's development?
   1   increasing agricultural and industrial productivity
   2   increasing population of subsistence farmers
   3   expanding religious diversity
   4   establishing greater power for local village councils

19 The United States became involved in the supporting the French in the Indo-Chinese independence movements because
   1   they involved Christian missionary work.
   2   it wished to eliminate French economic competition.
   3   it was committed to containing communism.
   4   the movements were essentially democratic.

Essays

1   The Indian government has attempted reform and social change since independence was granted in 1948. Progress has often been hampered by traditionalists.

    a   Why has the government tried to control the population growth? [6]

    b   Discuss *three* reasons why India's population growth continues. [9]

2   Democracy has been difficult to establish in Southeast Asia.

Nations

    · The Philippines   · Indonesia
    · Vietnam   · Cambodia (Kampuchea)

Choose THREE of the nations above and discuss why each has had difficulty in achieving democracy. [5,5,5]

IV. Economic Development In South And Southeast Asia

A. Economic Conditions

Since independence, economic development has been the most crucial challenge to "**Third World**" nations (underdeveloped) like India. The imperial system kept control of national resources and decision making in the hands of British policy makers, giving Indians little experience. India was often forced to import its most commonly used items from elsewhere in the empire. The domestic economy could not meet the population's basic needs once independence arrived.

Some segments of the Indian economy are managed by government agencies in the socialist manner, while some are based on free enterprise. This "**mixed**" **economic system** often reflects the varied views on economic life held by diverse leaders. The majority of India's agriculture and industry is managed by the private sector.

Nehru

The government has invested public funds in railroads, irrigation, power production, steel, nonferrous metals, basic chemicals, and heavy machinery. Leaders have used democratic means to promote development. Gandhi advocated small scale craft production in the nation's villages, while **Jawaharlal Nehru**, who was Prime Minister from 1947 through 1964, stressed development of western-style heavy industry and power plants. Wealthier classes supported free enterprise, and in recent years, the government has lightened its management of the economy.

B. Nature Of Decision Making In Less Developed Countries (LDCs)

Because the economic systems of the modern world are extremely interdependent, the choices of "Third World" nations in South and Southeast Asia are highly sensitive to the conditions of the world in general.

Basic or heavy industries like mining, nuclear and conventional energy production, and transportation are extremely important for less developed nations. The Indian government has attempted to develop these basic industries by state-run projects, supplementing private projects with government funds, and encouraging private efforts.

The growth of India's urban middle class has encouraged expansion of consumer goods production. India's cotton goods industries have expanded to meet domestic needs, but the industry is also dependent on foreign markets, especially in the western world. The rise and fall of textile exports make India's economy dependent on economic conditions abroad.

LDC's must also compete at home with the exports of more developed nations. When a country's products are not as attractive to consumers at home or abroad as those of other nations, the domestic economy suffers.

Developed countries are powerful enough to manipulate world markets to the disadvantage of competing underdeveloped nations. Such "trade war" tactics as "dumping" or "hoarding" can undermine the economies of the LDCs.

When another nation "dumps" goods it greatly increases the supply and forces world prices down, driving out competing nations. Japan frequently has done this. Holding supplies back, or "hoarding" them, artificially creates scarcity, making prices go up. Both tactics can have disastrous effects on vulnerable economies.

To indicate the extent of the LDCs economic problems, the table below compares (1990) annual **per capita income*** of the countries of South and Southeast Asia with some of the more developed nations.

Comparison Of Per Capita Income			
South & Southeast Asia		**Developed Nations**	
Bangladesh	$ 180.00	Austria	$17,360.00
India	350.00	Israel	9,460.00
Pakistan	370.00	Japan	15,030.00
Philippines	667.00	Switzerland	30,270.00
Vietnam	180.00	U.S.A	19,343.00

*(total national income ÷ population = share per person)

C. Economic Planning In India

Decisions made by India's leaders today will affect both the country's standard of living and its future status in the world. India's role as a power in Asia and the Third World depends on its leaders' ability to develop modern industrial capacities. As a "mixed" system, the economy combines elements of the **free market** and **command** systems.

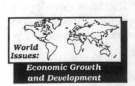

World Issues:
Economic Growth and Development

Free market systems operate according to the relationship of supply and demand in the economy.

Government planning and operation of the economy constitute **command systems**. Since independence, the Indian government has indicated a desire to reduce dependence on outside nations.

Beginning in 1951, it set official production goals in a series of five-year national economic plans. The first placed emphasis on agricultural development. The second focused efforts on heavy industry. The third (1961-66) was a revision of the first because food shortages had become life-threatening.

D. Agricultural Advancement In India

"The Green Revolution" is a term social analysts have applied to a worldwide effort that focuses scientific and technological efforts on overcoming food shortages and starvation. Thanks to the "Green Revolution," India has been using hybrid wheat and rice seeds superior to older types, which has actually allowed the country to build up grain reserves in recent years. However, the technological problem in India is intertwined with social and economic difficulties.

Culture

Reasons for Failure to Meet the Food Shortage

- cultural and religious traditions affect the raising and utilization of certain animals (pork is banned by Muslims, and beef and dairy products are banned by Hindu custom)
- shortage of and resistance to animal or chemical fertilizers
- lack of capital for improvement and mechanization
- land held in tiny parcels
- acceptance of famines as natural

E. Technological Progress In Industry

India has managed significant gains in technological progress since independence. It is now the tenth largest industrial power in the world in terms of GNP (total value of goods and service produced annually). Major industrial production includes jute fiber, processed food, steel, heavy machinery, and cement. This rapid growth has had an uneven effect on the standard of living. Two distinct classes are emerging. An educated urban class is prospering, while the rural poor are experiencing a decline in the quality of life.

Technology

F. India's Economic Struggle To Succeed

Fulfillment of its economic planning goals has caused India to borrow heavily from the western world. Besides debts to Britain and other Commonwealth nations, India has relied on grants and food supplies from the United States.

In 1955, Nehru began receiving Soviet assistance. The government also encourages privately owned foreign companies to build plant facilities if they compliment government planning goals.

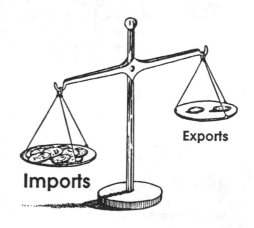
Imports   Exports

The 1970's were exceptionally bad years. Drought and crop failures forced importation of food, and the increase in oil prices drained investment capital. Today, the economy is growing at a healthier rate (8% in recent years), but India still suffers from an **imbalance in trade** (imports exceeding exports). India's major trade is with Japan, Saudi Arabia, and the U.S.

G. Economic Development In Other Areas

Continued domestic and foreign problems plague the other economies of this region. Vietnam and Kampuchea suffer from the long years of fighting. The economies are primarily agrarian and the per capita income of communist nations is generally very low. Agriculture is generally a collective as opposed to individually owned enterprise. Most economies follow the strict plans common to socialist economies, with the labor force expected to achieve set production goals.

Non-communist nations have organized their economies in varying ways. After **Indonesia's** independence, Sukarno launched a **nationalization** program. This was a government confiscation of the property of the Dutch and other foreign investors. Under Suharto's military control, some private enterprise has emerged, but the government still controls major industries like petroleum production.

Singapore enjoys a per capita income of $8,792.00 (1990), second only to Japan's in Asia. It has a free-enterprise industrial economy with petroleum refining, rubber processing, and electronics prominent. Only 10% of its land is under agricultural production. Malaysia is also a free-enterprise system, but the imbalance of wealth in the hands of the urban Chinese minority has caused the government to institute costly rural development programs. The Philippines also follow capitalist economic principles, but the per capita income is low and only 12% of the population is engaged in industry. Major products are sugar, timber, nickel, coconut products, bananas, and textiles.

Interdependence

The nations of Southeast Asia are often linked commercially to Japan, and that country's investment capita is to be found throughout the region. Japanese industries purchase much of the raw material produced, especially petroleum, rubber, tin, and bauxite. Japan exports heavily to these areas, especially its electrical products. These nations also use Japanese shipping and financial services.

Questions

1   Which person is correctly paired with the economic development theory he favored?
   1   Suharto — green revolution   3   Nehru — five year plans
   2   Gandhi — trade imbalance   4   Sukarno — free enterprise

2   Third World nations are dependent on the developed nations for
   1   financial resources.   3   agricultural workers.
   2   raw materials.   4   cottage industries.

3   "Cottage industry" was a system in which
    1   overseas trade was discouraged.
    2   piecework was done by hand craftsmen.
    3   agriculture was the only means of making a living.
    4   workers contract for their wages.

4   What has been an important result of the "Green Revolution?"
    1   Agricultural productivity has increased.
    2   Slavery has been abolished.
    3   Large estates have become unprofitable.
    4   Commercial farming has become collectivized.

5   India's first economic five-year plan emphasized
    1   military production.
    2   development of heavy industry.
    3   improvement of food supply.
    4   production of consumer goods.

6   Which is common to current economic development in South & Southeast Asia?
    1   exhaustion of natural resources
    2   interference by the U.N.
    3   oppression of European imperialists
    4   imbalance of trade

7   Which is the primary reason why India often has difficulty adding to its supply of capital equipment?
    1   Most members of their professional classes emigrate.
    2   It has a scarcity of unskilled labor.
    3   Its government tends to promote a free market system.
    4   Much of its productive capacity is used to provide the bare necessities.

8   The term "LDCs" is used primarily to refer to countries which
    1   lack extensive natural resources.
    2   have Christianity as their established religion.
    3   are in revolt against control by communist foreign powers.
    4   have underdeveloped industrial and financial resources.

9   Currently, which situation in developing nations of South and Southeast Asia hinders efforts to raise their standards of living?
    1   continued high rate of population growth
    2   lack of adequate rainfall
    3   inability of scientists to increase crop yields
    4   rejection of Western technology by nationalist leaders

10   Which is the major problem facing many developing nations today?
    1   resolving conflicts between church and state
    2   adjusting traditional life to new technological advancements
    3   gaining political independence from colonial powers
    4   obtaining membership in the United Nations

11 Which is most characteristic of a command economy?
1   resources are allocated by government direction
2   a variety of economic incentives encourage private business growth
3   there is a high rate of unemployment
4   prices are set by interaction of consumers and producers

12 An economic structure in which there is both private and government ownership of industry is known as
1   collectivization.   3   free enterprise.
2   mixed economy.   4   command system.

Base your answers to questions 13 through 15 on the statements below and on your knowledge of the social studies.

Speaker A: Increased contact among nations and peoples is characteristic of our times. A single decision by OPEC or a multinational corporation can send ripples of change throughout our global society.

Speaker B: If the last 500,000 years were divided into lifetimes of years, there would be 800 such lifetimes. Humans spent the first 650 of these in caves, and the most important changes occurred only during the final lifetime.

Speaker C: If we are to survive, all passengers on our Spaceship Earth must participate in efforts to solve the issues that threaten mankind - poverty, resource depletion, pollution, violence, and war.

Speaker D: We must understand that no single culture's view of the world is universally shared. Other people have different value systems and ways of thinking and acting. They will not see the world as we do.

13 Which concept is discussed by both speakers *A* and *C*?
1   self-determination   3   conservation
2   nationalism   4   interdependence

14 Which statement best summarizes the main idea expressed by speaker *B?*
1   Humans have always had to deal with many changes in their lives.
2   The rate of change has increased rapidly in the 20th century.
3   Throughout history there has always been great resistance to change.
4   Conditions in the modern world are better than in any prior era.

15 Speaker *D* indicates a desire to reduce
1   ethnocentrism.   3   social mobility.
2   globalism.   4   religious tolerance.

16 Which situation has brought about changes in traditional Indian society?
1   existence of cultural isolation
2   establishment of local governments
3   dependence on subsistence agriculture
4   increase in industrialization

17 To which situation has the growth of industrialization in many South and Southeast Asian nations led?
1 weakening of family and village ties
2 reductions in the standard of living
3 strengthening of ethnic loyalties
4 increase in the influence of traditional religions

18 A chronic problem facing most Asian countries since World War II has been a shortage of
1 natural resources.
2 unskilled labor.
3 investment capital.
4 markets for agricultural products.

Essays

1 The Industrial Revolution continues to change the world. Choose THREE specific countries in South or Southeast Asia and describe two ways in which they have attempted to meet the challenge of industrializing. [5,5,5]

2 Technological problems are intertwined with social and economic difficulties in India. Describe THREE ways religious and cultural traditions have affected the economic development of India. [5,5,5]

V. Global Context:
South And Southeast Asia

Various foreign policy issues have affected South and Southeast Asian nations since the time of their independence. Their international policies today are largely outgrowths of many factors in their history.

A. Basic Approaches
To Foreign Relations

The political and strategic concerns of South Asia's countries have historically been shaped by their relationships with major world powers: the Peoples' Republic of China, the Soviet Union, and the United States.

After independence, India's leaders committed the nation to a policy of **non-alignment**. Nehru wished to devote the nation's attention to domestic development. India accepted U.S. economic aid under President Truman's **Point Four Program** for less developed countries. However, Nehru refused to join the **Southeast Asia Treaty Organization**, a regional military alliance sponsored by the United States. The U.S. and its allies formed S.E.A.T.O. (1954) as a **multilateral security agreement** to help nations resist communism.

Pakistan, which had been defeated by India in the 1948 war over Kashmir, did move toward alliances with the west. President Ayub Kahn joined S.E.A.T.O. in 1954, and the following year, committed his nation to membership in the **Central Treaty Organization.** C.E.N.T.O. was an alliance of Britain, and several Middle Eastern nation — including Turkey and Iran. Although these alliances became weak, when war with India broke out again in 1965 and 1971, Pakistan was able to hold its own with the equipment and training its military had received from the west.

The major powers have had an even more direct impact on events in Southeast Asia.

The French fought to retain its Indo-Chinese colonies after World War II, and the U.S. attempted to restrain the communist akeover of South Vietnam. The United States suffered 57,702 dead and 153,303 wounded in the nine-year involvement.

America operated on the "Domino Theory" — a communist victory in one of these small, weak states would lead to other nations falling. After the U.S. withdrawal, Laos and Cambodia did fall to communist insurgents who had received aid from Red China and the U.S.S.R.

After the fall of Vietnam and Cambodia, **Thailand,** once a strong U.S. ally and S.E.A.T.O. member, requested the U.S. military personnel and bases be withdrawn. In 1975, S.E.A.T.O. was formally disbanded. The following year, Thailand reached a formal diplomatic accommodation with communist Vietnam.

B. India's Foreign Policy Reflects Its Geopolitical Concerns

During the Cold War period, India used many strategies to avoid superpower conflicts.

United States	Soviet Union	Red China
(1950's) Nehru feared Western colonialism more than communist aggression. He refused defensive treaties.	Negotiated aid treaty in 1955.	Generally friendly relations until 1959. After Tibetan revolt, China occupied territory in north India.
(1960's) accepted arms from U.S. to defend against Chinese. Suspicious of continued U.S. aid to Pakistan.	Continued cordial relations. Technological assistance accepted.	Fought with China, lost more territory.
(1980's) U.S. - Red Chinese detente and U.S. aid to Pakistan strained relations.	Soviet invasion of Afghanistan cooled friendship.	More cordial and friendly relationship after Soviet action in Afghanistan.

C. Pakistan's Geopolitical Concerns

External threats have modified Pakistan's foreign policies. The border wars with India and the Indian interference during the secession of Bangladesh moved Pakistan to ally itself with Western nations. The 1979 Soviet invasion of neighboring Afghanistan increased security fears.

D. India And Today's World

During the Cold War period, India tried to lead the less developed nations ("Third World") as a neutral bloc. India plays a leadership role in shaping the United Nations General Assembly's policies. It condemned the nuclear arms race of the superpowers in the Cold War. However, India has nuclear weapons of its own. It is also in an intense nuclear weapons competition with its neighbor, Pakistan.

E. Foreign Policies: Cultural Differences

Hostility to imperialism and superpower interference are not the only contexts in which students can view the behavior patterns of Southeast Asian nations. It is impossible to understand affairs in Southeast Asia unless ancient rivalries and cultural differences are taken into account. Cambodia (Kampuchea) has long been the target of invasion from people in the area of Vietnam. Similarly, most Southeast Asian countries have historically been invaded by China, and are often prejudiced against those of Chinese ancestry living in their countries. This can be seen by the hostilities which caused Singapore to leave the Malaysian Federation in 1965. Traditional rivalries were also evident when, in that same year, Indonesia resigned its seat on the United Nations Security Council when rival Malaysia was admitted.

G. General Foreign Policy Alignments

Nations With Close Ties to the West	Nations With Close Ties to the Communist Bloc	Unaligned Nations
Pakistan Philippines	Cambodia (Kampuchea) Laos Vietnam	Burma (Myanmar) India Indonesia Sri Lanka Thailand

Questions

1   Which is an example of Cold War neutrality?
    1   France's attempt to hold its Indo-Chinese colonies after WW II.
    2   The 1979 Soviet invasion of Afghanistan.
    3   U.S. sponsorship of the S.E.A.T.O. alliance in 1954.
    4   India's decisions to avoid S.E.A.T.O. and C.E.N.T.O.

2   Which event strained Chinese-Indian relations?
    1   impositions of tariffs
    2   India's adoption of a pro-Western foreign policy
    3   border disputes
    4   India's participation in the Vietnam War

3   The purpose of S.E.A.T.O. (1954-1975) was to solve problems through
    1   peaceful negotiation.   3   free trade.
    2   religious toleration.   4   military defense.

4 Newly formed nations sometimes choose to remain non-aligned because
   they
   1 wish to ignore world problems.
   2 are concerned with internal problems.
   3 believe U.N. involvement might hamper relations.
   4 combine both public and private economic planning.

5 The United States helped create S.E.A.T.O. after
   1 the communist victory over France in Vietnam.
   2 India's defeat of Pakistan in Kashmir.
   3 China's invasion of India in 1959.
   4 The Soviet invasion of Afghanistan in 1979.

6 After gaining independence from Britain, India chose to
   1 end relations with all European nations.
   2 not join the United Nations.
   3 ally itself with the communist bloc.
   4 steer a neutral course.

7 The "domino theory" on communist insurgency in Southeast Asia held
   that
   1 India would seek to become a major world power.
   2 cultural rivalries would be a continual source of friction.
   3 imperialism would be a constant threat.
   4 when one small nation falls, others will follow.

8 For much of Southeast Asia, the three decades since World War II may
   best be described as a period of
   1 economic independence.   3 social unification.
   2 cultural isolation.   4 political instability.

9 Which Cold War event strained relations between India and the Soviet
   Union?
   1 the Soviet invasion of Afghanistan
   2 the Soviet take over in Bangladesh
   3 Indira Gandhi's assassination
   4 Soviet-Chinese raids on the Indian border

10 Which nations were closely tied to the communist bloc?
   1 Pakistan, Burma, India   3 India, Thailand, Philippines
   2 Cambodia, Laos, Vietnam   4 Indonesia, Laos, Philippines

Essay

Discuss an issue of conflict for each of the following pairs of nations.
[5,5,5]

· Indonesia — Malaysia
· India — Pakistan
· Singapore — Malaysia

Unit Three

East Asia

China

	BC AD			
3000	←◆→	800	1500	1700

Dynasties: • Chin   • Han   • Tang   • Mongol   • Manchu

     • Confucius   • Feudal Japan   • European Spheres

           • Shintoism

   • Buddhism

                  • Tokugawa Shogunate

• Yaoi (Japan)

Shinto
Dynasty
Hiroshima
Confucianism
Ethnocentrism
Great Leap Forward

Japan

1900	1950	2000

- Japan Industrializes   • WW II   • Communist China (Mao)
  - Boxer Rebellion   • Democracy in Japan
    - Republic of China   • Chinese Cultural Revolution
      - Russo-Japanese War   • Deng Xiaopong

Unit Three: East Asia
I. Physical/Historical Setting Of China

Physical, historical, social, and economic elements have shaped the culture of China. To understand the events in China today, the actions of its government, and the expressions toward or against other nations, it is necessary to look at the cultural forces which shaped Chinese society.

A. Geography And Early Development

There is a strong relationship between the physical environment of China and the development of its civilization.

Development Of Civilizations In The Yellow (Huang), Yangtze (Chang Jiang), And The West (Xi) Rivers

The earliest civilizations developed over 4,000 years ago in the Yellow River Valley. Gradually the civilization expanded outwards and the land known as China began. The major river valleys are still the heart of China's agricultural economy. They have been the basic framework for the growth of Chinese population and culture.

B. Geography And Chinese Culture
Geographic Isolation

China's topography and location have given it physical isolation from other civilizations. These physical features have separated China from the development of Western Civilization in Europe, the cultures of South Asia, and to some extent, from the island peoples of Japan and Taiwan. In some instances, the separation has discouraged Chinese movement outside its borders; in other cases the physical barriers discouraged invasion by outsiders.

Population Density And Demographic Patterns

Over 90% of China's more than one billion people live on less than one-half of the land. China has the highest population of any nation and is very homogeneous, despite the constant influx of non-Chinese invaders.

Rivers Of China

The mountainous west has a very low **population density** (number of people per square mile), while the eastern river valleys have very high density. **Shanghai,** the major port on the Yangtze, has over 12 million inhabitants.

Ethnocentric Conception Of History

Ethnocentrism is a form of prejudice. It means viewing all other cultures as inferior to one's own. Traditionally, the Chinese referred to their country as the **Middle** or **Central Kingdom** because they believed it to be the center of the world. They lacked any interest in foreign cultures as they regarded them as "barbarian" or uncivilized.

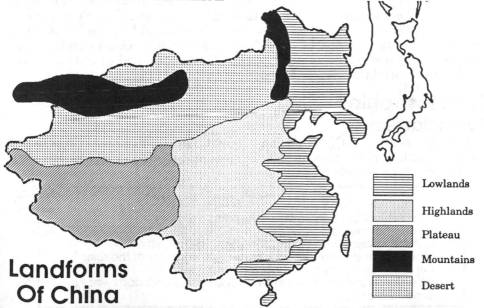

Lowlands

Highlands

Plateau

Mountains

Desert

Landforms Of China

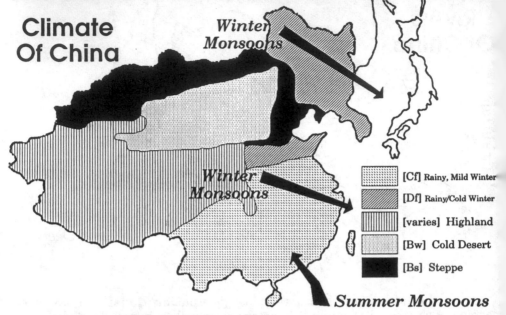

Climate Of China

Winter Monsoons

Winter Monsoons

Summer Monsoons

[Cf] Rainy, Mild Winter
[Df] Rainy/Cold Winter
[varies] Highland
[Bw] Cold Desert
[Bs] Steppe

Physical factors favoring the formation of a homogeneous culture and an ethnocentric attitude include:
- settlement in the deltas and river valleys
- ease of contact with other cultures afforded by a network of rivers
- discouragement of Western infiltration

Recurring Droughts And Floods

Environment   Geography has posed a challenge to China's economic development. Much of North China receives low irregular rainfall. Irrigation canals are necessary throughout the area. Droughts have often led to famine and death. China's major rivers have frequently caused floods. The **Yellow (Huang)** has flooded so often through the centuries that it is called **"China's Sorrow."** Great efforts by the Communist regime to construct dams, run-off trenches, and irrigation canals have helped control this river's destruction.

C. Philosophies
Confucianism

In the 6th century B.C., Confucian thought came to dominate Chinese social organization, political structure, educational system, and was the very foundation of its civilization.

Basic Beliefs Of Confucianism

Culture

- humanity as the center of heaven and earth
- human nature is essentially good
- cultural evidence of respect for age and authority
- success of the state depends on proper conduct of the ruler
- the family group as the foundation of society
- an ordered society in which everyone knows and does what is expected of them

Natural Order Reflected In Human Relationships

Confucius taught that society would be orderly if everyone knew their proper rank or place. The social classes in descending order of importance were: scholars, peasants, artisans or craftsmen, and merchants. The Five Human Relationships are found in the *Analects*, a collection of Confucius' sayings which are the guide to correct behavior.

Identity

The Five Human Relationships	
1 Ruler and Subject 2 Father and Son 3 Husband and Wife 4 Older Brother and Younger Brother	The first person was the superior and was to set a good example and take care of the inferior. The second person, the inferior, owed respect and obedience to their superior.
5 Friend and Friend	Friends were social equals who owed each other respect and courtesy.

Emperor's Pivotal Role In Social History

Confucian philosophy taught that society would be in harmony if everyone performed their proper duties. If the ruler was good, his people would naturally follow his example and also be good. The ruler was the Son of Heaven. If he was just, he received a **mandate** (right or command) to rule which came from heaven; if he was unjust, he was denied the mandate. The people had the right of rebellion against an unfair ruler.

Taoism

The **Taoist** philosophy emerged around the 3rd century B.C. It revered nature, self-knowledge, simplicity and non-action. One should follow instinct and not live a highly-organized or activist life. If the natural order was upset by humanity, troubles would develop.

Legalism

Legalism also emerged around the 3rd century B.C. It was developed in response to the lawlessness which plagued China. According to legalism, punishment should be very severe for even minor offenses. Legalists believed the best government was one in which the ruler had much authority. War was regarded as good for society as people would become even more obedient and submissive to the ruler's commands.

Introduction Of Buddhism From India

Buddhism, imported from India during the 3rd century A.D., widened contacts with the non-Chinese world through such experiences as pilgrimages to India and Southeast Asia, and missionary trips to Korea and Japan. Buddhism remains the predominant religion in the Province of Tibet.

Early Chinese Contacts With The West

Despite geographic conditions that favored a degree of isolation, civilization in China progressed as a result of contacts with other cultures.

Conquest Of Central Asia
And Establishment Of A Silk Route

A number of strong dynasties (succession of rulers belonging to the same family) created a centralized rule and far-ranging trade contacts.

The **Chin** Dynasty (221 B.C. - 206 B.C.) united China, created an empire under a strong ruler whose central government reflected legalist ideas.

The **Han** dynasty (206 B.C. - 220 A.D.), expanded China's control over Central Asia. Chinese products, tea, silk, porcelain, were carried on the Silk Route, the route which connected China with India and the Mediterranean world.

The **Tang** dynasty (618-907) followed four centuries of internal disorder. After the Tangs established strong central government, its soldiers expanded the Empire into Mongolia, Tibet and the vast deserts of Central Asia. Their trade along the **Silk Route** continued to flourish.

Sea Routes

The **Ming** Dynasty (1368 - 1644) showed interest in maritime expeditions but these had little lasting effect other than to widen the tribute system. The Mings financed expeditions throughout Southeast Asia and to the Somali coast of Africa. In the 15th century, China had over one hundred ships and a force of over 27,000 men. But financial support ended with the demise of the Mings. Most of the contacts with Europe only tended to reinforce China's ethnocentric attitude toward foreigners.

Chinese Empires

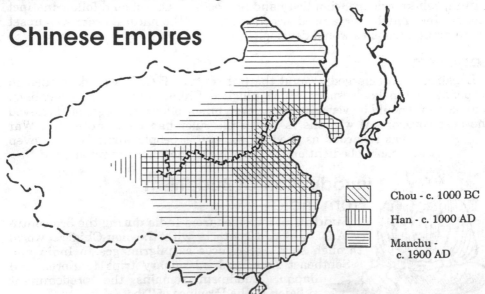

Chou - c. 1000 BC

Han - c. 1000 AD

Manchu -
c. 1900 AD

D. Chinese Dynasties: Social Changes

In order to rule successfully, a political system must be responsive to its society's needs and desires.

Chin (Qin) Dynasty (221 B.C. - 210 B.C.)

Legalism was created at the end of the Chou (Zhou) Dynasty by scholars concerned about lawlessness. Although the Chins only lasted fifteen years, their adherence to Legalist principles greatly changed China. Their strong central government structure survived under succeeding dynasties. The Chins began construction of the **Great Wall**, regulated coinage but also burned the books of rival philosophies.

Han Dynasty (210 B.C. - 220 A.D.)

Political Systems

The Han Dynasty blended Legalist structure with Confucian tradition. The major Legalist contribution of strong central government remained but the philosophy itself was banned. A main contribution was the establishment of the civil service examination system. Workers were needed to direct the Empire's expanding **bureaucracy** (civil servants). These government workers took competitive examinations testing their knowledge of Confucianism. To prevent any one bureaucrat from becoming entrenched in his office, no official served in the province of his birth, or in any province longer than three years. In this period a calendar was drawn up, sunspots recorded, and paper and the seismograph were invented.

China's Golden Age: Tang Dynasty (618 - 907)

During the Tang Dynasty, Chinese society served as a model for Japanese, Korean and Southeast Asian peoples. Literature and the arts flourished. The imperial armies conquered parts of today's Korea and Tibet. Domestically, Tang rulers revived Confucianism as the dominant philosophy and stressed the civil service examination system.

Periods Of Foreign Domination:
Mongol (Yuan) (1279 - 1368) And Manchu (Ching) (1644 - 1912)

For almost a century after the fall of the Tangs, **Mongols** from the north ruled China. The Mongol (Yuan) Dynasty, led by **Genghis Khan** and his successors, maintained contacts with the world. One famous emissary from Europe was **Marco Polo,** an Italian visitor to the court of Kublai Khan. Mongol rule was successful for a time as they adopted Chinese form and tradition. In the 14th century, their over-lordship fell to the **Mings.**

The Mings were committed to keeping Chinese traditional society and regarded all others as barbarians. The Mings, in turn, were conquered by invaders from Manchuria, who established the **Manchu (Ching)** Dynasty. The Manchus preserved, as had earlier conquerors, the Confucian-dominated society. Until the 19th century, the Chinese continued to absorb their conquerors.

Genghis Khan

Power

The Manchu Empire was organized according to the **tributary system**, meaning that conquered regions were required to send tribute (gifts) to the Manchu overlord. Areas dominated were: Nepal, Manchuria, Mongolia, Burma, Thailand, Laos, Vietnam and Korea. During the 19th century, the Manchu Empire declined. Modern Chinese history was shaped by the Manchu policies toward the Western world. The Manchus treated the Europeans as inferiors, and displayed attitudes ranging from indifference to hostility.

Questions

1   The Taoist philosophy taught humanity would only attain peace and happiness by
   1   accepting his lot in life and by not struggling against nature.
   2   depending entirely on the government.
   3   fighting to reform the nation.
   4   seeking glory and wealth.

2   In which river valley did the first Chinese Civilization develop?
   1   Yellow   3   Yangtze
   2   Mekong   4   Xi

3   Confucianism was noted for promoting loyalty to a person's
   1   nation.   3   family.
   2   empire.   4   caste.

4   Confucianism encouraged its followers to
   1   experiment with science.   3   respect traditional customs.
   2   travel to foreign countries.   4   conquer East Asia.

5   Western contacts with China can be traced to the famous merchant who visited Mongol China,
   1   Lao Tze.   3   Confucius.
   2   Genghis Khan.   4   Marco Polo.

6   Genghis Khan is remembered as a famous conqueror who
   1   united China under Mongol rule.
   2   introduced Buddhism.
   3   created the basic philosophy of China.
   4   isolated China from the outside world.

7   The attitude of Manchu China to the Western world can best be described as
   1   curious.   3   tolerant.
   2   welcoming.   4   hostile.

8   China fortified its northern border to
   1   protect Silk Route.   3   withstand barbarian attacks.
   2   provide irrigation.   4   for flood control.

9   What is China's current rank in world population?
   1   first   3   third
   2   second   4   fourth

10 In Confucian society, a member of the "elite" class would be the
   1   soldier.   3   scholar.
   2   farmer.   4   landlord.

11　In regard to China's population distribution,
　　1　approximately half live in rural areas and about half in cities.
　　2　90% or more of the people live in less than half of China.
　　3　the largest cities are clustered in the west.
　　4　10% live in rural areas and 90% live in cities.

12　Historically, China's agriculture over the centuries
　　1　yielded a good crop per acre.
　　2　was unimportant in Chinese economy.
　　3　usually produced surplus crops.
　　4　was insufficient to feed the population.

13　Who is described here? "China's classical period (1027 B.C. - 220 A.D.)
　　produced its greatest philosopher. His rules for correct behavior set the
　　pattern of China's society for 2,000 years."
　　1　Lao Tze　　　　　　　　　　3　Chiang Jiang
　　2　Genghis Khan　　　　　　　4　Confucius

14　The strong ethnocentrism encountered by European traders in early 19th
　　century China was primarily due to China's
　　1　economic superiority.　　　3　historic geographic isolation.
　　2　artistic excellence.　　　　4　overwhelming military strength.

15　Social control in traditional China was chiefly the function and
　　responsibility of the
　　1　established church.　　　　3　central government.
　　2　extended family.　　　　　4　village communes.

16　In Chinese history prior to the 20th century, cultural traditions were
　　transmitted primarily by
　　1　the government.　　　　　3　the schools.
　　2　the family.　　　　　　　4　invading foreigners.

17　Which was an important teaching of Confucius?
　　1　Intellectual knowledge is secondary to one's emotions.
　　2　The family group can often hinder the smooth functioning of the
　　　　society.
　　3　All persons must accept and perform their duties in society.
　　4　Those who have military power have earned the right to govern.

Essays

1　Geography has been a major influence on Chinese history.

　　a　Explain how China's geographic isolation shaped its culture. [6]

　　b　Discuss the effect that China's three major rivers have had on the
　　　　country's development. [9]

2　Confucian, Taoist, and Legalist ideas influenced the development of
　　Chinese civilization from earlier times.

　　a　Describe the three philosophies which appeared during China's early
　　　　history. [9]

　　b　Describe two qualities an ideal person would have according to these
　　　　early philosophies. [6]

II. The Dynamics of Change

The Chinese people have experienced almost constant social upheaval, war, and political unrest during the years since 1850.

A. China's Relationships With The West

China disagreed with the Western powers on the conduct of international relationships and on what constitutes justice in these relationships.

World Issues:
World Trade and Finance

Reasons For Western Interest

Chinese tea, silk, porcelains and various luxury goods were in great demand in the West. A growing number of merchants and missionaries tried to enter China. The 19th century saw the rise of European Imperialism and the desire for Western capitalists to open up the Chinese markets and raw materials.

Chinese Interest In Foreign Trade Was Limited

Although contact with Europeans became more frequent, the development of foreign relations was limited. China continued to regard its civilization, culture, and knowledge as superior to that of the West. It wished to protect its culture from "barbarian" influences and was not interested in utilizing Western ideas or products. Manchu officials restricted European ships to the one port of Canton, demanded bribes, and treated the Westerners as inferiors.

Identity

Foreign Relations And The Tribute System

One major area of friction between China and the outside world was China's insistence of the **tributary system**. This was the act of showing homage to the Emperor by bringing gifts and performing the **kowtow** (deep ceremonial bow). By 1795, Westerners were demanding diplomatic relations based on equality.

Failure To Develop Modern Armaments

Despite the fact that China had invented gunpowder in the 6th century, the low priority placed on technological development, especially in arms, eventually compromised its power.

B. The West Carves Up China

China's traditional ways of repelling foreign dominations proved ineffective against nations that had entered the Industrial Revolution. Events that led to the final humiliation and defeat of the Manchus included:

The Opium War (1839 - 1842)

In order to upset China's favorable balance of trade (more exports than imports), Britain sold opium, grown in India, to the Chinese. After British opium stored in Canton was destroyed by the Manchu government, the war began. Superior British warships and military firepower defeated the Manchus.

Unequal Treaties

Chinese acceptance of the first of the unequal treaties ended the Opium War. By the **Treaty of Nanking** (1842), China ceded the island of Hong Kong to Britain and opened five treaty ports to foreigners. More unequal treaties with Britain, France, and the United States followed.

China was forced to accept **extraterritoriality** (foreigners are not subject to Chinese law), allow foreign gunboats in her waters, and accept the right of foreigners to set tariffs. These treaties (1842-1860) reduced the Manchus' prestige and helped ignite over half a century of peasant uprisings. The most serious was the Taiping Rebellion (1850-1864).

Spheres Of Influence

The technologically superior European governments forced China to open to its trade. The **sphere of influence** was created. This was a diplomatic agreement which carved up a weaker area's territory into spheres where one imperialist nation was allowed to dominate. China was also forced to accept Christian missionaries. Their presence and the treaty ports functioning as centers of westernization caused friction.

Perhaps China's greatest shock was delivered by another Asian nation — Japan. The **Sino-Japanese War** (1894-1895) ended Chinese claim of dominance in East Asia. Japan easily won Taiwan, the Liaotung Peninsula, and a sphere of influence over Korea.

C. Response To Foreign Imperialism

The imposition of Western and Japanese political, economic and social demands had great impact upon Chinese consciousness. Yet the Manchu attempts at reform and their efforts to modernize were largely ineffective.

Attempt At Western Learning

Economic concessions to the principal European powers convinced some Manchu officials that reforms were needed. An attempt was made to adopt Western technology without disturbing traditional Chinese social and political order. Between 1861 and 1895, guns and steamships were manufactured, telegraph lines and railroads were constructed. Chinese went to universities in Europe and the United States.

Empress And Confucian Scholars Fight Reform

The Empress Dowager, who ruled through a **regency** (governing for a child monarch) and then directly for 47 years, preferred to manipulate supreme power rather than institute reform. The many Confucian scholars who dominated the bureaucracy opposed new Western learning as they saw their power decline. The reform movement was further hindered as treaty concessions and peasant revolts had drained the government's resources.

D. Overthrow Of The Emperor (1911 - 1912)

The final collapse of the Manchu Empire brought political confusion and ineffective moves to establish the Parliamentary government desired by Sun Yat-sen and other reformers.

Establishment Of The Republic Of China

Throughout the 19th century, there was growing opposition to the influence of Western nations. A secret resistance movement (**Boxers**) led a rebellion in 1900, which captured Peking for several months. The Boxers isolated the Western diplomatic community, seeking to force them out. A combined force of Germans, Russians, British, Japanese, Americans, and French managed to free the city and its rail links. Following the crushing of the Boxer Rebellion, the Manchu dynasty attempted reform.

In 1911, a middle class and student revolt became the final crisis of the Manchus when the revolution gained army support. The revolutionary spokesman, Sun Yat-sen (1866-1925), abroad raising funds, rushed home to try to take control.

Three Principles Of Sun Yat-sen

Sun's revolutionary speeches were printed in *Three Principles of the People.* He wished to create a democratic republic based on:

- **Nationalism:** the overthrow of all spheres of influence, and the restoration of Chinese rule

- **Democracy:** the establishment of a democratic constitution and an elected President and Legislature

- **Livelihood:** the redistribution of the large estates.

Sun Yat-sen

China's 1st President: Yuan Shih-kai

In order to hold the army's support, General **Yuan Shih-Kai** was chosen President of the new Chinese Republic. He dissolved the new legislature, bribed or murdered his opposition, and used the army to back his rule as a dictator until his death (1916). Sun Yat-sen and his followers formed the **Kuomintang**, or Nationalist Party, dedicated to reforming China.

Civil War Between The Warlords

Power

The local military dictator of each province was called the warlord. After General Yuan's death, no one was strong enough to unite China. Each warlord ruled by terror and extortion. China was torn by their territorial wars. In the 1920's, Sun asked for Western help to defeat the warlords, but only the Soviet Union sent arms and military advisers.

E. Nationalist Party Rule (1928 - 1949)

To follow the history of the Nationalist Party is to understand the reasons for the communist triumph in China.

Leadership Of Chiang Kai-shek

In 1924, **Chiang Kai-shek** was named military leader of the Kuomintang. The following year, after Sun's death, Chiang became political leader also. With Soviet help, Chiang broke the power of the warlords. He then turned on the communists and tried to destroy them.

Nationalist Party Corruption

Under Chiang, the Kuomintang entrenched its power and sought the eradication of the Chinese communists. Chiang abandoned the principles of Sun Yat-sen and allied with the wealthy who opposed land reform. Under his leadership, China was a dictatorship with progress only in the areas of industrial growth.

Chiang Kai-shek

F. Victory Of Communists (1920 - 1949)

The Chinese adopted Marxism hoping to accomplish industrialization while sharing the benefits of economic development equally among the proletariat and peasantry.

Political Systems

Marxism appealed to different classes of Chinese because it:
- forecast the worldwide collapse of imperialism
- promised land reform and the end of poverty
- appeared successful in the large, backward nation of Russia
- promised industrial development and more employment
- rejected Confucian thought which supported acceptance of established authority
- had strong leadership

Mao Zedong

Leadership Of Mao Zedong

Mao emerged as the leader of the communist forces at the time of the **Long March**, 1934 - 35. This was the 6,000 mile flight of the communists from southern to northern China to escape the Kuomintang army (see map following page).

The survivors became the dedicated core of the Communist Party. Because of Mao's political programs, the party gained enormous strength among the peasants.

Long March 1934-1935

Mongolia

Korea

Japan

Mao Zedong's Communist Forces flee the Chiang Kai-shek's Kuomintang Army

Taiwan

Japanese Invasion Weakened The Nationalist Government

Japanese imperialism brought a halt to internal conflicts. Japan occupied the northern province of Manchuria (1931). In 1937, the Second Sino-Japanese War began with their aerial attack against Chinese seaports. Japanese armies marched into the Yellow and Yangtze valleys. Chiang was forced to form a "united front" with the communists to fight the Japanese invasion. Each knew that civil war would resume once Japan was defeated. Much of the Nationalist Army was destroyed fighting in WW II in China.

Civil War Escalated After World War II

Kuomintang weaknesses in the 1940's set the stage for the communist victory:

- corruption and inefficiency with no apparent efforts to correct
- suppression of democratic practices which alienated the intellectuals
- mismanagement and ineffective use of American aid
- alienation of business interests through misguided fiscal policies
- endorsement of business practices that stifled competition
- not dealing with peasant pressures for land during recurrent famines

As discontent with the Kuomintang grew, the communists gained support. In areas they liberated from the Japanese, communists divided the property among peasants, began political education programs, and raised the status of women. The Kuomintang Party lost because they did not develop programs for economic and social reform.

People's Republic of China Proclaimed

The Soviets supplied Mao's forces with substantial amounts of weaponry. By 1949, Peking fell to the Chinese communists. Chiang and his forces fled to the island of Taiwan. Both governments claimed to be the legal government of China.

Questions

1 Imperialist nations in the 18th and 19th centuries generally attempted to acquire or control areas that had
  1 highly developed technology.
  2 undeveloped natural resources.
  3 literate populations.
  4 stable centralized governments.

2 Which would be the most difficult to prove?
  1 The revolutions of 1911-1912 in China overthrew the Manchus.
  2 Russia's Communist Party is more ruthless than China's Communist Party.
  3 Mao Zedong came to power in 1949.
  4 China's population is larger than Japan's.

3 Which statement best applies to the Chinese Empire after 1885?
  1 The Chinese welcomed the economic imperialism of the Europeans.
  2 The Boxer Rebellion successfully drove out the Europeans.
  3 European powers carved China into "Spheres of influence."
  4 The Open Door Policy of the United States ended imperialism.

4 Who led the Chinese government forces in the 1925-50 era against both Japan and the communists?
  1 Sun Yat-sen   3 Chiang Kai-shek
  2 Mao Zedong   4 Yuan Shih-kai

5 China was an easy victim of Western Imperialism despite its size and population because it
  1 lacked effective central governments and technology.
  2 was peace-loving and nonaggressive.
  3 welcomed Western influence.
  4 hoped to profit from lessons to be learned about Western science.

6 The right of extraterritoriality in the 19th and early 20th centuries allowed a Westerner in China to
  1 establish an export-import business.
  2 be tried for crime under laws of his own country.
  3 take out temporary Chinese citizenship.
  4 serve as an advisor to the Chinese government.

7 The Western nations became interested in China in the 19th century because China
  1 had large reserves of oil.
  2 had recently discovered large gold fields.
  3 exported tons of surplus crops.
  4 could serve as a market for trade.

8 Which characteristic of Western European nations allowed them to dominate the Chinese Empire?
  1 rigid social class structures
  2 self-sufficiency in natural resources
  3 frequent political revolutions
  4 advanced technological development

9   The primary usefulness of the spheres of influence acquired by foreign nations in the late 19th century was to provide
    1   aid for the Chinese in developing their industrial capacity.
    2   assistance in resisting communist insurgents.
    3   sources of raw materials and markets for the foreign nations.
    4   new settlements for the growing Chinese population.

10 A basic aim of Sun Yat-sen was to
    1   declare war on Japan.
    2   end foreign domination of China.
    3   execute Christian missionaries.
    4   overthrow the Dowager Empress.

11 Philosophically, Chinese communists accepted the beliefs of
    1   Marx.   3   Sun Yat-sen.
    2   Gandhi.   4   Confucius.

12 A major reason for the defeat of the Kuomintang during the Chinese Civil War was that they lost the support of the
    1   Buddhists.   3   army.
    2   factory workers.   4   peasants.

13 Which best accounts for the lack of political unity in China between 1912 and 1937?
    1   religious warfare
    2   little popular loyalty to the central government
    3   nonrecognition of the Chinese government by foreign powers
    4   the declining strength of Chinese communism.

14 One factor explaining the 1949 communist victory in China was that
    1   the United States would not aid the Nationalists.
    2   Mao Zedong promised to drive out all foreign powers.
    3   Soviet Russia sent aid to Mao's forces.
    4   Japan had eliminated all of the Nationalist armies.

Essays

1   China fell victim to Western imperialism in the 19th century.
    a   Why had the Chinese first placed restrictions on Western traders? [5]
    b   Why are the Treaty of Nanking (1842) and others of that period referred to as "unequal?" [5]
    c   Why were the Manchu attempts to reform China unsuccessful? [5]

2   To know Chinese history in the 20th century is to understand the reasons for the communist victory.
    a   Discuss the problems of Nationalist-Kuomintang government in the 1930's. [5]
    b   Why is the Long March important in this period of Chinese history? [5]
    c   Marxist revolutionary philosophy deals with economic alteration in industrial societies. Why did the communist philosophy appeal to the Chinese peasants? [5]

III. Contemporary China

Under the leadership of Mao Zedong, social, political, and economic changes occurred in China. Even more dramatic change followed his death, as his successors wished to modernize China without his strict revolutionary ideology.

A. Rule Of Mao Zedong (1949 - 1976)

From the founding of the People's Republic of China until the death of Mao Zedong, his vision of the Chinese Revolution dominated goals and developments in China.

Reestablishment Of China's World Prominence

China's image of itself has influenced the definition of national goals in the People's Republic of China. Starting in the 1950's, China increased its influence over the newly independent nations of Asia and Africa. It presented itself as a successful model of a native revolution against imperialism. Chinese leaders also restored China to its pre-eminent position in East Asia and became involved in the area's international diplomacy questions. China supplied arms to both North Korea and North Vietnam in their struggles with the United States.

Economic Reform And Development

Mao desired to move China from its technological backwardness. Inflation was an early problem, but it was controlled by the mid-1950's. Industrial production began to surpass prewar levels.

Improvement Of The Quality Of Life

Sanitation, medical facilities, and education improved gradually. Illiteracy was reduced. Women received full equality with men. Although the peasants did not receive individual plots of land, they did enjoy a higher standard of living in the communes.

Political Regions Of East Asia

Mongolian People's Republic

People's Republic of Korea

Japan

Republic of Korea

People's Republic of China

Taiwan (Republic of China)

Hong Kong

Changes In Agriculture

Collectivization programs were begun in an attempt to solve several basic agrarian problems:

- controlling population increases which strained food supplies
- generating capital for importing needed industrial materials
- training workers in new technologies
- controlling the migration of rural labor to the cities

In 1958, Mao Zedong ordered the cooperative farms merged into **communes** of at least 20,000 people. The commune system was part of the ambitious program called the **Great Leap Forward**.

Need To Industrialize

Under the Great Leap Forward, the factory workers were forced to work long hours in order to meet demanding goals. The major efforts of Mao's regime to industrialize were:

- implementing **Five Years Plans** which focused upon heavy industry
- expanding transportation facilities
- spreading industry more evenly throughout the country
- reforming the banking and financial systems

Thought Reform Movement

A major focus of both foreign and domestic policies was an attitude of constant alertness to dangers from without and within. Dedication to the ideals of the new regime was stressed in all phases of the domestic program. The government's position was strengthened by:

- encouraging of voluntary campaigns to improve production
- identifying all who subjected themselves to the new regime of Mao as "the People"
- labelling "landlords," and "capitalists," as symbols of those who exploited Chinese in the past
- using of psychological techniques to reinforce communist ideology and lessen the ties with Confucian thinking
- emphasizing literacy, particularly for adults
- employing "street committees" to provide surveillance of neighborhoods and disseminate propaganda

The Cultural Revolution

By the 1960's the failure of the Great Leap Forward and the Sino-Soviet split caused a big division in the Chinese Communist Party. President Lin

World Issues:

Determination of Political and Economic Systems

Shao-qi and others were disturbed by Chairman Mao's collectivization of agriculture, rapid industrial growth and heavy propaganda campaigns. A battle for control of China erupted in 1965. Since it involved education, government, science, and culture, it became known the **Cultural Revolution**.

Mao was supported by the army while Lin Shao-qi was backed by various party officials. Mao ordered the removal of this opposition from power. He closed schools so that students could mobilize into political groups called the **Red Guards**. By 1968, the army ended the street violence and Mao's victory assured that China would continue on her revolutionary path. His book, *Quotations of Chairman Mao*, continued to be required reading with its condemnation of the old ways.

B. Problems In Achieving Goals
Population Increases
A large population requires substantial resources for subsistence, making development difficult. China's large population and the level of education within the country are both important factors affecting development. The communist government has discouraged early marriages among its citizens and encouraged people to have only one child.

Agricultural Base
No more than one-third of China's vast territory has proved arable. Some characteristics of China's past agricultural pattern were:

- intensive cultivation of small plots of land with almost no mechanization (labor being the cheapest factor in production)
- widespread irrigation
- very little animal husbandry because of a lack of land for pasturage

The pressure to produce enough to sustain the largest population in the world has always been great. China's principal crops are rice, wheat, grains, and cotton. It does not enjoy the security of having large food reserves.

By 1985, in spite of intensive efforts, only 11% of the land was used for agriculture and yet 75% of the labor force was engaged in agriculture. Annual per capita income that same year was only 330 dollars.

World Issues: Population

C. Internal Policies Since Mao
Trial Of The Gang Of Four
Following Mao's death, a power struggle began between moderates and radicals, led by his widow **Jiang Qing**, and three conspirators. After this "Gang of Four" tried to force a return to the violence of the Cultural Revolution, they were put on trial in 1980. They were found guilty of undermining the party and government and were sentenced to life imprisonment.

In 1981, the Central Committee of the Chinese Communist Party issued a statement that Mao Zedong was responsible for the "grave blunder" of the Cultural Revolution. The years of the personality cult which idolized China's revolutionary leader were over.

Moderate Policies Under Deng Xiaopong

Changes in the Legal System. While there has been some loosening of control, there is still no freedom of speech or press.

- **The Four Modernizations.** Deputy Premier Deng Xiaopong, announced a 1978 plan to modernize China by the year 2000. Major improvements were forecast in four fields: agriculture, industry, science and technology, and military. (See discussion in IV of China).

- **New Education and Cultural Policies.** China's Confucian tradition, which had been rejected by Mao Zedong as unsuitable to modern China, is now being reevaluated by Chinese intellectuals.

The Chinese communist leaders wish to maintain strong ties with China's past and continue some cultural traditions as long as they can be adapted to Marxism. Two such areas are:

- the persistence of a pyramid of political control, traditional from the time of the Han Dynasty;

- the continued subordination of the individual to the group, with the communist state now substituted for the family.

Culture

In the 1980's, China expanded its cultural contacts with other nations. Ten thousand Chinese students were permitted to study abroad at foreign universities and technological schools in 1984.

Tiananman Square Massacre

In recent years, the new economic and social reforms and the intensified contact with the Western world have triggered more and more political unrest, especially among the young. The Spring of 1989 saw massive pro-democracy student demonstrations in Beijing's Tiananman Square against the slow pace of Deng's political reform. Party leader **Zhao Ziyang** was forced to resign from the leadership for failure to control democratic movement among the people. Premier **LiPeng**, with Deng's backing, unleashed troops on the demonstrators, killed many and followed with harsh political repression, executions, and banishment of demonstration leaders.

Questions

1   Soon after coming to power, the government of the People's Republic of China tried to make significant changes in the traditional family structure because
   1   it was an obstacle to communist plans for modernization.
   2   there was too much decision-making power in women's hands
   3   the structure was based on Western values of self-reliance.
   4   it did not encourage sufficient acceptance of authority.

2 Which is a major reason why families are smaller in China today than in the past?
  1 Religious beliefs encourage small families.
  2 The government offers incentives for smaller families.
  3 widespread disease and famines have reduced the population.
  4 educational facilities are limited.

3 Which has been an effect of the communist revolution on the status of women?
  1 Women's legal rights have been diminished.
  2 Less emphasis is placed on women receiving higher education.
  3 There have been more employment opportunities for women.
  4 The percentage of women in domestic occupations has increased.

4 Which basic agrarian problem was collectivization of agriculture supposed to solve?
  1 a surplus of trained workers
  2 huge surpluses of agricultural produce
  3 inflation caused by overabundance of investment capital
  4 the flooding of rural workers into the cities

5 Which factor is common to both Confucian and communist Chinese societies?
  1 decentralized government
  2 welfare of the group more important than the individual
  3 frequent internal conflict preventing stability
  4 stress on reverence for the past

6 Which is an accurate statement about art and music during the Cultural Revolution?
  1 Government programs fostered creative expression.
  2 Government banned them as culturally useless.
  3 Development of the arts followed government policies.
  4 A special emphasis was placed on cultural diversity.

7 The fact that political controversy often occurs when governments try to solve complex economic problems indicates that
  1 proposed solutions often generate new problems.
  2 the government should never interfere with economic life.
  3 democratic governments handle economic decision-making best.
  4 political and economic issues are not related.

8 Currently, which situation in China hinders efforts to raise the standard of living?
  1 continued high birth rates
  2 widespread disease and starvation
  3 inability of scientists to increase food supply
  4 government reluctance to adopt Western technology

9 Which group achieved victory in the Cultural Revolution?
  1 Kuomintang   3 Red Guards
  2 Boxers   4 Gang of Four

10 The trial of the Gang of Four symbolized a struggle between
  1 communism and capitalism.   3 moderates and radicals.
  2 religious groups.   4 Confucian & Marxist philosophies.

IV. Economic Development Of China

A profound economic transformation is taking place as China attempts to move rapidly from an agrarian economy to an industrialized one.

A. Resource Potential For China

Throughout its history, China has relied upon the use of human energy as the chief productive factor in the creation of wealth.

Mineral Wealth

China has a limited amount of the natural resources which are important in today's world. Known mineral wealth includes: tungsten, antimony, iron ore, oil, and scattered coal deposits. Manchuria has one of the richest coal deposits in the world.

Agricultural Wealth

Agriculture is China's main source of income. Since no more than one-third of the land is arable, every acre must be carefully used. In South China, extensive irrigation and terraces carved out of the hillsides have increased land use. The rice crop requires much intensive human labor. Because of its temperate, drier climate, North China grows wheat, corn, and soybeans. Not only must Chinese agriculture feed a large population, but it must provide food for export. Such exportation is necessary to obtain foreign currency necessary for capital investment.

B. Huge Population

The availability of natural resources can help economic development, but a large population can have such great demands on available resources leaving little for anything else. China is attempting to utilize technology to overcome problems of scarcity in both food and consumer goods.

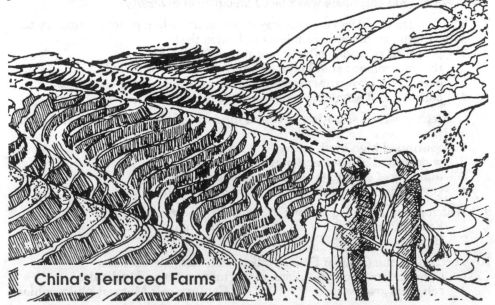

China's Terraced Farms

C. Changes Under Mao Zedong

Hoping to achieve greater production, the communists introduced far reaching changes in the traditional landlord-peasant system.

Land Redistributed. All land, farm animals, and equipment were taken from landowners and given to peasants. If they did not confess to the crimes of which the peasants accused them, the land-owners were tried and executed.

Cooperatives Established. In the early 1950's, farmers were forced to join their lands together and form cooperatives. The land was still considered privately owned, but the farmers had to work together. Farmers could sell a small part of their produce, but the government's share was still not large enough to feed the city workers.

The Great Leap Forward. This movement established large scale agricultural communes (1958) and set heavy production demands on the peasants sent to labor in the factories. Although it managed significant economic gains, the program suffered from peasant resentment, mismanagement and shortages.

Commune System Established. All the peasants' private property was turned over to the commune. Family living was all but destroyed as dining halls, dormitories, etc., replaced private homes. Each peasant received a government wage, could not sell any produce for himself, and was completely under the direction of the commune leaders. The commune system was a failure. Peasants hated the loss of privacy and of their homes. They resented their heavy workloads. Resistance, plus disastrous weather conditions, caused the government to ration food and purchase foreign grain.

Ideology Versus Expertise Controversy. Some officials believed a person's loyalty to Marxist doctrine should be the first criteria for appointment to government positions. Others took another view and believed ideology should sometimes bend to knowledge and expertise. Since Mao's death and the rule of the more moderate politicians, the government has permitted greater economic freedom and even implemented some capitalist methods.

D. Changes Under Deng Xiaopong

In 1978, Deng announced the "Four Modernizations," a program designed to modernize communist China by the year 2000. The major difference from Mao's economic program is the use of incentives to encourage Chinese to increase production.

Farming, Management Of Small Business In Hands Of Individual Or Family

In agriculture, the commune organization was disbanded in favor of family-directed farming. The **Family Responsibility System** began in 1981, and allows the peasant some produce to be sold for his own profit. This incentive has steadily increased food production.

Small private enterprise has been allowed in cities. This also has served to raise the family or individual's standard of living.

Responsibility For State Factories To Factory Manager

In 1984, hoping to make industry more productive, a series of reforms was announced. The government cut back on its industrial planning. The factory managers would decide the amount of goods to be produced, set salaries, and select the workers. Rather than all profits being handed over to the central government, the managers must only pay a tax on their income.

Stress On Consumer Goods

Chinese industry is working to produce more consumer goods. Their prices have risen steadily because of the law of supply and demand. Television and radios are top priority items for manufacture. Making more consumer goods available also meets the goals of communist leaders to show the system can provide for the people.

Relationships With The Outside World

The communist leaders realize that they will modernize more quickly and efficiently with technical help from the West. They have consistently worked to normalize relations with the free, capitalist countries. Today, among China's major trading partners are the democracies of Japan, Hong Kong, the United States, Germany, Australia and Canada.

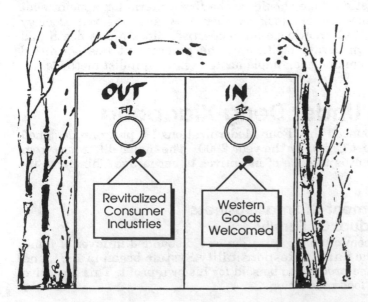

New China Trade Policy:

"Swing Doors"

Questions

1 The recent encouragement of private enterprise in the People's Republic of China is a shift from that country's
   1 mercantilism.   3 imperialism.
   2 command system.   4 free market system.

2 A major consumer complaint about the centrally planned economy of Communist China has concerned
   1 overemphasis on agricultural production.
   2 scarcity and the lack of variety of products.
   3 rapid fluctuations of prices.
   4 overproduction of consumer goods.

3 Which is a characteristic of command economies?
   1 Decision making is concentrated in the hands of government officials.
   2 Major industrialists make all economic decisions.
   3 Colonial officials dominate the economic structure.
   4 Consumer choices indicate use of economic resources.

4 Which is a current economic problem of the People's Republic of China?
   1 internal interference by the United Nations
   2 peasant rebellions
   3 oppression by Western imperialists
   4 lack of consumer goods

5 Which problem undermined Mao Zedong's goals in the *Great Leap Forward?*
   1 landlord manipulation of food prices
   2 overproduction and massive farm surpluses
   3 peasant resentment and resistance
   4 interference from the Kuomintang

6 Since the death of Mao Zedong, elements of which philosophy have been permitted in China?
   1 socialism   3 totalitarianism
   2 fascism   4 capitalism

7 A major difference between Chairman Mao's *Great Leap Forward* and Deng Xiaopong's *Four Modernizations* policy is the
   1 creation of forced labor camps for dissenters.
   2 use of incentives to increase production.
   3 introduction of a pure free-market economic structure.
   4 importation of skilled labor.

8 Which situation in the People's Republic of China best illustrates the concept of interdependence of nations?
   1 expanded participation in international sports events
   2 sale of food by China to obtain technology from other nations
   3 establishment of high protective tariffs
   4 persecution of landlords by the government

9   A chronic problem for the People's Republic of China since 1949 has been a lack of
1   important mineral resources.
2   markets for agricultural produce.
3   unskilled labor.
4   government direction of the economy.

Essay

1   Today, developing nations seek to improve the quality of life for their inhabitants through economic development. To achieve such improvement, the People's Republic of China must face decisions about modifying the way it makes basic economic decisions.

    a   Define and compare the concepts of command economy and free-market economy. [6]

    b   Explain why the Great Leap Forward and the Commune system failed as command economic structures. [4]

    c   Discuss how China is now modifying its command economic structure. [5]

V. China In The Global Context
China has not abandoned its claim to international leadership and cultural greatness. The present regime in China has reorganized society, the economy, and the state toward the reassertion of the nation's role as a world power.

A. Chinese Influence Upon East Asia
Historically, China was one of the world's leading civilizations in terms of technological development.

Literary Chinese As International Language
Chinese writing developed over 3,500 years ago and began with the drawing of objects. Chinese script spread beyond its borders and was used by Koreans, Japanese, and Vietnamese. Although these civilizations later developed their own writings, they never discarded the concept of **pictographs** (pictures used for writing) and **ideographs** (pictures used for concepts or ideas).

Pictographs

日

Represents:

"SUN"

月

Represents:

"MOON"

Ideograph

明

Represents:

"Brightness"
(SUN-MOON)

Buddhism Spread From China To Korea & Japan
During one of China's periods of disunity (220 - 581) many Chinese adopted **Buddhism.** The Tang dynasty persecuted Buddhists as the Confucian bureaucrat-scholars worried over its popularity. Buddhism never regained the number of converts it had previously. Between the 7th and 9th centuries, Buddhism was spread by merchants and missionaries to Korea and Japan.

B. U.S. - China: 1945 To The Present
There has been movement from hostility to tolerance in United States - Chinese relations.

Civil War In China: 1945 - 1947
At the end of World War II, as the Japanese withdrew from eastern China, both the Nationalist and the communist  forces rushed to control the area. The armies of Chiang Kai–shek used war material supplied by the United States during WW II, to fight Mao's communists.

In 1946, President Truman sent General George Marshall to negotiate between the communists and the Kuomintang and end the civil war. Neither side would compromise. The communists accused the United States of supporting Chiang Kai-shek with military and economic aid. After thirteen months of frustration, Marshall returned to the United States without a settlement.

The Break-off Of Relations: 1949 - 1972
Victory Of Mao Zedong, China: Totalitarian State

Supporters of the Kuomintang were arrested and many were executed. Diplomatic relations with the United States were broken when America refused to recognize the People's Republic as the legitimate government of China. By stationing its 7th Fleet off the coast of the Republic of China, the United States prevented the invasion of Taiwan, where Chiang Kai-shek had retreated in exile.

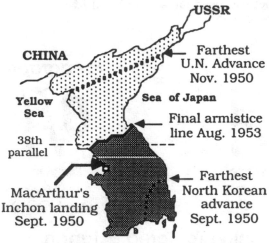

CHINA

USSR

Yellow Sea

Sea of Japan

38th parallel

Farthest U.N. Advance Nov. 1950

Final armistice line Aug. 1953

Farthest North Korean advance Sept. 1950

MacArthur's Inchon landing Sept. 1950

The Korean Conflict

Korean War (1950-1953)

After World War II, the Korean peninsula was divided at the 38° parallel; the North under Russian troops, the South occupied by American troops. Two separate governments developed: communist and anti-communist. In 1950, communist North Koreans had launched an invasion which nearly pushed the South Korean army into the sea. The United Nations' Security Council condemned the aggression and voted to enter the war. Within a few months, U.N. forces (American, South Korean, and 15 member nations) under the command of U.S. General Douglas MacArthur had penetrated deeply into North Korea. As the U.N. force drew close to the Chinese border, Red Chinese soldiers invaded Korea. Because of this escalation of the war, three years of heavy fighting and casualties resulted. In 1953, a truce was reached and the division at the 38° parallel was restored.

Vietnam War

In the mid-1960's, as the United States dispatched soldiers and equipment to combat communist insurgency in South Vietnam, Red China aided North Vietnam and the Viet Cong rebels in the south. President Nixon, who had campaigned promising to work for peace in Vietnam, sent his aide, Henry Kissinger, to secret negotiations with Russia and Red China. After these discussions, public negotiations followed with North Vietnam. In 1974, American troops were finally withdrawn from Indochina.

Current Relations And The Taiwan Issue

While present foreign relations between the United States and Red China are good, there are areas of disagreement. The largest issue is the question of Taiwan. Red China claims it belongs to the People's Republic, while the United States recognizes it as the democratic **Republic of China**, independent of the mainland. In 1982, a joint communique signed by the United States and the People's Republic promised gradual reduction of American aid to Taiwan.

C. Sino-Soviet Relations

With the defeat of the Kuomintang, the Soviet Union welcomed China to the world stage as a second major communist power. In the four decades since then, this friendship soured.

Sino-Soviet Disagreements (1950's-1980's)	
Peoples' Republic Of China	**Soviet Union**
Mao defended Stalin's image, policies, and personality cult.	1956 - Official attacks on late Soviet dictator Josef Stalin.
Mao claimed Chinese communism was the true version of Marxism-Leninism.	Claimed to be true leader of world communist movement as oldest Marxist nation.
Rejected "peaceful coexistence" with Western democracies; supported spreading Marxist revolutions throughout the undeveloped world.	Promoted idea of "peaceful coexistence" and avoidance of nuclear warfare.
Detonated first nuclear bomb in 1964.	Refused to aid China in nuclear technology after 1959.
Denounced U.S.S.R. for refusing to help communist China against non-communist India.	Sent aid to India in its 1961 border war with China

Continuing Problems

From the days of the Chinese Emperors and the Tsars, there have been many sources of friction: border disputes, claims to the Amur River Valley, support for the communist groups in Southeast Asia. China strongly condemned the 1979 Soviet invasion of Afghanistan.

The two communist giants clashed less frequently in the 1980's. Internal problems preoccupied the two rivals. In the late 1980's, Gorbachev visited Deng to ease some of the traditional tensions. They made some progress. Their wars of words eased. However, when Gorbachev resigned, most of the old problems remained. In the 1990's, the collapse of the Soviet Union and Russia's economic and governmental problems kept leaders from addressing problems.

Chinese Border Disputes

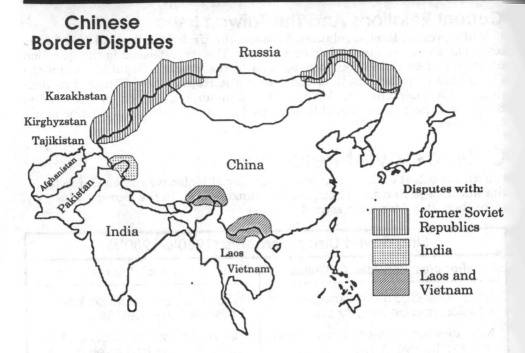

Disputes with:

- former Soviet Republics
- India
- Laos and Vietnam

D. Relations Between People's Republic And Third World After WW II

The communist regime has tried to claim a leadership role for China among the Third World nations.

China And "Wars Of Liberation"

China has become the strongest military power in East Asia. In the 1950's, Mao Zedong held the view that war with capitalism and imperialism was inevitable. He described the U.S. as a "paper tiger," and believed China should

World Issues:
War and Peace

support wars of liberation for the oppressed throughout the world. Chinese military aid and technical training has been sent to struggling Marxist rebels in Africa as well as other areas of Asia and the Pacific.

Korean And Vietnam Wars

Involvement in the Korean and Vietnamese wars showed that Mao Zedong intended that China was to play a major role in foreign affairs.

Chinese Role In The United Nations

In 1971, the Peoples' Republic of China was admitted to the U.N., and replaced the Republic of China (Taiwan) as the government officially representing mainland China. Not only is China represented in the General Assembly, it also has a permanent seat in the Security Council. Since that time, China has consistently supported anti-colonialism and other Third World interests and voted against Western democracies and Israel.

E. China's New Status In The Pacific

The People's Republic of China has reestablished itself in Asian affairs.

Trade And Diplomatic Ties With Japan

Red China's foremost trading partner is its former enemy, Japan. Japan imports China's agricultural products and also exports machinery and metal products to the Chinese. Diplomatic relations between mainland China and Japan were re-established in 1972.

Agreement With Britain: Hong Kong

Hong Kong had been permanently ceded to the victorious British at the close of the first Opium War (1842). An agreement was reached in the mid-1970's which set a lease on Britain's possession of the island. The accord states that the Chinese flag will be raised but British social, economic, and legal systems will exist until its lease expires in 1997. With the signing of the accord concerning Hong Kong's future, China and Great Britain ended the division that 19th century imperialism caused.

Questions

1   In the 1970's and 1980's, the U.S. and the People's Republic of China moved toward establishing better relations mainly because
   1   China has democratized its government and seeks to preserve human rights.
   2   both countries fear the rising industrial strength of Japan.
   3   the U.S. needs vital supplies of raw materials from China.
   4   both wish to balance the power of the U.S.S.R.

2   In the 1990's, Great Britain plans to return its Hong Kong colony to China. This planned event can be considered a victory of
   1   free trade over tariff restriction.
   2   nationalism over imperialism.
   3   communism over capitalism.
   4   ethnocentrism over internationalism.

3   An area of ancient China whose possession is a troubled issue for the U.S. and China is
   1   Manchuria.   3   Hong Kong.
   2   Korea.   4   Taiwan.

4   Since their victory in 1949, a major goal of China's communist leaders in Asia has been to bring about
   1   peaceful settlement to all Asian conflicts.
   2   permanent U.N. control of disputed regions.
   3   establishment of China as a global power.
   4   ownership of the Korean peninsula.

5   The introduction of Buddhism to Japan and Korea by ancient China is an example of
   1   cultural diffusion.   3   acculturation.
   2   assimilation.   4   ethnocentrism.

6   Which is an example of improved relations between the People's Republic
     of China and the United States?
     1   sale of U.S. products in China
     2   continued U.S. recognition of Nationalist China's government
     3   increased U.S. support for Vietnam in its struggles with China
     4   restrictions on Chinese immigration to the U.S.

7   The most accurate description of Chinese foreign policy today would be
     1   deep friendship with former Soviet republics in north and west.
     2   suspicion and coolness toward former Soviet republics in north and
          west.
     3   deep friendship and military alliance with the United States.
     4   suspicion and increasing hostility toward the United States

8   During the 1950's, United States' policies toward the People's Republic of
     China was influenced primarily by
     1   existence of Soviet power over Eastern Europe.
     2   fear of further communist expansion into critical areas of Asia.
     3   a close alliance between Japan and China.
     4   the stormy relationships between China and Vietnam.

9   Which foreign policy did both Chinese and Soviet communist leaders use
     during the Cold War?
     1   They supported African and Asian "wars of liberation."
     2   They promoted peaceful coexistence with Western democracies.
     3   They provided aid for India against Pakistan.
     4   They remained neutral in Southeast Asian communist revolutions.

10   Even after the collapse of the Soviet Union after Gorbachev, China and
     Russia still have problems on
     1   whose communist system is better.
     2   who should control Vietnam.
     3   control of former Soviet naval bases.
     4   their borders.

11   The purpose of China's intervention in both the Korean and Vietnam
     Wars was to show the Chinese
     1   resistance to imperialism.
     2   disdain for the United Nations.
     3   intention to act as a regional power in Asia
     4   possessed advanced nuclear technology.

Essay

The People's Republic of China is considered one of the world's major
powers.

   a   Discuss *two* issues which have caused friction between the U.S.A. and
        China. [5]

   b   Discuss *two* problems which caused friction between the communist
        regimes of China and the Soviet Union. [5]

   c   Discuss communist China's policies toward less developed countries.
        [5]

East Asia

JAPAN

HOKKAIDO

HONSHU

SHIKOKU

KYUSHU

VI. Physical/Historical Setting

Geography, climate, and location are keys to understanding the historical and cultural development of Japan.

A. Location And Size

Japan is an archipelago lying off the eastern coast of Asia. It extends 1,500 miles and covers over 142,000 square miles. Because it is an island nation, it has been able to isolate itself from invasion and commercial contact for long periods. This **insular** (separateness) behavior pattern is important to understanding Japanese culture.

Four Main Islands

The three southernmost islands: Honshu, Kyushu, Shikoku, are where Japan's civilization developed. Hokkaido, settled only in the 19th century, is the northernmost island. It has a rough terrain, severe winters and is still considered a frontier area. Adjacent to the four main islands are about 3,400 smaller islands, many of which are uninhabited.

Edge Of The East Asian Culture

Located off the eastern coast of Asia, Japan's position compares with Britain's off the coast of Europe. Despite the geographic conditions that favored isolation, Japanese civilization was influenced as a result of contact with China. Korea and the East China Sea served as the avenues of contact.

Political And Cultural Independence

Japan's insular physical geography has allowed it to observe and borrow selectively from other cultures without being overwhelmed by them. While Japan absorbed much of its culture from China and Korea, it was never controlled by these states.

Culture

B. Topography, Climate, And Resources

The secure boundaries and remoteness of their islands permitted the Japanese to develop a sense of cultural identity at an early period.

Mountainous Terrain, Small Percentage of Land Suitable for Farming. Eighty-five percent of Japan is mountainous. Agricultural land is at a premium. Since Japan has a high population density, it has had to look to the sea to sustain its people. Fortunately, the waters surrounding Japan are one of the world's richest fishing grounds.

Environment **Many Rivers, Favorable Climate Support Traditional Agrarian Economy.** Rivers are short with rapids and are not widely used for navigation. They are important for irrigation, and in the 20th century for hydroelectricity. The islands of Kyushu, Shikoku and more than half of Honshu are categorized as Tropical Rainy Climate (**Am-Monsoon type**). The northern section of Honshu and Hokkaido are Mid-Latitude Wet-and-Dry Climate (**DF-Rainy, cold winter type**).

Scarcity **Japan Lacks Resources Needed For Modern Industry.** Japan has copper and some small deposits of iron. Its coal deposits are not of the quality needed for steel production. About 90% of Japan's petroleum needs are met by Middle East imports. Japan's lack of natural resources was a major reason why it adopted aggressive policies towards Asian nations in the 20th century.

Prone to Natural Disasters. Japan suffers from volcanic eruptions and periodic earthquakes. It is also frequently struck by typhoons (hurricanes) and tidal waves from the Pacific Ocean.

C. Early History: Japanese Origins

Little archaeological research was done in Japan prior to World War II. Information about early Japan is still incomplete and rests heavily on Korean and Chinese written records. It seems that Japan's earliest settlers entered the islands of Sakhalin and Korea. Later migrations from other Pacific islands and southeastern Asia reached Japan's southern islands.

Yayoi Culture: Example of Cultural Diffusion. Between 300 B.C. and 300 A.D., new invaders from the Asian mainland, the **Yayoi**, sailed to Japan. They introduced wet rice cultivation and bronze, iron working.

Tomb Period (300 A.D. - c. 650) Marked by Tribal Society. The **Tomb Culture**, most advanced of early Japan's societies, developed from the Yayoi culture. It took its name from the high mounds of earth which were the tombs of the local chiefs. It was during the Tomb culture that references to Japan are found in Chinese sources.

Yamato Clan Leaders First Emperors of Japan. By the year 220 A.D. there were about 40 tribal communities in the Japanese islands. For the next two hundred years, the **Yamato**, from Honshu, were the most powerful and were accepted as the first imperial clan. Japan's political organization was an outgrowth of the tribal and clan societies.

Power Of The Imperial Family

While Chinese history is divided by dynasties, in Japan it is divided by the family names which actually held power behind the emperor.

Religious Role. Scholars were appointed to write an official family history for the **Yamato** imperial family. The result was the *Nihongi* or *Chronicles of Japan*, finished in 720 A.D. According to this history, the emperor traced his ancestry to various **Kami**, or spirits, who had created the islands of Japan. With the acceptance of this myth, the emperors were regarded as divine and the complete owners of all land. No one could question their authority.

Emperors Have Reigned But Rarely Ruled. While the prestige of the emperor was enhanced by legends of divine ancestry, noble families actually usurped the emperor's power. Indications of the minor role of the emperor are:

- the enormous power by the **Fujiwara** family, from the 10th through the 12th centuries
- the rise in influence of the military families in the 12th century and their extension of feudalism
- the long-term control of the **Tokugawa Shogunate** of 1603 - 1868 and its development of feudal institutions
- the force of the **Meiji Restoration** - This nominally returned power to the emperor, but actually permitted the rise of new coalitions of political leaders, industrialists, and the military
- the postwar parliamentary system, established by the Constitution of 1947, which placed power in the hands of the people

D. Religion In Japanese Culture
Buddhism Introduced In 552 A.D. By Koreans

The Japanese branch of Buddhism used the Chinese language, ceremonies, and architecture but it had no real influence among the common people in its early stage.

Shintoism: "The Way Of The Gods"

The development of **Shintoism** is an example of how physical geography and beauty influenced Japan's aesthetic values.

Shintoism has no founder or sacred writings. It is a religion based on **animism** (belief that objects contain a spirit) and the worship of nature. Shintoism does not accept the existence of one personal, all-powerful God. Shintoism looks to the physical world for meaning and stresses the individual's duty to live in harmony with his surroundings. Shintoism served to deepen the bond between the Japanese people, their family, and their nation.

Culture Shinto blended with Buddhism through most of Japan's history. Japanese religions became assimilations of several beliefs. A combination of Buddhism and Shintoism remains the major religious form today.

E. Chinese Influence

While the Japanese learned much from abroad, they have changed what they import to suit their own needs and tastes.

First Contacts With Chinese Civilization Via Korea. Most of Japan's contact with China's civilization came by way of Korea, Japan's closest neighbor. An appreciation for Chinese civilization gradually took root in Japan. During the reign of **Shotoku** (592-621), students were sent to the "Middle Kingdom" (as China referred to itself) to study Buddhism, art, Confucian philosophy, and government.

Diversity **Nara Period (710-794) Represents High Point of Chinese Culture in Japan. Nara** was Japan's earliest capital city. It was patterned after the Chinese capital Chang-an. Nara's imperial court became strongly influenced by Buddhist monks. In reaction to this domination, a new city, **Kyoto**, was built and served as the capital until 1868.

Japanese Developed Script From Chinese Characters. Written Japanese is partly based upon Chinese writing. Japan adopted pictographs and ideographs but found Chinese writing did not meet all the needs of the Japanese language. In the 9th century, Buddhist monks developed two writing systems in which the characters represented Japanese syllables rather than objects.

The Heian Classical Period (794-1185) Lessened Chinese Cultural Domination. Japan alternately encouraged and rejected outside contacts. During this time, Japan had less contact with China and adapted a broad variety of cultural borrowings.

F. The Feudal Period (1185 - 1600)

During Japan's feudal period, power rested in the hands of military strong-men, rather than in those of the emperor.

Samurai (the warrior class) Governments Replaced Court Nobles. The dominance of the warrior in feudal times made a deep impression on Japan's future. The power of the emperor's court declined as the samurai became the elite.

Shogun Wielded Supreme Power. The real power in Japan was the warrior-noble who led the samurai. In 1185, a noble by the name of **Yoritomo**, obtained the title **Shogun** (military ruler) from the emperor. It was an hereditary title, and future emperors were deprived of the power of selection and control over this supreme military ruler. Shoguns would rule Japan for 700 years.

Bushido, the Way of the Warrior. The **Code of the Warrior** (Bushido), developed during the mid-17th century. It was the guide to the ideal warrior, a blend of military discipline, Confucian thought, and Zen Buddhism. Bushido emphasized Confucianism's stress on the individual's duty to his superior. **Zen Buddhism** was popular among the samurai because its required meditation called for much self-discipline.

Samurai Bands Saved Japan from Mongol Invasions in the 13th Century. Kublai Khan, Mongol emperor of China, launched armadas against Japan in 1274 and 1281. Both fleets were heavily battered by typhoons. (This is the origin of **kamikaze**, meaning winds of the kami or divine winds). The Mongols who survived the storms were defeated by the samurai. At this time, only Japan, India, and Southeast Asia were able to withstand the demands of the Mongol overlord.

Cultural Developments Of Feudal Period (1185-1600)

Trade Flourished Between China and Japan. Silk, porcelain, and pottery were imported from the Middle Kingdom in return for Japanese swords and lacquer-ware. This commercial contact increased cultural borrowing and caused Japanese culture to bloom.

Art Forms Imported From China. Two examples of artistic efforts were flower arrangement and miniature **bonsai** cultivation (the technique of arresting the growth of trees). Another popular import was the Chinese tea ceremony. The Chinese-influenced land-scape painting, scroll painting, and architecture of the **Ashikaga Shogunate** (1338-1567) have never been surpassed.

Interdependence

Japan Developed Two Forms of Drama During the Feudal Period. The **Noh** play, which arose in the 14th century, dealt with Japanese myths and history. The second form of drama was the **Kabuki**, which originated in the 16th century. The Kabuki was directed towards the common people and was easier to understand.

Political Power Shifted To Local Authorities

The **Ashikaga Shogun** was never able to exert much political control beyond Kyoto. From the standpoint of peace and security, this was a disorderly time in feudal Japan. From 1333 to 1600, Japan suffered from internal wars. The local aristocracy, the **Daimyo** ("Great Lords"), fought among themselves for political supremacy.

Strong Military Government (1600)

General Tokugawa Ieyasu won the battle of Sekigahara, one of the most decisive battles of Japanese history. He then created the last of the military dynasties of Japan, the **Tokugawa Shogunate** (1603-1868). **Edo**, later called **Tokyo**, became the center of Tokugawa government.

Power

A Rigid Social Structure Imposed by Tokugawa Shoguns. The Classes of Japanese society, in descending rank, were: warriors, farmers, artisans, merchants. All positions were hereditary and duties belonged exclusively to each class.

Tokugawa Seclusion Policy. By the mid-17th century, newly established European contact with Japan was regarded as a threat to the Tokugawa Shogunate. It is seen by the following sequence of events:

* Portuguese traders arrived in 1542 and gradually increased their numbers

* European Jesuit missionaries accompanying the traders converted many Japanese (The most famous Jesuit was **Francis Xavier** who died at Macao in 1552). It is estimated that by 1600 there were 300,000 Christians in Japan

* Dutch traders arrived shortly thereafter, and began trade wars with the Portuguese

* Japanese authorities became fearful that Christianity and European traders would introduce social and political disorders, if not outright conquest. The Shogun forbade missionaries to enter Japan on pain of death; authorities also banned all contact with foreigners, except for very limited Dutch and Chinese trade in 1639.

Questions

1   Most of the Japanese terrain can be described as
    1   desert.   3   marshland.
    2   steppe.   4   mountainous.

2   Which would be correctly associated with Japanese culture?
    1   cultural diffusion   3   democracy
    2   monotheism   4   social equality

3   By the 12th century, Japan had
    1   accepted elements from Chinese culture.
    2   driven out Christian missionaries.
    3   conquered Korea.
    4   begun to industrialize.

4   Which figure would compare best to Japan's Shogun?
    1   a corporation president   3   a military dictator
    2   the President of the U.S.   4   a Christian missionary

5   What was the result of the Tokugawa Shogunate's seclusion policy?
    1   delayed Japan's development as a modern nation
    2   conquest of most of civilized Asia
    3   widespread competition with industrial nations
    4   a golden age of Japanese art and literature

6   The heroes or elite of the Tokugawa Shogunate would have been
    1   scholars.   3   merchants.
    2   Shinto priests.   4   samurai.

7   Japan's suicide pilots in the WW II were named "kamikaze" after the
    1   most famous Shogun.
    2   highest mountain peak of Japan.
    3   chief Buddhist deity.
    4   winds that destroyed Mongol armadas.

8   Why did Japan isolate itself in the 17th century?
    1   It feared a European conquest.
    2   Few Japanese were interested in Christianity.
    3   Europeans brought infectious diseases.
    4   It believed its civilization was superior to that of Europe.

9   Which was Shintoism's major teaching?
    1   achievement of human perfection
    2   reincarnation of the soul
    3   love for fellow humans
    4   reverence for the land

10   Yoritomo, who became the first Shogun,
    1   outlawed further cultural borrowing from China.
    2   took political power away from the emperor.
    3   helped establish Christianity as a major religion.
    4   began to build Japan into a modern industrial nation.

11   Which island is one of Japan's main islands?
    1   Hong Kong   3   Taiwan
    2   Honshu   4   Korea

12 Korea, Japan's closest neighbor, has often served as a
   1   home for the Japanese Emperor.
   2   buffer zone against European invasion.
   3   climatic barrier.
   4   bridge for cultural diffusion.

13 The rivers of Japan
   1   originate near the seacoast.
   2   all flow northward.
   3   are important for hydroelectricity.
   4   serve as ocean highways for many miles up-river.

14 The geographic relationship of Japan to the continent of Asia is most
   similar to the relationship of which country to Europe?
   1   Spain   3   Britain
   2   Denmark   4   Italy

15 In the 16th century, Francis Xavier altered Japanese culture by
   1   helping to develop its industrial base.
   2   leading a joint-European military conquest of Japan.
   3   establishing a French sphere of influence.
   4   helping to introduce Christianity.

16 Which natural resource is one of Japan's most crucial imports?
   1   diamonds   3   oil
   2   copper   4   silver

17 Which natural disaster strikes Japan frequently?
   1   blizzards   3   drought
   2   earthquakes   4   dust storms

18 To which famous writing did the Japanese trace the divinity of their
   Emperor?
   1   *Chronicles of Japan*   3   *Bushido*
   2   *The Analects*   4   *Tales of the Genji*

19 The Daimyo or "Great Lords" of the 14th century were involved in
   1   feudal wars for control of Japan.
   2   spreading Chinese culture.
   3   converting Japan to Buddhism.
   4   defending Japan against European conquest.

20 Asiatic invaders of Japan established the Yayoi culture. Which was not a
   feature of their civilization?
   1   feudalism   3   bronze working
   2   rice cultivation   4   use of iron implements

21 Which adjective would be an accurate description of Japan's climate?
   1   dry   3   temperate
   2   frigid   4   polar

Essay

Identify *three* important geographic (physical) features of Japan and in
each case, show its relationship to the country's cultural development or
history. [5,5,5]

VII. The Dynamics Of Change

Japan's cultural borrowing and long-established sense of cultural identity spurred the drive for industrialization and modernization to achieve world power status in the late 19th and 20th centuries.

A. Expedition Of Perry (1853)

American Motives for Perry's Action. The main purpose for Matthew Perry's expedition was to negotiate a treaty to protect American sailors shipwrecked in Japan's territorial waters. Because of Japan's hostility for foreigners, he was sent with a squadron of steamships as a show of force. Perry also requested that Japan open its ports to American ships and trade.

Japanese Response. After Perry refused demands to sail away, the Tokugawa officials, frightened by American warships, accepted his letter from American President Franklin Pierce. Perry announced he would return in one year to receive the Japanese response. The resulting agreement was the **Treaty of Kanagawa** (1854) in which Japan acceded to American demands.

B. Meiji Restoration (1868)

Japan modernized rapidly. A high literacy rate, urbanization, and a large pool of skilled labor indicated swift progress.

Overthrow of the Shogun. Signing of the Treaty of Kanagawa hastened the fall of the Shogun. Many samurai resented the presence of foreigners and wanted to unify behind the divine emperor in order to avoid the kind of experience the Chinese were having. Violence began and the last of the Tokugawa Shoguns surrendered Edo to imperial forces in May 1868.

Change

The result was a period which became known as the **Meiji** (Enlightened) **Restoration.** Modified political power was returned to the emperor and the last traces of Japanese feudalism began to dissolve.

Changes By 1912

The Meiji Restoration helped to provide the necessary political revolution to free the population from feudal restrictions and permit its participation in the economic modernization. The developments which accelerated changes were:

- establishment of a highly centralized bureaucratic government (an **oligarchy** which concentrated real power in the hands of a small group)
- establishment of a constitution which called for elected an parliament
- development of an **infrastructure** (transport and communication system)
- development of public education, free of feudal class restrictions, development of industry
- establishment of a powerful army and navy which virtually controlled the government. Although the divine emperor was considered "restored," he was still not the real power in Japan.

C. Japan As An Industrial Power

In the late 19th and early 20th centuries, scarcity of raw materials was a major factor in Japan's international relations and in its strategy of economic development. The quest for raw materials led Japan along a dangerous path:

Sino-Japanese War (1894-1895)

Meiji statesmen feared a Western imperialist nation would seize Korea from the decaying Manchu Empire. This growing unease led to the Sino-Japanese War, which Japan's modernized forces quickly won. The **Treaty of Shimonoseki** (1895) granted Japan the island of Formosa (Taiwan), and a large indemnity (war damage payments). Korea became independent of China. Japan began to create its own sphere of influence there.

Russian Empire

Manchuria (disputed)

Chinese Empire

Korea

Japan

Ryukyu Is.

Japanese 19th & 20th Century Expansion

Formosa (from China)

Russo-Japanese War (1904-1905)

Japanese rulers viewed Russian advancement in Asia with apprehension. Russia had acquired a foothold in the Liaotung Peninsula and wanted Korea. Meiji leaders feared any foreign power taking over Korea would be a "dagger pointing at Japan's heart." Too often in the past, Korea had served as a launching place for foreign assaults on

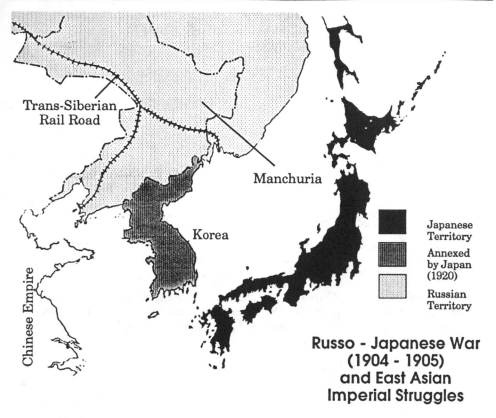

Trans-Siberian
Rail Road

Manchuria

Korea

Chinese Empire

Japanese
Territory

Annexed
by Japan
(1920)

Russian
Territory

**Russo - Japanese War
(1904 - 1905)
and East Asian
Imperial Struggles**

Japan. To block Russia from entering Korea, Japan launched a sneak attack on the Russian Pacific fleet anchored at Port Arthur. To the world's surprise, Russia was forced to sue for peace. By the **Treaty of Portsmouth**, Japan gained Port Arthur, territory in southern Manchuria, and the southern half of Sakhalin Island. In 1910, Japan annexed Korea and neither China nor Russia could do more than protest.

World War I And The 21 Demands

In World War I, Japan joined the Allies and declared war on the German Empire. It seized German treaty areas in China and some small Pacific islands. **The 21 Demands** were delivered to the Chinese Republic in 1915. If accepted, China would have become a Japanese protectorate. International outcry forced Japan to reduce its demands. Most of the remaining demands were incorporated into treaties with China. By the end of World War I, Japan was the dominant power in East Asia.

"Greater East Asia Co-prosperity Sphere"

Encouraged by their easy successes, Japanese nationalists pro- posed the creation of a new international order. Under their plan **Power** for a Greater East Asia Co-Prosperity Sphere, Japan would supply manufactured products and capital for underdeveloped areas. Korea, Formosa, and other less developed countries would provide food and raw materials for Japan.

D. Japan's Pre-WW II Expansion

Japanese aggressions against weaker nations were modeled after earlier imperialist actions of Western powers. Japan desired raw materials, markets, and the rank of a world power.

After World War I, Japan became upset with discriminatory Western policies (for example, the **Washington Naval Arms Conference** agreements of 1922 limiting Japanese naval power in comparison to that of Britain, France, and the U.S.). Hurt by the Great Depression, Japan used military production to recover. Aggressive acts against Asian neighbors revealed Japan's goal to become supreme in the Pacific.

Attack on Manchuria (1931). The **"Mukden Incident"** was an alleged Chinese attack on a Japanese train. Claiming riots were erupting, Japan overran the province of Manchuria and set up a puppet state, Manchukuo.

League of Nations Condemns Japanese Aggression. The **Lytton Commission** was established by the League to examine Japan's conquest of Manchuria. Its report in 1932 condemned Japanese actions. In answer, Japan withdrew from the League of Nations.

Marco Polo Bridge Incident. In 1937, Japanese army units on maneuvers, clashed with Chinese soldiers at a bridge near Peking (Beijing). Blame has never definitely been assigned, but from this incident grew the **Second Sino-Japanese War (1937-1945).**

Formation of the Axis. In 1940, Nazi Germany, Mussolini's Italy, and Imperial Japan signed the **Tripartite Pact**. Commonly known as the **Rome-Berlin-Tokyo Axis**, it joined three aggressor nations. In reaction, the United States banned the export of war materials, scrap iron, and steel to Japan.

Conquest of Southeast Asia. In 1941, Japan began seizing sections of Southeast Asia, gaining vital rubber, tin, and oil supplies. Since France and the Netherlands had been conquered by the Nazis, and Britain was fighting for her survival, almost no resistance was offered.

U.S. Reaction: Embargoes on Trade. U.S. officials condemned Japanese aggression in China and Southeast Asia. In the summer of 1941, America **embargoed** (refused to sell) oil, scrap iron and steel, hoping to halt the Japanese attacks.

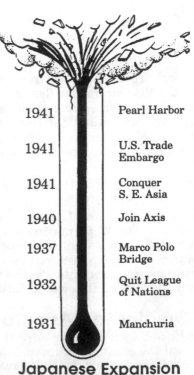

1941	Pearl Harbor
1941	U.S. Trade Embargo
1941	Conquer S. E. Asia
1940	Join Axis
1937	Marco Polo Bridge
1932	Quit League of Nations
1931	Manchuria

Japanese Expansion Leads to an Explosion

Pearl Harbor Attack, 7 December 1941

As American and Japanese diplomats prepared to confer in Washington, D.C., to resolve current tensions, news came of the "sneak attack" on Pearl Harbor. Over 2,000 Americans died on what President Franklin Roosevelt referred to as a "Day of Infamy." This surprise attack led to the American Congress declaring war against Japan.

E. Japanese Expansion During WW II

By 1942, Japan had captured Hong Kong, Malaysia, Thailand, Burma, Indonesia, the Philippines, and part of New Guinea. The tide of Japanese expansion was halted at the battle of **Midway** (1942). U.S. forces, then on the offensive, adopted the tactics of "island hopping."

This was an all-out assault on key islands, with high American casualties, while leaving other isolated islands to "wither on the vine." Japanese soldiers were indoctrinated in Bushido and chose "**banzai**" suicidal attacks rather than face the dishonor of surrender. Over 1,200 Japanese became "kamikaze" pilots in 1944-45, sacrificing their lives by crashing bomb-laden planes into American ships.

The Pacific Theater

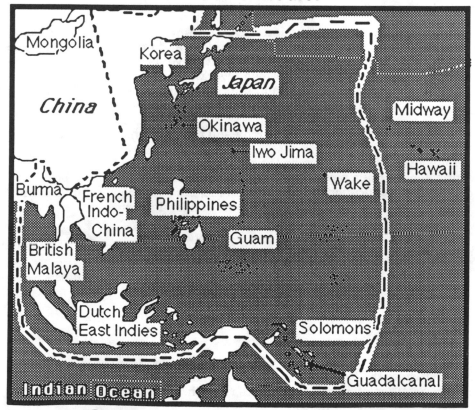

– – – – Farthest extent of Japanese conquest (1942)

F. Bombing Of Hiroshima And Nagasaki

American Rationale For Dropping the Atom Bomb. Japan had been pushed back to her home islands, regarded as sacred by the Shinto religion. The American military advised Truman that Japan would never surrender and would have to be invaded. Possible American casualties were estimated at one million, with hand to hand combat lasting one year. Truman ordered the use of a new secret weapon, the atom bomb. The military selected the city of Hiroshima as the target. Although the city was obliterated, Japan would not surrender until a second city, Nagasaki, was destroyed. As the world moves further from World War II days, the tendency has been to increase condemnation of Truman's decision to use nuclear weapons to end the war.

G. U.S. Occupation Of Japan, 1945-1952

The post World War II occupation reforms had great economic, political, and social impact upon Japan. Reforms which produced lasting change in Japan, were those for which there were bases of support in Japanese society.

Role of the U.S. Military. American troops occupied Japan until 1952. During this time, Japan's government was subordinate to the Supreme Allied Commander, General Douglas MacArthur, who was responsible for sweeping reforms.

U.S. Influence on Constitutional Development. United States occupation led to the diffusion of some American ideas and practices into Japanese culture. The objective was to give Japan a democratic government that would work toward social reform and reestablish Japan in the community of nations. The results of American occupation of Japanese government were:

Political Systems

- establishment of a limited monarchy and reform of the parliamentary system
- elimination of domination by the military
- promulgation of a new constitution (1947), including provision for compulsory education, women's rights including suffrage, establishment and protection of rights of labor unions, and land reform

Questions

1   Political power concentrated in the hands of a very few constitutes
    1   representative democracy.
    2   constitutional limited monarchy.
    3   limited democracy.
    4   an oligarchy.

2   An important reform in Japan following World War II was the
    1   return to the Emperor the powers he had lost during the war.
    2   recognition of Shinto as the state religion.
    3   nationalization of industry.
    4   adoption of a constitution which established democracy.

3 Created before the outbreak of the Second World War, the Tripartite Pact linked the Japan to the
   1 Communist nations.
   2 Axis Alliance.
   3 League of Nations.
   4 East Asian Co-Prosperity Sphere.

4 Economic conditions in Japan during the period 1920-1940 contributed to the
   1 strengthening of parliamentary government.
   2 growth of political stability.
   3 rise of an expansionist party.
   4 success of the League of Nations.

5 Which was the chief victim of imperialistic aggression in Asia during the years 1915-1939?
   1 China   3 Japan
   2 Thailand   4 Soviet Union

6 Which describes Japanese policy in the early 20th century?
   1 Spreading Shintoism was a motivating force in its expansion.
   2 Proclamations of neutrality amid European power struggles in China.
   3 Lack of basic raw materials led to aggressive action.
   4 Military alliances were necessary because it was surrounded by hostile powers.

7 Which event convinced Western nations that a new imperialistic power had developed in the Far East?
   1 Russo-Japanese War
   2 Boxer Rebellion in China
   3 French annexation of Indochina
   4 Great Britain's control of Hong Kong

8 China, weakened by concessions and economic privileges granted to foreign powers became an easy prey for Japanese aggression. Which event best portrays this idea?
   1 the Meiji Restoration   3 the Pearl Harbor Attack
   2 the Sino-Japanese War   4 Perry's Expedition

9 During World War I, Japan
   1 joined forces with Germany.
   2 participated in the war in order to gain territory.
   3 was forced into the war by direct attack on its land.
   4 declared its position only in the last year of the war.

10 Before 1945, modern Japan
   1 exported large quantities of wheat.
   2 needed raw materials and markets.
   3 discouraged farming.
   4 wanted to maintain China's territorial integrity.

11 Manchuria became a symbol of Japan's
   1 attempts to aid underdeveloped regions.
   2 desire for empire.
   3 religious conversion to Christianity.
   4 experimentation with socialist government.

12 One reason why modern Japan came into conflict with China was that
    China
    1   possessed one of the oldest civilizations.
    2   was overpopulated.
    3   possessed natural resources.
    4   was too friendly with Russia.

13 Which headline could have appeared during the first decade of the 20th
    century?
    1   *Treaty of Portsmouth Ends Russo-Japanese War*
    2   *Lytton Report Condemns Japanese Aggression*
    3   *War Ends - Japan Loses Empire*
    4   *Rome-Berlin-Tokyo Axis Announced*

14 The Russo-Japanese War
    1   resulted from rivalry for control of Korea.
    2   grew out of Japan's alliances in World War I.
    3   saw Japan fighting to defend China.
    4   made Western powers force Japan to reduce its naval power.

15 Japan's "21 Demands" were an attempt to
    1   ally itself with Germany and Italy.
    2   gain entry into the League of Nations.
    3   establish a protectorate over China.
    4   defeat the United States at Midway.

16 U.S. General Douglas MacArthur was the Allied Commander in World
    War II and
    1   directed the postwar reconstruction of Japan.
    2   forced Japan to withdraw from the League of Nations.
    3   opened Japan to Western trade.
    4   supervised the Meiji Restoration.

17 Kanagawa Treaty in 1854 was responsible for "opening" Japan to
    1   Russian conquest.
    2   Confusian philosophy.
    3   the East Asian Co-Prosperity Sphere.
    4   Western trade, ideas, and technology.

18 Which strategy did American commanders use in the Pacific
    from 1942-1945?
    1   guerrilla warfare   3   saturation bombing
    2   island hopping   4   naval blockade

Essay

The Industrial Revolution greatly changed the course of Japanese
history.

 a   Explain how Western technology entered Japanese society in the
       19th century. [5]

 b   Describe *two* changes made in Japan under the Meiji Restoration. [5]

 c   Discuss the foreign policy goals of Japan between World War I and
       World War II. [5]

VIII. Contemporary Japan And Culture

Japan is a technologically advanced society, democratically governed, and primarily urban.

A. Japan Population Characteristics

Size, Distribution

Japan is a densely populated nation having 122 million inhabitants in an area about the size of California. The population density is 846 persons per square mile (1986). Seventy six percent of the population lives in urban areas; twenty four percent lives in rural areas. Japan's literacy rate and per capita income are the highest in Asia.

Homogeneity

Because of their insular geography and centuries of seclusion, the Japanese are a homogeneous people. Although they were willing to adopt western methods for efficiency and modernization, they have retained much of their traditional life. A study of Japan reinforces the message that westernization and modernization are not always synonymous.

B. Democratic System Of Government

Postwar Japan might be likened to the phoenix of Greek legend which rose triumphant from the ashes. What has emerged from the shock of defeat and occupation after World War II has been a new Japan which has moved ahead under a strong, democratic system of government.

Parliamentary System Of Government

Japan is now a constitutional monarchy under an **Emperor** and a two-house, democratic legislature (the **Diet**) which produces a **Prime Minister**, the nation's chief executive. The **Cabinet of Ministers** assists the Prime Minister, and is responsible to the Diet.

Political Parties

The major parties are the **Liberal Democrats** and the **Socialists**. There have been occasional crises precipitated by leftist parties and movements, but Japan has remained a functioning democracy.

C. Educational System

Japan places much emphasis on education and enjoys a literacy rate of 99%. While Japan has produced a literate, skilled work-force, some Japanese criticize the pressure which the educational system places on youth. Japan's educational system is characterized by high standards and competitiveness. To qualify for admission to high schools and universities, Japanese students must pass difficult examinations. Since the number of openings are limited, competition is fierce. Because a university degree is the major means to a good job and income, education has become one of the most competitive areas in Japanese life.

D. Social Conditions And Social Relations

Urban Issues And Problems

Rapid industrial growth has been at the expense of public services. Japan has serious housing shortages. Areas where more public spending are needed are health care and pollution control. While the cities are overcrowded, there are few actual slums, and Japan enjoys a lower crime rate than the United States.

Evolving Role Of Women

The male's power as head of the family has declined as the male now spends more time at work. While fewer marriages are still arranged by family and friends, arranged marriages still account for over 50% of Japanese unions. The average age of bride and groom has risen to the mid or late 20's as more women are in the work force. Officially, women have been given equal rights with men. While their status has risen, few females are in leading positions in business, government or science.

Work Relations

Employees identify strongly with their employer. Corporations offer workers lifetime employment until retirement at about age 55. As a result of this security, workers in Japan have not formed militant labor unions nor do they change jobs as frequently as Americans.

Changing Social Conditions

Social conditions showing the transition to modern Japan, include: change to nuclear families in urban areas, declining birth rates, and decreasing support of household religious rites among the young.

E. Impact Of Japan's Aesthetic Ideas

Continued Use Of The Haiku

The Japanese people have a rich literary heritage. Since the 17th century, Japanese poets have expressed their thoughts by means of the **Haiku,** a short poem of only 3 lines which usually expresses a mood. In contemporary Japan, it is still a creative medium.

Leisure Activities

Some of the most notable changes in Japan have been in the field of recreation. Japanese flock to movies, watch television, and enjoy spectator sports. The increasing effect of industrial "mass culture" can be seen. There are more modern comforts and conveniences in most homes. The middle class of Japan has become more and more consumption oriented.

Questions

1   Which change in social living patterns has occurred in industrialized Japan since World War II?
   1   increased leisure time
   2   lower standard of living
   3   decreased emphasis of material goods
   4   increased emphasis on hereditary status

2   The introduction of karate into the U.S. and baseball into Japan are
    examples of
    1   cultural diffusion.   3   acculturation.
    2   assimilation.   4   ethnocentrism.

3   The best evidence that Japan has been greatly influenced by Western
    values and ideas is Japan's
    1   strengthening of the old family system.
    2   efforts to increase the power of landlords.
    3   insistence upon rigid job definitions and work rules.
    4   adoption of parliamentary democracy.

4   A major barrier to equal rights for women in Japan today is in
    1   advancement to executive positions.
    2   ownership of private property.
    3   political party enrollment.
    4   admission to higher educational institutions.

5   The real political power today in Japan is held by the
    1   high military officials.   3   Emperor.
    2   shogun.   4   legislature.

6   Which characteristic best describes education in modern Japan?
    1   medieval   3   dominated by militarists
    2   religiously oriented   4   highly competitive

7   The government of contemporary Japan is a functioning
    1   federal union.   3   socialist state.
    2   constitutional monarchy.   4   democratic republic.

8   Which factor helps explain the growth in Japanese industrial
    productivity since World War II?
    1   emphasis on employment of unskilled workers
    2   high rates of unionization
    3   low tariffs
    4   strong worker identification with employers

9   In which urban problems category does the U.S. and Japan differ most?
    1   crime rates   3   housing shortages
    2   pollution   4   overcrowding

10 What is an accurate description of life in Japan today?
    1   Japanese are still a rural people.
    2   Japanese continue to isolate themselves from other nations.
    3   Japanese have eliminated all social and economic classes.
    4   Japanese are blending Western culture with their own.

Essay

Since 1945, industrialization has had a major impact on Japanese social,
political, and economic forces and institutions.

Forces and Institutions

· labor unions   · public education   · urbanization
· women's rights   · leisure activities

Select *three* of the items listed above. For *each one*, discuss *two* ways in
which industrialization has had an impact on that force or social
institution. [5,5,5]

IX. Economic Development Of Japan

Trade has been the lifeblood of modern Japan, crucial to its prosperity and growth.

A. Economic Recovery After WW II

In 1945, Japan was one of the most devastated nations in the world. One-fourth of Japan's manufacturing capacity and communications network was destroyed. Its maritime fleet was devastated.

Goals Of Occupation Government

Economic goals included at making Japan self-supporting and reducing the domination of farm and factory by the privileged few. To achieve these goals:

* American investments were provided to re-establish industry
* land reforms were instituted to increase food production
* contract incentives were given to labor unions
* attempts were made to break up large corporations (**zaibatsu**) and to encourage small industries

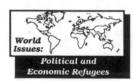

World Issues:

Political and Economic Refugees

Effect Of Korean War

The 1949 communist takeover in China persuaded the United States to seek a new ally in Asia. Japan received over two billion dollars in aid and loans directed toward its economic reconstruction. Japan also benefited by selling much food and equipment to American forces in the Korean conflict (1950-53).

After Occupation, Rapid Industrial Expansion Occurred

Technology was needed to overcome problems posed by the physical environment, particularly a lack of natural resources. Reasons for Japan's re-emergence as a great industrial power were:

* Technological Innovation (New, efficient factories were built.)
* Skilled Labor Supply (Japan's greatest resource has been its hard-working, highly motivated labor force)
* Substantial United States aid

B. Japanese Economy

Increasingly, Japan has turned to advanced technology to improve its economic position in the world market.

Tremendous Growth

Japan has been one of the world's leaders in technology and trade since the 1960's. Its total production of goods and services is second only to that of the United States. The domination of the zaibatsu has reappeared. Large corporations, such as Mitsui, Mitsubishi, and Fuji, dominate the economy and drive out competition.

Emphasis On Electronics And Heavy Industry

Japan is world famous for its electronics and other technology-related products. In heavy industry, it is one of the major world producers of steel, machinery and ships. Its automobile industry is one of the most profitable in the world.

C. Continuing Needs And Problems

The health of the economy depends on world trading conditions and on Japan's capacity to maintain and extend its exports.

Need For Industrial Raw Materials

The scarcity of raw materials and oil has affected the pattern of economic development. Because Japan's major imports are metal ore, raw materials, and food, it has become the best customer of Australia and the underdeveloped nations of Southeast Asia.

Dependence On Imported Petroleum

As a major importer of fossil fuels, the Persian Gulf is a crucial waterway to Japan's economic health. Over 90% of Japan's oil requirements are met by imports from the volatile Middle East.

Food Supply

Only 13% of Japan's land is used for agriculture and as few as 9% of the work force, including fishermen, work to produce food. Japan cannot sustain its growing population. Major suppliers of food for Japan are the United States, People's Republic of China, Australia, and Canada.

Oil-dependent industrial nations held hostage by Persian Gulf politics.

Environmental Concern

Ecology (preserving the natural environment) has become a major political issue among the younger generation of Japanese. They see conservation as vital to survival.

Population Changes

Japan's population continues to decline. It has one of the lowest birth rates in the world. This has caused a shortage of labor. Survival may require allowing more foreign labor into Japan. Many critics fear that Japan's traditions and culture will suffer if immigrants flood the country.

D. U.S. - Japan Economic Interactions

The trade imbalance experienced by the United States in its trade with Japan, and by Japan in its quest for raw materials, show the **interdependence of nations** in the global economy.

Interdependence   **Imbalance in Mutual Trade Relationships.** The United States suffers from a trade deficit in its trade relationship with Japan. While Americans purchase many Japanese products, Japan has high tariffs to prevent domestic consumption of foreign goods. While the Japanese government aids its businesses with tax breaks and low cost loans, it has also made it difficult for foreign firms to prosper.

World Issues:

World Trade and Finance

Trade with Japan accounts for nearly half of the U.S. trade deficit. Japan's restrictions on American products create many problems. Recent economic recessions caused increased tension between the two countries. U.S. Presidents placed high priorities on working with Japanese leaders to reduce the trade imbalance. Both countries want trade to remain open.

Japan needs to maintain a favorable balance of trade with some wealthier nations, such as the United States, in order to pay for the raw materials and oil it imports. In response to American threats of import quotas on its products, Japan's government promised to increase its defense spending, relax trade barriers for foreign businesses, and make its economy less export-intensive.

Questions

1   Which is the best definition of the zaibatsu?
    1   philosophers who believe true knowledge can only be derived from science
    2   a laboratory equipped by industrial corporations
    3   one of the major corporations which control Japan's economy
    4   an important principle of economics

2   What is a tariff wall?
    1   high taxes on imported goods
    2   a favorable balance of trade
    3   alternate period of prosperity and depression
    4   a barrier to stock brokers

3   How did the Korean War benefit Japan?
    1   Communist expansion was broken in Asia.
    2   Japanese industry sold to the American military forces.
    3   Red China bankrupted its economy helping North Korea.
    4   Southeast Asia looked to Japan for protection.

4   Japan is dependent on which unstable world area for its petroleum supply?
    1   Western Europe   3   the Middle East
    2   Indonesia   4   Mexico

5 Which is the best explanation for Japan's current industrial success?
1 need to support heavy military expenses
2 vast reserves of raw materials and fossil fuels
3 the government's role in setting and supporting national goals
4 emphasis on individual achievement rather than group effort.

6 A chronic problem which has always faced Japan has been a shortage of
1 natural resources.
2 unskilled labor.
3 investment capital.
4 markets for their manufactures.

7 Which statement is most accurate regarding Japanese industrial success?
1 Japan began to industrialize before European nations.
2 The traditions of hard work and discipline are built into its industrial life.
3 Industrialization has had little effect on its foreign policy.
4 Its industry has solved the problem of endangering the environment.

8 One goal which the American occupation government failed to meet after World War II was
1 construction of new factories.
2 land reform.
3 establishment of labor unions.
4 breaking up the zaibatsu.

9 Crucial to Japan's economy is continued reliance on
1 heavy defense industry spending.
2 unskilled foreign labor.
3 imported petroleum.
4 foreign investment capital.

10 A major supplier of food for Japan is
1 India.
2 Bangladesh.
3 Australia.
4 Philippines

Essay

Today, Japan ranks third in the world in total production of goods and services. Discuss *three* characteristics of the modern Japanese economy which have raised it to this status. [5,5,5]

X. Japan In The Global Context

Japan now relies on its economic power rather than military strength in its global relationships.

A. Anti Nuclear Policy

When nuclear tests are carried out by the world powers, protests follow from the Japanese government and general public. Many Americans today have empathy for the Japanese in their concern about nuclear warfare.

B. Present Military Status Of Japan

Although Japan's Constitution outlawed war as an instrument of national policy, Japan, under steady U.S. prodding, has increased its armed forces.

Article 9 Of The Japanese Constitution Of 1947 Outlawed War

In part, Article 9 reads:

> *"...the Japanese people forever renounce war as a sovereign right of the nation and the threat or use of force as a means of settling international disputes... In order to accomplish the aim... land, sea, and air forces... will never be maintained."*

Self-Defense Forces

With the outbreak of the Korean War in 1950, the United States withdrew occupation troops from Japan. Japan was permitted to organize small army, navy, and air units.

C. U.S. - Japanese Mutual Security

One term of the U.S.-Japanese Mutual Security Pact (1951) was that the United States agreed to take the major responsibility for defending Japan. While the treaty has been revised, this essential provision remains in force.

Protected By United States "Nuclear Umbrella"

Despite a steady military build-up, Japan insists its armed forces are only for its defense. Any attempt to amend Article 9 has been defeated as a majority of Japanese prefer to rely on the United States.

With U.S. protection, Japan has had to spend relatively little on defense, freeing investment capital for industry. As the Asian power structure has changed, the United States has pressured Japan to increase its defense spending by announcing a cutback in U.S. troops in Japan.

Interdependence

D. Japan's Role In World Organizations

Since the beginning of its modernization, Japan has sought international influence.

Termination Of Membership In The League Of Nations

When the League condemned Japanese occupation of the Chinese province of Manchuria, Japan withdrew from that international organization (1932).

Soviet Veto Of Japanese Admission To The U.N. (1952)

Although the Soviet Union regained territory from Japan at the close of World War II, the Soviets refused to sign a formal peace treaty. Relations were strained until 1956 when the two nations resumed diplomatic relations. Russia permitted Japan to join the United Nations in 1956, although it disapproved of Japanese-U.S. defense arrangements.

E. Japanese Relations: Asian Nations

Japan has had to overcome hostility which persisted in those parts of Asia it conquered in World War II.

Japan Controls Significant Economic Power In Asia

While Japan may be dependent on other countries for resources, its industrial strength gives it power in international relations.

World Issues:

World Trade and Finance

Present Japanese Relationships:

With Southeast Asia: Japan has paid reparations for war damages and given economic aid to Southeast Asian nations. Important trade relations exist with Japan dominating the economy of the region.

With People's Republic of China: Trade between the two nations has grown since Japan's trade embargo against Red China during the Korean War. Diplomatic relations were not instituted until 1972.

With South Korea: Relations were poor until 1965 when Japan and Korea set a World War II reparations figure and restored diplomatic relations. Japan agreed to pay for its exploitation of its former colony.

Interdependence

F. Japan's Role In Global Economics

Japan wields enormous economic strength. Japan's Gross National Product in 1990 was $1.8 trillion. The GNP for the U.S. was $2.5 trillion. Japan participates in summit conferences with the heads of state of the most powerful industrial democracies.

Questions

1   The purpose of Article 9 of the Japanese Constitution was to
    1   build an international police force.
    2   establish high tariff walls.
    3   outlaw war as an instrument of national policy.
    4   abolish tariffs on grain.

2   The United States gave economic aid to Japan after World War II to
    1   create an ally against the spread of communism.
    2   strengthen Japan against British power.
    3   help Japan socialize its industry.
    4   raise the Japanese standard of living.

3   Following the Korean War,
    1   Korea was unified.
    2   Japan built up its armed forces.
    3   communist influence in Asia ended.
    4   Japan joined NATO.

4   Which is most characteristic of Japan's foreign policy?
    1   voting with Russia in the United Nations
    2   spreading communist propaganda in Asia
    3   offering aid to communist Vietnam
    4   broadening trade relations in Southeast Asia.

5   From which international organization, formed after World War I to preserve peace, did Japan withdraw in 1932?
    1   League of Nations
    2   Security Council
    3   Mandate System
    4   United Nations

6   Which event occurred last?
    1   Twenty-one Demands
    2   Japan's admission to the U.N.
    3   Bombing of Pearl Harbor
    4   Japan's surrender to the U.S.

7   According to the post World War II peace treaty with the U.S., Japan
    1   was required to pay reparations.
    2   retains ownership of Taiwan.
    3   has the right of military self-defense.
    4   could not trade with communist China.

8 Which Asian nation, formerly an enemy of Japan, is now a major trading partner?
1 People's Republic of China
2 Cambodia (Kampuchea)
3 Pakistan
4 Vietnam

9 Japan's successful advancement to major global status proves which factor is critical for power and prestige?
1 abundant natural resources
2 charismatic leadership
3 strong military
4 technology

10 Japanese foreign policy toward other nations since 1945 has been generally motivated by
1 social and humanitarian concerns.
2 a desire for isolationism.
3 a desire to spread its ideology.
4 economic advancement.

Essay

Japan has significantly improved its foreign relations since the end of World War II. Discuss the status of contemporary Japanese relations with *three* of the following: [5,5,5]

- Southeast Asia
- People's Republic of China
- Republic of (South) Korea
- Western Europe
- The United States of America

Unit Four

Latin America

Barrio
Caudillo
Machismo
Assimilation
Urbanization
Mercantilism
Pan-American
Fragmentation
Pre-Columbian
Encomienda System

		BC	AD			
3000	1000			1000	1500	1600

• Mayans   • Olmecs   • Aztecs (Mexico)   • Spanish Conquistadores

• Chavin - Nazca - Huari - Inca (Peru)   • Portugese

1800 — 1900 — 1950 — 2000

- Indepencence Movements
  - Gran Columbia
  - Monroe Doctrine
  - Juarez & Diaz
- Spanish–American War
  - Panama Canal
  - Mexican Civil War
- OAS
  - Castro
- Contra Affair
  - Norlega Drug Arrest
- Alliance For Progress
- Good Neighbor Policy

Unit Four: Latin America

Latin America is a region that has had significant influence on the other regions of the globe. That influence, and the physical, historical, political, and social elements which make up the cultures of the variety of peoples that live in this vast region, will be the focus of this unit.

I. The Physical/Historical Setting

A. Geography And Resources

Political Subdivisions

Latin America is located south and southeast of the United States. Latin America consists of thirty-three independent nations and three **dependent states** (colonies). Geographers usually sub-divide the region into Mexico, Caribbean America, Central America, and South America.

These sub-regions are extremely diverse, each having different cultures and traditional development. Colonization by the nations of the Iberian Peninsula in Europe (Spain and Portugal) in the 15th and 16th centuries A.D. has created a cultural connection which often oversimplifies our view of the region. The dominance of the **Latin-based (Romance) languages** (**Spanish** throughout most of the region, **Portuguese** in Brazil), have led to the general description of the region as "Latin America." However, there are areas where English, Dutch, and French are also official languages. The Iberian Spanish/Portuguese dominance in the colonial period also accounts for the dominance of the **Roman Catholic** religion in the region. In modern times, groups like the **Organization of American States** (OAS) have drawn the nations of the region together to solve mutual problems.

Physical Features

Diversity   The physical and political maps in this unit indicate this is a large region, encompassing almost eight million square miles (1/6th of the Earth's land surface). It runs nearly six thousand miles from north to south and is over three thousand miles at its widest point.

Much of the region lies in the tropics. Severe winters are not usually found. However, due to the **variety of elevations** in its rugged topography, nearly every major climate except the polar types can be found. The amount of rainfall areas receive varies greatly. Such variations in climate and topography have significant influence on the lives of the people.

For centuries, the people of Latin America have been separated by the vast mountain ranges, dense rain-forests, and unnavigable rivers which have blocked the establishment of a good **infrastructure** (transportation and communication system).

Latin America
Political Features

Latin American Landforms

Atlantic Ocean

Caribbean Sea

Sierras

Pacific Ocean

Orinoco River

Amazon Basin

Andes Mts.

Lowlands

High Plateaus

High Plains

Mountains

Rio de la Plata

Pampas

DP

Most of the population lives on the plateaus that range from 4,000 to 9,000 feet above sea level and offer a temperate climate. The latitude, altitude, and prevailing winds have had much to do with the patterns of life in the region. A unique feature of Latin America is the **vertical environmental zones**. In mountainous regions, all three of these zones can be found within a few square miles. There, they are major determinants of human activity.

The physical features of Latin America include its massive mountain ranges, lengthy river systems, extensive plateaus, and small plains. The coastal **Sierras** of Central America and **Andes Mountains** of South America form a cordillera ("backbone" mountain chain) along the entire western coast of Latin America that is an extension of the Rocky Mountains of North America. The highest peaks in the Andes are over 20,000 feet above sea level and are exceeded in height only by the Himalayas in Asia. The highest peak is Argentina's **Aconcagua** (22,831feet). East-west travel in the Andes is limited to a few narrow passes.

Diversity   The river systems of South America are critical to the region's development. The **Orinoco River** in the north winds its way from the Guiana Highlands through 1,500 miles of Venezuela before emptying into the Atlantic.

The **Amazon River** system in the center drains from the Andes into the vast lowland basin occupying the northern half of Brazil. The Amazon is over 3,000 miles long and has nearly 200 tributaries. It is second in size only to the Nile system in Africa. The Amazon River system drains over 2% of the world's fresh water into the Atlantic Ocean. Farming is nearly impossible, but this huge tropical rain-forest yield large supplies of natural rubber and carnuba.

The **Rio de la Plata** (River of Silver) is actually an **estuary** (broad, shallow bay) in the southern part of the continent formed by two other rivers which drain from the Andes — the Parana and the Uruguay.

This river system provides an irrigation basin for one of the most productive agricultural regions in the world.

Two large plateau regions contain rich farmlands and mineral reserves. The **Brazilian Highlands** in the south-central region near the Atlantic coast contain Brazil's major population centers. **Gran Chaco** is a 200,000 square-mile flatland shared by Argentina, Bolivia, and Paraguay. Here, cotton and yerba mate (a native tea) are grown extensively.

The plains areas are savannas. They are used for raising livestock and grains. They include the **Llanos** of northern Venezuela and Columbia, Brazil's **Mate Grasso**, the huge **Pampas** of Argentina, and the cold, barren **Patagonia** on the southern tip of the continent.

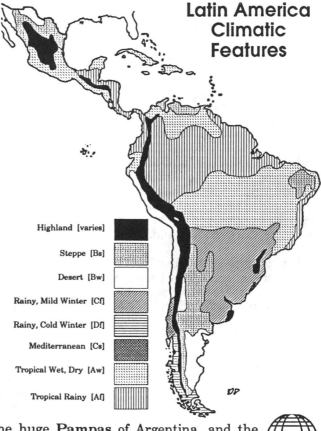

Latin America Climatic Features

Highland [varies]

Steppe [Bs]

Desert [Bw]

Rainy, Mild Winter [Cf]

Rainy, Cold Winter [Df]

Mediterranean [Cs]

Tropical Wet, Dry [Aw]

Tropical Rainy [Af]

Diversity

Resources

Latin America is fortunate to have abundant natural resources. Its soils produce 75% of the world's coffee, 60% of its bananas, and 25% of its sugar cane. Other staple crops include cacao, tobacco, cotton, maize, and rice. There is extensive herding of beef cattle, sheep, llamas, alpacas, and goats for food,

Land of Contrasts

Gaucho rides the Argentine Pampas   Denseness of the Amazon Rain-forest hides and fur. Mexico, Venezuela, and Ecuador are major producers of petroleum and natural gas. From South American mines come great quantities of iron ore, manganese, tin, bauxite, copper, silver, and gold. The region suffers from lack of adequate technology, and many farmers exist at a subsistence level, forcing some nations to import food supplies.

People

The region has a variety of racial and ethnic mixtures. Over the centuries there has been much blending of racial groups. Three main peoples have formed the historic background of the area: Indians, Europeans, and Africans. The Indians were the earliest inhabitants, migrating down the American continent from the Asian interior in prehistoric times. Today they make up the bulk of the population of Mexico, Guatemala, Ecuador, Peru, and Bolivia. Most of the descendents of African slaves brought by Europeans live in Brazil, Colombia, Venezuela, Haiti, Cuba and the other Caribbean islands.

The original European colonizers intermarried with Indians forming a mixed group, commonly called **mestizos**. Mestizos make up about one third of the Latin American population. The major portion of the fifteen million **caucasians** are found in the southern areas (Argentina, Chile, Uruguay). In recent years, there has also been significant immigration from Asia.

Seventy percent of all Latin Americans live in urban areas, and twenty cities exceed one million in population. It is here that the contrast between rich and poor is most dramatic where modern high-rise apartments share neighborhoods with squatter slums, called **barrios**.

Compared to other regions of the world, race prejudice is rather minimal in Latin America. Discrimination is more evident among economic classes than racial or ethnic groups.

B. Early Civilizations

Traditionally, Indians have suffered the most from discrimination. This is ironic, for these peoples had high civilizations of amazing accomplishment in **pre-Columbian times** (before the first voyages of European discovery by Columbus in 1492). Three of the most highly developed Indian civilizations were the Maya,

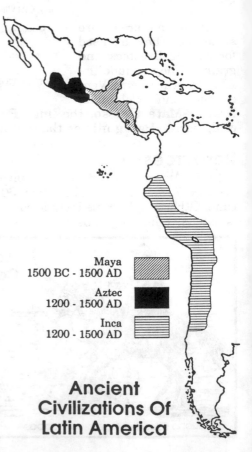

Maya
1500 BC - 1500 AD

Aztec
1200 - 1500 AD

Inca
1200 - 1500 AD

**Ancient
Civilizations Of
Latin America**

the **Aztec**, and the **Inca**. They were highly advanced and had well-developed **pyramidal social structures** which were the forerunners of Latin American structures of today.

Each culture developed in isolation from the others and from the rest of the world. Not until the European Age of Discovery did they become known, and they disintegrated rapidly after the European colonization began.

The Maya Civilization (c.1500 B.C. - 1548 A.D.)

The **Maya** civilization began in Mesoamerica (a region of Central America) as an agrarian economy, relying on the production of maize. Villages were shifted frequently as their "slash and burn" agrarian techniques quickly wore out the infertile rain-forest soils.

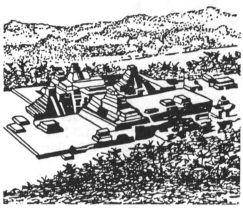

Their great ceremonial center became the city of **Tikal**, with its palace and pyramid temples arranged in a great forum. A polytheistic religion was the unifying social institution. Its major deities were connected to planting and harvests, and guided the sun, moon, soil, rain, etc.

Tikal

Historians claim that, at its peak in 300-900 A.D., Mayan culture appears to be the most advanced of the pre-Columbian civilizations. They excelled in mathematics, astronomy, architecture, ceramics, and sculpture. They had a complex writing system that combined phonetic symbols with **ideographs** (picture writing) which astounds linguists and is still being translated today.

The Aztec Civilization (1200-1535 A.D.)

The **Aztec** civilization emerged from a nomadic warrior group which settled in central Mexico about 1200 A.D.

Tenochtitlan (the present site of Mexico City) was the magnificent center of the Aztec state. It had an estimated population of 100,000 people and was built on a lake with an ingenious series of moveable bridges connecting its islands. It became the capital of an empire that ruled over five million people. It had an elaborate legal system, with liberal use of capital punishment.

The principal deity of the Aztecs was **Huitzilpochtli**, god of sun and war. Aztecs frequently waged war to expand their empire and to capture prisoners from neighboring tribes for human sacrifices at their annual religious rites.

Mayan Stone Carving

Aztec Temple - Tenochtitlan

An estimated 20,000 such sacrifices were made annually. The Aztecs engineered elaborate reservoirs and floating gardens to supplement their maize production. They adopted many of the cultural advances of their southern neighbors, the Mayas. Aztec artisans created exquisite gold and silver jewelry as well as carved jade, crystal and wood sculpture. Their most sacred activity was warfare, and this would lead to their downfall when the European colonizers arrived in the 1500's.

The Inca Civilization (1200 - 1535 A.D.)

The **Inca** Empire (1200-1535 A.D.) was built in the Andes Mountains of Peru. The name means "children of the sun." At its peak, the empire ruled about 15 million people. It included much of what is present-day Ecuador, Peru, Chile, and Bolivia. From the capital at Cuzco, an emperor ruled over a totalitarian state.

The Inca civilization was known for its vast supplies of gold and silver which were used in jewelry of stunning quality. Although the Incas learned about roads, irrigation systems, and imperial administration from previous tribal empires, it is apparent that their own original achievements were equally impressive. Their agricultural terracing in the mountainous terrain and the assigning of different crops to different elevations, making each dependent on the other, was astonishing. They domesticated llamas and alpacas to transport goods on a magnificent network of roads. Relay runners were constantly traveling these roads carrying messages throughout the empire. They kept official records on bundles knitted and beaded strings called **quipu.** Their spoken language, **que chua**, was highly developed. They used anesthetics in medicine and had developed brain surgery techniques.

Inca Engineering - Roads and Bridges

Fortress City Of Machu Picchu

Machu Picchu, their famed fortress city, sits in the Peruvian Andes 6,750 feet above sea level. The city's stone monuments and buildings were the Incas' crowning achievement. Just prior to the arrival of the European colonizers in the early 1500's, a royal family struggle erupted into a civil war and made the weakened empire easy prey for outside conquest.

The historical development of Latin America is rich and diverse. A variety of environmental conditions make this region a fascinating blend of diverse people and culture.

Questions

1 Geography has often caused people in Latin America to experience
  1 environmentalism.   3 urbanization.
  2 agrarianism.   4 isolation.

2 The llanos is an area of South America known for its
  1 grasslands.   3 rain-forests.
  2 mountainous terrain.   4 deserts.

3 The Aztec civilization was known to neighboring people for
  1 irrigation programs.   3 ritual animal sacrifices.
  2 warlike behavior.   4 peace efforts.

4 The Inca Empire was centered in the
  1 Amazon Basin.   3 Gran Chaco.
  2 Yucatan Peninsula.   4 Andes Mountains.

5   In the 20th century, the flow of population into the cities has led to
   1   deeper economic class divisions.
   2   decreased pressure on rural regions.
   3   greater isolation.
   4   more European colonization.

6   The landform that has been a barrier to cultural and economic development in Latin America is
   1   cordilleras.   3   estuaries.
   2   llanos.   4   mestizos.

7   Latin America produces three-fourths of the world's supply of
   1   corn.   3   rice.
   2   tea.   4   coffee.

8   The Amazon Basin is being developed by Brazil as a new
   1   defense installation.
   2   wildlife preserve.
   3   agricultural and industrial area.
   4   historic Indian memorial.

9   The dominant cultural characteristics common in Latin America are
   1   English language and parliamentary government.
   2   French language and Protestantism.
   3   Spanish language and Roman Catholic religion.
   4   African language and Islamic religion.

10 The main racial and ethnic groups in Latin American history have been
   1   Africans, Europeans, and Indians.
   2   Asians, Muslims, and Europeans.
   3   Indians, Arabs, and Africans.
   4   Europeans, Indians, and Asians.

Essay

Three great Indian civilizations existed during the Pre-Columbian era of Latin American history: Inca, Mayan, Aztec. Choose *one* of these, and discuss the following aspects of the civilization:

a   the major achievements [5]

b   the economic livelihood [5]

c   the influence of geography [5]

II. The Dynamics Of Change

A. European Colonialism
The Age Of Discovery
The European "**Age of Discovery**" had a dramatic impact on the historical development of Latin America. In 1492, Christopher Columbus, searching for a short water route to the "East Indies" of Asia, discovered the islands of the Caribbean Sea. Numerous explorers followed.

In the 15th and 16th centuries, Spain and Portugal became major colonial powers because of the might of their **armadas** (navies). In this **Age of Exploration**, they were the two nations that led Europe in efforts to colonize the "New World."

Date	Explorer (Nation)		Discovery
1492-1504	Columbus	(Spain)	West Indies & Central Am.
1500	Cabral	(Portugal)	Brazil
1513	Balboa	(Spain)	Panama / Pacific Ocean
1519-21	Magellan	(Spain)	circumnavigated the globe
1519	Cortes	(Spain)	Mexico
1524-35	Pizarro	(Spain)	Peru

Colonial Development
As more knowledge about the Americas emerged, the crowns of Europe desired more and more control over the newly discovered lands. After Columbus' sensational discovery, intense competition between the Catholic sovereigns of Spain and Portugal had to be arbitrated by the Pope. In the **Treaty of Tordesillias** (1494), an imaginary line was drawn through the Atlantic. Spain was allowed to make claims to the west of it and Portugal to its east.

Two factors promoted rapid colonization by Spain and Portugal in the 15th and 16th centuries. The first was a strong **mercantilist** economy (establishing colonies as government-sponsored private business enterprises to bring wealth to the mother country). The second was high degree of Catholic **missionary zeal**. During this time, Latin American societies were influenced more by the new economic structures than racial differences. Indian labor was scarce and proved difficult to manage. The colonizers began importing slaves from Africa to work their farms. This led to even more racial variety and mixture.

Change

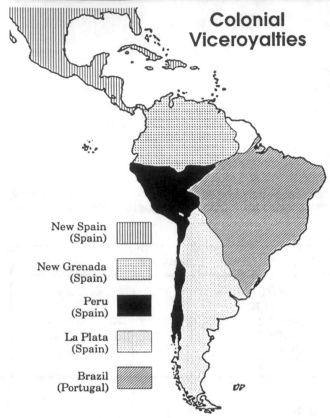

Colonial Viceroyalties

New Spain (Spain)

New Grenada (Spain)

Peru (Spain)

La Plata (Spain)

Brazil (Portugal)

This treaty arrangement explains why Portugal claimed the large area of Brazil, while most of the rest of Latin America (including much of the southern area of North America) fell into Spanish hands. Spain also moved more quickly to explore the New World.

Portugal was more interested in trade routes around Africa to India and the rest of Asia. Portugal did not start to develop its Brazilian lands until the Mid-Sixteenth Century.

Spain sent out fortune seekers and **conquistadores** (conquerors) immediately. The Spanish were consumed by Indian myths like that of **El Dorado**, the fabulous city of gold.

Filled with the spirit of the **Counter-Reformation**, Catholic Church officials felt an obligation to Christianize the local population and save them from the **Protestantism** of northern European nations like England.

Power

Missionaries were sent to build churches and schools in the settlements. They taught Iberian languages and culture to the local peoples. Because of this, the Roman Catholic church became the dominant social institution of Latin America.

Mercantilist ventures in "New Spain" involved plantation agriculture, mining, or cattle ranching. These were rural enterprises and few large settlements were built. Spanish rule was through authoritarian crown governors called **viceroys**. There were also crown appointed boards, called **audiencas**, to watch over the viceroys and advise them.

Between 1505 and 1700, Spain divided its New World holdings into four huge **viceroyalties**: New Spain, Peru, New Grenada, and LaPlata. The wealth of the empire depended on the forced labor of the Indians, and few laws protected them.

Although some Africans had been with the earlier explorers and conquistadores, the Spanish colonists began importing slaves in large numbers to work the mines and land in 1522.

Political Authority And Social Classes

A distinct social class system began to emerge. It was based on birth and resembled the Hindu caste system. Vast tracts of land, called **encomiendas,** were controlled by Iberian-born nobles (**peninsularies**), or American-born sons of such nobles (**criollos**). These colonists were pledged to protect the social welfare of the Indians on their assigned holdings. This rarely occurred.

One of the most bitter protests over the mistreatment of Indians and African slaves was led by a priest, **Bartolome de las Casas.** **Empathy** However, the church was generally neutral in such matters or acted as a tool of colonial administrators. As the titular head of the church within their empire, the Spanish rulers had the power to appoint all pastors and other church officials. The crown granted permission to collect special church taxes. The church did serve as a unifying element for the society, but it also accumulated vast wealth through inheritance of estates and the **tithe** (10% of a person's earnings were to be donated).

Initially, there was less domination in the huge Portuguese colony of Brazil because of official neglect. In 1555, a **Political Systems** French attempt to move into the area was prevented, and the Portuguese began to strengthen their rule. They divided the huge colony into districts they called **captaincies.** Towns, ranches (**fazendas**), and other business operations began to emerge along the Atlantic coast. An overall **Captain-General** (governor) was appointed by the Portuguese crown.

Sugar cane, grown on the fazendas, was the first profitable crop. Indians would not adjust to plantation life, and West African slaves were imported. Inter-marriage became common. It led to a high percentage of **mulattoes** in the Brazilian population.

The blurring of racial groups meant that class lines were drawn more as to one's wealth and occupation, rather than race. There was slightly more religious toleration in Brazil, but the Roman Catholic church was still the major unifying force in Brazil as it was in the Spanish territories.

In addition to Spain and Portugal, there were colonies of other European states. On the northern coast of South America and in the Caribbean, **England**, the **Netherlands**, and **France** established small, profitable colonies whose economies depended on sugar plantations.

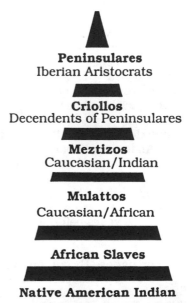

Peninsulares
Iberian Aristocrats

Criollos
Decendents of Peninsulares

Meztizos
Caucasian/Indian

Mulattos
Caucasian/African

African Slaves

Native American Indian

B. Independence Movements

Historians consider it ironic that the first outbursts against colonial rule in the late 18th century did not come from the strictly ruled Spanish or Portuguese regions, but against the French on the island of **Hispaniola**. In **Saint - Dominique**, a self-educated black slave, **Toussaint L'Overture**, led an insurrection in 1791. It was suppressed, but inspired a series of revolts which ended in independence for the new nation of **Haiti** in 1804.

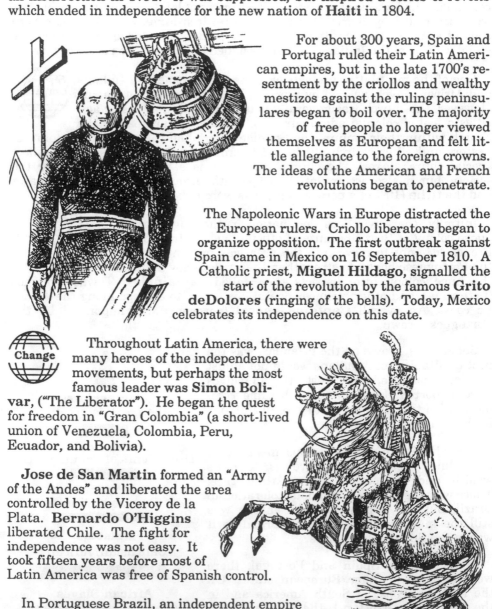

For about 300 years, Spain and Portugal ruled their Latin American empires, but in the late 1700's resentment by the criollos and wealthy mestizos against the ruling peninsulares began to boil over. The majority of free people no longer viewed themselves as European and felt little allegiance to the foreign crowns. The ideas of the American and French revolutions began to penetrate.

The Napoleonic Wars in Europe distracted the European rulers. Criollo liberators began to organize opposition. The first outbreak against Spain came in Mexico on 16 September 1810. A Catholic priest, **Miguel Hildago**, signalled the start of the revolution by the famous **Grito deDolores** (ringing of the bells). Today, Mexico celebrates its independence on this date.

Change   Throughout Latin America, there were many heroes of the independence movements, but perhaps the most famous leader was **Simon Bolivar**, ("The Liberator"). He began the quest for freedom in "Gran Colombia" (a short-lived union of Venezuela, Colombia, Peru, Ecuador, and Bolivia).

Jose de San Martin formed an "Army of the Andes" and liberated the area controlled by the Viceroy de la Plata. **Bernardo O'Higgins** liberated Chile. The fight for independence was not easy. It took fifteen years before most of Latin America was free of Spanish control.

In Portuguese Brazil, an independent empire under **Pedro I** was proclaimed without bloodshed in 1822. Spain was weak and exhausted by 1821, and most of the Central American countries were able to announce the formation of a short-lived federation and achieve independence without a struggle.

The European colonial powers were more resistant to independence when it came to the Caribbean islands. It would take several generations more for them to win their freedom.

In a span of 300 years, Latin America experienced dynamic changes. The region had endured the Age of Discovery, harsh colonial rule, exploitation, and finally, independence. For all the negative elements of the colonial experience, the Iberian nations had left a legacy of cultural unity and enrichment through their social structure, traditions, language, religion, and the arts.

Questions

1   Mercantilism was an economic philosophy in which colonies existed for the economic good of the
   1   colony's population.   3   middle class merchant.
   2   mother country.   4   Christian churches.

2   The king's representative in the Spanish colonies of Latin America was called a
   1   Captain.   3   mulatto.
   2   Viceroy.   4   Criollo.

3   The first independence movement in Latin America occurred in
   1   Brazil.   3   Bolivia.
   2   Haiti.   4   Central America.

4   Mixed marriages of European settlers and Indian natives produced
   1   criollos.   3   mulattos.
   2   slaves.   4   mestizos.

5   The largest racial group of people in Latin America are
   1   Blacks.   3   mestizos.
   2   Spanish.   4   mulattos.

6   The term *conquistador,* as applied to Spanish colonization in the New World, refers to
   1   large land grants.   3   expert navigators.
   2   plantation owners.   4   military explorers.

7   "Grito de Dolores" signifies
   1   a colonial treaty between Spain and Portugal.
   2   the beginning of Mexico's revolution.
   3   Bolivar's war cry.
   4   the conquest of the Aztecs by Cortes.

8   Portuguese sugar cane plantations in Brazil ware called
   1   fazendas.   3   peninsulares.
   2   viceroys.   4   audiencas.

9   The Spanish colonial empire in Latin America lasted
    1   400 years.   3   200 years.
    2   300 years.   4   100 years.

10. An encomienda represented
    1   a tax paid to the Roman Catholic Church.
    2   an Andes mining operation.
    3   a vast land grant to peninsulares.
    4   a slave revolt.

Essay

During the colonial period in Latin American history, a distinct social-economic structure emerged which was to limit advancement for a majority of the people. Certain groups became dominant, while others suffered.

Groups

- Peninsulares   • Mestizos
- Criollos   • Mulattoes
- Indians

a   Use *all* of the groups above to explain the social structure that emerged in the colonial era. [9]

b   Select *two* of the groups and discuss their living standards within the social structure. [6]

III. Contemporary Latin America: Nations And Cultures

Political independence brought much change to Latin America. Population shifts from the rural areas to the cities, a high birth rate, and nationalism have simultaneously helped and hindered progress. There has often been resistance to change. Social institutions, like the close-knit family structure, the landed aristocracy, the military, and the church, have sometimes combined to slow the process of change. Regional culture and geographic barriers have also blocked progress. Political analysts call this division **fragmentation**. To achieve progress, government leaders must try to bridge this fragmentation between the strong traditions of Latin America and the urban-industrial pattern of growth.

A. Initial Attempts At Unification

In the early 1800's, strong nationalism in the newly independent countries prevented early leaders from uniting the countries into larger groupings. Simon Bolivar's **Gran Columbia** and the **Central American Federation** both met with poor financing, intense regional jealousy, and internal power struggles among leaders. The fragmentation was difficult to overcome.

Bolivar himself provides an example. He had used the noble ideals expressed in the United States Constitution to rally the people against the Spanish rulers. When he assumed the presidency of Gran Columbia, he had himself declared president-for-life, and concentrated power in his own hands, abandoning democracy. The country was later torn by civil war.

Latin America After Independence Movements c. 1830

B. Obstacles To Change

Unity was difficult to achieve in these early stages because of the rugged terrain and the great travel distances. Democracy was also frustrated by the lack of preparation people had for self-rule. Power seemed to remain in the hands of those who owned the fazendas and encomiendas. They made up a **landed aristocracy, or oligarchy** (governing body of a small, elite group), which had no interest in creating democratic reforms which might undermine their wealth and position. The landed elite were supported by the military

Power and the church that did not want disruption of the **status quo** (the current power structure). In this alliance of social and political interests, the military kept law and order so that the other groups could keep their property and wealth. Strong military leaders, dictators called **caudillos**, were kept in power by the landowners and the church. Few democratic elections were held. They were usually managed by the caudillos to preserve their power. While democratic leaders have often led opposition to this structure, it still remains in effect in many Latin American nations.

Citizenship The church lost some of its power after the overthrow of the colonial powers. It did not adjust to meeting the needs of the new societies. Church **hierarchy** (leaders) wished to hold on to the land and wealth they had accumulated in return for services to the colonial rulers. Church leaders often allied themselves with the wealthy land owners and lined up behind the absolute power of the new dictators and their supporting **juntas** (military committees). Since these systems were built on the personality of the individual caudillos, **coups d'etat** (internal power struggles), have become a frequent and familiar scene in Latin America.

C. Political Evolution
Since Independence

Political Systems This generalized view of political structures does not give a clear picture of the varied systems in Latin America. A look at situations in Mexico, Argentina, Cuba, Puerto Rico, and Nicaragua will be useful.

Central America

Mexico

Some nations have done better in establishing democratic systems than others. Mexico is a case in point. Mexico became a dictatorship after independence in 1821. Antonio Lopez de **Santa Anna** managed to rule for nearly thirty years, losing Texas and most of the northern half of the original nation to the United States in the 1840's.

Benito Juarez, a liberal reformer, emerged in the 1850's. Mexicans regard him as their greatest President. He struggled against conservatives and the church to gain reforms for the lower classes, especially Indians. The result was a new constitution, but foreign intervention delayed the reform program. In 1863, an Austrian archduke, **Maximillan**, was set up by the French as emperor of Mexico with the help of local conservatives. He was overthrown shortly afterward with the help of the United States. Juarez died just after re-establishing independence.

After Juarez' death, **Porfirio Diaz** became the "law and order" caudillo of Mexico from 1876 until he was forced to resign in 1911. During his rule, there was superficial peace and prosperity, but peasants and factory workers were not sharing in the prosperity. Living conditions were very poor for the lower classes.

A six-year civil war, that saw some of the landholders' private forces fighting the national army, ended with a new constitution. The new government under President **Venustiano Carranza** guaranteed all Mexicans the right to vote. For the first time mestizos began to dominate the country's political life.

Argentina

Political evolution in Argentina occurred differently. Following the dictatorship of **Juan Manuel de Rosas** (1829-1852), a new constitution modeled after that of the U.S. was approved. A period of stability and prosperity followed, attracting a large number of European immigrants.

By 1900, Argentina had become the wealthiest nation in Latin America. As happened in Germany, Italy, Spain, and many countries during the worldwide depression in the 1930's, the economic collapse set the scene for Argentine political upheaval. A military coup d'etat overthrew the civilian government and began a half century of decline.

During World War II, a local caudillo, **Colonel Juan Peron**, emerged as a favorite of the middle classes and the militant labor unions. While he promoted higher wages and fringe benefits for the working classes, he quelled the opposition by cutting back freedom of speech and the press. His popular wife Eva, (known to the people as **"Evita"**) a dynamic Minister of Health and Labor, had succeeded in getting women the right to vote. When Evita Peron died at age 33 in 1952, Juan Peron's regime was shaken. Living in fear, he lost considerable support by weakening the power of the church and then alienating the military. Peron was deposed and exiled to Spain in 1955.

Cuba

The island nation of Cuba has also experienced a dramatic political evolution. It was liberated as a result of U.S. intervention in the Spanish-American War of 1898. The U.S. granted Cuba independence in 1902, with the agreement that the U.S. would be able to intervene if it felt it was necessary. A series of "do-nothing" dictators ruled until 1933, when **Fulgencio Batista** seized control. Batista catered to American business interests, allowing them to take huge profits in sugar and tobacco, but little of the money earned ever got to the laboring classes.

In 1956, Fidel Castro began a revolt against Batista. Castro succeeded in 1959. Castro then set up the first communist state in the Western Hemisphere. The United States cut off relations. Cuba used aid from the Soviet Union to build its military and help communist rebels elsewhere in Latin America and Africa.

Communism declined in the U.S.S.R. and Eastern Europe in the 1980's. Gorbachev cut aid to Castro. Castro's regime began to run into trouble. He cut aid to Ortega in Nicaragua, and the communists there lost power (see below). In recent years Cuba has appeared less hostile. It has been trying to improve relations with neighboring countries.

Fidel Castro

Nicaragua

The most successful of Castro's revolutionary ventures has occurred in the Central American nation of Nicaragua. A communist guerrilla movement called the **Sandinistas** (in memory of a 1920's rebel, Augusto Sandino), used Cuban-Soviet aid to overthrow the dictatorial **Somoza** regime in the late 1970's. Sandinista leader **Daniel Ortega** became President and created a military state with increased aid from Cuba and the Soviets.

World Issues:

Determination of Political and Economic Systems

In 1981, relations with the U.S. came to a crisis as **President Reagan** approved a plan to have the American Central Intelligence Agency give aid to an opposition force, the **Contras**. The 1990's began with Nicaraguans going to the polls and unseating the Sandinista Party in favor of a moderate coalition party. **Violeta Chamorro**, wife of a slain opposition leader, was elected President. The Chamorro government is pledged to end the contra rebellion and revive the war-ravaged economy.

Panama

On November 3, 1903, Panama declared its independence from Columbia. United States President Theodore Roosevelt had sent American gunboats to the region and recognized the new nation almost immediately because he wanted to negotiate a treaty to build an interocean canal through the region. Almost simultaneously, Panama became an independent nation and granted the U.S. the right to create a Canal Zone through the middle of the country.

By 1978, the Canal had become less useful to the U.S. and a treaty signed by President Carter arranged for a gradual transfer of the Canal Zone back to the Panamanian government by the year 2000.

Power

Over the years, a series of anti-communist military governments in Panama had been given U.S. support. However, in late 1989, President Bush authorized an invasion of U.S. troops to protect American lives and property in the Canal Zone from the threats of sabotage by forces under a hostile dictator, **General Manuel Noriega**.

Noriega had been under indictment for narcotics smuggling into the United States. The U.S. invasion resulted in Noriega's capture and restored civilian control of the government.

D. Urban Versus Rural Change

The movement from the farm to the city has also caused problems for the agricultural areas. As governments channel their funds into relieving the cities' problems, they are forced to neglect the farmers. Funding for education and technology to help increase agricultural production has been cut drastically. This causes divisions in the society between urban and rural groups competing for the governments' attention.

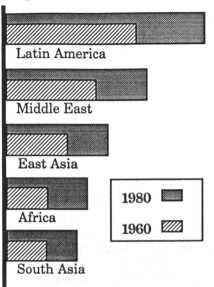

Regional Urban Growth

Latin America

Middle East

East Asia

Africa

South Asia

1980
1960

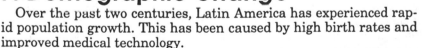

0 10 20 30 40 50 60 70 80
Percent of Population in Cities
Source: World Bank, 1983

E. Changing Social Institutions

As seen in the examples of political evolution, patterns of national change are not always clear. The experiences of these nations reflect the variety of roles played by the military, church, landowners, and labor organizations. There are constant struggles over land, wages, working conditions, education and social, economic, and political equality.

F. Demographic Change

Over the past two centuries, Latin America has experienced rapid population growth. This has been caused by high birth rates and improved medical technology.

In certain regions, such as the southern countries, European immigration has added to this rapid population growth. In Central America and the northern region of South America, Asians have been entering in large numbers. Many of the immigrants have settled in urban areas.

Since World War II, Latin American cities have grown nearly twice as fast as the rest of the other cities of the world. Most of this growth has been caused by internal migration from rural areas. Victims of poverty and illiteracy who lack job skills have moved to the cities seeking work. Most migrants are forced to live in the **barrios** (poor squatter settlements), often in cardboard or tin shacks with no water or electricity.

Recent projections show that, by the year 2000, Sao Paulo, Brazil and Mexico City, Mexico will be the two largest cities in the world with over twenty million people each. (Note: New York City has 7.2 million people.)

Many governments have tried to relieve the enormous problems by building public housing. It is estimated that one-third of Latin America's urban population live in the barrios. The consequences of this urban population explosion can be clearly seen. Shortages of food and other goods, congestion, disease, and pollution are ever present in the run-down overcrowded sections.

G. Other Social Factors

Within this growing political and economic gap, the family has remained the cornerstone of stability and security in Latin American society. Personal ties are seen as more important than political affiliations.

The extended family is still found throughout the region at all levels of society. Clannish family pride is very strong. The families are male-dominated (**patrilinial**) and a **machismo** attitude (exaggerated sense of masculine dominance) pervades most of the social life.

Culture

In the past, marriages were arranged for women, and the role of the female was always as support to the male. Some of this male dominance has begun to erode. Economic prosperity among the urban middle and upper classes has opened employment and educational opportunities for females. By 1961 women in all nations of Latin America had achieved the right to vote. Conditions vary, and Latin American women generally lag behind in the progress women have achieved in other western societies.

Industrialization and **mobility** (moving physically and socially to gain better economic and political positions) have had enormous impact on Latin American societies. Migrations of people always cause upheaval, and in the more industrialized nations of Argentina, Uruguay, Brazil, and Mexico, its effect on the social structure is becoming more evident.

The middle classes are beginning to make their presence known in politics. The small elite land-owning families are beginning to be challenged. The urban middle class identifies more closely with the needs of the poorer levels of laboring classes. Expenditures for education are increasing. Few people go beyond elementary levels, but literacy is still approaching 75%. This can provide a vital link between the middle and poorer groups seeking justice.

Questions

1 Which happened in most new Latin American nations following the
   independence movements of the 19th century?
   1 monarchies were re-established by European powers.
   2 liberal reform movements began.
   3 communist guerrillas launched counterrevolutions.
   4 dictators called caudillos emerged.

2 Elitist groups which exercised great power in the newly independent
   Latin American republics were the
   1 artisans.   3 subsistence farmers.
   2 landed aristocracy.   4 intellectuals.

3 An oligarchy refers to rule by
  1 the majority.   3 a single person.
  2 a small group.   4 the military.

4 A group of military commanders that reinforces a dictator is called
  1 a monarchy.   3 a senate.
  2 a commonwealth.   4 a junta.

5 Puerto Rico's official political classification is a
  1 state.   3 nation.
  2 colony.   4 commonwealth.

6 When Fidel Castro came to power, U.S.- Cuban diplomatic relations were
  1 improved.   3 established.
  2 broken.   4 liberated.

7 The squatter settlements in large urban centers of Latin America are often called
  1 juntas.   3 barrios.
  2 coups d'etat.   4 contras.

8 In Nicaragua, the guerrilla revolutionaries that took control after the overthrow of the Somoza regime were called
  1 Sandinistas.   3 Machismos.
  2 Contras.   4 Hierarchy.

9 Why was Argentine dictator Juan Peron overthrown?
  1 He could not defeat the communist guerrillas.
  2 He insulted the United States.
  3 He alienated the church and the military.
  4 He would not allow women voting rights.

10 A major change after Mexico's 1914-17 civil war was that power passed to
  1 male-dominated families.
  2 a committee of military commanders.
  3 liberals and communists.
  4 those with Indian blood.

Essays

While the revolutions against European colonialism were successful, most new Latin American countries experienced great difficulties.

a Explain why the countries were so poorly equipped to govern themselves. [5]

b Discuss *two* specific instances of Latin American nations struggling to establish democratic government after independence. [5,5]

IV. Economic Development

A. Capital And Manufacturing

Latin America's economic development has both great potential and severe limitations. There is an uneven distribution of most resources in the area as a whole, and an uneven pattern of development within each of the nations. There is a significant gap between the general economic growth and the quality of life of the majority of the inhabitants. There have also been positive and negative effects of a recent wave of international immigration.

The Colonial Period

Latin America has had a pattern of economic dependence since the days of European colonization. The colonies first relied on the mother countries. In the mercantile system, the colony exported raw materials and cash crops and imported the mother country's goods. As the Spanish and Portuguese control eroded, U.S. and European trading partners emerged (England, France, the Netherlands). In the two centuries since independence, most Latin American nations have relied chiefly on the United States.

Post - Independence Era

Under the 19th century trade situation, young Latin American nations remained largely undeveloped and highly dependent on imports from abroad, while their trading partners prospered. Only minor industrial development occurred in the areas of tanning, pottery and weaving.

Interdependence

Dominance Of U.S. Capital In The 20th Century

In the 20th century, increased foreign capital brought industrialization. Substantial profits were enjoyed by investors in Argentina, Brazil, Chile, and Mexico. However, industrial development actually occurred in very limited areas. In the 1930's, worldwide depression caused foreign nations to slow down or halt their enterprises in Latin America.

During and after World War II, European investment declined rapidly. The United States emerged as the foremost foreign investor. Latin American nations adopted policies that favored industrial growth by offering outside investors tax incentives. To protect new industries, restrictive tariffs were developed. Tariffs are import taxes on foreign goods being shipped into a country. At this time, a **substitution policy** restricted imports and encouraged local manufacturers to produce similar consumer goods which could be made efficiently in Latin America.

B. Agriculture

Fifty percent of the labor force remains engaged in the agricultural sector, while agricultural production makes up less and less of each nation's **Gross National Product** (sum of all goods and services produced in a year).

There have been modern technological advancements in agricultural productivity, but they have occurred more in connection with export crops rather than food staples for the local populations. The region supplies 75% of the world's coffee, 60% of its bananas, and 25% of its sugar cane. Yet, like many underdeveloped regions, it is unable to feed its own growing population.

World Issues:

Economic Growth and Development

The reason for this dilemma can be traced to the Latin American **encomienda system** of landholding that began with the peninsulares in the colonial era. The management of the encomiendas was eventually taken over by criollos for absentee landlords in Spain or Portugal. The wealthy landlords across the ocean knew little of conditions on the encomiendas and failed to provide proper support.

Campesinos (paid laborers — peasants) were tenants who lived on the land but did not own it. Poorly treated and without the motivation that comes from owning their land, these campesinos had little desire to produce more than just a bare subsistence.

Human Rights

In no other area of the world has so much land been owned by so few people. The problem continues today. Caudillos grasp at land for themselves and their families as did the Somozas in Nicaragua. There have been only a few successful land-reform programs in the 20th century, and even in these, the results have been mixed. Governments have been quick to break up encomiendas, but have not had the resources to educate and equip campesinos to achieve success.

The climate and topographical variations limit the supply of arable land. Despite the diversity of geographic conditions, most countries have developed into **one-crop economies** (coffee, bananas, or sugar). This can be dangerous, in that the entire economy is linked to fluctuating world market prices. Also, natural disasters have often destroyed the entire crop and plunge the nation's economic structure into long-term debt.

Mineral Production

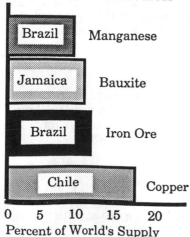

Brazil	Manganese
Jamaica	Bauxite
Brazil	Iron Ore
Chile	Copper

0 5 10 15 20
Percent of World's Supply

C. Minerals And Energy Sources

Minerals and energy sources are another important source of economic development in the area. Vital ores are concentrated in only a remote few areas and are often impossible to develop. The **infrastructure** is inadequate to move these minerals to industrial processing centers.

There is also a lack of high grade fossil fuels (coal and oil) necessary for industrial development and most countries must import them.

Scarcity

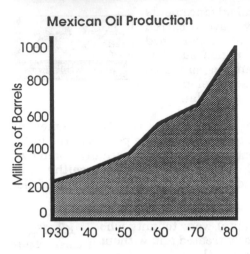

Mexican Oil Production

Millions of Barrels

1000, 800, 600, 400, 200, 0

1930 '40 '50 '60 '70 '80

On the positive side of this situation, Brazil has the world's largest manganese deposits, Chile is the second largest copper producing nation, and Mexico, Ecuador and Venezuela have vast oil reserves that may even surpass those of the Middle East. These petroleum resources have been a mixed blessing. In the 1970's when oil prices soared, oil producers borrowed huge sums to develop Latin American sources. When prices declined in the 1980's, an economic crisis developed over this foreign debt to international banks. Inflation in other sectors of the countries' economies worsened the situation.

D. Tourism

Many areas of Latin America that lack mineral resources or sufficient tracts of arable land have turned to tourism. Sunny climates, beautiful beaches, historic ruins, and cultural festivals, such as Brazil's "Carnival," continue to attract foreign tourists. As an economic mainstay, however, tourism has its problems. The high costs of advertising, building modern facilities, and the large numbers of people employed in tourism cut profits. Mexico earns the most of any nation from tourism.

E. Search For Paths To Development

Increased Industrialism

Many Latin American leaders continue to search for a solid path to development. Industrialization is critical to providing the increased employment their rising populations need. It will fill domestic demands and diversify national exports. Finding foreign investment capital for development other than raw material exports is difficult. The **multinational** corporations, having worldwide manufacturing and distribution capabilities, are blamed for interfering with the launching of new industries.

Interdependence

Regional Cooperation

Since 1950, attempts to achieve regional economic cooperation have been somewhat limited. The Latin American Trade Association, the Central American Common Market, and the Caribbean Free Trade Association have not lived up to their founders' expectations.

Major Industrial Regions

Argentina, Brazil, and Mexico account for 70% of the region's industrial output. Added to these are the five nations of Venezuela, Chile, Uruguay, Colombia, and Peru which produce about 22%. All of the other nations combined account for only 8% of the region's output.

F. Migration

Migrations to the cities as well as immigration from other nations is often motivated by desires for better jobs. Certain patterns have emerged:

Migration Patterns

From:	To:
Mexico & Central America	United States
Central America	Mexico
Colombia	Venezuela
Paraguay	Bolivia, Brazil, Argentina
Caribbean	U.S. and Great Britain

In seeking greater economic opportunity in their new lands, immigrants often face resentment from groups competing for jobs, and discrimination from employers and governments. Those who oppose immigrants claim their willingness to work for lower pay keeps wage levels down and depresses living standards for local lower classes.

New immigrants often resist **assimilation** (blending into a new culture). The hostility and resistance they meet as they settle in large urban areas causes immigrant groups to isolate themselves. They band together in ethnic enclaves (often called **"barrios"**).

An estimated one million people from Mexico, Central America, and the Caribbean attempt to enter the United States illegally each year. Many are caught by the **U.S. Immigration and Naturalization Service (INS)** officials and deported, but many avoid border patrols and find work as migrant farm workers or in unskilled jobs in cities. U.S. immigration laws have recently been revised to deal with this problem, but this pattern of immigrant labor is similar in other countries of the western hemisphere as people seek to break out of the poverty cycle.

Serious economic problems persist in many areas of the region. One problem is **economic nationalism**: the effort to stimulate internal development by using government policies to eliminate outside competition. Many nations like Cuba have learned that **nationalizing** foreign owned-industries (confiscating them) drives out the foreign capital needed to maintain them.

Nations that borrow heavily from foreign bankers at high interest rates often **default** (cannot make debt payments). This earns them ratings as bad credit risks. Even the more prosperous nations like Argentina, Mexico, and Brazil have huge debt burdens, widening the gap between themselves and economic progress. Their debt-ridden connection to the wealthier countries makes their problems global in nature.

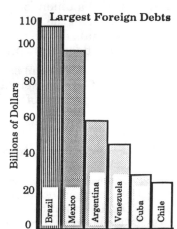

Questions

1 The major source of wealth for most Caribbean island nations is in
  1 heavy industry.   3 mining.
  2 tourism.   4 food processing.

2 Unlike the United States, the internal migration pattern in most Latin American nations is from
  1 rural to urban areas.   3 urban to rural regions.
  2 cities to suburbs.   4 suburbs to rural regions.

3 The largest segment of the labor force in most Latin American nations is engaged in
  1 governmental work.   3 agriculture.
  2 industrial production.   4 mining.

4 Even the most effective Latin American land reform programs in have failed because they cannot adequately meet the need for
  1 fossil fuels.   3 education.
  2 industrial support.   4 military protection.

5 Venezuela, Mexico, and Ecuador are major world suppliers of
  1 copper.   3 coffee.
  2 magnesium.   4 petroleum.

6 Which essential industrial resource is generally lacking in Latin America?
  1 fossil fuels   3 tariff protection
  2 unskilled labor   4 urban centers

7 Capital needed for industrial development has usually come from
  1 juntas.   3 encomiendas.
  2 campesinos.   4 foreign investment.

8 Which is an example of attempted cooperation in Latin America?
  1 Multinational Corporation
  2 Organization of American States
  3 Central American Common Market
  4 Gran Colombia Union

9 Collectively, Mexico, Argentina, and Brazil have
  1 formed a union for economic cooperation.
  2 generated the most illegal aliens to the United States.
  3 nationalized the most industries in Latin America.
  4 debt ridden economies.

10 Latin American campesinos' problems stem from
  1 lack of land ownership.   3 union strikes.
  2 mechanization of agriculture. 4 refusal to accept church authority.

Essays

One-crop economies have often meant disaster for Latin American countries.
  a Choose *two* crops (eg. coffee, bananas) and explain the problems of one-crop economy nations dependent on them. [5,5]
  b Discuss what can be done to broaden the economic base of the nations discussed in part a. [5]

V. Latin America: Global Context

A. Regionalism Grows To Globalism

Observing Latin America within a global context can be a difficult task since there is considerable geographic, political, and cultural diversity. In addition, long before the industrial era, most Latin American countries adopted policies that involved only their neighbors in the western hemisphere, virtually isolating themselves from other global regions. There was outside contact but it was usually limited to former colonial masters.

It is important to understand that the region has begun to take on an increasingly important role in the global economy in recent times. Increased interdependence of the entire world has linked the region to more developed nations. The strong anti-imperialist feelings that prevail in the region must be seen in the light of the increased interest of the two superpowers. This has caused political realignments sometimes resulting in civil wars and border disputes. This situation resulted in Cuba being largely excluded from contact with the other nations in the hemisphere.

Diversity

B. Inter-American Relations

One positive arrangement that offers a legal channel for resolving disputes is the **Organization of American States** founded in 1948. It is a mutual defense and peace-keeping union of thirty two North and South American nations (Cuba was excluded in 1962).

C. Economic Integration

As a region, Latin America has made substantial cultural contributions to the world. Since the beginnings of European settlement in the region, there has been a slow but steady interdependence between the two areas. Economic integration has occurred through trade relations which centered on cash crops and minerals being exchanged for the finished products of Europe. As foreign investment grew, and returns were substantial. There has been a considerable growth of **multinational corporations** (Unilever, Mitsubishi, ITT, General Motors, Exxon, Philips-Gloeilampenfabrieken, Royal/ Dutch Shell). In the past twenty years Japan has increased its investments in Latin America not only for natural resources, but for the considerable market for its industrial products.

Interdependence

D. Relations With The United States

Although politically independent, most Latin American nations continue to be heavily influenced by the **"Colossus of the North,"** the United States. Both regions share geographic similarities and European heritages, but historically, their relations have been marked by misunderstanding and resentment. It is difficult to define U.S. policy toward Latin America. Actually there have been a number of policies over the years.

Originally, the U.S. encouraged the early 19th century independence movements. A policy was formulated in President Monroe's term (1823). It became known as the **Monroe Doctrine** and warned European nations against trying to reestablish colonies in the area.

But the Monroe Doctrine has often been misused as an excuse for intervention in Latin American affairs by the U.S. At the end of the 19th century it was used by the U.S. in going to war against Spain over its treatment of Cuba and Puerto Rico. Teddy Roosevelt used it to intervene on behalf of American business interests in Cuba, the Dominican Republic, and against Columbia to aid a revolt in Panama so that the canal could be built in 1903. Armed intervention on behalf of U.S. businesses continued under Presidents Taft, Wilson, Harding, Coolidge, and Hoover. This pattern of **"Dollar Diplomacy"** convinced many Latin American leaders that the U.S. was practicing a new form of colonialism.

In an effort to improve relations, President Franklin D. Roosevelt developed the **Good Neighbor Policy** in 1933. He attempted to create a feeling of **"Pan-Americanism"** by granting favorable trade policies with Latin American countries and halting armed intervention.

F. Role In The United Nations

After World War II, most Latin American nations joined the U.N. and have since been enthusiastic supporters of the world organization, often voting with other LDCs of the Third World.

G. Communism In Latin America

A major problem since the second World War has been the growing attractiveness of communism to certain groups in the region. Fidel Castro's revolution in 1959 established the first communist state in the western hemisphere.

In the early 1960's President Kennedy's **Alliance for Progress** promoted large scale foreign aid grants in Latin America to make communism less attractive. Unfortunately, the land-holding aristocracies which dominated politics resisted land reform, and much of the money found its way into the hands of military juntas who used it to strengthen their power and brutally suppress reform movements. Frustration drove more people toward revolutionary movements, some being financed by the Soviets through the Cubans. For example, the communist **Sandinista** movement in Nicaragua converted the country into another Marxist-Leninist state.

The many differences among the nations of Latin America and their numerous problems have often led to conflicts. The Organization of American States attempts to foster peaceful resolutions of inter-American disputes. Like the U.N., it also sponsors humanitarian projects to improve health, education, and scientific research to improve living conditions in the region. It has not satisfied everyone. Sporadically, Cuba has tried to form a new inter-American organization which would exclude the "Colossus of the North."

Some other regional organizations have been formed to foster cooperation: The Organization of Central American States (1951); The Central American Common Market (1980); The Latin American Integration Association (1980); and the **Contadora Group** (1983). The Contadora Group was named after a Panamanian island where leaders from Colombia, Mexico, Venezuela, and Panama met to seek solutions to frequent outbreaks of violence in Central America.

Interdependence

While these organizations have worked for peace, the pro-communist activities of Cuba remain a problem. Cuba promoted insurgency to advance communism throughout Latin America, and, with the aid of the U.S.S.R., sent technical aid and troops to help Marxist revolutionaries in Africa (Angola, Mozambique, and Ethiopia).

H. Latin American Cultural Contributions

Beyond its global economic and political connections, Latin America has contributed much to world culture. It blends Native American, African, and European cultures. From the days of colonization to the modern era, Latin American influence has been felt in the world's art, music, and literature. Its contributions are many:

• **Weaving** - native American patterns are prominent in plain, patterned, loop pile, and tapestry masterpieces.

Culture

• **Metalwork** - the silver jewelry of Mexico and the Peruvian Incas are incomparable.

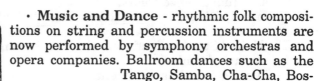

• **Music and Dance** - rhythmic folk compositions on string and percussion instruments are now performed by symphony orchestras and opera companies. Ballroom dances such as the Tango, Samba, Cha-Cha, Bossa Nova, and Merengue are performed throughout the world.

• **Ornate Religious Art** deeply influences many Christian portrayals of the religious saints and Biblical themes.

• **Murals** - artist **Diego Rivera**'s huge and powerful scenes of Mexican battles, legends, and traditions are admired and imitated worldwide.

• **Architecture** - unique Hispanic cathedrals blending Native American styles with Iberian-Moorish-Romanesque traditions of the Catholic past. The ultra-modern forms of the government buildings in Brasilia by **Oscar Neimeyer** are a magnificent use of concrete, glass, and bronze.

• **Literature** - oral literature and folk tales of the Incas, Mayas, and Aztecs blend with modern themes in celebrated poetry of Nicaragua's **Ruben Diario** emotionallly portray Latin American nationalism and Central American regionalism. *Ariel*, by Jose Rodo, is a brilliant questioning of the values of modern life.

The poems of Chile's Nobel Prize winner, **Pablo Neruda**, express the feelings of common country folk of Chile, while **Jorge Luis Borges** portrays the rugged lives of Argentine gauchos. Another Nobel Prize winner, Guatemala's **Miguel Asturias** writes vividly of the Central American Indians' culture.

In the latter half of the Twentieth century, Latin America has been drawn into the global context. It is a not quite a Third World region, but it stands politically and culturally as a bridge between the developed and the underdeveloped regions of the global community.

Questions

1 Pan-American refers to Latin American nations which have
1   a unified military force.
2   economic tariff agreements.
3   communication and cooperation.
4   U.S. aid grants.

2 The Contadora group refers to a group seeking
1   a common market for Latin American countries.
2   to coordinate communist revolutionary activities.
3   a mutual defense treaty.
4   to end violence in Central America.

3 The United States gained control of the Panama Canal by helping
1   victims of famine.
2   in agricultural development.
3   European powers to conquer it.
4   a rebel group in launching a revolution.

4 A major cause of quarrels among Latin American nations in the past two centuries has been
1   language differences.
2   cultural differences.
3   boundary disputes.
4   unfair trade practices.

5 Which country became an ally of the Soviet Union during the Cold War?
   1 Brazil   3 Puerto Rico
   2 Mexico   4 Cuba

6 The Good Neighbor Policy of Franklin D. Roosevelt was a departure from the policy of
   1 intervention.   3 mercantilism.
   2 Dollar Diplomacy.   4 Alliance for Progress.

7 Cuba and Puerto Rico came under U.S. control as a result of the
   1 Alliance for Progress.
   2 Spanish-American War.
   3 Organization of American States.
   4 Monroe Doctrine.

8 The Latin American nations' borrowing from foreign banks has resulted in
   1 an increase in the standard of living.
   2 cultural diffusion.
   3 a build up of nuclear weapons.
   4 enormous debt problems.

9 The Alliance for Progress was President Kennedy's attempt to abolish
   1 the Monroe Doctrine.
   2 anti-American feelings in Latin America.
   3 Fidel Castro's communist government forcefully.
   4 the Organization of American States.

10 The "Colossus of the North" is a term used to portray
   1 suspicion of American interventionism.
   2 traditional Latin American isolationism.
   3 the power of multinational corporations.
   4 the revolution in Latin American architecture.

Essays

Despite the great mineral wealth and agricultural production of the region, for the majority of Latin Americans, being able to obtain enough food to avoid hunger is a daily task.

a Use any *two* of the following countries to discuss the validity of the above statement: Brazil, Chile, Cuba, Mexico. [7]

b Choose *two* of the following and explain how they have either helped or hurt the development of Latin American nations. [8]

   · United States foreign policy
   · United Nations programs
   · regional organizations
   · communism

Unit Five

Middle East

4000		BC AD		600		1400

- Sumerians   • Hebrews   • Byzantine Empire   • Ottoman Empire
  - • Egyptian Civilization   • Christianity Begins
    - • Islamic Empire

Jihad
OPEC
Zionism
Terrorism
Monotheism
Arab Socialism
Heartland Theory
Cradles of Civilization
Islamic Fundamentalism

1900   1950   2000

• European Mandates

• World War II

   • Israel

    • Suez Crisis   • OPEC   • Iranian Revolution

   • Six–day War

    Persian Gulf War •

    • Camp David Accords

Unit Five: The Middle East

American Naval Captain Alfred Thayer Mahan coined the term "Middle East" in the beginning of the 20th century when he described this region's strategic location in the world. He saw it as a "heartland," a crossroads for the three continents: Africa, Asia, and Europe. He believed that whosoever controlled this area would have immense advantages in trade, political, and economic control.

Many physical, historical, social, and economic aspects have contributed to the diversity of cultures, and it is important to see these inter-relationships. The Middle East culture has contributed much to human civilization. Like Europe, the region has always been the center of struggles between competing power groups.

I. The Physical/Historical Setting

A. Geography And Resources

Although most Westerners would classify the Middle East as one big desert, the fact remains that the region has great geographic diversity. Encompassing an area twice the size of the United States (approximately six million square miles), the region extends from Morocco to Afghanistan, and from Turkey to Oman.

Physical Features

Environment   The **Sahara**. This region has the world's largest desert which covers an area of 3.5 million square miles in Northern Africa. **Sahara** comes from the Arabic word meaning "emptiness." Only a third of the Sahara is shifting sand dunes. Much larger regions have rocky plateaus, and barren plains strewn with pebbles and boulders. The common feature throughout this region is a lack of water, and only a few fertile oases (regions where underground water is close to the surface) exist in this desert.

Desert Oasis

The **Nile River Basin.** Egypt has often been called the "Gift of the Nile." Along its banks is one of the world's most fertile agricultural regions. The Nile has annually provided Egypt with rich **alluvial soil,** and it has irrigated the four percent of Egypt not claimed by the desert.

The **Arabian Peninsula.** This area has mountain ranges in the west along the Red Sea, but a huge desert called the **Rub al Khali** ("empty quarter") in its large interior plateau. Only in the extreme South where monsoons water the regions and in the Oasis of the North is the land suitable for cultivation.

The **Fertile Crescent.** Some of the richest soil of the region is found here, and much of it is irrigated by the Tigris, Euphrates, and Jordan Rivers. This is a region of Valleys, and plateaus with rich alluvial soil. The **Levant** (a rich agricultural plateau of Syria, Lebanon, and Israel bordering the Mediterranean Sea) is found in the Western portion of this region.

The **Northern Tier.** The **Anatolian Plateau** of Turkey and high plateaus and mountain regions of Iran and Afghanistan are found in this region. Turkey is in a strategic location as it controls the important waterways linking the Black Sea and the Mediterranean Sea. This area has long been coveted by the Russians who have wanted warm water ports.

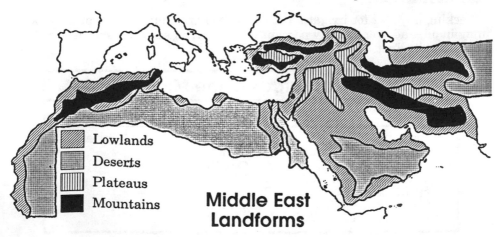

Lowlands
Deserts
Plateaus
Mountains

Middle East Landforms

Climate and Natural Resources

The climate for most of the region reflects dry hot summers and warm winters, (Koeppen "B" Types) but some areas do have extremes in temperatures such as Turkey and Iran that have cold winters and snow in the mountain regions. In the Levant region along the Mediterranean Coast, rainfall can be as high as 40" a year with cool pleasant spring weather (Cs).

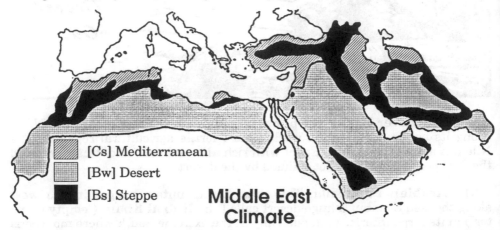

[Cs] Mediterranean
[Bw] Desert
[Bs] Steppe   **Middle East Climate**

The heavily populated areas of the region remain along the three major river systems in Egypt and Iraq: the **Nile**, the **Tigris**, and the **Euphrates**. For centuries these waterways have been used for irrigation and transportation. More recently, hydroelectric power has been generated by these rivers. The **High Aswan Dam** in Egypt created both electric power and irrigation control for the people of the Nile Valley. Most of the nations have a minimal amount of water resources and only 15% of this region has land suitable for cultivation. Subsistence agriculture and herding remain prevalent in most of

World Issues:
Economic Growth and Development

the region, and every nation (except Turkey) has to import food products. Agricultural products that are shipped to the rest of the world are cotton from Egypt and Iraq, tobacco from Turkey, Syria, and Lebanon; and dates (75% of the world's supply) from Iraq.

Lacking in water for irrigation of its limited arable lands, the area is swimming in oil, and over seventy percent of the world's known reserves are found in the Middle East.

Mineral Resources of the Middle East	
Nation	*Mineral Resources*
Turkey	Coal, Iron, Chrome, and Copper
Israel	Phosphates
Iran	Iron Ore, Coal
Saudi Arabia	Gold
Egypt	Coal
Morocco	Phosphates
Algeria	Natural gas

Population Distribution

The population distribution is uneven in the region. Three nations (Egypt, Turkey, and Iran) have more than half of the Middle East's 240 million people. Many of these people live in the large metropolitan centers which have more than a million people.

The people of the Middle East are of the widest possible mixture of races, nationalities, religions, and ethnic groups. The largest ethnic group, the **Semites**, is primarily made up of the Arab, Assyrian, and Hebrew peoples. Two other large groups are the Iranians and the Turks. Most people reside in and around large cities of the region such as Baghdad, Cairo, Damascus, Teheran, and Tel Aviv. Rural inhabitants constitute less than 2% of the population. Today, only a very few follow nomadic lives. These are the people of the dry plateau regions who follow seasonal migration for water and pastures.

Diversity

Trade has always been an important vehicle for cultural diffusion in the Middle East, and this is most visible in the population centers in the Nile, Tigris, and Euphrates River Valleys. Since the dawn of civilization, these areas have been centers of great cultural achievement. Today, two of the largest metropolitan areas of the Middle East are found at Cairo, Egypt, and Baghdad, Iraq.

The Nile has been one of history's most important rivers, and the Egyptian civilization could not have existed without its rich deposits of silt and irrigation.

Environment

The Tigris and Euphrates Rivers in Iraq served as "the fertile crescent" for numerous civilizations from the Sumerians and Babylonians to the present. Some of the most productive agricultural centers of the Middle East are located in these river valleys as elsewhere there is such a scarcity of water.

B. Earliest Civilizations
First Cities And Trade

Agriculture and technology began in the Middle East when humans began to cultivate crops and domesticate animals. The technological developments from stone hunting and farming implements contributed to the establishment of small farm communities. From 6000 B.C., this **Neolithic Revolution** saw life begin to center on agricultural pursuits.

The oldest settlement to be uncovered and documented by archeologists has been **Jericho**, but the two earliest centers of civilization were the Egyptian and the Sumerian. Both began approximately in 4000 B.C.

World Issues:

World Trade and Finance

As trade developed in the region in response to a scarcity of resources, a third area emerged along the eastern end of the Mediterranean Sea extending from Turkey south to Palestine. This was to become the area dominated by the Phoenicians. It was headquartered in what is modern-day Lebanon.

Invention Of Writing Systems

Our knowledge of these three great civilizations has been enhanced through each society's development and diffusion of writing systems.

- **Sumerians** developed **cuneiform,** a system of writing that used a wedge-shaped implement to create more than 350 designs carved in clay tablets to represent syllables, sounds, persons, places, and things.

- **Egyptians** developed **hieroglyphics**, which is an elaborate system of picture writing that suggested ideas, objects, syllables, or words.

Sumerian Cuneiform

- **Phoenicians** developed **phonetics**, which is an alphabet code in which each letter stood for only one distinct sound.

Culture   By recording information pertaining to trade, government, and religion, their ideas could be transmitted to other regions, and even more important, their languages provided a historical legacy. Furthermore, the invention of writing made more complex civilizations and more advanced technology possible. It must be noted however, that many of those ancient languages have been difficult to translate, and one of the greatest breakthroughs occurred in the early 1800's when the Frenchman **Champollian** deciphered Egyptian hieroglyphics on the **Rosetta Stone.**

Early Middle Eastern Empires And Their Contributions To The World

People	Area	Contributions
Sumerians	*Southern Iraq*	Political City-State; Formalized religion with a 7 story temple called a **Ziggurat**; Cultural Center at Ur; Writing - Cuneiform; Developed the wheel and a numbers system based on 60, and geometrics
Egyptians	*Nile River, Egypt*	Political kingdoms dominated by the Pharaohs (kings); Religion based on many gods, immortality, and mummification to protect the soul; Huge tombs called pyramids built to preserve honored Pharaohs; Cultural centers -- Memphis and Thebes; Writing - hieroglyphics; Skilled engineers with knowledge of algebra and geometry demonstrated in architectural art forms
Babylonians	*Mesopotamia*	King Hammurabi's Code of Laws (an "eye for an eye"); Central City - Babylon: famous Hanging Gardens at Babylon - one of the 7 wonders of the ancient world
Hebrews	*Palestine*	Monotheism - The belief in one God; The Old Testament - written book of scriptural teachings
Lydians	*Western Turkey*	Coined money used in place of bartering
Phoenicians	*Lebanon*	A maritime empire; Commercial center was Tyre; Extensive use of purple dye - indigo; Phonetic alphabet
Persians	*Iran*	Conquered and united fertile crescent

Contributions Of The Early Empires

The chart of Early Middle East Empires demonstrates that the early history of the Middle East was marked by numerous peoples that helped shape the area's unique identity and political systems.

The groups in the region of the **Tigris-Euphrates River Valley** were often overcome by the advanced technology of a neighboring civilization. Conquered people were placed into slavery to build the empires. As civilizations spread, they became increasingly diversified. Control over each empire was administered by a political code of laws that reflected the needs of the society that had formulated it.

Centers of Civilizations

C. The Hebrews Of Ancient Israel

A close examination of the region's first major religion, Judaism, will demonstrate that values play a major role in shaping the character and identity of a culture.

The Hebrews, who founded ancient Israel about 1400 B.C., were both a culture and a nation. Judaism, in its rejection of polytheism and its insistence upon the belief in one God, social justice, and moral law, established itself as significantly different from the previous religions of the other ancient Middle Eastern cultures.

Symbols of Judaism

The Hebrews called their God Yahweh, and believed that this supreme being created the human race and the entire universe. Their religious literature, the **Old Testament** (*Bible*), contained the teachings and law required for the moral behavior of the Jews.

In later years, Christianity and Islam were greatly influenced by these teachings, and the following Judaic ideas: belief in the compassion of God, belief in the **Torah** (first five books of the Old Testament), belief in the Ten Commandments, and belief in the dignity of the individual.

However, the Hebrew nation lasted only a short time before it was destroyed by the Roman Empire in 70 A.D. This date signaled the beginning of the **Diaspora**, or great dispersion of the Jews from Palestine to all areas of the world. In keeping their traditions alive in their new surrounding, the Jews relied on **rabbis** (religious teachers) to interpret Judaic law and to determine new decisions for the situations.

These rabbinical decisions were written in a multi-volume text called the **Talmud**, a repository of knowledge and ethics. This law was to establish an identity for Jews of the world and kept them together for almost 2,000 years even though they had been scattered throughout the world. Although the Jews were without a nation of their own, many still remained in the area. The independent nation of Israel was eventually established here in 1948.

D. The Growth Of Christianity

During Roman rule in Palestine, a new religion was created based on the teachings of a Jew named **Jesus Christ**. This occurred nearly 2,000 years ago when Jesus preached about the way God wanted people to act toward each other. Jesus was crucified by the Romans for his teachings. Much of what we know of his life and teachings can be read in the first four books of he *Bible's* **New Testament** (the Gospels of Matthew, Mark, Luke and John). Christianity's basic principles included the beliefs that:

- there is only one God
- Jesus Christ is the Son of God and a member of the Holy Trinity
- Christians must practice Jesus' teachings: to love God, to promote brotherhood, to acknowledge divine judgment of one's actions on Earth, and to accept Christ's death as atonement for sins

Christianity spread rapidly along the trade routes of the Roman Empire as many followers were attracted to its teachings by special messengers called Apostles. The universal appeal of the Christian ethic and the promise of salvation was actually a blend of Judaic and Greek philosophy. By the 3rd century, Christian communities were to have spread from Palestine to Syria, Turkey, Egypt, Greece, and even Rome itself. Initially, Roman authorities persecuted and even killed Christians because they worried about the religion's threat to their rule.

In the 4th century, Christianity's popularity grew even greater among the educated and upper classes, and when the Roman Emperor **Constantine the Great** issued the **Edict of Milan** in 313, he granted freedom of worship to all Christians. By the end of the century, Christianity was adopted as the established religion of the Roman Empire, and worship of all other deities was declared illegal. Over the centuries, the **Judeo-Christian ethic** has continued to shape the values, ideals, and cultures of the western world.

E. The Byzantine Empire
The Roman Empire Moves Eastward

Prior to Constantine's rule, his predecessor, Diocletian, had divided the Roman Empire into two parts. The Eastern part was centered at **Byzantium** and consisted of Greece, Asia Minor, and the Middle Eastern territory which bordered the eastern end of the Mediterranean Sea. The western segment of

*Santa Sophia
in Constantinople*

the empire remained centered at Rome but was to decline during the 4th and 5th centuries as Constantine dedicated a new capital, **Constantinople** (formerly Byzantium). In his effort to push the Roman Empire eastward, it soon became apparent that the two regions were vastly different in culture and language.

The Byzantine Empire, with an emperor that presided over Church and State, and who was regarded as God's agent on earth, combined a unique synthesis of Hellenistic and Eastern Mediterranean Culture. The Christians in this eastern region called their church **Eastern Orthodox** to distinguish it from the Roman Church.

Although a formal split between the two churches occurred 500 years later, Christianity continued to experience growth in both regions. While Western Europe fragmented into small feudal units, the political system of Byzantium and the Church-State relationships in this area created a model for future power relationships in Russia and the Middle East. Constantinople became the crossroads of global trade and the flourishing Hellenistic culture.

The Rule Of Justinian And Theodora

The Byzantine Empire reached its peak during the rule of **Justinian** and his wife **Theodora**. Under their rule, great attention was granted to Byzantine Law, religion, and art. The largest and most beautiful church (**Hagia-Sophia** - "Holy Wisdom") in the Byzantine Empire was constructed during Justinian's rule, and is considered one of the world's great architectural wonders. But the **Justinian Code**, a written collection of civil law preserving the Roman legal heritage, was to be Justinian's legacy to future judicial systems of Western Europe and Latin America as it had the greatest impact on the concept of human rights.

After Justinian's death in 505 A.D., the Byzantine Empire encountered invasions from Eastern Europe, Persia, and the Arab World. These invasions tended to change the political and cultural institutions of both the conquered and the invader, and left the Byzantine Empire with territories that were primarily Greek, and a diminished international character.

Justinian **(Byzantine Mosaic)**

Although the economy of the Byzantine Empire would never recover, the Church had missionary successes. Most notable of these successes was the dispersing of Orthodox Christianity and Byzantine culture into the **Slavic** core-land of Russia, the Ukraine, and Eastern Europe. This was accomplished by the use of the Cyrillic alphabet, a modified form of the Greek alphabet which was introduced to the Slavs by two Byzantine missionaries, **Cyril** and **Methodius**. Many Slavs were then converted to the Eastern Orthodox Church.

The Ottoman Conquest

By 1453, the Byzantine Empire had declined to such a point that the Ottoman Turkish Sultan laid siege to **Constantinople**, and shortly after, victoriously entered the city. The Byzantine Empire that had lasted over 1,000 years had passed into history. The **Ottoman Turks** were Muslims and when they made Constantinople their new capital, they converted the famous Hagia Sophia into a **mosque** (a house of worship for Moslems). The new leaders permitted religious freedom for the Orthodox Christians in Greece and in Eastern Europe but installed a new Patriarch to supervise their religious and political life.

In reviewing the physical and early historical setting of the Middle East, it is evident that the region has a great geographical diversity, and a vast heritage as traced through the rise and fall of numerous empires. Beliefs and value systems developed through the cultural diffusion of many philosophies and cultures of the region. Many of these religions, political beliefs, and value systems have been incorporated into the cultural patterns of the western world.

Questions

1   The land area of the Middle East is
   1   twice the size of the United States.
   2   four times the size of the United States.
   3   about the same size of the former Soviet Union.
   4   twice the size of the former Soviet Union.

2   The Nile River Basin has been a home to civilization since early times because of its
   1   rich alluvial soil.
   2   wealth of minerals.
   3   temperate climate.
   4   access to Africa's interior.

3   Because of the Rub al Khali or Empty Quarter in the Saudi Arabian peninsula,
   1   settlement has remained along the coast.
   2   the country is the major agricultural producer in the region.
   3   the people are the most isolated in the world.
   4   constant flooding makes permanent settlement difficult.

4   Which of the following indicates the importance of cultural diffusion in the Middle East?
1   the Judaic-Christian tradition.
2   the dominance of polytheism.
3   a single common language for all the diverse people.
4   peace and harmony with little warfare.

5   An oasis is a
1   large oil well.   3   the mouth of a large river.
2   fertile region of the desert.   4   religious shrine.

6   The largest ethnic group in the Middle East is called
1   Bedouins.   3   Semitic.
2   Arabs.   4   Jewish.

7   The Sumerians' cuneiform was
1   one of the earliest forms of writing known on Earth.
2   a seven story temple.
3   a form of government
4   an ingenious irrigation system.

8   Judaism, the ancient Hebrews' religion, was significantly different from that of other civilizations that preceded it because
1   the religion's prophets became their ruling council.
2   it required worship of a sacred stone called the K'aaba.
3   it rejected polytheism.
4   the central belief was in a three-person divinity.

9   Talmudic law was significant for the Hebrew people because it created
1   an identity and cultural basis despite a 2,000 year dispersal.
2   a major reason for persecution of their culture.
3   a rigid social class structure
4   the first written code of law in history.

10   Justinian's Code is significant because it was
1   an effort to make Roman architecture uniform in size.
2   the first attempt of a civilization to keep laws secret.
3   an attempt to organize and preserve the Roman legal heritage.
4   a collection of the military strategies that built the Roman Empire.

Essays

Geographic factors often determine the founding and development of civilizations.

Civilizations

- Egyptians
- Hebrews
- Babylonians

- Sumerians
- Phoenicians

Choose *three* of the civilizations above and for each one discuss why geography played an important role in their development. [5,5,5]

II. Dynamics Of Change

A. Mohammed And The Rise Of Islam

Almost 600 years after Christianity had begun in the Middle East, another of the world's great religions, Islam, began in an Arab society inspired by the teachings of Mohammed, the Messenger of God. **Islam** (an Arabic word meaning "submission to the will of God"), has played a major role in shaping the culture and value system of the Middle East. It became one of the fastest growing religions in the world, and its numbers today exceed 750 million.

Within a few centuries, Mohammed's followers eventually spread Islam throughout the known world. Islam played an important role in preserving Greek and Roman cultures and advancing the arts and sciences while Europe was in its dark ages.

In modern history, the unity of Islamic culture allowed the Ottoman Empire to survive into the 20th century long after its political structure had declined. Islam has preserved a cultural identity through a common language, and common religious beliefs, values, and ethics. Over the past 1,400 years, Islam played a formidable role in shaping the Middle Eastern social structure and to understand the region, it is important to observe the strong grasp that Islam has held over its people.

Identity

Islam's founder, **Mohammed**, was born in the city of **Mecca**, Saudi Arabia, in 570 A.D. Islamic scripture indicates he was selected by God to be his prophet. Mohammed's early converts were poor townspeople who focused on his teachings of the one God, Allah, the Creator of all. But the wealthy merchants and town leaders opposed him. They had grown prosperous from the pilgrims who came to Mecca to worship the many gods (in particular, the famous black meteor at the Kaaba Shrine). They feared his teachings (that all believers in Allah were equal, and that the rich should share their wealth with the poor) would take away their power.

Mohammed and his followers were persecuted and forced to flee to a neighboring city, Medina, to seek converts. This was the famous "Hegira" (flight) migration in 622 A.D. which signaled the beginning of the Islamic Era. Mohammed's following rapidly grew among the many Arab tribes as he established a reputation as both a religious leader and a warrior.

B. Muslim Beliefs And Practices

To his followers, Mohammed was known as the last in the succession of the great prophets that began with Abraham, Moses, and Jesus. Mohammed's revelations are recorded in the **Qur'an** (*Koran*), the sacred book of Islam. Muslims believe the *Qur'an* is the word of God spoken to Mohammed by the Angel Gabriel.

The **Five Pillars of Wisdom** of the Islamic Faith govern the conduct of all Muslims:

---

1. **Faith** - recital of the Creed, "There is no God but Allah; and Mohammed is his prophet."

2. **Prayer** - praying five times a day (dawn, noon, mid-afternoon, sunset, and nightfall). Services are held in mosques (houses of worship) at noon on Friday.

3. **Alms-giving** (charity) - sharing to help the poor.

4. **Fasting** - renouncing food, drink, and other pleasures from sunrise to sunset during the ninth month of the year (Ramadan).

5. **Pilgrimage** (hadj) - visiting the sacred Kaaba Shrine at the Great Mosque in Mecca once in one's lifetime.

Mohammed established basic religious obligations for his followers which have remained remarkably intact throughout Islamic history. The *Qur'an* (*Koran*) is a guide to Islamic a religious and civil behavior. Islamic moral rules are incorporated into a code of law called the *Shari'a*, which covers all aspects of private and public life. In Islamic culture, there is no separation of religious and political activities.

When Mohammed died in 632 A.D., most of the Arabian Peninsula was under Islamic religious, social, political, and economic control. Now the question surfaced as to who would succeed him. A group of Muslim leaders met and chose a new type of leader called a "**Caliph**" ("the successor").

The first Caliph was **Abu Bakr**, the father-in-law of Mohammed, who was elected for life. The Caliphs were to strengthen the Muslim community by developing strong civil and military governments. The followers of Islam united to spread the religion beyond Arabia in a series of holy crusades called **jihads**. These jihads sought converts as they swept throughout the Middle East and across Northern Africa.

As the jihads progressed, the Islamic empire became a rich mixture of cultures. By the end of the 8th Century, the Omayyad dynasty consolidated power over a a huge territory (see map, page 201). When this occurred, a religious split developed within Islam.

C. Expansion And Consolidation Of Power

In 661 A.D., disagreements concerning the succession of the Prophet caused a **schism** (split) in Islam between the "**Sunnis**," who believed in orthodox Islamic doctrine, and "**Shi'ites**," who believed that Mohammed's son-in-law Ali, and his descendents, should be Caliph (Islam's leader). In this power struggle, Ali was assassinated. His followers founded the minority Shi'ite group which was primarily located in Mesopotamia and Persia.

Power

Under **Caliph Muawiyah**, the Sunnis established the Omayyad dynasty and moved the Muslim capital from Medina to Damascus, Syria. It was a more centralized location for the empire. In their search for additional converts, the Omayyad Caliphs extended the boundaries of Islam westward to Egypt, across North Africa to Spain, and eastward to the Indus River Valley. This empire was organized into provinces led by governors who reported to the Caliph in Damascus.

The Omayyads employed numerous artists and architects to build beautiful mosques, palaces, and fortresses, and much of their work featured classical Greek and Byzantine architecture.

Jerusalem's famous **Dome of the Rock Mosque** was built during this dynasty. However, there were many groups that were dissatisfied with the highly centralized rule of the Omayyads. In 747 A.D., a Shi'ite revolt was successfully staged in Persia and Mesopotamia bringing to power a new dynasty called **Abbasid**.

Intricate interior architecture of a mosque in the Omayyad Period

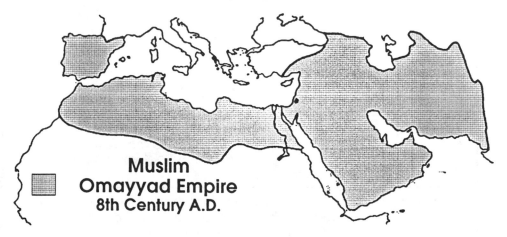

Muslim Omayyad Empire 8th Century A.D.

D. The Golden Age Of Muslim Culture

The "Golden Age" of Muslim culture occurred during this time (750-1258). Under its second Caliph, **Al Mansur**, a new capital was established at Baghdad (the modern-day capital of Iraq). The founding of Baghdad shifted the Muslim empire's center of power to the eastern sector of the Middle East and marked a turning point in Arab control.

Although the religion of Islam and the use of Arabic as a language brought unity to the empire, other cultures were beginning to exercise considerable influence. The **Persians** became the most powerful force in the government, the **Turks** dominated the military organizations, and the **Arabs** continued to control religious institutions and the administration of law.

Culture   The eighth through thirteenth centuries were an age of toleration and Muslims and non-Muslims alike were given equality. It was also an age of prosperity as increased shipping and camel caravan trade brought wealth and luxuries from all over the world. Baghdad emerged as a brilliant cosmopolitan civilization and tales of this wealth were documented in the famous literary work *Arabian Nights* (a collection of stories told at the Caliph's Court in the 8th and 9th centuries).

More time and energy were devoted to preserving the earlier cultures of Greece and Rome, and this intellectual awakening also saw Persian scholars introducing the Arab world to Persian history and literature, and Indian science and philosophy. With this type of interest and support, Muslim scholars and scientists began to develop their own innovations and lay the foundations for today's modern science and mathematics.

Contributions of Muslim Civilization

Area	Achievement
Medicine	Surgery with anesthetics; Understanding of the functions of internal organs; Science of Optics - study of sight; Written Medical encyclopedias; Advanced use of drugs and therapy.
Mathematics	The concept of zero, and Arabic numerals (0-9); Algebra and Trigonometry.
Chemistry	Laboratory equipment (beakers, vials, etc.); Alchemy - turned base metals to compounds; distinguished between acids and alkalis.
Astronomy	Mathematical models of the universe with charts giving distances to stars and planets; and described solar eclipses and the moon's effects on ocean tides.

From the 8th to the 10th centuries, while Western Europe was in its "Dark Ages," the Islamic world had become unique in its religious tolerance and a new-found acceptance of cultural diversity. The Muslim cultural advances during this golden age eventually reached Europe by way of Spain and Sicily, through increasing trade.

E. Invasions Weaken Muslim Hegemony
Seljuk Turks

Eventually, the wealth and luxury that accumulated in Baghdad led to corrupt rule by the Caliph and his associates. The Islamic Empire became too large to be governed effectively. Slowly, regional ruling families began to set up their own independent states in Persia, Morocco, Tunisia, Spain, and Egypt.

One Persian **Buyid** dynasty even went so far as to seize Baghdad, and force the Caliph to accept their rule. During the disunity, a nomadic people from Central Asia called the **Seljuk Turks**, began a systematic conquest of the region. They took control of Baghdad in 1055 allowing the **Abbasid Caliph** to keep his religious authority but established their own political control through their leader who was given the title of **Sultan** ("he who has authority").

The Seljuk Turks converted to Islam and continued their territorial expansion southwestward to Jerusalem and into Egypt, crushing the Christian Byzantine armies of the region. Alarmed that the Seljuk Turks controlled the Christian Shrines in Palestine, and threatened the rest of the Byzantine Empire, the Eastern Orthodox Emperor appealed to the Roman Catholic Pope for assistance.

Crusades

In 1095 A.D., a call went out from Pope Urban II for a crusade to drive the Turks out of the Holy Land. Religious-military expeditions were organized by European nobles and common people who hoped to free Jerusalem and the surrounding area.

Over the next 200 years, eight major crusades were launched and these became holy wars for Christian and Muslim alike. Each side's religious leaders promised their supporters that if they were to die in battle, they would go directly to heaven. The Crusaders left a legacy of mistrust between Muslims and the Western Europeans, and many Middle Eastern cities were pillaged and innocent people killed by Crusaders who were more interested in wealth than religion.

Perhaps the most significant impact was the cultural diffusion brought to Western Europe by the returning Crusaders. European trade with the Middle East became important as a demand was created for the luxuries that had been discovered: spices, sugar, exotic foods, and fine fabrics. Also, the Europeans borrowed extensively from the knowledge that the Islamic world had developed in the arts, literature, and sciences.

Mongols

The Seljuk Turks lost control of the Middle East in the early 13th century when the **Mongols**, a Central Asian nomadic group, began their conquest of the region. In 1258, the Mongols destroyed Baghdad and ended the Abbasid dynasty. For the next hundred and fifty years, the Mongol-Muslim empire included Iran, Iraq, Turkey, Syria, Afghanistan, and the Indus River Valley.

Ottoman Turks

When the Mongol influence declined, the **Ottomans**, another group of nomadic Turks from the Anatolian Plateau region began a rise to power. Their rule would influence the Middle East until the 20th Century. The Ottomans established a small, powerful state in Turkey, and, as the power of the Abbasid and the Byzantine Empire declined, theirs rose. They took Constantinople in 1453. This began a land empire which extended far beyond the territories controlled by either of these earlier empires. The Ottoman Turks had adopted Sunni Islam as their religion and often assumed the role of defenders of the faith.

16th century Mosque

F. The Ottoman Empire

Dreaming of an empire that would connect Europe and Asia, the Ottoman Sultan and his forces dominated much of Eastern Europe and the Middle East in the 16th and 17th centuries. By fusing Byzantine and Muslim cultures, the Ottoman Turks realized important achievements in literature, especially in the field of poetry and civil law. As master architects and builders, the Ottoman Turks constructed beautiful mosques and palaces. The Ottomans reached their peak under their most famous Sultan, **Sulieman the Magnificent** (1520-1566).

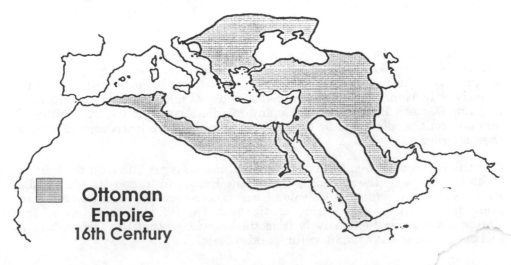

Ottoman Empire 16th Century

Known as "The Codifier," Sulieman organized Ottoman laws, and presided over a vast bureaucracy of officials that were promoted by a merit system. This bureaucracy contained a variety of nationalities that represented the other ethnic groups in the Ottoman Empire.

The defeat of the Ottomans in the famous **Battle of Vienna** in 1683 signaled the beginning of their decline. Only intense rivalry among the European nations saved the Ottoman Empire from total collapse. In the 1800's, the Ottoman Empire was forced to withdraw from many territories that it had ruled for centuries. It became nicknamed "the Sick Man of Europe," and other European nations eagerly awaited the opportunity to assert their **spheres of influence** in the Middle East.

At one point in the mid-1800's, Austria and Russia made an agreement to divide the Ottoman Empire, but France, Britain, and the others thwarted this plan in the Crimean War. They felt that this would upset the delicate **balance of power** in Europe. Throughout the 19th century, Russia fought several wars against Turkey in hopes of obtaining warm-water ports to its south. Only through the support of England and France was the Ottoman Empire able to survive.

G. European Imperialism
Russian - British Rivalry

In the 19th century, European imperialism expanded in the Middle East. The Europeans held the upper hand with their modern military, technological, and administrative policies. However, they did little to change the Islamic culture.

The British wanted to rule over, and invest in, the less developed regions to obtain resources for their factories and markets for their goods. The Russian Tsars saw the British ambitions as a threat to their own goal of expanding toward the warm-water ports of the Mediterranean.

An intense rivalry developed in the region, as Britain successfully denied Russian expansion. In 1907, the two powers reached an agreement regarding spheres of influence in Persia whereby the Russians gained the northern section, the British operated the southern tier, while the middle of the country remained neutral.

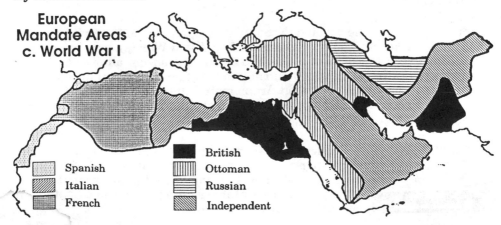

European
Mandate Areas
c. World War I

Spanish	British
Italian	Ottoman
French	Russian
	Independent

In Afghanistan, the two powers warred against each other for their own spheres of influence. At the close of the 18th century, local rulers remained in their respective offices in the Middle Eastern States. They were often puppets of Western European nations who exercised true political and economic control.

The Ottomans: Pawns In The Balance Of Power

The Ottoman Empire collapsed at the end of World War I with the defeat of the Central Powers by the Allies. The English had openly encouraged the Arabs to fight on their side against the Ottoman Turks in the Middle East with vague promises of an independent Arab nation being granted to the Arabian Peninsula. This did not occur as the League of Nations established **mandates** (territories ruled others until they were considered ready for independence).

Feeling betrayed, the Arab world reacted bitterly towards what they considered imperialism by France and Great Britain. This became a unifying factor among the Arabs, giving rise to nationalist movements in the Islamic World.

H. Rise Of Nationalism

In the Middle East, nationalism has been used as an agent of change not only by those who favor tradition, but also by those that favor modernization and westernization.

Zionism And The Balfour Declaration

Two excellent examples of the rise of Middle East nationalism in the late 19th and early 20th centuries are Zionism in Palestine, and Turkish secularism under Ataturk.

Zionism was founded in 1897 by **Theodor Herzel,** an Austrian who sought a Jewish homeland. This idea gained great impetus when the British issued the **Balfour Declaration** (1917) in an attempt to gain Jewish support for their War effort. The Declaration called for... *"the establishment in Palestine of a national home for the Jewish people..."*

Yet, 90% of Palestine was inhabited by Arabs, and when the British set up their mandate government in Palestine after World War I, a growing conflict emerged between Palestinian Arabs and Jews. Jews from all over the world thought of Palestine as their true homeland, and as Jewish immigration and nationalism increased, Palestinian Arabs feared that they would soon be outnumbered. Palestinian Arabs demanded that the British end this Jewish immigration, and Arab nationalism grew stronger.

World Issues:
Political and Economic Refugees

Requests for an independent Arab state in Palestine were interrupted by the outbreak of WW II. The British realized that they had made conflicting promises, but could provide no suitable solution that was acceptable to both the Arabs and the Jews.

Ataturk And Turkish Nationalism

Political Systems

It is ironic that Turkey, the home of the crushed Ottoman Empire, became the first Middle Eastern nation to move toward modernization and establish its own form of national identity. **Mustapha Kemel Ataturk**, a Turkish war hero, established the **Republic of Turkey** in 1923 and became its President from 1923-1938 and gave his people purpose and direction.

Ataturk told them that in order to survive as an independent nation, they would have to adopt the ways of the Western World which he identified as **Ataturk's Six Principles:**

---

1. **Nationalism**-- unification of the Turkish people with common land, culture, language
2. **Secularism** - separation of religion and government
3. **Populism** - election of officials by the people
4. **Republicanism** - formation of representative government
5. **Statism** - nationalization of Industries
6. **Revolutionism** - acceptance of reform in all phases of social, political, and economic life

---

Often these ideas were in conflict with Islamic traditions and customs that the Turks had observed for centuries, but "secular nationalism" succeeded. Within twenty years, Turkey changed from a defeated medieval empire to a 20th century nation. Ataturk was often severely criticized for his reforms (especially the ending of Islam as a state religion and the limiting of authority of Muslim religious leaders). To his credit, Turkey became the first Middle East Nation to be independent of foreign control.

Arab Nationalism

Nationalist movements were slower to occur in other areas of the Middle East. It was evident in the independence of Egypt in 1922, Iraq in 1922, and Saudi Arabia in 1927. The French held absolute power in Syria and Lebanon until the end of World War II, and it was only after the war that the region as a whole achieved real independence.

Questions

1 Mohammed was persecuted because his new religion taught
    1   all believers in Allah were equal.
    2   polytheism was better than monotheism.
    3   the rich must give up their wealth to the poor.
    4   European imperialism must be overthrown.

2 Which occurred during the Islamic "golden age" under Al Mansur?
    1   huge sculptures were dedicated to the many gods.
    2   Islam's center of culture shifted to Baghdad.
    3   Mongols used slave labor to build temples to their gods.
    4   Arabs conquered most of Western Europe.

3   The ***Qur'an*** (***Koran***) contains
   1   over 500 chapters called psalms.
   2   the laws that govern a Muslim's daily life.
   3   the legendary stories of the ***Arabian Nights.***
   4   the history of the Muslim conquest of North Africa and Spain.

4   The religion of Islam began in this Middle Eastern country.
   1   Egypt   3   Saudi Arabia
   2   Iran   4   Kuwait

5   Which indicates why the Islamic Empire grew rapidly under the highly centralized rule of the Omayyads?
   1   An organized political system was established with provincial governors reporting to the Caliph.
   2   A caste system forbade social advancement.
   3   Intense religious persecution began against non-Islamic groups.
   4   Nationalism became a major stabilizing force.

6   Which is the main reason why the Popes organized the Crusades?
   1   They wanted to promote missionary work.
   2   They wanted to drive the Turks out of the Holy Land.
   3   They wanted to expand commercial activities.
   4   They wanted to conquer more land for the Popes.

7   "Caliph" was the title given to the chief Muslim
   1   priest.   3   tax collector.
   2   religious leader.   4   chanter of prayers.

8   The "Sick Man of Europe" was a title associated with
   1   the Ottoman Empire.   3   the Mongol Empire.
   2   the Holy Roman Empire.   4   the Byzantine Empire.

9   In 1917, the British gave support to the creation of a homeland for
   1   the Ottoman Turks.   3   a central Islamic mosque.
   2   the Jews in Palestine.   4   the Byzantine Empire.

10 A major change that Ataturk brought to Turkey in the 1920's was
   1   the separation of religion and the government.
   2   forced collectivization of farms.
   3   the national income tax.
   4   adoption of the Cyrillic alphabet.

Essays

1   The "golden age" of Islamic culture (7th to 10th centuries A.D.) demonstrated that the Muslims could contribute many ideas to the rest of the world in science and mathematics, philosophy, literature, architecture, and government.

   a   Explain in detail how contributions in *three* of these fields influenced civilization. [12]
   b   This golden age also saw a serious split in the Islamic religion. Discuss this schism's impact on the Arab world. [3]

2   At the beginning of the 20th century, European nations were eager to establish "spheres of influence" in the Middle East. Explain who the leading nations involved in this policy were and the territories that they were to control. [15]

III. Contemporary Middle Eastern Nations And Cultures

Prior to 1945, the European powers exerted their influence and control over the Middle East. In the two decades following World War II, most of the countries became independent. In studying the contemporary nations and cultures of the Middle East, it is important to analyze conflicts. In most contemporary societies, there are groups seeking to maintain their traditional cultures and values while experiencing rapid change. Ethnic diversity, independence, and traditional values have a widespread impact on the region. Shifting power structures have affected Muslim nationhood and the struggle for human rights. The rebirth of Israel as a nation-state has had an especially significant effect on regional affairs.

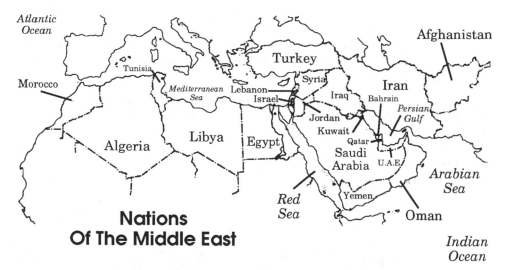

Nations Of The Middle East

A. Independence Movements After 1945
Clash Of Nationalisms In Palestine

Perhaps the greatest conflicts in the Middle East since World War II have centered on the possession of the land of **Palestine**. Jewish Zionists and Arab Nationalists saw no improvement when the British withdrew from the area and turned the problem over to the newly formed United Nations.

Worldwide support for the Zionist movement had grown as a result of the Nazi persecution of Jews during the Holocaust of World War II. In 1947, the U.N. Security Council voted for separate Jewish and Arab states in Palestine. A United Nations' supervised international zone was created in the city of Jerusalem. The plan was immediately accepted by the Zionists, but rejected by the Arabs.

World Issues:

Political and Economic Refugees

In May of 1948, a Jewish nation was declared, signaling the rebirth of Israel. The Jews, whose history had witnessed the Diaspora in 135 A.D., and the dispersion of their people throughout the world, returned to their ancient homeland. Arab neighbors refused to recognize Israel. Neighboring nations immediately provided military aid to Palestinian Arabs to block Israel's independence.

Diversity

The **Israeli War of Independence** (1948) became the first of a series of Arab-Israeli wars. Outnumbered by about 50 to 1, the Israelis fought for their survival with vastly inferior military equipment. Surprisingly, Israel proved to be more than a match for the Arabs, and held out until a U.N. truce was established in 1949. Israel gained an additional third of the land in Arab Palestine, and control of half of Jerusalem. The conflict resulted in a great loss of prestige for the Arab nations.

Culture

Another problem emerged for the Arab world when over one million Arabs left Palestine and settled in refugee camps in the neighboring Arab nations. These camps intensified the conflict. The more radical Palestinians used these camps for terrorist training centers. A truce was signed, but the Arab world refused to recognize Israel. They have also boycotted commercial products of nations which trade with their enemy.

In 1956, Egypt nationalized the Suez Canal and prohibited Israel from using it. Israeli forces then invaded Egyptian territory in the Sinai Peninsula. Within five days, the Israeli military marched to the Suez Canal. Great Britain and France also invaded Egypt in an effort to promote equal access to the canal. The U.N. stepped in and arranged a truce, and sent in a peace-keeping force to prevent further clashes.

In June of 1967, a third war erupted as Israel retaliated against its neighbors for the continuous terrorist attacks on its borders. Egypt ordered the removal of the United Nations peace-keeping force in the Sinai Peninsula, and closed Israel's vital oil supply depots on the Gulf of Aqaba.

With lightning speed, Israel conducted an all-out attack on Egyptian and Syrian targets, capturing vast quantities of the Soviet-supplied equipment of their enemies.

1967 Arab – Israeli War

By the time a truce was made in what became known as the **Six-Day War**, Israel occupied a land area four times its original size, including the Gaza Strip, Sinai Peninsula, Golan Heights, the West Bank, and all of Jerusalem.

Despite diplomatic efforts by the U.N. and major world powers, it was inevitable that the Arab nations would mount another military effort to reclaim their lost territories. In October 1973, Egypt attacked Israel's occupation troops in the Sinai Peninsula. Syria attacked Israel's occupation troops in the Golan Heights (see map page 210). Israel was caught off guard. Global alarm spread as the U.S. began sending massive aid to Israel, and the U.S.S.R. did the same for Egypt and Syria. In this war, the greatest tank warfare in military history occurred in the three weeks of fighting between the Egyptians and the Israelis. Finally, after enormous pressure was exerted by the Soviet Union and the United States, another uneasy cease fire was arranged through the U.N.

In March 1979, the historic **Camp David Accords** were signed by Israeli Prime Minister **Begin**, Egyptian President **Sadat**, and U.S. President **Carter**. For the first time, an Arab nation had recognized Israel as a nation.

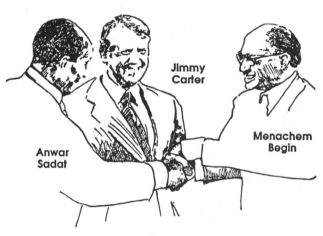

Jimmy Carter

Menachem Begin

Anwar Sadat

The **Camp David Accords** provided for:

- withdrawal of Israel from the Sinai and a return of the U.N. peace-keeping forces
- normalization of diplomatic and economic relations
- negotiations on Palestinian self-rule

Throughout most of the world, the 1979 agreement was welcomed as a positive step. Within the Arab and Islamic world, Sadat's actions were looked upon with disdain. To date, the Palestinian portion of the accords has not been implemented. Until there is a solution to this question, there can be little hope for a lasting peace.

For many years, the United Nations issued resolutions that brought the Arab-Israeli Wars to a halt through cease-fires and truces. The most famous document was **U.N. Resolution #242**, passed by the Security Council in 1967. It called for acknowledgement of the sovereignty, territorial integrity, and political independence of every state in the region.

The U.N. also requested that Israel withdraw from the territory that it attained in 1967's Six-Day War. Israel has refused to comply until the Arab nations recognize its existence as a nation in permanent peace settlements.

World Issues: Terrorism

There are over three million displaced Palestinian Arabs, many of whom belong to a coalition, the **Palestinian Liberation Organization**. The **PLO**, headed by **Yassir Arafat**, has continued to press for a sovereign Palestinian nation. In order to emphasize their cause, the displaced Palestinian groups have launched terrorist attacks against Israel from their refugee camps in Jordan and Lebanon. Israel's military retaliation has been swift and violent.

The Israelis want security and recognition as a nation, and the Arab Palestinians want nationhood on the West Bank and the Gaza Strip — regions which Israel now claims are vital to its defense. Palestinian Arabs and their allies want the return of East Jerusalem and territories occupied by Israel since the 1968 war. A major breakthrough occurred in September 1993 when Israeli Prime Minister **Vitzhak Rabin** and PLO Chairman Yassir Arafat signed a *Declaration of Principles for Palestinian Self-rule* in Washington, DC under the watchful eyes of President Clinton. It may have been the initial step to ending over forty years of Arab-Israeli conflict.

Human Rights

Middle Eastern governments often fail to protect the human rights of people. This has been accentuated by the miserable living conditions in the refugee camps which serve as breeding grounds for revolutionary and terrorist activities. These are the unresolved issues in this region of the Middle East that will continue to remain volatile.

New Political Leadership In The Middle East

After World War II, the spirit of nationalism grew rapidly in the various Arab countries, and this brought new political leadership which has often looked to western technology to cure social, political, and economic problems.

At the same time, the leaders recognized the necessity of maintaining their own culture and value systems. In attempting to maintain this delicate balance, many of the leaders were victimized by revolutions, which caused considerable political instability.

Following World War II, Egypt assumed the early leadership role on the promotion of Arab unity (**Pan-Arabism**) under the guidance of a charismatic military leader, **Gamal Abdul Nasser**. Although Egypt had been independent since 1922, it had been ruled by a monarchy and a class of wealthy land owners that were heavily influenced by the British.

In 1952, Nasser led a coup d'etat of army officers in the ousting of Egyptian King Farouk and proclaimed a republic.

Abdul Nasser

Nasser helped create a modern, mixed economy for Egypt. One of his first achievements was land reform accompanied by extensive irrigation projects. This significantly increased agricultural production. Seeking self-sufficiency for his nation, Nasser accepted aid from both the free world and the communist nations.

Nasser's social, political and economic reforms strengthened Egypt's nationalism. Perhaps his greatest project was the construction of the **Aswan High Dam** which was built with Soviet financial aid and technical supervision. The project would provide the energy source for the growth of Egyptian industry. His social reforms promoted educational, health care services, and more equality for women. Nasser endeared himself to the Arab world when he spoke of **Arab socialism** (improvement of the social and economic conditions for all Arabs).

World Issues:

Economic Growth and Development

Interdependence

Despite losing two costly wars to the Israelis, Nasser remained a hero in the Arab world, and over two million people joined his funeral procession in Cairo when he died in 1970.

Nasser's successor, **Anwar Sadat,** broke relations with the Soviets, and Egypt established closer ties with the United States. In a bold move, Sadat journeyed to Jerusalem in 1977 to negotiate with Israel in an attempt to resolve the Arab-Israeli conflicts. When he signed the **Camp David Accords,** the Arab world became angry that he was making a separate peace and destroying Arab unity. A year later, Muslim extremists assassinated Sadat.

In recent years, Islamic fundamentalists in Egypt have begun to exert pressure on the government to refrain from secularization and have urged the political leaders to turn back to the more traditional Islamic teachings and culture. Conflicts have continued to develop over the roles of men and women in the Muslim society, and over guarantees of individual rights.

In other nations of the Middle East, similar military coups ousted traditional monarchs who favored former European colonial regimes. In Libya, military leader **Muammar Qaddafi** successfully overthrew the monarchy in 1969. Since then, he has used Libya's vast oil reserves to promote revolutionary politics in the Middle East.

Military revolutions were also frequent in Syria, Lebanon and Iraq. In recent times, Iraq's dictator, **Saddam Hussein,** attempted to become the new leader of Arab Nationalism by building his country into the most powerful military force in the Middle East.

Saddam Hussein

B. The Islamic Revolution:
Iran's Conflict: Modernization And Fundamentalism

In Iran, **Shah Muhammed Reza Pahlavi** ruled as a figurehead until 1953. With the help of his military, and the support of western governments, he was able to overthrow the nationalist regime of Prime Minister **Mohammed Mossadegh.**

The Shah repealed many of Mossadegh's anti-western measures, and announced the plans to modernize his country which included the introduction of land reforms for the peasants, the reformation of the legal status of women, and the improvement of educational and health standards. Although some of these goals were achieved, much of the money from sale of Iran's oil and natural gas was spent on the Shah's grand building projects in the cities, lavish government ceremonial events, and armaments.

There was extreme poverty among the lower classes. Rural villages lacked running water and other basic facilities. The Shah's efforts at westernization alienated his people. He had not consulted Iran's Islamic religious leaders. He had exercised absolute rule. His government was rampant with corruption. To preserve his hold over the people, the **Savak** (secret police) used terror and torture.

Opposition to the Shah became overwhelming. In 1979, strikes in Teheran became bloody riots. The Shah fled the country. In March, **Ruhollah Khomeini**, an exiled **ayatollah** (Shi'ite religious leader) returned to Iran and rallied his followers. Their revolution succeeded in taking control of the government. They declared Iran an Islamic republic. Khomeini's group began reforms which reflected the strict Shi'ite teachings and political structures.

Khomeini

Identity

The new government pursued an anti-western and anti-modern-ization policy. The economy was greatly weakened in the aftermath of this Islamic revolution. Many Iranian women who had grown accustomed to western dress and a sense of freedom under the Shah's modernization policies saw these gains removed by the Ayatollah Ruhollah Khomeini's Shi'ite fundamentalists.

The Iran-Iraq War

Iran and its neighbor, Iraq, have had border disputes for many years over the control of land on the Persian Gulf and its many islands. In 1975, they had signed an agreement which seemed to settle their differences. However, when the Khomeini regime took over the government of Iran, tension mounted between the two rivals over traditional border disputes. Khomeini's agents tried to rally Iraqi Shi'ites in a revolution. In September 1980, Iraq's military leadership under **Saddam Hussein**, launched a full scale war against Iran.

World Issues:
War and Peace

The war raged throughout the 1980's, severely straining each nation's economy and claiming more than a half million lives. The U.N. eventually worked out a truce in the summer of 1988.

Iraq's Invasion Of Kuwait

In August,1990, Iraq began a new crisis in the Persian Gulf. Saddam Hussein used his military power to overrun and annex a neighbor, Kuwait. The United States immediately sent a large military force to defend Saudi Arabia from Iraqi threat ("Operation Desert Shield"). The U.N. Security Council authorized a trade embargo and finally condemned Iraq's aggression. Early in 1991, U.S.-led coalition of 28 nations began a relentless air attack ("Operation Desert Storm"). This was followed by a 4 day ground invasion which destroyed Saddam's forces and freed Kuwait.

Social Changes In The 1980's

Today, much of the Middle East is experiencing social changes through industrialization and rapid urbanization. Four good examples of these changes follow:

Role of Women. Despite the opposition of fundamentalist Muslims, large numbers of women are receiving more education and have become valuable members of the work force, and in many nations have earned the right to vote and hold political office. In Israel, equality is guaranteed by law, and women serve side by side with men in the military.

Democratic Reforms. Centralized schools have provided education and have dramatically improved literacy rates creating more social equality in the labor force. In most nations voting is granted to all citizens, and women have been granted improved social, economic, and legal equality.

Role of Religion. Many religious leaders of the region (Muslim, Jewish, and Christian) have attempted to block modernization and keep their conservative fundamental value systems. An excellent example is the Ayatollah Khomeini's movement in Iran.

Causes and Results of Terrorism. Terrorists have represented many different ethnic, religious, and nationalist causes and have resorted to surprise attacks of violence to achieve their ends. In coping with these threats, many nations have met violence with violence; yet others support these terrorist factions as tools of revolutionary freedom fighters.

As a result of these changes, many people of the Middle East are attempting to balance traditional culture which is heavily influenced by religion with the forces of modernization which are secular in nature. Revolutionary groups have used any conflict as an opportunity to support terrorism as a means to their nationalistic goals.

Questions

1 The nation of Israel was created in 1948 as a homeland for the Jews in Palestine because
   1 this was the only territory the British would give up.
   2 Arab Palestinians wanted to help Jewish refugees from Nazi camps.
   3 the U.N. recognized a separate Jewish state.
   4 the U.S.S.R. needed a place to send Jewish dissenters.

2 Egyptian leader Gamal Abdul Nasser nationalized the Suez Canal
   1 to give the Soviets a strategic base in the Middle East.
   2 to close it off to all but Mediterranean countries.
   3 because he resented American dominance in the region.
   4 to prevent Israel from developing its national resources.

3 The U.S.S.R. helped Egypt construct the Aswan High Dam because
   1 they needed the electric power generated from the project.
   2 they wanted a stronger alliance with Nasser.
   3 it was a stepping-stone to conquer Central Africa.
   4 they wished to repay their World War II debts to Egypt.

4 In the 1967 War, the Israelis captured the Golan Heights from Syria. This was a valuable area because it had
   1 the richest oil field in the Middle East.
   2 potentially rich deposits of uranium for nuclear development.
   3 the holy shrines of three major world religions.
   4 a strategic observation point to view Syria.

5 Yassir Arafat leads Arab World opposition to Israel because of
   1 the Judaic belief in monotheism.
   2 his jealousy of Israel's wealth.
   3 opposition to the kibbutz system.
   4 his demands for an independent Palestinian-Arab state.

6 The 1979 Camp David Accords called for
1 the sovereignty, territorial integrity, and political independence of every state in the region.
2 establishment of a new Arab-Palestinian state.
3 withdrawal of Israeli troops from the Golan Heights.
4 a joint development project on the Jordan River.

7 Libyan leader Muammar Qaddafi is typical of
1 strong Islamic nationalists in the Middle East.
2 pro-Western leaders in the Arab world.
3 a group which wants general peace with the Israelis.
4 Arabs who wish to strengthen ties with the United States.

8 Many Arab nations felt that as a result of the Camp David Accords,
1 President Sadat had betrayed them.
2 the United States turned away from its ally, Israel.
3 The colonial powers would return.
4 Menachem Begin was their new spokesman.

9 The Islamic Revolution occurred in Iran as a result of
1 the Shah's insensitivity to traditional customs.
2 an invasion by their Soviet neighbors.
3 the popularity of the Shah.
4 demands by the PLO.

Essay

Contemporary problems in the Middle East revolve around Israel and Islam.

a Explain why there has been a resurgence of Islamic fundamentalism in the Middle East in recent years. Include an example of a country where this has occurred. [6]

b The key to peace in the Middle East rests in the resolution of the Arab-Palestinian homeland problem. Discuss the reasons why the solution to this problem is so difficult. [6]

c Discuss one other problem that has been caused by modernization of life in the Middle East in the past generation. [3]

IV. Middle East:
Economic Development

For centuries the major economic activity in the Middle East has been agriculture. Today, extensive capital has been generated from the region's vast oil reserves. This money has often been used to modernize and broaden the industrial base in the region. With improved educational systems and modern technology, the Middle East is witnessing major transformations. Industrialization has brought employment and economic development, but often is accompanied by problems.

Throughout its long history, the Middle East has witnessed a deterioration and loss of suitable land for farming. This has occurred through overpopulation, overgrazing, and an overall lack of conservation. Turkey is the only nation in the region that is self-sufficient in agriculture. All other nations of the Middle East must import much of their food supplies.

Scarcity

The scarcity of water resources has traditionally been a concern, but in certain areas such as the Jordan River Basin, it has become a more vital issue than oil. In the next century, the need for irrigation and hydroelectric power in Jordan, Israel, and the West Bank will provoke additional conflict for the area ready to explode over the Palestinian homeland question. Population pressures on water supplies in nations such as Saudi Arabia and Kuwait have caused them to launch expensive projects to arid desert lands for agriculture.

A. Barriers To Development

With wealth from oil revenue in the hands of only a few Middle East nations, power and control of the distribution of this money is critical. It has often been used as a political weapon. The 1960's saw the creation of **O.P.E.C.** (Organization of Petroleum Exporting Countries). OPEC is a **cartel** (an international business group which forms to control prices and production). OPEC includes member nations from South America, Africa, Asia. However, the Middle Eastern nations have had the most influence on OPEC policies.

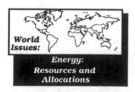
World Issues
Energy: Resources and Allocations

As OPEC's financial reserves grew, oil-producing nations became increasingly powerful in world politics and economics. Many countries of the region are not as fortunate, and lack resources. This has fostered regional rivalry and political instability.

B. Arab Socialism

Some countries of the Middle East have attempted to further their economic development by nationalizing industries, businesses, and resources. An example of this policy occurred in Egypt in the early 1950's under Colonel Nasser. A mixture of ideologies was used by Nasser under the title of **Arab Socialism**. Nasser created a mixed economy. He broke up the large estates the rich had accumulated under the monarchy. He established public ownership of farmlands, but he also encouraged private ownership of industry and invited foreign investment.

When the Egyptian economy failed to meet Nasser's lofty goals, he abruptly nationalized the Suez Canal. Revenue from its tolls added 200 million dollars to Egypt's treasury.

In 1957, many banks and insurance companies were nationalized. By 1961, the Egyptian government controlled all of the nation's light industry. Nasser then proceeded to provide more and more public services and education for Egyptians, and became a hero for his policies.

C. A Mixed Economy In Israel

Israel, with limited raw materials and energy sources, has achieved success through economic planning that has stressed a mixed economy of industrialization and agricultural development.

Maintaining the highest literacy rate in the region, Israel has developed successful diamond cutting, food processing, fertilizer, textile, and chemical industries. Israel has wisely used the skilled immigrants in its labor force, and has acquired vast amounts of foreign investment and loans.

Remarkable gains have been achieved in Israeli agriculture through strict control of limited water resources. Food sufficiency has almost been achieved through successful irrigation and fertilization which has expanded this nation's arable land. Cotton and citrus fruits have been produced in such abundance that these products are now exported throughout the world.

The **moshav** also serves to increase Israeli agricultural output. It is a cooperative settlement where land is rented by the state to individuals. Farmers may purchase or rent their supplies through a regional cooperative agency. Israel's agricultural success story can be attributed to these two systems which use only ten percent of its population.

Another unique Israeli agricultural system is the **kibbutz**, a system of collective farms where all property is owned indirectly by the Israeli government. Early Zionist settlers originated this system to encourage shared work and communal living, and it is strictly a voluntary system, where its members are free to join or leave. In return for their labors, members are provided with food, clothing, social services, and education for their children. Recently, the kibbutz system was expanded to include light industries such as radio and television manufacturing.

Israel does have a serious inflation problem caused by its huge defense budget, and the inability to maintain a stable industrial force. To broaden its economic base, Israel has turned to tourism, but there is too much tension and insecurity in the region, and this financial venture has proven to be very unpredictable.

Israel still depends heavily on over a billion dollars in U.S. government aid and private donations by U.S. citizens each year for its survival.

D. Political And Economic Problems

Many other issues will continue to shape economies and politics in the Middle East, and there will be a wide diversity of living standards in the region. Social scientists have focused on several major concerns.

Population Growth. Urbanization has happened very quickly as rapid population shifts have occurred from rural areas to the region's cities. While people are seeking educational opportunities and better jobs, new nations

World Issues: *Population*

have been unable to keep up with housing, education, or health and sanitation conditions. Overcrowding has caused miserable slum conditions, and food shortages. The exception to this situation has occurred in the newly created cities of the wealthy oil nations.

Rise of the Middle Class. In the large, cosmopolitan urban centers, a new class has emerged of highly educated professionals and bureaucrats who have distanced themselves from traditional religious customs and family traditions. Their new found independence has resulted in marriage by choice and smaller, nuclear families. This new class has assumed political leadership in many of today's nations.

Identity

Impact of Islamic Fundamentalism. Conservative Muslim leaders have been alarmed at today's secular laws and reforms. They have rallied their supporters in an attempt to return to a strict adherence to Islamic law and traditions. The best example of this was when the Ayatollah Khomeini's Shi'ite group led its revolution in Iran in 1979.

Impact of Western Values. Since World War II, Middle Eastern women have achieved more equality in the large urban centers where there are influences from the western world. Women have achieved the right to vote, and in some nations have been politically active. Through education, many members of society have moved rapidly toward a professional work force. In Israel, equality is guaranteed by law, and women have always served beside men in the work force and in the military. Many of the newly organized political systems of the Middle East have borrowed ideas from western nations, yet Israel is the only true democracy in the region.

Global interdependence is assured by the energy dependent world's reliance on Middle East oil, and the Arab world's dependence on the technology and foodstuffs of the world's industrialized nations.

Questions

1   A rising middle class has emerged in the Middle East among the
   1   religious leaders.   3   military forces.
   2   urban professionals.   4   independent farmers.

2   The most rapid change from traditional to modern societies in the Middle East is occurring in Israel because it has
   1   large oil deposits.   3   a balanced, planned economy.
   2   high mineral wealth.   4   the most advanced military.

3   OPEC is a group of nations that formed an agreement to control
    1   the Olympic games.
    2   the price and production of oil.
    3   traditional Islam.
    4   nuclear weapons.

4   There is intense interest in the Middle East in desalination, an expensive process used in converting
    1   petroleum to unleaded gas.   3   salt to gold.
    2   seawater to freshwater.   4   coal to gasoline.

5   Nationalization of an industry means that
    1   the government takes control.
    2   it is sold at an auction.
    3   a government loan is being guaranteed.
    4   the industry has gone bankrupt.

6   A kibbutz is an Israeli economic institution primarily used to organize
    1   agricultural production.   3   oil marketing with Arab nations.
    2   military training skills   4   trade with Western nations.

7   One economic consequence of Israel's high defense budget is
    1   loss of traditional values.
    2   high inflation rates.
    3   decrease in leisure time.
    4   decrease in domestic oil production.

8   The goal of Islamic fundamentalists in the Middle East is to
    1   revert to traditional Muslim laws.
    2   encourage the secular middle class.
    3   support Israel.
    4   encourage women to be active in politics.

9   With the exception of Israel, most of the labor force in the Middle East is involved in
    1   the tourist industry.   3   agriculture.
    2   the oil industry.   4   commerce or business.

Essay

In the last 20 years, oil has been used as a political and economic weapon in various conflicts involving Arab nations and groups

Conflicts

- OPEC v. Western Nations (1970's)
- Iran-Iraq War 1980-1989
- Arab-Israeli War of 1973
- Libya v. the U.S. (1980's)

Choose *three* of the conflicts above and discuss how oil was used as a weapon and how effective its use was in each conflict. [5,5,5]

V. The Middle East In The Global Context

A. Power Struggles In The Cold War

The Middle East always plays a central role in world affairs. In the decades after World War II, many Cold War struggles between communism and democracy centered there. The U.S. and Soviet Union aligned themselves with various groups. Each sent foreign, technological, and military aid into the region. The U.S. became the major ally of Israel and the Shah of Iran. The Soviets aided Syria, Yemen, and Afghanistan. In **Power** recent times, the U.S. became deeply involved in the Persian Gulf to protect the industrial world's petroleum supplies.

Strategic Location

The Middle East's strategic location in world affairs still reflects Mahan's heartland theory. The region remains the hub of three continents. Its waterways continue to serve as access to the major east-west trade routes. Since WW II, Middle Eastern wars, oil, and politics have greatly influenced the foreign policies of the world's superpowers.

Arab-Israeli Conflicts

Arab-Israeli confrontations constantly endanger the region. During the Cold War, the U.S. and Western democracies tried to support Israel while maintaining relations with Arab oil producing nations. The Soviets worked to undermine western activities. These outside influences sometimes prevented hostilities, but sometimes destabilized the region.

With its inception, the existence Israel as a nation has been a problem in the Arab world. Since 1948, neither Arab nor Israelis has enjoyed peace. After all the Arab-Israeli conflicts, Israel appears to have convinced much of the Arab world that with the support of the United States, it cannot be driven out of the region. This was made evident with the 1979 *Camp David Accords* (between Egypt and Israel) and the 1993 *Declaration of Principles for Palestinian Self-rule* (between the PLO and Israel).

Civil War In Lebanon

Another source of trouble in the Middle East has been the ongoing civil war in Lebanon. Many different religious and ethnic groups reside in this Mediterranean area which became a republic in 1942. Initially, Lebanon had lofty goals such as democracy, a strong economy, and harmony among its diverse groups, and for a short time these goals seemed to be accomplished.

The government was balanced by a unique leadership of a Maronite Christian President, and Sunni Muslims as Premier and Legislative President. Initially, the Christian population was the majority and retained the most seats in the legislature, but this was gradually reversed. During the 1940's and 1950's, the nation was prospering. Its capital, Beirut, became the commercial and financial center of the Middle East, even being called "the Paris of the Middle East."

Problems began to emerge in the 1970's, as the population quota shifted between Muslims and Christians. The Christian population had declined to 45% of the population, and the Muslims demanded a greater role in governing the nation. The situation grew worse with the

World Issues:
Political and Economic Refugees

additional presence of almost 400,000 Palestinian refugees from Israel who had settled in campsites in southern Lebanon. The political arm of the Palestinians, the PLO, began to use Lebanon as their base for staging terrorist attacks on Israel. The Israelis retaliated by bombing and invading the PLO refugee camps. This led to political strife in Lebanon with most of the Muslim population supporting the PLO and the Christian Phalangist group supporting Israel.

By 1975, civil war had broken out, and the Muslims vowed to fight on until they had achieved the dominant position in the Lebanese government. The once prosperous nation saw its businesses collapse and its capital ravaged by numerous bombings. By 1976, the Arab League and the Lebanese government asked neighboring Syria to intervene and restore order. A cease-fire was arranged, but in 1977, Syria sided with the PLO, the Israelis provided military assistance to the Christian Phalangists, and the civil war resumed.

In 1978, Israel began attacks on Lebanese PLO camps near its borders to retaliate for terrorist attacks. In 1982, an all-out invasion was launched against the PLO which drew it into the Lebanese Civil War. Eventually, the PLO agreed to withdraw its forces from Leb-

World Issues:
Terrorism

anon, and a multinational peace-keeping force of American, French, British, and Italian troops were sent to Lebanon in an effort to supervise the PLO withdrawal. These efforts were severely hampered by the continued terrorist efforts which succeeded in assassinating the Lebanese President and over 250 American Marines. By 1984, the peace-keeping force had withdrawn, and the civil war had resumed. Today, the situation remains tense, and Syrian troops have remained in the country to help keep the sporadic fighting from intensifying.

B. Struggle For Afghanistan

In 1979, the Brezhnev regime in the Soviet Union invaded Afghanistan. Brezhnev claimed a weak communist government needed reinforcement against Mujahidin rebels seeking an Islamic republic. The Soviets feared such rebellions spreading into their own Central Asian republics. They also thought the invasion could extend Soviet influence into the Persian Gulf area. In a classic Cold War response, the U.S. sent aid to the rebel groups. Islamic nations also sent aid to the rebels.

As with the U.S. in Vietnam, the Red Army became mired in the Afghanistan War. The rebels used hit-and-run guerrilla tactics then retreated into the mountainous terrain. Conventional Soviet military forces with high tech weaponry could not make any progress. The Soviets lost thousands of troops and poured millions into the effort to no avail.

The war became more unpopular in the U.S.S.R. Mikhail Gorbachev came to power in 1985. He struggled with military leaders to pull the Soviet forces out. In 1988, Gorbachev signed a truce agreement. The Red Army withdrew in 1989, but a general civil war continued into 1992.

C. OPEC And The Global Power Of Oil

Major Oil Reserves

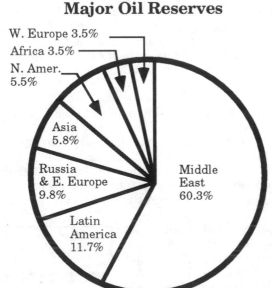

W. Europe 3.5%
Africa 3.5%
N. Amer. 5.5%
Asia 5.8%
Russia & E. Europe 9.8%
Latin America 11.7%
Middle East 60.3%

Recently, the concerted actions of the Middle Eastern oil producing nations have drawn attention to the political and economic power of the region. The strength of the 13-nation OPEC cartel was openly acknowledged in the mid-1970's with the use of embargoes and skyrocketing prices.

This caused grave concerns and much inconvenience to the United States, Japan, and an energy-starved Western Europe. OPEC, in exercising its control of petroleum reserves, was able to use oil as a weapon to achieve its nations political goals.

A vivid example of this occurred during the 1973 Arab-Israeli War when an embargo was placed on shipments of oil to those nations which aided Israel. As supplies began to dwindle, shortages forced up the price of oil. By 1979, prices had quadrupled. Fabulous wealth came to the oil-rich nations, but it caused severe inflation throughout the rest of the world. Conservation became the theme for world consumers. A trend developed for energy efficient automobiles, homes, and appliances.

World Issues:

Energy:
Resources and
Allocations

As demand for oil decreased, a glut developed which forced severe budgetary cuts among the OPEC nations. The non-oil producing Muslim nations of the Middle East suffered because they had grown extremely dependent on their oil rich neighbors for financial aid and employment for their people. Arab oil money, which had previously been invested in foreign countries and loaned to foreign governments and corporations, was restricted. Oil prices continued to decline.

The production and distribution of oil continues to affect the international financial situation. Dangerous conditions in the Persian Gulf led President Reagan to **re-flag** (re-register the ships as U.S. property) of Kuwaiti oil tankers in 1987 to insure the safe transportation of vital petroleum supplies to the free world.

World Issues:

World Trade and Finance

Saddam Hussein's 1990 invasion of Kuwait and the war it caused, involved nearly every nation in the Middle East and most of the major industrial nations of the world.

Interdependence

The Middle East remains an important crossroads in today's political and economic world. Numerous crises have disrupted the chances for the region's stability. The Palestinian question, superpower intervention, and religious upheaval are continuing problems.

The leaders in this region, which has enormous oil wealth and a vast historical legacy, must face the challenges of poverty, overpopulated urban centers, contrasting values, educational needs, modern technology, and social inequality. The direction that is chosen will be closely watched by the other nations of the world as this will shape international relations.

Questions

1   The U.S.S.R. sent its military forces into Afghanistan in 1979 to support
    1   the Mujihidin rebellion.
    2   the power of a rising capitalist class.
    3   its pro-Soviet Marxist leader.
    4   the cause of human rights under Camp David Accords.

2   OPEC is a *cartel,* this means that it seeks to dominate
    1   capitalists.
    2   communists.
    3   production and prices.
    4   the import-export business.

3   The Phalangists are important religious political figures in Lebanon because they are
    1   a fanatical terrorist group.
    2   dominant in the bureaucracy of the Middle East.
    3   a nonviolent-pacifist group.
    4   representative of the large Christian population there.

4   Beirut was given the name "the Paris of the Middle East" because
    1   of its financial and commercial successes following WW II.
    2   it has many evidences of Gothic architecture.
    3   French is the national language.
    4   it is the largest wine producing country in the region.

5   The Arab League asked Syria to intervene and restore order in Lebanon because
    1   it was feared Israel would continue to intervene in the nation.
    2   the major Arab military base is in the country.
    3   Syria wanted to control the mineral wealth of Lebanon.
    4   there was fear of a Shi'ite fundamentalist revolution there.

6   Israel invaded Southern Lebanon in 1982 to stop
    1   PLO terrorist camps threatening its security.
    2   Jordan from taking its land.
    3   attacks by the U.S. and U.S.S.R.
    4   the Lebanese from attacking its oil refineries.

7   In the 1980's, a multinational peace-keeping force was sent to Lebanon because
    1   it was the center of Arab League aggression.
    2   the withdrawal of the PLO needed close supervision.
    3   multinational corporations economic stabilization.
    4   it was about to become the site of a nuclear confrontation.

8   One of the major political goals of OPEC was to punish
    1   those who supported Israel.
    2   the Russians in Afghanistan.
    3   Arabs under Libya's Qaddafi.
    4   Islamic fundamentalism.

) America has assumed the major role in keeping oil from the Persian Gulf flowing to the rest of the world because
1 U.S. oil companies' high profits are paying for protection.
2 oil is the only industrial energy source.
3 Western nations and Japan are highly dependent on Middle East petroleum.
4 no other nations will accept military responsibility in the region.

Essay

During the Cold War the United States and the Soviet Union became involved in many Middle East conflicts.

a Explain the importance of this region to *each* superpower. [6]

b Select *three* of the following events and discuss a reason why one of the superpowers is concerned: [9]

- Nationalization of the Suez Canal (1956)
- Yom Kippur War (1973)
- Invasion of Afghanistan (1979)
- Lebanese Civil War (1982)

Unit Six

Western Europe

Parliamentary System
European Community
Mixed Economy
Codified Law
Cold War
Socialism

Feudalism
Absolutism
Totalitarianism
Market System
Industrial Revolution
Consent of the Governed

| 4000 | BC AD | 1000 | 1500 |

• Greek Civilization   • Christianity Begins   • Renaissance   • Elizabeth I

     • Roman Empire   • Feudalism   • Reformation

          • Charlemagne   • Crusades   • Rise of Nation-states

               • Middle Ages

1800   1900   1950   2000

- Enlightment
- French Revolution
- Napoleonic Wars
- Industrial Revolution
- Imperialism
- Bismarck
- WW I
- WW II
- Hitler
- Holocaust
- NATO
- Cold War
- Pro-democracy Movements
- Common Market
- German Reunification

Unit Six: Western Europe

I. The Physical/Historical Setting

Western Europe is a densely populated global region that encompasses twenty-six nations and dependencies. It is bordered by the Arctic Ocean on the north, the Atlantic Ocean on the west, the Mediterranean Sea on the south, and the region of Eastern Europe. It is subdivided by mountain ranges into northern, western, central, and southern sections.

Diversity

A. The Western Section

The nations of the **United Kingdom, Ireland, France, Belgium**, the **Netherlands**, and **Luxembourg** are included in the western section. While they are above 40° North latitude, the section has milder Type C climates (mid-latitude rainy) because of the influence of the **North Atlantic Drift** (warm Gulf Stream currents).

The **English Channel**, a narrow strait which separates the British Isles from the European mainland, has offered the United Kingdom (Great Britain) unique natural protection. It also fostered Britain's development as a seafaring nation with a massive overseas empire. Rich iron and coal deposits also allowed England to emerge as the world's major industrial nation in the early 19th century. The rapid depletion of these resources spurred development of **North Sea** petroleum drilling. Inland development was aided by a series of canals linked to the Thames River.

France's seacoast, rivers, fertile soils, and mineral deposits permitted a balanced economic development. Mountain boundaries inland (Pyrenees, Alps) have given the French some protection, but a relatively open plain in the northeastern section of the country has been a frequent invasion route.

Belgium, the Netherlands, and Luxembourg are lowland countries which are also located in the Northeastern European plain, and have been frequent battlegrounds in Europe's wars. They have excellent harbors and rivers which have helped their communication, trade and cultural development.

The Netherlands' low elevations have forced the people to employ dikes, canals, and windmills in constant battles to preserve the land from the encroaching seas.

B. The Central Section

Central Western Europe includes Germany, Switzerland, Austria, and the tiny country of Liechtenstein. This inland area basically has a Type D climate (mid-latitude wet-and-dry) climate with cold winters, but the topography modifies the wind currents from place to place within the section. The Ruhr and Saar areas of Germany provide rich coal and iron ore deposits which have been instrumental in industrialization. The Rhine River and its canal system have been a vital communication and transportation route for centuries. The river has also provided some natural protection against invasion from the west.

West European Nations

Despite Austria's mountainous terrain, the lengthy Danube River has acted as a major trade route. Because of the river, the country has a flourishing agricultural economy. Switzerland's Alps have not provided complete protection because of the many passes through them, but they are a source of hydroelectric power for the small nation. Despite poor soils, the Swiss dairy industry is famous, but its major source of wealth is found in its industrial, financial, and commercial enterprises.

C. The Northern Section

In the **Scandinavian countries** of Norway, Sweden, Finland, Denmark, Iceland, and Greenland, Type D climates prevail, except in the extreme northern polar regions (Type E). Short, cool growing seasons have caused the population to rely more on fishing and shipping for its livelihood. Mining and lumber industries are also sources of income.

D. The Southern Section

Spain, **Portugal**, **Italy**, and **Greece** are the major nations in this section. They have hot, dry summers and mild, sunny winters of the Type C climates (Mediterranean - Cs predominates). Spain and Portugal occupy the **Iberian Peninsula** which is separated from the rest of Western Europe by the Pyrenees Mountains. As a consequence, their development has been influenced by Muslim cultures of North Africa. The economy is largely agricultural, although Portugal has large fishing fleets, and Spain has considerable mining operations. The strategic **Strait of Gibraltar**, on the southern tip of Spain, controls the entrance to the Mediterranean, but it currently lies in British hands.

Italy is a mountainous, boot-like peninsula which juts out into the central Mediterranean below the Alps. The Po River valley is its most productive farming region. The northern section has fertile soils and is also industrialized.

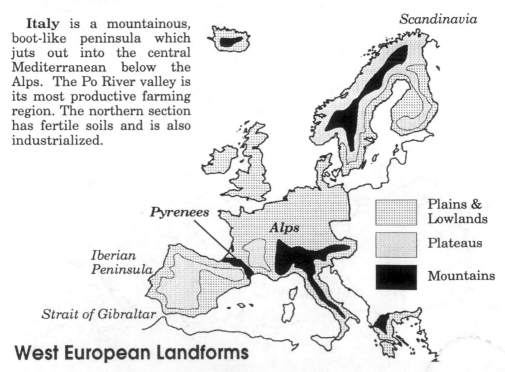

Scandinavia

Pyrenees

Alps

Iberian Peninsula

Strait of Gibraltar

Plains & Lowlands

Plateaus

Mountains

West European Landforms

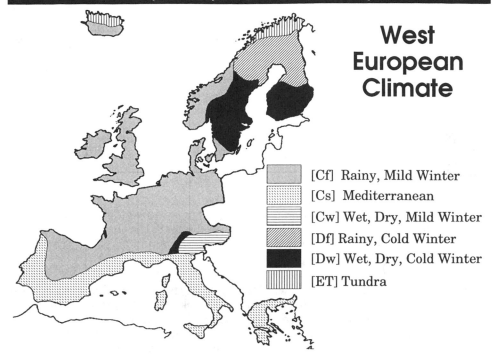

West European Climate

[Cf] Rainy, Mild Winter
[Cs] Mediterranean
[Cw] Wet, Dry, Mild Winter
[Df] Rainy, Cold Winter
[Dw] Wet, Dry, Cold Winter
[ET] Tundra

Southern Italy tends to have poorer soils and is less developed. Greece's mountainous terrain has limited its agricultural development, but numerous fine harbors and a commanding location in the eastern Mediterranean have made its people turn to seafaring for their livelihood.

E. Ancient Civilizations
Greece

Between 1500 and 1000 B.C., the invading Hellenes married with peoples at the tip of the Balkan peninsula, and began the Greek civilization. Unity was difficult because of the mountainous terrain. Therefore, a series of small, autonomous **city-states** emerged. Two of these city-states merit special attention: **Sparta** and **Athens**.

Sparta placed its emphasis on military prowess and aristocratic control of the government. It made few lasting contributions to western civilization.

Athens made significant contributions to government and western culture. From the 7th to the 5th centuries B.C., Athens took numerous steps toward a more democratic government. Laws were **codified** (organized and written) to insure equal treatment, and jury duty was created. Citizenship was still denied to women, aliens, and slaves, and punishments for crimes remained severe, but commoners were allowed to vote in the Assembly. This established a form of **direct democracy**, with citizens having direct say in the making of laws rather than being represented by officials. Under **Pericles** (461-429 B.C.), all restrictions on office-holding were removed, so that the poor could participate. The responsibility of service in office was taken seriously, and many served to protect their rights as citizens.

Citizenship

Athenian Contributions

The democratic environment in the **Age of Pericles** led to a spirit of questioning, individual expression, and creativity. Of the many philosophers, three stand out in laying the basis for modern thought: **Socrates**, **Plato**, and **Aristotle**. They concerned themselves with questions of justice, morality, government's purpose, and the interrelationship of human beings. Socrates held that individuals should know themselves and gave Plato, his student, a

Culture

method of seeking truth through constant questioning of life. Plato wrote his *Dialogues*, including *The Republic*, which described ideal social institutions. Aristotle's *Politics* and *Ethics* preached moderation in life as well as the use of logic and reason.

The ideas of all three of these philosophers continue to be studied to this day. Socrates himself was sentenced to death for encouraging his students to question authority. He accepted his sentence for he believed that civilization rested on the principle of law and people should not put themselves above the law.

Modern mathematics and science developed in the questioning atmosphere of Athens in this age. Examples include the work of **Pythagoras** (principles of geometry), **Hippocrates** (medicine - natural causes of disease, and the oath physicians take to serve the best interests of their patients), and **Democritus** (elementary ideas about the basic composition of matter).

Greek ideals of simplicity, perfection, realism, balance, and symmetry can be readily seen in the architecture of this age. The **Parthenon** was erected on the Acropolis, the city's highest hill, to honor Athena, the patron goddess of the city. It still stands and is considered one of the most beautiful structures in the world. Its **Doric columns**, **pediment** (low triangular roof), and **decorative friezes** (wall sculptures) are still copied in modern structures.

The Greeks of this age also laid the groundwork for modern theater. Plays were performed in outdoor arenas (amphitheaters) and it was viewed as a civic responsibility to attend performances. **Aeschylus**, **Sophocles**, and **Euripides** wrote tragedies, while **Aristophanes** wrote comedies. All are still performed to this day.

Ruins Of The Parthenon In Athens, Greece

The **Olympics**, the international games of today, date to the Greeks also. The ancient games were dedicated to the gods, especially **Zeus**. All fighting between men was stopped for their duration. Athletes who won in foot races, discus throwing, wrestling, and other sports were rewarded with crowns of laurel or olive leaves and the admiration of the crowds.

The location of Greece, with its good harbors, promoted much trade and travel. As a result of the contacts made throughout the Mediterranean, Greek culture became diffused and was preserved and copied by others.

The Hellenistic World

The disunity of the Greek city-states led to their eventual conquest by **Philip of Macedonia** (359-336 B.C.). After Philip's assassination, he was succeeded by his son, **Alexander the Great** (336-323 B.C.).

Alexander conquered a vast region stretching from the Balkan peninsula across Egypt and the Middle East to Persia and the Indus River in India. His conquests led to a **cultural fusion** between the Greeks and the people of the Middle East. It resulted in a culture that became known as **Hellenistic**, and made lasting contributions to civilization in many fields.

Field	Contributor	Contribution
Philosophy	Diogenes	**cynic** - humans should see truth and not be driven to seek wealth, power, and pleasure.
Natural Science	Archimedes	circumference of a circle; use of pulley, lever; theory of flotation
Philosophy	Epicurus	**epicurian** - the proper end of life is to seek knowledge; seek happiness in moderation.
Mathematics	Euclid	Euclidean geometry
Philosophy	Zeno	**stoicism** - humans must rise above misfortunes; seek harmony and equality.

Disunity among Alexander's followers made it easy for the ambitious Romans to seize control of the Hellenistic conquests.

Ancient Rome

Rome was founded by the **Latins**, on the hills above the Tiber River in Italy c. 1500 B.C. Initially, the government was an **aristocracy** with power in the hands of the landed **patricians** (nobles). The **plebians** (common people) had few rights, and they demanded reforms.

This resulted in admission of their representatives into the lawmaking assembly, the right to hold government office, and a veto power over the patrician consuls and patrician-dominated senate. Rome became a **republic** (representative democracy).

Justice

One of the most important achievements of the plebeians was to secure codification of the law into **Twelve Tables,** ensuring them that arbitrary unwritten acts would not be used. The modern word **justice** comes from the Latin *Ius*. The Roman ideal of the individual's equality before the law comes to us from this source.

The Twelve Tables concerned themselves with civil law, primarily the rights of individuals. For example, a murdered person's family had the responsibility of demanding satisfaction for its loss. Both sides appeared before a judge who decided whether the murder was deliberate. If the judge decided in favor of the accusers, the accused lost the protection of the gods and the murdered person's family could legally take revenge.

Citizenship

Around 340 B.C., Rome began to expand, seizing control of all of Italy, then the entire Mediterranean basin, Western Europe, and even England. As a consequence of this expansion, Greek civilization was absorbed and diffused.

On the negative side, great differences began to separate the rich from the poor and the composition of the Roman army changed from one of citizens to professionals. The common people demanded more reforms, and civil wars broke out in which military men sought control of the empire. As a result of one of these struggles in the first century B.C., **Julius Caesar** emerged as dictator, and the ideas of a republic faded.

Shortly after Caesar's assassination, the first Roman Emperor, **Caesar Augustus** was crowned, and the **Roman Empire** was established.

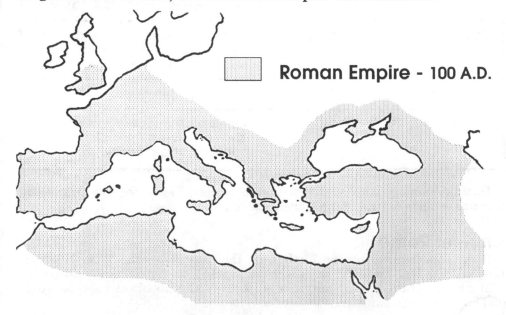

Roman Empire - 100 A.D.

The Senate became an advisory group and the government a military dictatorship. It lasted from 27 B.C. to 476 A.D.

The Romans enforced a **Pax Romana** (Peace of Rome) for over 200 years by using their armies, road systems, language, and broadened citizenship to unify the Mediterranean world.

Progress was made in many fields. Individual rights were protected by organizing imperial laws. The codes specified the freedom of thought and expression, placed the burden of proof on the accusers, and considered age in giving out punishments.

During the early years of the Empire, Christianity spread rapidly, despite government persecutions. Its emphasis on the (**Judeo-Christian**) belief in one God, human brotherhood, and the immortality of the soul won converts among the poor. It became the official religion of the empire in 392 A.D.

Roman achievements in the practical art of engineering are noteworthy. Even today their roads, aqueducts, and buildings (employing the round arch, dome, and Greek columns), stand as reminders of their skill. However, in terms of sculpture, painting, drama, and literature, they tended to imitate Greek patterns.

The Decline Of The Roman Empire

The Roman Empire declined in Western Europe due to the combination of internal weakness and attacks by outside peoples. Politically, the military dictatorship left little room for citizen participation, and failed to provide effective protection.

Economically, expensive imports undermined the value of currency and led to barter systems. Large estates at the edges of the empire became more self-sufficient and began to break away from the empire. Socially, a rigid class structure developed, crime increased, and the population declined. Under such circumstances, Rome became easy prey for **Germanic tribes**. The last emperor was overthrown in 476 A.D., and the empire disintegrated.

In the 4th century A.D., the eastern area of the Roman Empire broke away from Rome's control and set up its capital in **Byzantium** (in modern Turkey) The eastern emperor dominated both the government and the **Eastern Orthodox Church**. The Byzantine Empire's active commerce with India and the Orient led to substantial riches. Its own craftsmen made luxury items which were exported to the west and into the interior of Eastern Europe. It continued the Greek classical heritage. Many manuscripts were preserved for later generations. This Byzantine-Roman Empire also made many of its own cultural contributions, especially in mosaic art.

The Middle Ages

After the fall of Rome, Western Europe fell into a period of disorder and chaos marked by the lack of a strong central government, a decline in trade, and little cultural progress. The period has become known as the **Dark Ages**, or the **Early Medieval** period. It lasted from 500 to 1000 A.D.

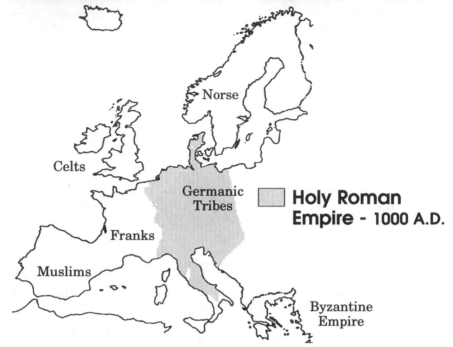

Holy Roman Empire - 1000 A.D.

Charlemagne

There were some notable exceptions to this general period of decline in the west. In the 8th century A.D., after Frankish Chieftan **Charles Martel** turned back the Muslim invaders at the **Battle of Tours**, a strong kingdom emerged in the central and western sections of Europe. This Frankish kingdom reached its zenith under **Charlemagne**. His empire extended from the Pyrenees and northern Italy north to the English Channel and eastward to modern Czechoslovakia.

The empire was divided into provinces and governed by nobles who were loyal to Charlemagne. His power rested in traveling investigators, or **missi dominici**. These agents kept the emperor informed of the actions of the provincial nobles. Conquered people were forced to convert to Christianity under pain of death. His conquest of the Lombards of Northern Italy provided lands for the Pope who crowned Charlemagne the first **Holy Roman Emperor** in 800 A.D. Charlemagne established a Palace School for the children of his loyal nobles. He was only partially successful in getting monasteries and churches to start schools for the young. His empire disintegrated amid struggles by his heirs for dominance.

Feudalism

A series of violent invasions in the 9th and 10th centuries by raiders from the northern regions of Europe (**Norsemen**, or **Vikings**) destroyed the larger kingdoms and principalities of Western Europe. Local lords who could defend their small holdings drew loyalty from local people. Frequently, landholders signed over their lands to these local lords in exchange for protection. These interrelated local loyalties evolved into a political, economic, and

Political Systems

social structure called **feudalism**. It provided strong local government, a connected system of self-sufficient manors, and a rigid class structure. Most important was its military protection for the individual in a perilous time of disorder.

Land-holding nobles became fighting men (**knights**) providing defense for those who worked their lands. Nobles usually allied themselves with some powerful **overlord**, serving in his army in exchange for the overlord's protection for his manor. Thus, the knights became **vassals** of the overlords and swore oaths of loyalty to them.

On the individual manors, people were bound to the land as **serfs** giving their labor in exchange for land to work and for protection. Serfs were considered property to be passed on as part of an inheritance. They could not leave the estate, marry, or change their trade without the noble's permission. In this rigid class structure, the only way serfs could possibly change status would be to enter the service of the Church.

The feudal manor was self-sufficient. Trade was minimal, since travel was dangerous. Agriculturally, a three-field system was used so as not to wear out the land. One field was **Interdependence** left vacant (**fallow**) each planting season to restore its fertility. Tools were crudely fashioned of wood because metals were scarce and needed for battle weapons. Consequently, the farms offered low yields. The serf could maintain some personal livestock on the lord's pastures, gather firewood, and fish. However, hunting game was restricted for the lord. The **manor house** was usually walled in for protection, and perhaps surrounded by a moat, or at least on high ground. Under siege, the people of the manor would gather behind the walls.

On his lands, the lord was absolute. For the serf, justice often took the form of a trial by some brutal **ordeal**. Survival would **Power** indicate God's blessing of the innocent, but often badly injured the serf. The social needs of the manor were often met by the Church's ceremonies, services, and festivals. Manor lords were sometimes entertained by traveling bands of troubadours, jesters, jugglers, and other wanderers.

The Church

In many respects, the Church was the dominant social institution of the Middle Ages. Its governmental structure had survived the fall of Rome and its teachings did provide some sense of universal law and order. Church courts and canon law provided a background for the inevitable clashes between the Church's spiritual power and the secular power of local overlords.

Monks decorated manuscripts with beautiful illumination.

The Church had economic power also. The **tithe** (10% of one's wealth was donated to the Church), and **Peter's Pence** (obligatory donations to the Pope) yielded vast amounts. Much of this wealth was used to benefit others, particularly monks in monasteries. They, in turn, provided care for the sick and lodging for travelers, copied ancient manuscripts, chronicled events, and introduced new farming techniques.

Culture
    Wealth was rather static because the church forbade **usury** (lending money at interest). Since Christians could not engage in such financial dealings, many of the Jews of Europe became money-lenders and later established banking houses. This often led to prejudice and jealousy against Jews since they were able to accumulate wealth. They were often expelled from regions where nobles who had borrowed did not wish to repay them.

To Christian Europe, the Church provided the services necessary for the faithful to achieve eternal life. The Mass and the sacraments were important rituals in these times. **Excommunication** was greatly feared because it denied the Church's services to a person. The cultural role of the Church is evident when one views the enormous Romanesque and Gothic cathedrals built in Medieval times. The donations of wealth, artisanship, and creativity in these structures, which sometimes took centuries to build, indicate the powerful position of the Church as a social institution. The painting, sculpture, and writing of the age had God or Church teachings as major themes.

Questions

1   Which of the following contributed most to the industrial development of Great Britain?
    1   iron and coal deposits   3   lumber industry
    2   Rhine River   4   mild, sunny winters

2   The Great Northern Plain played a significant role in European history because it
    1   provides France with access to Spain.
    2   has been a major invasion route into France.
    3   blocked German expansion to the east.
    4   allowed the spread of industrial development.

3   The Ruhr and Saar areas of Germany are
    1   Western Europe's major agricultural region.
    2   areas of mineral wealth.
    3   on the border of Russia.
    4   along the Danube River.

4   Which of the following rivers is correctly associated with a country through which it flows?
    1   Po River - Great Britain
    2   Rhine River - Germany
    3   Danube River - France
    4   Thames River - Austria

5 Fjords are most closely associated with
   1 Great Britain.   3 Italy.
   2 Germany.   4 Norway.

6 Southern Europe is an area which
   1 depends on large scale industry as its major source of wealth.
   2 has lagged behind other areas of Europe in industrial growth.
   3 derives little of its income from agricultural production.
   4 has a moist, cool climate during the summer months.

7 Which is true of a direct democracy?
   1 The people elect representatives who make decisions.
   2 Government officials are appointed by a groups of elders.
   3 Citizens vote on laws themselves.
   4 Juries are selected by the defendants.

8 In *The Republic*, Plato wrote about
   1 a system for international peace.
   2 monotheism.
   3 new methods of scientific farming.
   4 ideal governmental forms.

9 The Parthenon is noted as
   1 the site of a major European battle.
   2 a Roman governmental building.
   3 a Spartan monument to their dead warrior heroes.
   4 an example of the ancient Greek ideals.

10 The diffusion of Greek culture was aided by
   1 a series of rivers linked by canals.
   2 location and good harbors.
   3 a lack of mountain barriers.
   4 widespread acceptance of the Greek religion.

11 Alexander the Great's conquests led to
   1 development of the Hellenistic culture.
   2 the spread of Christianity.
   3 the establishment of feudalism.
   4 a cultural decline called the "Dark Ages."

12 The Twelve Tables are important because they were
   1 a written statement of Roman law.
   2 an important Greek archeological find.
   3 written by the Greek philosopher Plato.
   4 a statement of religious doctrine.

13 Preservation of the classical heritage, the use of mosaic decorations, and
   the spread of the Eastern Orthodox religion can be attributed to
   1 the Byzantine Empire.
   2 the Roman Empire.
   3 Alexander the Great.
   4 Charlemagne.

14 Which was true of Early Christians in the Roman Empire?
1　They were exempt from taxes in the Roman Empire.
2　They first attracted followers among the poor.
3　They were basically polytheistic.
4　They denied the existence of life after death.

15 Rome's major contributions were in the field of
1　literature.　　　　　　　　3　engineering.
2　drama.　　　　　　　　　4　sculpture.

16 Feudalism might best be described as a system designed to
1　provide protection through interdependence of classes.
2　increase the power of absolute monarchs.
3　oppose the spread of Christianity.
4　protect the trade of merchants.

17 A fighting man, head of the local government, and major landowner are all terms that could be used to describe medieval
1　nobles.　　　　　　　　　3　serfs.
2　merchants.　　　　　　　4　troubadours.

18 Tithes, Truce of God, usury, and canon law are terms connected with
1　Charlemagne.　　　　　　3　feudalism.
2　the medieval Church.　　　4　architecture.

Essays

1　Select *three* major geographic features of Western Europe listed below and for each one selected, explain how it affected the development of the area in which it is located. [5,5,5]

· The Great Northern European Plain
· The English Channel
· The Alps Mountains
· The North Atlantic Drift

2　Select *three* of the fields listed below and for each one selected, discuss *two* contributions that the ancient Greeks and/or Romans made in that field to modern civilization. [5,5,5]

· Philosophy　　　　　　· Science and Mathematics
· Government　　　　　　· Architecture
· Sculpture　　　　　　　· Literature

3　Feudalism and the Roman Catholic Church were the dominant institutions in Western Europe in the Middle Ages.

a　Explain how each affected the economic, political, and social structures of the era. [6,6]

b　Explain why the Church also dominated the cultural achievements of the age. [3]

II. The Dynamics Of Change

A. Effects Of Cross Cultural Change

The Crusades

In 1095, Pope Urban II called for a crusade to regain control of the Holy Land from the Muslim Turks. It had other purposes: to increase the power of the Church, to reunite the Roman and Eastern Orthodox churches, and to unify the warlike nobility of Western Europe in a church cause. Ultimately, the crusades obtained the right for Christian pilgrims to visit the area. They brought about far reaching social, political, and economic results that moved Europe from the Middle Ages into modern times.

Both the Byzantines and the Muslims had preserved much ancient Greek and Hellenistic culture and used it as a starting point for their own contributions, including advances in mathematics and science. They also brought the Europeans into contact with the spices, silks, and porcelains of the Far East as well as block printing, gunpowder, and the compass. The increased knowledge, the desire for the new products, and the wealth gained from the resulting trade, did much to bring about the Renaissance in Western Europe.

Woodcut of the Crusades

Cultural Changes: The Renaissance

The **Renaissance** (14th -17th centuries) first appeared in the Italian city states which had extensive contacts with the Middle East. They acted as middlemen for the rest of Western Europe. Popes and families, such as the **Medici** of Florence, used the wealth to sponsor artisans.

The word **Renaissance** means "rebirth," and this time period was one in which men once again became interested in education and learning. They were inspired by classical Greek and Roman civilizations to follow interests in mankind, nature, and individualism.

It was also a period of transition when characteristics of both the Middle Ages and Modern Times mixed. The interest in mankind was particularly evident in the movement called **humanism** which placed an increased emphasis upon individual uniqueness and worth. Both characteristics were reflected in the literature and art of the period.

Writer	Work	Ideas
Dante	*Divine Comedy*	Described imaginary trip through Hell, Purgatory, and Paradise using people such as the Roman poet, Virgil, as guides.
Erasmus	*In Praise of Folly*	Satirized the professions, but reserved special criticism for the clergymen whom he found to be uneducated and worldly.
More	*Utopia*	Proposed an ideal society in which there was no unemployment and everyone had equal possessions.

Artist	Work	Characteristics
Da Vinci	*Mona Lisa*	Used triangular composition & landscape background, famous smile, expressive eyes.
	Last Supper	Depicted Last Supper at moment when Christ announced betrayal by Judas. Famous for portrayal of apostles' characters, triangular composition and perspective.
Michelangelo	*Sistine Chapel*	Combined the Bible story from the creation to the flood with figures from ancient Greece.
Raphael	*Disputa*	Showed Greek philosophers holding a discussion. Used overlapping figures and extended limbs to hold multi-figured picture together.

Da Vinci's *"Mona Lisa"*

The magnificent pieces of sculpture such as the *Pieta* and *David* by Michelangelo were known for their accurate rendition of human anatomy and their expressive portrayal of people. In addition to this work, Michelangelo was responsible for much of the planning of **St. Peter's Basilica** in Rome which was closely modeled on Greek and Roman buildings, but with the addition of a Renaissance touch, the **cupola**.

However, the ideal Renaissance man was **Leonardo Da Vinci**. He excelled as an artist, writer, scientist, inventor, sculptor, and engineer. He produced designs for a tank, an airplane, a parachute, and the chain drive for bicycles.

Religious Change

People began to question the practices and doctrine of the Roman Catholic Church and placed an increased emphasis on the role of the individual in religion. In 1517, a German cleric, **Martin Luther**, formalized the **Protestant Reformation** with his *95 Theses* in which he questioned Church practices such as selling indulgences, the role and power of the pope, the way to attain salvation, the value of some of the sacraments, the interpretation of the *Bible*, and the role of clergy. He gave rise to the **Lutheran** Christian sects.

John Calvin, another religious reformer, went further than Luther in proposing changes. His followers founded the **Presbyterian** and **Congregational** churches.

Most of the Protestant groups denied the power of the pope, believed that faith alone was sufficient to achieve salvation, accepted only the sacraments of Baptism and the Lord's Supper, encouraged self-interpretation of the *Bible*, and believed in the priesthood of all believers.

Michelangelo's
"David"

Many rulers began to question the political power of the Church and saw it as competing with their attempts to centralize their governments. For example, in order to obtain a male heir for the throne of England, **Henry VIII** wished to annul his marriage to Catherine of Aragon in order to marry Anne Boleyn. The Pope refused.

The English Archbishop of Canterbury, Thomas Cranmer, helped King Henry secure a divorce independently of the pope. Cranmer helped to persuade Parliament to pass the **Act of Supremacy** in 1534. It established the **Anglican Church** (Church of England). It made Henry the head of the Church in England. Henry was able to seize the Church property. He kept some to increase his power, and he gave some to important nobles to win their support.

Martin Luther *protesting church practices by posting his grievances on the door of the Roman Catholic Church in Wittenberg.*

Culture   The Catholic Church responded to these threats to its power with the **Catholic Counterreformation** in the 16th century. The Church convened the **Council of Trent**. It reaffirmed basic doctrine and took steps to eliminate abuses within the Church.

The results of the Reformation were far reaching and have affected Europe to the present day. The Protestant emphasis on self-interpretation of the Bible, combined with the invention of the movable-type printing press by **Gutenburg** (1447), increased the literacy rate. The religious unity that had prevailed in Western Europe disappeared. A number of devastating religious wars were fought. The last of these wars ended in 1648. There was a period of uneasy toleration, but in parts of Europe, the animosity between the religions continued.

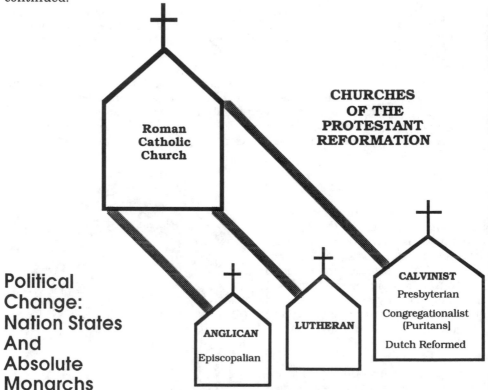

CHURCHES OF THE PROTESTANT REFORMATION

Roman Catholic Church

ANGLICAN
Episcopalian

LUTHERAN

CALVINIST
Presbyterian
Congregationalist (Puritans)
Dutch Reformed

Political Change: Nation States And Absolute Monarchs

The rise of nation states and the development of **absolutism** (all power in hands of a single party) occurred during the Renaissance. The philosophical basis can be found in the writing of Niccolo Machiavelli and Bishop Bossuet of France among others.

Power   **Machiavelli** (1469-1527) wrote *The Prince* to give advice on how to increase and hold power. Later rulers frequently followed his advice. He stated that "the end justifies the means" (anything that a ruler does to keep or increase his power is justified). He suggested that a ruler use the more reliable citizen armies rather than mercenaries. Machiavelli believed that rulers should be perceived as cruel and tight-fisted by their subordinates (as opposed to kindly and generous). Numerous rulers used these ideas as justification for increasing their power.

Although the **Tudor** rulers of England never claimed to rule by **divine right** ("God bestows ruling power on a person or family"), they did come very close to absolute power.

Elizabeth I (1558-1603) was very powerful, and popular with the people. However, she had difficulty living within the income Parliament granted her. Because she feared a loss of power, she seldom called Parliament to meet or to give her more money.

Religion was a controversial issue during her reign, but her policy of limited toleration for the private practice of religion, as long as no threats were made to her power, was wise. Her policy of encouraging trade won her support from the vital middle class. She used marriage negotiations to secure temporary alliances. She provided secret aid to Protestant groups fighting the Catholics.

Queen Elizabeth I

By 1588, Philip II of Spain was tired of Elizabeth's policies and after the execution of Mary, Queen of Scots (in his eyes, the legitimate Catholic ruler of England), he sent his Armada against the English. A combination of good English seamanship, the use of fire-ships, and winter storms resulted in the defeat of Spain. Elizabeth helped to develop an sense of English nationalism that was reflected in the literary works of **Shakespeare**, **Spenser**, and **Marlowe**.

Louis XIV of France (1643-1715) is considered to be the best example of a divine right ruler. He never called the **Estates General** (the French Parliament) to meet. Nobles were replaced by middle class officials appointed by the king. Louis built the magnificent **Palace of Versailles** to serve as a "gilded cage" for his nobles.

The nobles were drawn to the Palace by the lifestyle which involved banquets, dances, gambling, fireworks, theatrical performances, and the opportunity to be in the presence of the **Sun King** (the absolute center of French life). In the meantime, their estates were often mismanaged. The resulting decrease in their income limited their ability to challenge the power of the king.

Louis established considerable control over the economy by the use of mercantilist policies under

King Louis XIV

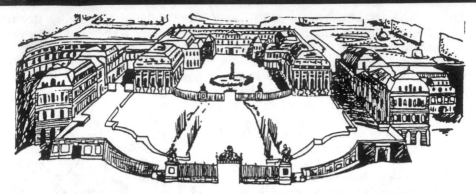

Palace of Versailles - *The Sun King's* **"Gilded Cage"**

Power the supervision of his able minister, **Colbert**. The increased revenues of the government were needed to pay for the major wars Louis fought to eliminate the Netherlands as a commercial rival and to gain the Rhine River as a boundary for France. Colbert could not stimulate enough revenue to cover the heavy costs of the wars. King Louis' expulsion of the economically important middle class **Huguenots** (French Calvinists) made the situation worse.

France gained little. A few small territories near the Rhine were obtained, and a French prince was allowed to rule Spain with the proviso that the two countries would never unite. France emerged from the wars heavily in debt and lost valuable colonies on the North American continent to England. French pride and nationalism did develop as a result of Louis' reign. Many rulers attempted to imitate his lifestyle. French became widely spoken in Europe and French fashions and cooking standards were adopted.

Political Change: Limits On Absolutism

Change Despite the nearly absolute power of the Tudors, there had been earlier attempts to limit the power of English monarchs. For example, in 1215, King John had been forced to sign the **Magna Carta** by his rebellious nobles who thought that he was infringing on their rights.

The **Model Parliament** in 1295 under Edward I established the concept of the **power of the purse**. Later Parliaments were able to use this to decrease the power of kings who were in need of additional revenues. It became a very important weapon in the hands of Parliament in the 17th century.

The Stuart rulers, who succeeded Elizabeth I, were from Scotland. They did not fully understand the English system of government. James I and Charles I tried to rule without consulting Parliament and claimed divine right. They also persecuted the **Puritans**. Puritans were Anglicans who sought Calvinistic reform within the Church of England. They were often persecuted despite their power in the House of Commons.

Political Systems

The Stuart kings' involvements on the European continent, and their inability to live within their income, brought frequent clashes with Parliament. Charles I was forced to call Parliament to meet in 1628 because of his need for funds. Parliament used this opportunity to force him to sign the **Petition of Right** in exchange for new revenues. This document reiterated some of the principles found in the Magna Carta. Charles then attempted to rule without calling Parliament until a revolt in Scotland forced him to do so. Charles attempted to arrest some of the House of Commons' Puritan leaders and caused the outbreak of the Puritan Revolution.

The **Puritan Revolution** (1642-1653) resulted in the defeat of the king's supporters (**Cavaliers**) at the hands of the Puritans (**Roundheads**) and the execution of Charles. A new government (commonwealth) was established under the Puritan leader **Oliver Cromwell** who was declared **Lord Protector**. One interesting result of this government was the first modern written constitution, the **Instrument of Government**. It was later used as a model for the writing of the American Constitution.

Cromwell's commonwealth was not popular with the English people because of its imposition of the Puritan lifestyle on the largely Anglican population. Shortly after Cromwell's death in 1658, Parliament voted to ask Charles II (son of the executed king) to return to rule England.

In the **Restoration** period, Charles II wished to avoid the fate of his father. He did little to interfere with Parliament. During his reign, the **Habeas Corpus Act** was passed. It guaranteed arrested Englishmen a statement of charges, bail, and a fair and speedy trial.

Charles II was succeeded by his brother, James II. James II claimed divine right rule, flaunted his Catholicism, and disobeyed English law by appointing Catholics to high positions. His overly harsh suppression of minor uprisings also brought criticism, but the birth of a Catholic son to succeed his Protestant daughters as his heir was sufficient to move Parliament to the **Glorious Revolution** in 1688.

Parliament deposed James and asked his older daughter and her husband, **William and Mary of Orange**, to rule England. This unmaking one ruler and making a new one estab-

lished the supremacy of Parliament. To further ensure its power, Parliament required the new rulers to sign the **Bill of Rights** in 1689. This document, combined with the earlier *Magna Carta* and *Petition of Right*, points to justice and the control of finances as vital in the fight to limit the power of the monarchy in England.

Most of the progress toward democracy in England was achieved through evolutionary means and rarely involved the type of intensely violent revolution seen in France and other countries. But these developments did provide a philosophical basis for the later revolutions in the American colonies, France, and elsewhere. In fact, some provisions of the *English Bill of Rights* were virtually duplicated in the *American Bill of Rights,* enabling American revolutionaries to claim that they were simply seeking their rights as Englishmen when they took up arms against George III.

Document	Justice Provisions	Money Provisions
Magna Carta 1215	Guarantees judgment by peers for all freemen. Justice may not be denied, delayed, or sold.	Taxes can be levied only with the advice of the Great Council (Parliament).
Petition of Right 1628	No imprisonment without a charge and provision for trial by jury.	No taxes without the consent of Parliament.
Bill of Rights 1689	Guarantees a speedy trial, protection against excessive fines and bail, and cruel or unusual punishment.	No taxes without the consent of Parliament.

Economic Change:
The Age Of Exploration And Discovery

The Age of Exploration and Discovery was an extension of the Renaissance. It reflected Renaissance interest in questioning formerly accepted authority and improving life. The Crusades exposed Europeans to the goods of the Far East. A demand emerged for the new products that could only be partially met by the expensive overland routes dominated by the Muslim middlemen.

The sea routes across the Mediterranean were controlled by the Italian city states. Limited accessibility added to the high cost of goods handled by numerous middlemen. This was made worse after the fall of Constantinople to the Ottoman Turks in 1453. The improvement of navigational devices such as the astrolabe and compass, as well as better ways of rigging ships, encouraged Europeans who already believed that the earth was round to support exploration ventures.

As a consequence, the European countries and their rulers were desirous of finding an all water route to the Far East. The search for such a route was started by the Portuguese under **Prince Henry**. Gradually, the Portuguese inched their way down the African coast claiming all the good harbor areas as they went. Finally, **Vasco da Gama** reached India in 1498. The goods that he brought back paid for the voyage several times over.

The Spanish looked to the West for a route to the Orient. In 1492, Isabella of Spain agreed to finance the first voyage of **Christopher Columbus**. After solving domestic problems, England, France, and the Netherlands also joined in the search for colonies, looking for passages through North America and Russia. Explorers claimed the areas they found for their respective countries.

Age Of Discovery

Explorer	Country	Area Claimed Or Discovered
Diaz	Portugal	Cape of Good Hope
da Gama	Portugal	India
Columbus	Spain	Caribbean islands, parts of northern South America and Central America
Cortes	Spain	Mexico
Pizarro	Spain	Peru
Magellan	Spain	Philippines
Cartier	France	St. Lawrence River (Canada)
Champlain	France	Eastern Canada and northern U.S.
Cabot	England	Northern U.S. and Labrador
Hudson	Netherlands	Hudson River

In their attempts to obtain their goals of "Gold, God, and Glory," the European countries came into conflict. They frequently seized each other's colonies. The most noteworthy conflict was between England and France from 1667 to 1763. This conflict was fought worldwide and terminated with the **Seven Years War** (1757-1763), or the French and Indian War, as it is called in American History. As a consequence of this war, France lost Canada, all the land east of the Mississippi (in what is now the U.S.), and was all but pushed out of India. England emerged as the dominant colonial power.

Economic Change: Commercial Revolution

Diversity

The domestic economic movement associated with the Renaissance is called the **Commercial Revolution**. It was brought about by the increase in trade that resulted from the exploration.

In order to finance exploration and colonization, a new form of business organization was started: the **joint stock company**. The sale of shares of stock made it possible to raise the necessary amounts of capital to undertake exploration and the following trade ventures. Modern banking began to develop to meet the needs of the emerging **capitalist system** (private enterprise) and insurance companies were started.

As demand for European products increased, some areas began to abandon the **guild system** (small groups of highly trained craftsmen) of production in favor of the **domestic system** (also called the "putting out system"). Production was done in the home and coordinated by a private capitalist financier.

In England, where much of the domestic system revolved around the production of textiles, changes were also made in agriculture to facilitate the production of wool. Farm lands were fenced for pasture purposes under **Enclosure Acts** and there was a resulting increase in unemployment among agricultural laborers. Some were able to find employment in the new domestic system, but economic hardships were frequent.

Governments, already trying to centralize political power, now tried to do the same with the economy. Many of them adopted **mercantilism** as their economic policy. The chief objective of this policy was to increase the gold and silver that a country possessed. In order to do this, countries tried to limit imports and encouraged exports by using subsidies and bonuses.

Sometimes, as in France under Louis XIV and Colbert, improvements were made in roads, bridges, and canals. Attempts were also made to establish government regulated standards of quality. Colonies were sought as sources of raw materials and controllable markets for finished products. Colonies were expected to serve the economic interests of the mother country, a policy that led to the American Revolution.

B. Political Revolutions

The Enlightenment

Change

An intellectual revolution in the 17th and 18th centuries began a search for natural laws that governed man's existence. It was called **the Enlightenment**.

Most of the philosophers believed that men were rational, thinking beings. They felt that governments and the Catholic Church often interfered with man's ability to use his power of reasoning. They questioned the idea of divine right, and some felt that men should participate in their government. Many of them questioned the Church, but continued to believe in God.

There was an acceptance of the idea of **natural law** which developed out of **Sir Isaac Newton's** discovery of the **universal law of gravitation**.

Some thinkers, called **Deists**, embraced the idea that God created the first life, established the laws governing the universe, and then left it to run according to His established rules. They believed that if man was allowed to use his reason, he would uncover the natural laws that governed his existence and progress would result.

The American Revolution

The political impact of these men's ideas was enormous. Repercussions could be seen not only in the American and French Revolutions, but also in many later revolutions. In the U.S. _Declaration of Independence_ (1776),

Thomas Jefferson reflected the ideas of John Locke when he indicated that the denial of natural rights was responsible for the Revolution. The U.S. *Constitution* used Montesquieu's ideas of separation of powers and a check-and-balance system. Not surprisingly, a strong impact was also felt in France which was home for most of the Enlightenment philosophers (*philosophes*).

Enlightenment Philosophies

Philosopher	Work	Ideas
Locke	*Two Treatises of Civil Government*	Thought men established a government to protect their natural rights of life, liberty and property. If the government failed to do this, the people have the right to revolt.
Voltaire	*Letters on the English*	Believed in enlightened despotism; government in which the ruler used his power for the benefit of people. Admired the relative freedom of speech, press, and religion in England.
Montesquieu	*The Spirit of the Laws*	Suggested that there should be a separation of powers between the branches of government and a check and balance system.
Smith	*Wealth of Nations*	Believed in laissez-faire, the government should keep its hands off business. The natural laws of supply and demand would do the best job of meeting the needs of the people.
Paine	*Common Sense*	Blamed the hereditary monarchy of England for the problems of the American colonists. Supported the rights of mankind and urged independence from England.

The French Revolution

The French Revolution of 1789 had many causes, but the Glorious Revolution of 1688 in England and the success of American Revolution six years earlier were inspirational to the downtrodden French people. The ideals of these revolutions led many members of the rising **bourgeois** (urban middle class), to question the Old Regime in France: the absolute monarchy and privileged nobles and clergy.

Despite the fact that the economy of France was on the upswing, and many members of the middle class were wealthy, they resented the fact that their non-noble birth was sufficient to deny them many positions in France. When the French government under **Louis XVI** and Marie Antoinette, found itself unable to meet its financial obligations in 1789, Louis was forced to call the French parliament, the **Estates General**, to meet for the first time in 175 years.

World Issues:

Determination of Political and Economic Systems

In his famous work, **The Anatomy of Revolution**, historian Crane Brinton examines the patterns of modern national revolutions. He notes the early leadership of the French Revolution (1789-1793) was in the hands of the moderate middle class (**bourgeoisie**). It successfully demanded that the Estates General, with its system of one vote per estate, be replaced by a more democratic **National Assembly**, with one vote per representative. This body was replaced by the **Legislative Assembly**, still under the control of the moderate middle class, but with a limited, or constitutional monarchy. Internal economic problems and the negative reaction of Prussia and Austria resulted in a change of leadership.

Violence-prone city workers (sans-culottes), with middle class leadership of people such as **Robespierre, Danton**, and **Marat**, took control and established the **National Convention**. It was during this period that the **Committee of Public Safety** operated the **Reign of Terror** which resulted in the execution of between 15 and 45 thousand presumed opponents of the French Revolution. Included among the victims of the guillotine were Louis XVI and Marie Antoinette.

Once the threat of foreign invasion diminished, and the French people tired of the violence, the leaders of the Committee themselves were guillotined. Once again under the control of the middle class, with a government called **The Directory**, the Revolution returned to a more moderate position.

Despite the turmoil of five governments within ten years, the violence of the Reign of Terror, and foreign invasion, both the National Assembly and the National Convention were able to pass numerous reforms.

Gov't.	Control Group	Reforms
National Assembly	*Moderate bourgeoisie*	Declaration of the Rights of Man Civil Constitution of the Clergy Reforms of Night Session of August 4th Le Chapelier Law
National Convention	*Radical proletariat with middle class*	Abolished imprisonment for debt Established a citizen army leadership Established the First French Republic Planned a system of public education Granted women the same property rights as men

Despite these important reforms, the French people were tired of the violence and upheaval of the preceding ten years. As Brinton's pattern of revolution indicates, control shifted at this time to a central figure, **Napoleon Bonaparte**. To some extent, Napoleon represented a return to near Old Regime conditions. He was a military hero who seized power in a **coup d'etat** (1799). He seemed to promise not only glory, but the return of peace and stability.

Within France, Napoleon established a government that had a facade of democracy, but in reality, he held most of the power. When he made changes in the structure of the government, such as the establishment of the **First French Empire**, he allowed the people to have a voice in voting on issues. In his reforms within France, he appeared to be a true son of the French Revolution.

Napoleon

Merit was the basis for obtaining advancement and was recognized in the **Legion of Honor** which was established for those who performed important services for France. The **Bank of France** took important steps to stabilize the currency, and the **University of France** provided for a public system of education under government control. The **Concordat of 1801** established amicable relations with the Catholic Church on Napoleon's terms.

Perhaps the most significant reform was the **Napoleonic Code of Laws** which has been frequently copied since that time. It reflected the ideas of the Enlightenment and proclaimed such things as equality before the law, religious toleration, and equality of inheritance.

Initially, Napoleon was most successful in dealing with the enemies of France who seemed to be unable to unite against him despite the strong efforts of the British. In 1806, he established the **Continental System** to hurt British trade and to help France establish economic supremacy on the Continent. The British then retaliated with their **Orders in Council**. The economic war was won by the British, whose navy was able to enforce its laws.

The refusal of Russia's **Tsar Alexander I** to continue to abide by the terms of the Continental System led to Napoleon's ill-fated invasion of Russia.

Napoleonic Influence In 1812 Europe

The Russian winter, guerrillas behind French lines, and the **scorched-earth policy** (retreat and destroy) of the Russians led to a disastrous defeat for the French in 1812. Close to 500,000 men lost their lives in this campaign.

This defeat encouraged Napoleon's enemies to join forces. They defeated him at the **Battle of Nations** and send him into his first exile on the island of Elba. Later he escaped for the so called Hundred Days and assembled an army, only to be defeated by the Duke of Wellington at the **Battle of Waterloo** (1815). This time, he was exiled to the island of St. Helena in the South Atlantic, a place from which escape was virtually impossible.

While Napoleon's armies crisscrossed Europe, they spread the ideals of the French Revolution: nationalism and democracy. In those areas which came under Napoleon's control, reforms similar to those of the French Revolution were enacted. The Napoleonic Code was made the legal system, feudalism was abolished, and religious toleration was instituted.

However, the **Congress of Vienna** (1815) met just before the final defeat of Napoleon to establish the peace. It returned many of the pre-1789 rulers or their heirs to power. With them came the return of Old Regime conditions, but the people did not forget the French ideals, and a number of revolutions eventually broke out.

National Unification: Germany And Italy

The spread of nationalism in Europe during the Napoleonic Period was to have long term repercussions, not only in Europe, but also in non-Western areas that came under European influence. **Nationalism** is a force which binds people with the same or similar language, history, religion, institutions, beliefs, geographic area. It can act to unify people, but it also can serve to break up multi-national empires. In its most extreme form (**chauvinism**), it has the power for tremendous evil, as in the case of Hitler's Germany.

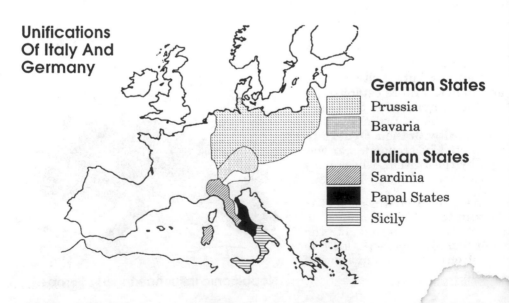

Unifications Of Italy And Germany

German States
Prussia
Bavaria

Italian States
Sardinia
Papal States
Sicily

During the 19th century, the new force of nationalism resulted in the formation of two new nation-states, Germany and Italy. In both cases, the process was accelerated by actions taken by Napoleon which decreased the number of states within each area. The arousal of the anti-French sentiment was also a unifying factor. Each area also had writers who encouraged the development of patriotism. People like **Fichte** in Germany and **Mazzini** in Italy did much to spur the movements toward national unification. There are, in addition, a number of other interesting parallels between the countries.

Germany		Italy
Prussia	**nucleus state**	Sardinia-Piedmont
Bismarck	**leader**	Cavour
Wars: Danish War Austro-Prussian War Franco-Prussian War	**means of achieving unification**	Wars: Austro-Sardinian War Austro-Prussian War Franco-Prussian War Plebiscites

In both cases, wars were important means of achieving unification, but in the case of Italy, the plebiscites added a democratic element which was not present in Germany. The German autocratic tradition was also apparent in the actions of **Otto von Bismarck** who is also known as the "Iron Chancellor." Denied additional tax revenue to increase and update the army, Bismarck simply collected the monies. His political philosophy was also apparent in his statement that major decisions were not made by parliamentary majorities, but "by blood and iron."

The unification of the German states upset the balance of power in Europe because the German Empire was considerably stronger than France in terms of manpower and resources. Later, Bismarck, fearing French revenge for defeat in the Franco-Prussian War (1871), began to establish the system of alliances that was to be a cause of World War I.

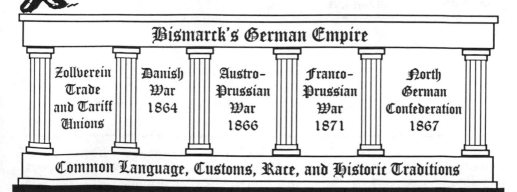

Bismarck's German Empire

| Zollverein Trade and Tariff Unions | Danish War 1864 | Austro-Prussian War 1866 | Franco-Prussian War 1871 | North German Confederation 1867 |

Common Language, Customs, Race, and Historic Traditions

C. The Industrial Revolution

The Industrial Revolution began in England about 1750. England had that unique combination of conditions that made this economic transformation possible. An agricultural revolution, which led to better methods of planting and hoeing (Tull), crop rotation (Townshend), and scientific breeding of cattle (Bakewell), resulted in an increased production per person. Better quality agricultural products made it possible for fewer people to supply the food needs for the nation. Many of the unemployed agricultural workers sought employment in the newly developing industries.

Technology

Other factors leading to industrialization include: excellent access to the seas, good harbors, coal and iron resources, capital to invest, a positive government attitude, and worldwide markets. These markets demanded goods that the English could not supply using the domestic system; creative men in England began to look for new ways to produce goods, particularly in the production of textiles, the first area to be affected by the new methods of production.

Inventor	Invention	Effect
Kay	flying shuttle	Doubled the speed of weavers
Hargreaves	spinning jenny	Could spin 8 to 20 threads at once
Arkwright	water frame	Use of water power; required development of factories. Could spin 48 to 300 threads at once
Crompton	spinning mule	Combines jenny and water frame; could spin fine thread
Cartwright	power loom	First application of power to weaving

Very quickly, new and improved methods of transportation were developed to speed the movement of goods around the country.

Inventor	Invention	Effect
Watt	steam engine	New source of power usable in many different places
Stephenson	steam locomotive	Faster land transportation
Telford and McAdam	hard surfaced roads	Faster land transportation in all kinds of weather

Initially at least, there were a number of detrimental effects of the Industrial Revolution. The **Sadler Report** on factories and **Ashley Report** on mines brought these to the attention of the English people.

It was not unusual to have young children 5 to 6 years old working 14 to 16 hours in factories where the machines had no safety devices. Poor ventilation, very warm temperatures, physical punishment for minor errors, and subsistence wages completed the picture. In the mines, conditions were no better. Possible explosions, lung diseases, back deformities, and miscarriages from pulling coal carriages through the mine tunnels were frequent.

Eventually, some political leaders began to empathize with the workers. This led them to investigate conditions. Laws such as the **Factory Act** of 1833, the **Mines Act** of 1842, and the **Ten Hours Act** of 1847 combined to limit the labor of women and children, and eventually men.

Reforms were also sought in the area of political democracy, but it was not until 1832 that the **Great Reform Bill** was passed. This lowered the property requirements for suffrage to give members of the middle class the right to vote. It also abolished most **rotten boroughs** (areas with little or no population and representation in Parliament) and gave seats in Parliament to the newly developed or greatly enlarged industrial areas. The workers were left out of this reform and started the **Chartist** movement to demand the suffrage for themselves.

A giant charter or petition was drawn up and presented to Parliament. It demanded universal male suffrage, annual elections of Parliament, payment of salaries to Members of Parliament, equal voting districts, and a secret ballot. Eventually, everything but the call for annual elections for Parliament became law. Especially important for the improvement of democracy were the laws that extended the right to vote.

Reform Bill	Group Obtaining The Right To Vote
1867	City workers
1884	Farm workers
1918	Universal male suffrage and all women over 30
1928	Universal suffrage
1969	Lowered voting age to 18

Gradually, improvements in the standard of living began to reach the working class, but real progress was not made until after the mid-19th century. At least in part, the industrialization of England was brought about by the sacrifices of the workers. This was because the laissez-faire economic policy of Adam Smith called for the government to keep its hands off business. This allowed the businessmen to disregard the safety and well being of the workers.

D. Socialism

People such as **Robert Owen**, **Karl Marx**, and **Frederick Engels** believed that the capitalist system was responsible for the evils of the Industrial Revolution. They advocated (argued for) alternative economic systems.

Robert Owen was called a **utopian socialist**. In hopes of proving to other capitalists that it would be possible to improve working conditions and still make a profit, he purchased the industrial town of **New Lanark**, Scotland. In his factory, he decreased hours, increased wages, and forbade the employment of young children. (Children were provided with a rudimentary education instead.) He built decent housing for his workers and even provided small garden areas.

Empathy
Owen proved he was able to make a profit, but few of his fellow factory owners followed his example. Later, he invested in a new enterprise in **New Harmony** (Indiana, USA) which operated according to the principle, "from each according to his ability, to each according to his need." Unfortunately, New Harmony was a dismal failure. Owen's last project was an attempt to organize English workers into one gigantic union.

Karl Marx and Frederick Engels proposed a different approach in their 1848 pamphlet, ***The Communist Manifesto***. Marx also wrote the multi-volume work, ***Das Kapital***, which further expanded on his socialist ideas. Essentially, he used past history and the current conditions in industrializing countries to predict what might happen in the future.

Marx did not wish to be associated with the utopian socialists. He referred to his ideas as **scientific socialism.** He left no clear description of what the communist society would be. He did indicate that initially, the government would own the means of production, the **dictatorship of the proletariat** would gradually abolish classes, and that eventually the government would "wither away." However, he gave no indication of how long this process might take.

Ironically, Marx's predictions may have been responsible for the failure of his ideas to come true in industrialized countries. Governments slowly began to act to alleviate poor working conditions, limit the role of big business, make provision for labor organizations to exist, and decrease "boom to bust" business cycles.

All of these actions helped to keep the conditions from reaching the stage that would cause Marx's proletarian revolution.

Marx's Idea	Explanation	Criticism
Economic interpretation of history	Economic factors determine the course of history and those who control the means of production will control the govern- ment and the society.	Does not account for such things as the Crusades, religious wars and the unifications of Germany and Italy.
Class struggle	Throughout history, there have been the "haves" and the "have-nots." In a modern industrial society the struggle is between the prole- tariat and capitalists.	Does not consider the cooperation between the proletariat and capitalists to increase production or profit- sharing arrangements.
Surplus Value Theory	*"Price of Product minus the Cost of Labor equals Surplus Value."* Here, Marx says the surplus value goes to capital- ist, but should go to the worker who produces the value.	Does not provide a return for the capitalist who risks his capital and provides management services.
Inevitability of Socialism	Over a long period of time, overproduction will result in bank- ruptcies, and depres- sions will occur. Conditions will get so bad that the proletariat will revolt and establish a dictatorship of the proletariat.	This has not come true. Communism has not gained control in countries already industrialized.

E. Imperialism

About 1870, approximately the same time that industrialization was making itself strongly felt in Britain, France, and Germany, a new wave of imperialism arose. Japan and the United States, both beginning to industrialize, would join the wave later. Many factors contributed to the movement to acquire colonial empires:

Power

- the demand for raw materials and markets
- the unification of Italy and Germany
- France's desire to restore prestige after the Franco-Prussian War
- the emergence of Japan as a power in international affairs
- the desire of humanitarian groups to help others

The biological theory of **natural selection** put forth by Charles Darwin in 1859 in his book, *The Origin of Species*, seemed to reinforce the idea that Europeans were a superior people and that they should control the resources of the world.

The combination of the technological supremacy of the Europeans with the weak governments and disunity that they often encountered in the less developed areas reinforced this concept of **Social Darwinism** and made it easier for them to gain control.

Conflicts rapidly developed among the imperialist countries over control of the desired areas. The British desire to control the north-south Cape-to-Cairo expanse in East Africa brought them close to conflict with both the Germans and French who were anxious to gain control of east-west belts. The French goal of obtaining North African colonies also led to disputes with both Italy and Germany. Imperialistic disputes among European countries were partially responsible for the outbreak of World War I.

In the 1890's, the United States abandoned its traditional isolationism to become a player in the world of international politics. American nationalism, combined with the "White Man's Burden" idea, led to armed conflict with Spain over its harsh repression in Cuba.

F. World War I (1914-1918)

World War I was caused by a variety of factors:

- competition for raw materials and markets
- acquisition of colonies for national prestige
- struggles for national independence in Eastern Europe
- competition among powers to build military power (militarism)

World
Issues:
War and Peace

As countries began to feel increasingly insecure, two alliance systems were developed in an attempt to achieve a balance of power. Germany, under the leadership of Bismarck, took the lead in establishing the **Triple Alliance,** largely in fear of French retaliation for the loss of the Franco-Prussian War. This alliance with Austria-Hungary and Italy was augmented by a secret agreement with Russia, eliminating the possibility of a two-front war.

However, when Bismarck was forced out of office by **Kaiser Wilhelm II**, the German alliance with Russia was allowed to lapse. The French were able to take advantage of this, and began the establishment of the **Triple Entente** alliance. Later, France and Russia were able to persuade the British to enter the Entente. Since the entente was not a firm commitment for action, some uncertainty remained about the British position right up until the outbreak of World War I.

A series of crises also preceded the outbreak of war and worsened relationships between the two alliance systems. There were two crises involving Morocco which pitted France against Germany and two Balkan Wars in Eastern Europe. The Balkan Peninsula was referred to as the "tinderbox" or "powder-keg" because of the explosive mix of nationalities there. Austria-Hungary wished to maintain the status quo in order to insure its existence.

The Russians were desirous of helping the Slavs to establish independent states under Russian influence. They backed the ambitions of Serbia, the leader of the Slavic movement. Two Balkan wars, fought by the small Balkan countries against the Ottoman Empire with Russian encouragement, further increased tension. The 1914 assassination of **Archduke Franz Ferdinand** (heir to the throne of Austria-Hungary) by a Slav who belonged to a Serbian nationalist organization, became the spark that set off the powder-keg.

Austria asked for German support. The Germans gave a "carte blanche" pledge to back anything Austria did. The Germans actively encouraged the Austrians to attack Serbia and were willing to aid Austria against Russia and France if the war could not be localized. However, they were concerned about the position of Britain, which did not make its stand clear until the war began. Ultimately, as mobilization began in Russia, Austria declared war. A chain reaction occurred as the alliances were activated. A regional crisis had become World War I.

Claiming that the alliance was defensive and their allies were the aggressors, the Italians refused to honor their alliance with Germany and Austria-Hungary. Later, Italy entered the war on the Entente side after receiving promises of land.

The Russians fought valiantly, but their failure to modernize, and their lack of equipment, resulted in heavy losses. The out-break of revolution, the abdication of the Tsar, and the rapid switch from the Provisional regime to the Bolshevik government led to the Russian withdrawal from the war in 1917.

However, most of the action occurred on the Western Front where a defensive war quickly emerged. The front lines hardly changed once they stabilized at the beginning of the war. Thousands of men died for less than a mile or two of land. During the course of the war, technological development of new weapons such as poison gas, the tank, large artillery, the airplane, and the submarine occurred. The real effect of these new weapons was not felt until 1939. They made possible the high mobility of World War II.

Despite early attempts to remain neutral, the U.S. entered WW I in 1917. Unrestricted submarine warfare by the Germans, loans made to the Allies, and the idea of the democracies (Allies) fighting the autocratic powers (Central Powers) drew America into the conflict.

During the course of World War I, **President Wilson** of the United States drew up his **Fourteen Points** which were designed to settle the issues that had caused the War and prevent wars in the future. He emphasized the ideas of self-determination of nations, freedom of the seas, equal access to trade, and the return of Alsace-Lorraine to France. The Allies accepted most of Wilson's ideas as the basis for a peace settlement, but indicated that they intended to obtain reparations or money payments for the war costs.

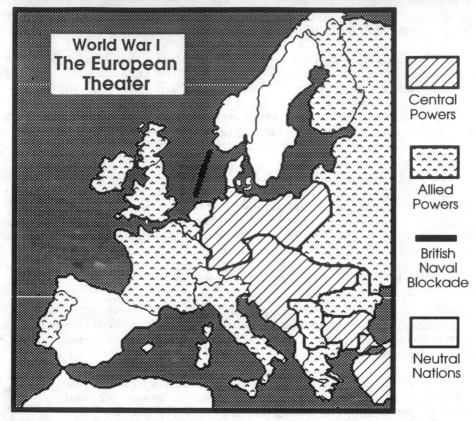

World War I
The European
Theater

Central Powers

Allied Powers

British Naval Blockade

Neutral Nations

By the fall of 1918, it had become apparent to the German military that they could not win the War. The Kaiser abdicated, and the government was persuaded to sign an armistice based on the Fourteen Points. At the Paris Peace Conference which followed, the Germans were not allowed to be present, and the basic decisions were made by Wilson, Lloyd George of Britain, Clemenceau of France, and Orlando of Italy. The resulting **Treaty of Versailles** required the Germans to accept responsibility for the war (war guilt clause), pay reparations, reduce its military, surrender all its colonies, return Alsace-Lorraine to France, and accept the loss of various territories in Europe.

Under protest and the threat of resumption of the war, the Germans signed the Treaty of Versailles. The resentment caused by the treaty's harsh terms was to be a major factor leading to World War II. The loss of lives caused by the war upset the demographic patterns in Europe leaving a large surplus of females over males and allowing younger people to emerge as national leaders.

Outside of Europe, the war resulted in an increase in a nationalist spirit in colonized nations hoping to achieve independence or a measure of self-government through the Paris Peace Conference. Although European domination began to weaken after World War I, it was World War II that dealt the fatal blow to European colonial empires.

Europe
After
World War I

Nor. — Sw. — Fin. — Estonia — Latvia — Lithuania — East Prussia — Ir. — Br. — Dk. — Germany — Pol. — U.S.S.R. — France — Czech. — Sz. — Aus. — Italy — Rom. — Spain — Yug. — Bul. — Gr. — Tur.

Questions

1 The Crusades helped begin the Renaissance because they
　1　opened trade with the Western Hemisphere.
　2　brought contact with the ideas and products of other people.
　3　increased the power of the Roman Catholic Church.
　4　freed the Byzantine Empire from Muslim control.

2 The Renaissance occurred first in Italy because
　1　the wealth from trade made sponsorship of art possible.
　2　the feudal system clearly dominated Italian life.
　3　censorship of new ideas was strong.
　4　there were many different religions.

3 Which of the following correctly associates a writer with his work?
　1　Dante - *Divine Comedy*　　3　Erasmus - *The Courtier*
　2　More - *In Praise of Folly*　　4　Castiglione - *Utopia*

4 Leonardo da Vinci was the ideal Renaissance man because he was
　1　extremely wealthy.　　3　multi-talented.
　2　an excellent athlete.　　4　very religious.

5 The Roman Catholic and Protestant religions differed in regard to
　1　monotheism.
　2　the role of Jesus.
　3　life after death.
　4　the value of some of the sacraments.

6   Henry VIII's actions regarding the Roman Catholic Church resulted in
   1   the establishment of the Anglican Church in England.
   2   the flight of most Protestants from England.
   3   a series of major religious wars.
   4   a loss of power for the English monarchy.

7   Rulers following the advice of Machiavelli would be most likely to
   1   listen to legislative bodies carefully.
   2   do anything necessary to keep or increase power.
   3   hire mercenaries to do the fighting.
   4   be merciful when handing down punishments.

8   Elizabeth I established the international power of England through the
   1   defeat of Philip II and the Spanish Armada.
   2   passage of the Act of Supremacy.
   3   defeat of the French in America.
   4   implementation of religious toleration.

9   To increase power, a Machiavellian ruler would most likely try to
   1   call the legislature to meet frequently.
   2   decrease the power of the nobles.
   3   support the power of the Roman Catholic Church.
   4   encourage free trade.

10   The English *Magna Carta*, *Petition of Right*, and *Bill of Rights* all
   1   limit the taxing power of the king.
   2   provide for universal male suffrage.
   3   prohibit excessive fines and bail.
   4   guarantee complete freedom of religion.

11   Developments in 17th century England are important because they
   1   established a direct democracy.
   2   made England a republic.
   3   influenced the American and French revolutions.
   4   resulted in an absolute monarchy.

12   The Commercial Revolution witnessed the establishment of
   1   the factory system.   3   a capitalist economic system.
   2   modern trade unions.   4   a self-sufficient economy.

13   The Protestant Reformation and the Age of Exploration and Discovery
   best illustrate which of the following characteristics of the Renaissance?
   1   questioning of formerly accepted authority
   2   interest in Greece and Rome
   3   progress in math and science
   4   attention to realism and detail

14   The Scientific Revolution helped start the Enlightenment because
   1   men began to search for universal laws in many fields.
   2   the Roman Catholic Church supported the findings of Galileo.
   3   men were willing to accept the teachings of the Church.
   4   scientists accepted the findings of the early Greeks.

15   The need for markets and raw materials, nationalism, and the concept of
   the "White Man's Burden" led to
   1   the Industrial Revolution.   3   imperialism.
   2   the Napoleonic Wars.   4   the unification of Germany.

16 An absolute monarch, privileged nobles and clergy, and an unfair tax structure for the Third Estate best describe
1   pre-1789 France.   3   pre-1776 America.
2   post-1688 England.   4   post-1789 France.

17 In *The Anatomy of Revolution*, Crane Brinton states that
1   radicals control the early phases of revolutions.
2   peasants provide revolutionary leadership.
3   revolutions often result in a return to one-man rule.
4   a revolution's initial result is a democratic government.

18 Two nation-states first established in the 19th century were
1   England and France.   3   Spain and Portugal.
2   Russia and Austria.   4   Germany and Italy.

19 Napoleon might be called a "son of the revolution" because he
1   established an absolute monarchy.
2   supported equality of law and religious toleration.
3   used birth as the criteria for advancement.
4   gave the Roman Catholic Church control of religion.

20 Which is a result of the French Revolutionary and Napoleonic Eras?
1   a spread of ideas of nationalism and democracy
2   a strengthening of religious forces
3   the expansion of communism
4   a new race for new colonies

21 An agricultural revolution, world wide markets, and good supplies of iron and coal made it possible for England to
1   begin the Commercial Revolution.
2   establish the guild system.
3   start the Industrial Revolution.
4   accept mercantilism.

22 Which did the British Great Reform Bill of 1832 achieve?
1   It abolished rotten boroughs.
2   It established universal male suffrage.
3   It set up annual elections of Parliament.
4   It gave women the right to vote.

23 Karl Marx believed that
1   capitalists would improve working conditions voluntarily.
2   bad conditions would cause the proletariat to revolt.
3   governments would act to improve working conditions.
4   large labor unions would protect worker interests.

24 Locke believed that
1   there should be a separation of powers in government.
2   rulers should have absolute powers.
3   the people have the right of revolution.
4   government power comes from God.

25 Bismarck established the Triple Alliance because he
1   feared the power of the British navy.
2   wished to avoid a two front war.
3   was afraid of an attack by Russia.
4   needed help against Austrian aggression.

26 The immediate cause of World War I was the
1 Moroccan Crisis.
2 British-French naval cooperation.
3 Balkan Wars.
4 assassination of the Archduke Franz Ferdinand.

27 Which statement is true about the Treaty of Versailles?
1 It placed no blame for starting the War.
2 It forced Germany to pay reparations.
3 It failed to return Alsace-Lorraine to France.
4 It allowed Germany to keep all its colonies.

28 Which statement is true of World War I?
1 It was a highly mobile, offensive war.
2 It produced new weapons technology used during World War II.
3 It resulted in few casualties.
4 It was fought mainly on the eastern front.

29 Which of the following pairs is correctly matched?
1 Watt - steam engine   3 Kay - cotton gin
2 Crompton - spinning jenny   4 Arkwright - sewing machine

Essays

1 The Renaissance is characterized as the Age of Transition, or the Age of Change. Major changes took place in many fields.

> · Religion   · Art
> · Science   · The Economy
> · Government or Politics

Choose *three* of the fields listed and discuss *two* changes that occurred during the Renaissance. Be sure to use specific examples for each change. [5,5,5]

2 European political philosophers have profoundly influenced the governments and social patterns of the Western World. Below are some major ideas of these philosophers:

· *Governments must protect the natural rights of the people or the people have the right to revolt.*
· *Governments should not interfere with the economic affairs of the country.*
· *Governments should be separated into three branches with a check and balance system.*

a Name the philosopher most closely associated with each of the ideas expressed. [3]

b Explain the meaning of each idea. [6]

c Discuss how each idea, properly implemented, could contribute to the development of democracy. [6]

III. Contemporary European Nations And Culture

A. The Rise Of The Modern Totalitarian Nazi State

Human Rights

Postwar Germany

In the period after World War I, Germans were dissatisfied with the Treaty of Versailles. Blame was placed, not on the earlier autocratic German Empire, but on the newly established **Weimar Republic**. The economic problems that usually occur at the end of a war were further accentuated in Germany by the reparation payments required by the Treaty of Versailles. The final sum had been set at thirty three billion dollars. The arrival of large numbers of displaced Jewish people from Eastern Europe further worsened the situation.

Anti-Semitism

Anti-Jewish feeling (**anti-Semitism**) was not new in European history. Much evidence of it can be found during the Middle Ages. Jews have been expelled from a number of countries at various times since. Russia, in particular, had a long history of anti-Semitism. Jews there were often required to live in **ghettos** (segregated areas). The Tsars subjected them to **pogroms** (violent purges) when they needed scapegoats to deflect attention from other problems. They were even forced to wear the Star of David as a means of identification. Anti-Semitism also went back for centuries in Germany.

Some 19th century philosophers, such as **Friedrich Nietzsche** made such strong points about the nationalistic virtues of the German people that they were later misinterpreted as anti-Semitic. Their ideas were further corrupted by some of the Nazis who were driven by the need to keep the Germanic race "pure" by attempting to annihilate the Jews.

World Issues:
Human Rights

Problems Of The Weimar Republic

The political situation in Germany after World War I made it relatively easy for a movement such as Nazism to develop. The democratic Weimar Republic had difficulty winning the respect of the German people who were used to an autocratic government. It was very tolerant, even when opposition bordered on treason. Movements from both the right and the left shook the Republic in its early years. Adolf Hitler's attempt to seize control of the state of Bavaria with his 1923 "Beer Hall Putsch" (uprising) is a good example. His prison sentence for the attempted overthrow of the government was five years, but he served only about eighteen months.

The **Ruhr Crisis** (1923) highlighted the Weimar Republic's difficulties in handling economic problems. France and Belgium claimed that Germany had fallen behind in reparations payments. French troops were sent to occupy the Ruhr.

The Weimar government encouraged the German workers in the Ruhr to refuse to work for France. It issued large amounts of printing press currency. The action backfired when massive inflation wiped out savings and seriously hurt people on fixed incomes. The middle class, in particular, was devastated. New currency was issued and some relief from the reparations schedule was obtained. But the vital middle class had lost faith in the ability of the government to handle economic crises.

From 1924 to 1929, things stabilized in Germany. The economic problems eased and international respectability was restored somewhat with the signing of the **Locarno Pacts**, admission to the League of Nations, and the signing of the **Kellogg-Briand Pact** (the Pact of Paris). However, the Great Depression changed the outlook completely.

Nazi Rise To Power

When the **Great Depression** made itself felt in Germany in 1929, the German people began to look to radical groups of the far left (communists), or the far right (the Nazis) for answers to their economic problems. The parties on the extremes saw a rise in their number of seats in the **Reichstag** (lower house of the German parliament). The multi-party

Power system kept any party from establishing a strong government and forced President von Hindenburg to govern by decree.

Hitler

In early 1933, the right wing **National Party** leaders were able to persuade Hindenburg to appoint a new chancellor. Hindenburg chose the leader of the **National Socialist German Workers Party** (Nazi Party), **Adolf Hitler.**

The Nazi State

Hitler's first move as chancellor was to call for new elections in hope that the Nazis could win an outright majority in the Reichstag. During the campaign, Hitler's mastery of political techniques was in evidence. Great outdoor rallies were carefully orchestrated by Nazi leaders. Hitler's aides knew how to use crowd psychology. The crowd was whipped into emotional frenzy by cheers, songs, etc. When he entered the stadium to speak, the crowd fell silent. His speeches were simple with only a few themes: abolish the Treaty of Versailles, restore German prestige, establish the supremacy of the Aryan Race.

Despite blaming the fire which destroyed the Reichstag building on the communists, the Nazis were disappointed in the election. Their coalition with the Nationalist Party represented only 52% of the vote. The Nazis never won the support of a majority of the German people in a free election. Hitler was still able to secure dictatorial powers for himself by using Nazi Storm Troopers to deny communist opponents access to the Reichstag.

Political Systems

Hitler immediately used these powers to centralize the government and wipe out any effective opposition. Next, without any effective opposition, a **totalitarian government** was established (total control over all aspects of the lives of the people) with Hitler as **Der Fuhrer** (leader).

To deal with the problems of the Depression, Hitler announced plans to re-build the German Army by enlarging the armaments industries. He removed most women and Jews from the work force. He began public works projects such as the autobahns and established a system of compulsory work service for all young people. By 1936, the number of unemployed workers had been reduced from six million to one million.

To control the cultural lives and minds of the people, **Goebbels** and his **Ministry of Propaganda and Enlightenment** were given extensive power. Censorship and book-burnings quickly resulted. Later, **Reich Culture Chambers** were established to control the work of artists, sculptors, and all others in the fine arts. Schools placed emphasis on physical education and obedience to the state. They discouraged young people from thinking for themselves. However, more than anything else, the presence and the tactics of Storm Troopers and the hated **SS** (Secret Police) invoked terror in the hearts of the people, violated human rights, and discouraged the opposition.

Many groups such as the Jehovah's Witnesses, gypsies, the handicapped, deformed, and the Slavic peoples of Eastern Europe were persecuted by the Nazis. The group that suffered most was the Jews. Hitler believed that the German people were a part of the Aryan Race, a superior group that should be kept pure to fulfill their mission of ruling the world.

The Jews were regarded as subhuman and not fit to survive. The Jews were driven out of the main stream of German life and reduced to the position of second class citizens. They could not be business executives. Their children were removed from schools. They could only shop at fixed hours. The **Jewish Star Decree** required them to wear a yellow Star of David on their clothing as a means of identification.

After World War II started, the Nazis developed the "Final Solution." It called for all Jews to be rounded up, forced to work in war related industries as long as they were capable. Then, they were sent to concentration camps, such as **Treblinka** and **Auschwitz.** Some received a short reprieve when they arrived at the camps. They were assigned to work crews or became the subjects of medical experimentation. Many were immediately sent to their deaths. This treatment was applied not only to German Jews, but to the Jewish people of all nations that came under Nazi control.

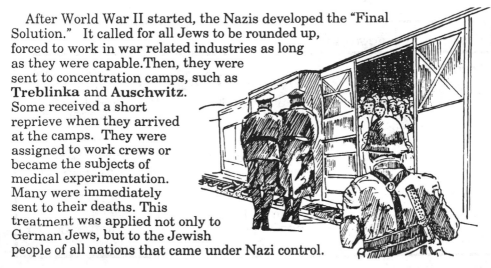

Human Rights   By the end of World War II, 6 million Jews had been killed in what is now known as **The Holocaust**. At the **Nuremberg Trials**, Nazi leaders were judged responsible for crimes against humanity. Their acts were not considered normal uner the accepted rules of warfare. The judges at the international trials said wholesale violations of human rights were really Nazi state-sponsored crimes. Since that time, **genocide** has been condemned and declared illegal by the U.N. Commission on Human Rights.

B. World War II
Causes

Many of the same factors that caused World War I helped to bring about World War II. Nationalism and imperialism were evident: the Italian desire for **mare nostrum** ("our sea," a reference to their power in Mediterranean); the German goal of **lebensraum** (living space, a reference to pushing into Eastern Europe); and the Japanese goal of **Asia for the Asiatics** (an expression of their desire to rid Asia of European/American influences).

Just as French concern about the loss of the Franco-Prussian War was a cause of World War I, the dissatisfaction of Italy, Germany, and Japan with the treatment they received at the Paris Peace Conference of 1919 was a cause of World War II. The League of Nations did not prove capable of dealing with the aggression of major powers or keeping a balance in world affairs.

However, there were some differences. There was no real arms race until war was about to break out in 1938-1939. This was largely because the democracies were not willing to acknowledge that another world war was possible. They were also busy fighting the effects of the Great Depression and lacked the economic resources for an arms build-up. Also, there was only one formal alliance system, that of the Axis powers. Germany, Italy and Japan had formed the Rome-Berlin-Tokyo Axis presumably to fight the spread of communism. As in the pre-World War I period, there were a series of crises that contributed to the outbreak of war:

Crisis	Aggressor	Results
Manchurian	Japan	League of Nations sent Lytton Commission to investigate. Japan condemned for aggression and no further action taken by League. Japan established puppet state of Manchukuo.
Ethiopian	Italy	Italian aggression condemned by League. Ineffective economic sanctions imposed and later lifted.
Austrian	Germany	German invasion and takeover condemned by League. No further action was taken.

In addition, there was a crisis over Czechoslovakia in 1938. Initially, Hitler demanded self-government for the Sudetenland, an area of Czechoslovakia inhabited by a large German population. Mussolini of Italy persuaded him to hold the **Munich Conference** to discuss the problem. Present were Hitler, Mussolini, Chamberlain of Great Britain, and Daladier of France. No representatives of Czechoslovakia were present nor of the Soviet Union, which had an alliance with the Czechs. Essentially, the decision was made by those present to give in to Hitler's demands.

This is considered to be the best modern example of **appeasement** (the policy of giving in to aggressors to avoid war). Shortly after the Munich Conference, Britain and France gave assurances of their support to Poland in case it became the next target of Hitler's aggression.

However, Hitler's next step was an understanding with **Premier Josef Stalin** of the Soviet Union, to avoid the possibility of a two-front war. The Nazi-Soviet Non-Aggression Pact was signed in August, 1939. Hitler began the invasion of Poland on 1 September 1939. France and Britain declared war, and World War II began.

The World At War

World War II was fought in Europe, Asia, and Africa. It resulted in the loss of approximately 40 million people and cost in excess of one trillion, one hundred billion dollars (not including the cost of destroyed civilian properties). It was very different from World War I because it was largely an offensive war.

The Nazi **blitzkrieg** (lightning war) offensive led to the defeat of Poland in approximately one month. The strategy was made possible by the use of motorized vehicles, tanks, and airplanes. Their military value was just beginning to be apparent during World War I. There was tremendous technological and scientific advancement in military techniques during World War II. Jungles were turned into airports. Roads were constructed across seemingly impossible terrain. Pontoon (floating) bridges appeared across rivers overnight. Harbors appeared where there had been none.

Technology

Radar was developed to locate approaching objects. It was a vital factor in helping the British Royal Air Force to win the **Battle of Britain**. **Sonar** helped the Allies control the Atlantic against German U-boats. The Nazis developed **V-1** and **V-2** jet-propelled bombs to terrify the British. They were forerunners of today's guided missiles.

Other developments included **magnetic sea mines** and the **Schnorchel device** allowing submarines to remain submerged for longer periods. The **atomic bomb** which was developed by the U.S. and dropped on the Japanese cities of Hiroshima and Nagasaki. It was the beginning of a new technological age in warfare.

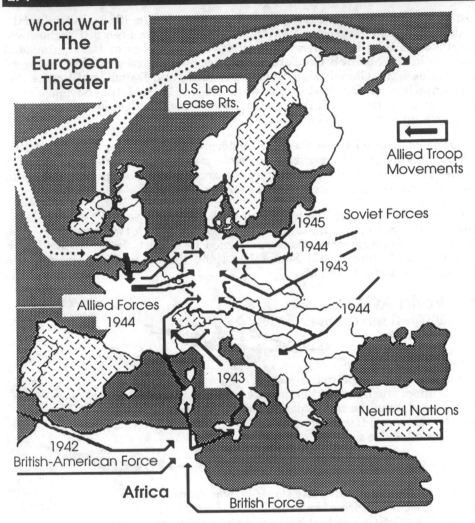

World War II
The European Theater

U.S. Lend Lease Rts.

← Allied Troop Movements

Soviet Forces

1945

1944

1943

1944

Allied Forces 1944

1943

Neutral Nations

1942 British-American Force

Africa

British Force

Global Impact Of The War

Power

By the end of World War II, a very different picture of international power was apparent. The world became polarized around two **superpowers** (the U.S. and the Soviet Union). The European countries were devastated by their war effort. Their decline in power, which started with World War I, was very apparent. Nationalist colonial rebel movements took advantage of the European inability to devote the necessary resources to hold them.

During the post-war period, many of the colonies gained independence. In some cases, the European countries struggled to hold their colonies. They became involved in long wars which further drained their resources. In the end, the colonies gained independence.

C. British Government
Historical Development

Modern British government is the product of countless changes that have occurred over centuries. These changes usually occurred without major bloodshed, therefore, the change is considered to be evolutionary, as opposed to the revolutionary process.

Event	Change
Establishment of royal court system (11th century)	Provided an alternative to feudal justice and Church courts. Began development of grand juries, trial juries and common law.
Signing of Magna Carta	King could not tax without advice of Great Council. Freemen guaranteed trial by jury, first time. Provided for power of purse.
Model Parliament (1295)	Led to the establishment of the Houses of Lords and Commons.
Glorious Revolution (1688)	Established supremacy of Parliament over king.
Cabinet system (17-19th century)	Provided for cabinet ministers to be selected from Parliament and to be responsible to it.
Reform Bills: 1832, 1867, 1884, 1918, 1928, and 1969	Extended the suffrage.
Parliament Acts: 1911 and 1949	Limited the power of the House of Lords to pass legislation.

Political Systems

Current British Government

Technically, Great Britain is a **constitutional (limited) monarchy**. Actually, it is a democracy. Human rights are guaranteed, and limits are placed on the power of the government. This is done by acts such as those listed above and **precedents** (past actions and decisions that act as models). Together, they compose the **unwritten constitution** of Britain. For example, the British ruler has the power to appoint the Prime Minister, but, by precedent, the ruler must appoint the leader of the majority party in the House of Commons. No bill can become law without the signature of the ruler, but none has refused to sign a bill passed by Parliament since the early 18th century.

The British Parliament has a **bicameral legislature** (two houses): the **House of Commons** (elective) and the **House of Lords** (hereditary or appointive). Since the passage of the Parliament Acts, power clearly rests with the House of Commons. The **Prime Minister** is the majority leader of the House of Commons. Other administrators, or members of the **Cabinet**, are from the House of Commons. Occasionally a cabinet member may be chosen from the House of Lords. The executive and legislative branches are not separated. Parliament also has certain judicial functions. This makes the British government **unitary** in nature.

British Parliament

Each cabinet member heads a department, draws up legislation to be presented to Parliament, and defends it before Parliament. If a major piece of cabinet (government) sponsored legislation is defeated in Commons, or if Commons votes "no confidence" in a government policy, the cabinet must either: 1) **resign** (in which case the opposition party forms a cabinet); or 2) **go to the country** (an election is held to determine the reaction of the country to the issue involved). If the people support the cabinet, it returns in office. If they do not, the cabinet resigns and the opposition takes over. Therefore, the government is directly responsible to the House of Commons and indirectly responsible to the people.

The parliamentary system of government has worked quite well in Britain. This is because there are only a few parties with any political strength and there is almost always a party with a majority. This avoids government by constantly changing coalitions. Currently, there are three major parties in Great Britain. The **Conservative Party** is closely allied with the U.S. and generally follows a capitalist economic policy with some government ownership and regulation. The **Labor Party**, favors socialist programs in Britain and opposes the American nuclear presence in the British Isles. Finally, the new **Social Democratic Party** includes many former Liberals and Labor Party members.

Problem of Northern Ireland

The question of Northern Ireland continues to plague Great Britain. The problem goes back almost 800 years to the first British attempts at conquest. In order to control the rebellious Irish, a number of English rulers, including Mary Tudor and Oliver Cromwell, set up large plantations with English and Scots as landowners. Many of these new landowners were Protestant and dispossessed the Irish Catholics who became landless tenant farmers or laborers. This is the basis of the religious and socio-economic problems in Northern Ireland today. During the 19th century there were partially successful attempts under the English leader, **William Gladstone**, to rectify some of these problems.

After the bloody **Easter Rebellion** of 1916, the Catholic-dominated **Irish Free State** (Eire) was proclaimed in the south. The north was given a separate government under Protestant control. Civil disorder resumed in the 1960's with the provisional wing of the **Irish Republican Army** (IRA) and various Protestant groups responsible. The British government sent in troops and assumed emergency powers to deal with the situation in 1976, but the violence has continued.

In 1985, an agreement was signed between the Republic of Ireland and Britain. This agreement called for the Irish Republic to have a voice in the administration of Northern Ireland. The Irish foreign minister and the British government's Secretary for Northern Ireland are to hold meetings in which the Irish foreign minister can bring attention to violations of the human rights of the Catholic minority in the North. Northern Ireland Protestants, under the leadership of **Reverend Ian Paisley**, protested strongly and resigned from the British Parliament. In the meantime, the violence continues.

D. European Peoples And Life
Ethnic And Religious Minorities

Western Europe is an area with many different ethnic and religious groups. This diversity has added to the rich cultural identity of the continent, but has also led to many problems.

The United Kingdom (Great Britain) remains 90% native, but there has been a heavy immigration from Commonwealth countries, especially the Caribbean, India, and Pakistan. Race riots have developed in major cities centered around the issue of unemployment. In 1962, Parliament passed the **Commonwealth Immigrants Act** which restricted immigration for those without means of support or likely employment. Further legislation established three categories of British citizenship (two of which may not live in Britain) and applied quotas for immigrants of different areas. Although most of the population of Britain is Protestant, there are large Catholic and Jewish minorities. A new controversy for Britain concerns admission of immigrants from the Crown Colony of Hong Kong when it returns to Chinese control in 1997 (see page 123).

France, with the fourth largest Jewish population in Western Europe, has recently seen a wave of anti-Semitism. During the 1980's, a number of synagogues were attacked by international terrorist groups. The French have not been totally sympathetic to the plight of the Jews. Like Britain, France also has a sizable number of immigrants from former colonies. There are a large number of Vietnamese, Algerians, and Moroccans living in France. In addition, Portuguese, Italians and Spanish are temporary immigrants because of seasonal unemployment in their home countries.

Large numbers of "guest workers" from Turkey, Yugoslavia, Italy, and Greece have increased Germany's workforce. There is some fear of ethnic strife as the two Germanies struggle to reunify the nation's economy. Anti-semitism and Neo-Nazism have been on the rise in recent years.

Spain is ethnically homogeneous in three-fourths of the country, but there are considerable differences between the north and the south. Groups such as the Basques, Galatians, and Catalans have been given considerable autonomy. The Basques remain dissatisfied and sometimes resort to terrorism. Population movements to urban areas, the coasts, and the islands have helped to decrease the differences.

Italy also has a high degree of ethnic homogeneity. There are Germans in the northern Tyrol area and Slavs in the area of Trieste. However, there are major socio-economic differences between the industrial north and the poor farm area of the south. These differences are decreasing with movement to the north and with the rural to urban migration.

Religion

There is a basic sense of shared values since most peoples of Western Europe share the Judaeo-Christian tradition even though they belong to different religious groups. Beginning with Pope John XXIII in 1959, the Roman Catholic Church has actively pursued **ecumenism**.

Recent Popes have met with representatives of the Orthodox Church and have taken steps to improve relations with the Jews. **Pope John Paul II** continued these dialogues both in the Vatican and on frequent visits to global regions. Critics see an inconsistency in Vatican policies. It encouraged the Roman Catholic clergy's involvement in pro-democracy movements in Poland. Yet, in Latin America, it warned priests against using "liberation theology" and involvement with political movements.

John Paul II

Urbanization

European countries have seen considerable rural-to-urban movement in the period since the end of World War II. This has brought about a number of concerns about pollution of the environment, causing governments to react.

The Ruhr River, center of the coal and steel industry of Germany, was an area of lung and bone diseases. The Ruhr was so polluted that few fish could live there. With help from the government, the Ruhr Association was established and began an anti-pollution program. Dues in the Association are

World Issues:
Environmental Concerns

paid by businesses in proportion to the amount of pollution they create. The cost of keeping the river clean is in excess of 14 million dollars per year. It is now one of the cleanest rivers in West Germany.

In Great Britain, the **Control of Pollution Act** of 1974, and other laws have decreased environmental pollution substantially. Since the 1950's, pollution of the Thames River has fallen by approximately 25%, and well over 75% of the population now has sewage treatment facilities available. A developing problem for the British, however, is control of oil spills in the North Sea fields.

The Arts

The arts reflect European values and the changing political, social, and economic scene. During the 19th century, romanticism and nationalism were reflected in the works of art and music. **Romanticism** idealized the beauties of nature and looked back on the Middle Ages with fondness. Strong feelings of nationalism were particularly evident in the music of the time.

Culture

The Impressionists

Late in the 19th century, the **impressionist school** of art was favorably recognized after an earlier period of considerable criticism. The impressionist artists tried to capture a moment in time and painted scenes of every day life. They painted pictures full of light and color, but the subjects might be somewhat blurred. In the 20th century, artists moved even further from reality. After World War I, this tendency increased and the art seemed to reflect the turbulence and uncertainty of the times. Surrealism emphasized the unconscious and was a totally subjective approach to art.

Artist	Country	Movement	*Work*
Delacroix	France	Romanticism	*"Abduction of Rebecca"*
Constable	England	Romanticism	*"Salisbury Cathedral"*
Monet	France	Impressionism	*"St. Lazare Railway Station"*
Renoir	France	Impressionism	*"The Rower's Lunch"*
Braque	France	Cubism	*"The Table"*
Picasso	Spain	Expressionism	*"Guernica"*
Dali	Spain	Surrealism	*"The Persistence of Memory"*

Modern Architecture

Modern architecture began to move away from traditional styles in the 1920's under the leadership of people such as the American **Frank Lloyd Wright**, the Swiss **Le Corbusier**, and the German, **Walter Gropius**. These men have done much to establish an **international style** of architecture in the 20th century. Much effort has gone into the design of skyscrapers which emphasize design with the efficient use of expensive city land. Extensive use of glass, steel, and reinforced concrete is evident in the simple and strikingly designed structures which carefully consider function and the modern life style.

City planning has also played a major role in architectural design as architects work with governments to redesign cities to fit modern needs.

E. Toward Political Unification

As a consequence of post-World War II problems, European nations began to realize that cooperation was necessary. Moves to establish a uniform European driver's license and increased educational exchanges were designed to increase the feeling of unity among the people.

The **Council of Europe** sets policy for the European Community (see section IV). The **European Court of Justice** handles controversies among the various branches of the European Community and interprets its agreements and treaties.

Questions

1 Factors which contributed to the rise of Nazism include
  1 unequal treatment of women.
  2 the autocratic Weimar Republic.
  3 economic problems of the Depression.
  4 religious differences.

2 Which is true of anti-Semitism?
  1 It first appeared in Nazi Germany.
  2 It was not apparent in Russia.
  3 It had existed for centuries.
  4 It was opposed by Luther.

3 Which is true of Adolf Hitler?
  1 He seized power in Germany in a coup d'etat.
  2 He won a majority of the vote.
  3 He was legally appointed as chancellor.
  4 He had no political allies.

4 The Reich Culture Chambers, the Storm Troopers, and persecution of the opposition were all used by Hitler to
  1 control the population.
  2 win support of the German Army.
  3 obtain foreign acceptance.
  4 show his support of religion.

5 The "Final Solution" involved a plan to
  1 deport all European Jews.
  2 eliminate the Jewish population of Europe.
  3 invade the Soviet Union.
  4 achieve economic self-sufficiency.

6 World War II was caused by
  1 many of the same things that caused World War I.
  2 religious differences among the European countries.
  3 the Soviet desire to spread Communism.
  4 the expansionist goals of France.

7 To avoid war during the 1930's, the democracies gave into Hitler's demands. Which of the following terms is associated with this policy?
  1 balance of power   3 imperialism
  2 detente   4 appeasement

8 A result of World War II was that
  1 Britain and France emerged as the major world powers.
  2 power shifted to the Southern Hemisphere.
  3 power was spread evenly among a number of countries.
  4 the U.S. and U.S.S.R emerged as the major world powers.

9 The British government has
  1 always been a republic.   3 a one-house legislature.
  2 no written constitution.   4 a monarch with absolute power.

10 In terms of population composition, Britain and France have
1   almost no Jews.
2   substantial colonial minorities.
3   a rapidly increasing birth rate.
4   a declining number of senior citizens.

11 The European countries are
1   experiencing a population return to rural areas.
2   having problems with environmental pollution.
3   refusing to construct new urban structures.
4   trying to limit the number of births.

Essays

1 Modern British government has had a long period of evolution.

   · Magna Carta   · Glorious Revolution
   · Model Parliament   · Use of precedents
   · Government or Cabinet responsibility to Commons

Select *three* of the factors listed above which contributed to the development of British democracy and for *each one* selected briefly identify it, explain why it occurred, and state why it helped to make Britain more democratic. [5,5,5]

2 The rise of Hitler to power in Germany and his establishment of a totalitarian government had a profound effect on the history of the 20th century.

   a Discuss the problems of the Weimar Republic which allowed the Nazi movement to take control of Germany. [6]

   b Explain how the methods employed by Hitler to control the German people fit the definition of totalitarian government. [6]

   c Describe the role played by Germany in causing World War II. [3]

3 Contemporary Europe has faced many changes and problems brought about by modern technology and a changing global world.

   · Problems in Northern Ireland
   · Urbanization
   · Diverse populations
   · Political unification
   · Environmental pollution
   · Decline in power

Select *three* of the above areas and for each one selected explain the nature of the change or problem, and how contemporary Europe has dealt with it. [5,5,5]

IV. Economic Development Of Western Europe

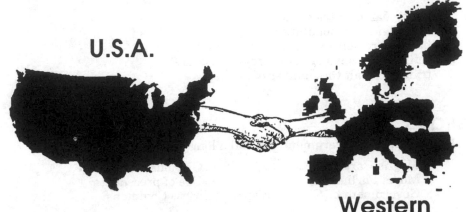

U.S.A.

Western Europe

A. The Marshall Plan

At the end of World War II, the economy of Western Europe was devastated. Much of the severe damage was repaired within a short time, but industrial Western Europe could not trade sufficiently with Eastern Europe or the rest of the world. Europeans had lost their overseas investments and could not afford to pay for vital imports. Many of the overseas areas developed their own industries during the war and were no longer interested in European products.

Interdependence

Supported by Moscow, Communist Parties in the devastated countries gained strength in the midst of the chaos.

The question for the United States was how to best help Europe recover. U.S. Secretary of State **George C. Marshall** proposed an answer. The U.S. Congress passed the European Recovery Act (the **Marshall Plan**), making approximately 12.5 billion dollars available to the war-torn nations of Europe providing they develop their own plan for economic recovery. Although the plan was offered to all nations, the Soviet Union put pressure on its Eastern European satellites to turn down the offer. The U.S.S.R. made available a scaled down version of its own, the Council of Mutual Economic Assistance (COMECON).

The Marshall Plan also aided American industry because much of the money had to be spent in the United States. It also fulfilled American humanitarian instincts. The program was successful. Western Europe recovered economically. American-Western European trade increased. The communist threat in Western Europe diminished and the European nations began to think in terms of economic cooperation.

B. European Development

Western European leaders began to see economic cooperation as critical in view of the diversity of the area and the distribution of resources. Britain, for example, lives largely from manufacturing and trade. Its major resources include coal, low grade iron ore, and the North Sea oil deposits. Other mineral resources vital to its industry must be imported.

Since the end of World War II, such traditional British industries have decreased in importance and their place has been taken by electronics, chemicals, and commercial services such as banking and insurance. In terms of agriculture, Britain currently produces only about two-thirds of its needs. The remainder must be imported.

France has a better balance between industry and agriculture. It is among the leading producers of coal and iron in Europe, and leads the world in the production of bauxite. Its industry has increased considerably since the end of the war. The electronics, transportation, and construction industries are highly productive. Much French industry tends to be smaller in scale and less inclined to use mass production techniques. Fashions, wine, cosmetics, and perfume are important. Agriculture employs only 9% of the population, but France is the only country in Europe self-sufficient in food production. The quality of the agricultural products is undoubtedly a factor in the famous French cuisine. France also exports products such as sugar, wheat, and beef.

Germany has the most significant coal deposits in Western Europe, but its iron ore is low in quality. Industry is well developed and diversified. Chemicals, iron and steel production, and engineering play important roles. Because agricultural production does not come close to meeting consumer demand, Germany is a major importer of food products.

Southern Europe provides a contrast with the north in that farming is a larger component of the economy and industry is less well developed. Since the end of World War II, the governments in the south have taken strong measures to improve both industry and agriculture. In Italy, the resource base is poor, but industry has continued to grow. Automobiles, precision machinery, chemicals, and rubber products are important, but much of the industry remains small and involves artisan-type production. Attempts to attract industry to the poorer areas are beginning to show some results.

Agriculture, on the other hand, has shown little growth in recent years. Italy is the largest producer of wine and olive oil in the world, and has good climatic conditions for two annual crops. It is a major cereal producing nation, although wheat yields have declined in recent years.

Most known minerals can be found in Spain, but mining has been decreasing in importance in the economy. Industrially, textiles and chemicals are significant. In agriculture, the use of fertilizers and mechanization has increased. A government agency regulates about 25 million acres of land and encourages the use of irrigation and new cultivation methods to increase productivity. As a consequence, there has been a decreasing number of farm workers, but the importance of farming in the economy has also declined.

Throughout most of Western Europe, governments have assumed major roles in economic development and planning. In Britain and France, the

World Issues:
Economic Growth and Development

governments have nationalized some major industries and resources while leaving the smaller concerns in private hands. The current government in Britain has tried to move away from a strong role in the economy, preferring to allow private enterprise to move in.

In France, a series of economic plans since the end of World War II have had the reverse effect. The French have been trying to decrease their reliance on imported oil, increase the use of advanced technology, and decrease unemployment and inflation. When these goals have not been met, austerity measures have been implemented, including new taxes.

With the exception of Britain, the West European countries were adversely affected by the oil price increases during the 1970's which led to recessions or depressions. The decline in oil prices between 1981 and 1985 improved economic conditions. Until recently, the U.S. dollar was increasing in value and this aided European exports.

C. Toward Economic Cooperation

The West European countries do have economies that can compliment each other if cooperation is achieved. The realization of the value of cooperation was made evident by the Marshall Plan and was continued by the European Communities. In 1951, the **European Coal and Steel Community** was established by Belgium, Netherlands, Luxembourg, France, and West Germany based on a plan proposed by Robert Schuman of France.

The **Schuman Plan** removed barriers to the movement of iron and steel workers among members countries. In 1957, **Euratom** was established to coordinate nuclear research and aid in the development of the nuclear power industry in the same six nations.

In the 1950's, Western European nations also established the **European Economic Community (EC)**. Today, we know it as **"The Common Market."**

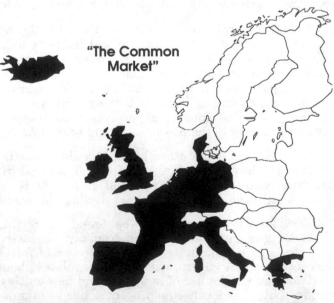

"The Common Market"

European Economic Community

The original EC were the six members of the European Coal and Steel Community. Later the EC expanded to include Iceland, Denmark, Greece, Portugal, Spain and Great Britain. The change in world economic markets and the decline of communist rule prompted other nations in Eastern and Western Europe to seek admission.

Common Market Goals	
Actions	**Goals**
Abolish trade barriers (tariffs, quotas) among EC members.	Raise member nations' standards of living.
Create standard trade rules for entire membership region.	Equalize competition in world markets.
Set up single money and credit system.	Strengthen competitive position with Japan and United States.
Allow free movement of workers into countries where needed.	
Create standard worker benefits and protections.	

Recent events present the European Community with many challenges. Economic conditions change. New situations influencing economic life include: the Soviet collapse, nationalistic movements, OPEC's actions, problems in the Middle East, behavior of multinational corporations, the unification of Germany. Economic growth and political stability are intertwined. For example, the EC played a major role in trying to solve Yugoslavia's recent civil war.

D. European Socialism

The 20th century added a third form of socialism to the utopian and scientific (Marxist) types already discussed. Sometimes called **democratic socialism**, it began to appear in a variety of forms. Most West European countries have **mixed economies** (capitalist and socialist). All have extensive social welfare programs. In addition, many have planned economies. Many have nationalized major industries and resources.

Great Britain is an example of democratic socialism. Its social welfare program dates from the early 20th century. It was extensively expanded after World War II as a result of the **Beveridge Report** developed during the war years. The Labor Party won the election of 1945, and developed the **National Insurance Service** and **National Health Service**.

The National Insurance program provides benefits for sickness, accident, old age, maternity, and disability. It is financed by contributions of employers, employees, and the self-employed. The National Health Service was established to provide free medical and dental care.

In terms of British industrial ownership, private, government, and cooperative owners can be found. Transportation, communication, fuel, power and the coal and steel industries are nationalized, but most other manufacturing industries remain in private hands. Both the Conservative and Labor parties support the social welfare program, but the amount of government owned industry has varied from time to time depending on the party in power. The

Conservative Party has frequently acted to undo nationalization or at least slow the process when it has been in power. The reverse has been true of the Labor Party.

E. Contemporary Economic Issues

Despite the increased role of the government in economic affairs and the establishment of the "safety nets" of social welfare programs, the Western European nations have faced a variety of contemporary economic problems. Inflation has been a serious problem at various times. In the 1980's, the British inflation rate reached 21.9%. By 1991, recessions and government efforts lowered it to 4.5%. The 1991 recessions caused concern as unemployment rose (Britain = 9%, Germany = 7%).

Political Systems

Much of the inflation was a result of the increase in oil prices. The situation was eased by a rising United States dollar, which increased European exports, and government sponsored programs to increase fuel self-sufficiency. Unemployment continues to be a serious problem. In 1985, British unemployment remained at 13% and West Germany had an unemployment rate of 9%. Both countries have felt the burden of increased unemployment compensation costs.

As the West European countries strive to remain competitive in the world market, governments have moved to subsidize certain industries and/or agricultural products. In Britain for example, the automotive industry has required government subsidies in order to survive. The French government offers financial assistance to companies that are relocating or modernizing.

F. Global Trading Network

West European countries that belong to the EEC do most of their trading with fellow members. In addition, the U.S. is a major trading partner for the Europeans. For those countries without sufficient oil, Saudi Arabia plays a major trade role. Britain, for example, carried on between 31% and 43% of its foreign trade with the EEC between 1972 and 1980. During the same time period, its trade with the members of the Commonwealth of Nations decreased from 18% to 13% (see page 291).

Spain trades extensively not only with the EEC, but also with the U.S. and Latin America. The economic power of Japan also concerns the EEC. In critical industries such as electronics and automobiles, Japanese products offer strong competition.

Recently, the British government vetoed the plan of a British corporation to purchase Norwegian gas. The Norwegians had to investigate other European sources of investment.

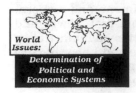
World Issues:
Determination of Political and Economic Systems

Trade with former communist bloc countries is increasing as Eastern Europe turns away from communism. There is only limited desire for most Eastern European manufactured products because quality standards are inferior. Polish hams, Russian vodka, and

Czech glass do find ready markets in the West. When the new pipeline is completed, Russian natural gas is expected to have a vast market.

Questions

1 At the end of World War II, Europe's economy was
   1 extremely prosperous.
   2 able to live off colonial investments.
   3 in a state of chaos.
   4 denied aid by the United States.

2 Since 1945, North European countries' economies have
   1 increasingly relied on agriculture as a source of income.
   2 experienced few unemployment problems.
   3 increased their "high tech" industries.
   4 discovered large new sources of coal and iron.

3 Which best describes the current economic system of most Western European countries?
   1 laissez-faire capitalist   3 mercantilist
   2 communist   4 mixed capitalist and socialist

4 The European Economic Community, Euratom, and the European Coal and Steel Community are all examples of
   1 European economic cooperation.
   2 plans to limit weapons production.
   3 European foreign aid programs.
   4 postwar American aid plans.

5 Democratic socialist countries usually have
   1 complete government ownership of industry.
   2 extensive social welfare programs.
   3 very low tax rates.
   4 one house legislatures.

6 A major economic problem for most European countries in the 1970's was
   1 the spread of communism.   3 the failure to subsidize industry.
   2 an increase in oil prices.   4 an insufficient supply of labor.

7 The major trading partner for most of West Europe (is/are)
   1 former colonies   3 Saudi Arabia
   2 the U.S.   4 EEC members

Essay

Economic cooperation is essential to the future development of Western Europe.

   a Discuss the success of the Marshall Plan and the role it played in promoting European economic cooperation. [3]

   b Using specific examples, explain why economic cooperation is essential in contemporary Europe. [6]

   c Explain the role of the Common Market and evaluate its success. [6]

V. Western Europe In The Global Context

A. Global Effects Of Allied Victory

After the dropping of the atomic bombs on Hiroshima and Nagasaki by the United States, international politics changed. The period of European dominance was over.

The Soviet Union exploded its first atomic bomb in 1949. Both of the atomic powers continued testing and developed hydrogen bombs with many times the explosive power of the bombs used against Japan. Atomic weapons were also miniaturized for use by troops under battlefield conditions. By the 1950's, people all over the world were concerned about the threat posed not just by the use of such weapons, but also the environmental threats resulting from nuclear tests.

Diplomacy slowly yielded results. In 1963, the **Limited Nuclear Test Ban Treaty** outlawed tests in the atmosphere. In 1967, the **Outer Space Treaty** prohibited the spread of nuclear weapons to outer space.

In 1970, the **Nuclear Nonproliferation Treaty** attempted to stop the spread of nuclear weapons to countries not already possessing them. Unfortunately, this has not been successful and a number of nations (India, China) have tested such weapons and a number of other nations are rumored to have nuclear weapon capability. The danger of multiple nuclear powers is obvious and a matter of concern to people of all nations.

B. Cold War Politics In Europe

During World War II, a number of conferences were held by the "Big Three" (the Soviet Union represented by Joseph Stalin, the United States by Franklin Roosevelt and later Harry S Truman, and Great Britain by Winston Churchill). The decisions made at these wartime conferences were to have a profound effect on shaping the post-war world.

World Issues:
War and Peace

The Allied decision to open the second front on the Italian Peninsula rather than the Balkan Peninsula left the way open for the Soviet Red Army to liberate most areas in Eastern Europe from Nazi occupation and to establish puppet governments in those nations. In fact, if one were to draw a line around the advances of the Red Army, they would coincide almost exactly with the areas later controlled by communists.

Churchill later coined the phrase **Iron Curtain** to denote the prevention the free flow of ideas between the West and the communist dominated East.

There was no European peace treaty signed at the end of World War II. Immediately after the war, Germany was divided into four occupation zones. The U.S., France, Britain, and U.S.S.R each controlled one. Berlin was completely surrounded by the Soviet Zone. The city was also divided into four sectors. West Berlin became a showcase for the better standard of living enjoyed by the areas under Western control. It became a constant source of irritation for the communists.

Wartime "Big Three" Conferences

Conference	Significant Decisions
Teheran - 1943	Agreed to open a second front against Germany on the continent of Europe and attack from all directions.
Yalta - 1945	Divided Germany into four occupation zones and pushed for denazification, democratization, and due punishment for war criminals. Guaranteed the Poles a broader based democratic government and free and fair elections. Russia promised to enter war against Japan in exchange for territory in the Far East.
Potsdam - 1945	Reconfirmed Yalta agreements and virtually gave the Soviet Union control of Eastern Europe.

Communist activities and the Soviet power moves in Berlin rekindled fears of totalitarian fascism. War-weakened Western European nations turned to the United States for help. The U.S. responded with the containment policy. The **Marshall Plan** (pg.282) and the **Truman Doctrine** were part of this policy. The Truman Doctrine (1947) gave financial aid and weapons to Greece, Turkey, and Italy to resist communist insurgency. **Containment** eventually became a global policy. Americans gave aid and fought the spread communism in every global region.

In 1948, the Russians closed off all surface routes to Berlin in an attempt to force the Western powers out of the city. The Allies responded with the **Berlin Airlift** which supplied the needs of the city for approximately a year. The embarrassed Soviets reopened access, but there were periodic closings after that time.

In 1949, the Soviet Union established the **German Democratic Republic** (East Germany) as a communist satellite country. In 1955, the Western Allies combined their occupation zones to form the **Federal Republic of Germany** (West Germany) which they recognized as an independent republic. Angered by the continued migration of educated people to West Germany, the Soviet leader Nikita Khrushchev ordered the East German government to erect the **Berlin Wall**, cutting the city in half in 1961.

After World War II, Soviet occupation forced insurgents to establish communist governments in other countries of Eastern Europe. The continued presence of Russian troops, economic dependence, and various treaties and alliances combined to give the Soviet Union great influence and control in these satellites.

In those cases where the people revolted against control by the Soviet Union, reaction was swift and often involved invasion. Czechoslovakia in 1968, is an example. **Alexander Dubcek** emerged as leader of the Communist Party with a proposed program of liberalization which included improved ties with the West and greater freedom for the people. The Soviet Union, with **Warsaw Pact** allies, invaded Czechoslovakia to force the reversal of the liberalization policy and removed Dubcek. This action was denounced not only by the West, but by communist parties in the West and several of the communist dominated countries.

After the Czech uprising, the Soviets announced the **Brezhnev Doctrine**. It said the U.S.S.R. would intervene if rebellions threatened communist regimes. Gorbachev later renounced this policy.

By 1989, economic problems had weakened the power of the Communist Party in many Eastern European nations. In addition, Soviet leader Mikhail Gorbachev's decision to diminish Soviet influence over the satellite countries, along with the examples set by his *glasnost* and *perestroika* reforms in the U.S.S.R., encouraged reformers. Mass demonstrations for reform began throughout Eastern Europe. By November of 1989, weeks of demonstrations weakened the hard-line communist regime. With hammers and chisels demonstrators broke openings in the infamous Berlin Wall, and free movement was allowed by East Germany. Political and economic barriers were cleared rapidly and the two Germanies reunited into one nation in 1990.

C. Collapse Of Colonial Domination

European imperialism suffered a severe setback at the end of World War II. It led to freedom for almost all of the pre-War colonies. Some colonies had to fight for their independence. In 1954 in Indochina, the communist Vietminh won the critical battle of Dienbienphu against the French.

The **Geneva Agreements** signed by Britain, France, the Soviet Union, Red China, and the Indo-chinese states provided for an independent and neutral Cambodia and Laos. Vietnam was to be divided at the 17th parallel with the North under communist control and the South under an anti-communist government. Plans were made to reunify the two Vietnams with elections in 1956. The elections were not held. By the 1960's, American involvement escalated into the Vietnam War.

The situation in the **Suez Canal Crisis** (1956) was somewhat different. Britain and France were angered by Egyptian leader Gamel Nasser's

The Berlin Wall Comes Down

nationalizing the canal. They feared that the Egyptians would not be able to run the vital waterway properly. The Israelis wanted to stop guerrilla raids into their country and open the Gulf of Aqaba to shipping. The three invaded the canal region. The U.N. with the affirmative votes of both the Soviet Union and the United States, condemned the attack and demanded the withdrawal of the invading forces. The countries complied and a U.N. Emergency Force was sent in to keep the peace.

Despite initial hostility that often developed between newly independent countries and their former colonial masters, the countries often established cordial relationships. In fact, many former colonies looked to the colonial power for economic and military aid. French aid to the government of Chad, now fighting a Libyan incursion, is one such example.

Interdependence

The **Commonwealth of Nations** established by Britain in the 1930's is still a viable órganization. It is made up of former members of the British Empire who are independent and have voluntarily chosen to join the organization. Certain economic and trade benefits are extended to the members, and regular conferences are held to discuss joint problems. The French first established the French Union, and then, the **French Community** to retain ties with former colonies. However, many members later chose to withdraw and the French Community no longer functions.

D. The United Nations

At the San Francisco Conference in 1945, final provisions for the charter of the **United Nations** were written. The purpose of the organization was to preserve international peace and security, to settle disputes between nations by peaceful means, and to encourage the development of friendly relations. It was also recognized that international cooperation was necessary to solve world social, economic, and cultural problems.

The **U.N. Security Council** was given the power to deal with threats to international peace and security. There are five permanent members of the Security Council: China, France, Great Britain, Russia, and the United States. Each has a veto power over the Council's actions. There are also ten members elected by the General Assembly for two year terms. Strong efforts are made to insure that various groups and areas are represented on the Council.

The **General Assembly** includes all member nations with one vote per member. It holds discussions and makes recommendations on world problems. The **Secretariat** handles the day to day operations of the organization, calls conferences and meetings, and distributes information. The **Secretary General** has the responsibility of calling Security Council attention to threats to world peace. The Secretary also undertakes special missions and heads U.N. Emergency Forces.

The **Economic and Social Council** coordinates the activities of the specialized agencies and tries to improve economic and social conditions. The **Trusteeship Council** oversees areas not yet independent, but under the control of major powers who are preparing them for self-government. The Council has done its job so well that almost no areas remain under its supervision today.   Finally, the Court of Justice decides disputes that member nations voluntarily submit to its jurisdiction and gives other U.N. organs advisory opinions.

The U.N. has had its greatest successes in the social and economic fields where it has successfully dealt with health problems, famine, crop production, labor conditions, and women's rights.   Politically, it has had difficulty dealing with nations and their claims of sovereignty. Numerous times nations have refused to obey U.N. resolutions, such as when India seized Goa, the Soviet Union invaded Hungary, or South Africa continued apartheid. However, in the case of the Korean War (1950-53), it did raise a U.N. Force to protect the independence of South Korea and it has used U.N. Emergency Forces numerous times to keep warring nations or factions apart.

Financially, the U.S. has accepted the largest burden. Some countries, including the U.S., have refused to contribute for U.N. actions of which they disapprove. Increasingly, the major powers have used forums other than the U.N. to settle their differences. All of these factors have weakened the ability of the U.N. to deal with international problems.

However, the U.N. has been more successful than its predecessor, the **League of Nations**. The League was established at the end of World War I in compliance with one of President Wilson's Fourteen Points. Its structure was very similar to that of the U.N., however, its Council required a unanimous vote of the members in order to act. The United States never joined. Countries such as the Soviet Union, Germany, and Japan joined late, left early, or were expelled for aggression as World War II approached. As a consequence, gaining adequate support for strong action was not easy to achieve.

The League did have the power to use diplomatic, economic, and military sanctions to punish those who disobeyed its resolutions. Its use of diplomatic and economic sanctions realized few effective results, and it never attempted to use military power. As is true for the U.N., its most effective work was in the economic, social and cultural fields.

The **Hague Conferences** of the pre-World War I period tried to limit the arms race without success. They did, however, establish "humane" rules of warfare that outlawed things such as bombing of civilian populations. They also established the **Hague Tribunal** to settle international disputes which still exists today.

Going back to the 19th century, after the Congress of Vienna in 1815, the **Concert of Europe** was established to try to preserve the peace in the face of potential revolutions by people seeking democracy and self-determination. For a brief period of time, the countries involved did cooperate to achieve these objectives, but the more liberal British, and at times the French, refused to continue their cooperation. By the time of the revolutions of 1848, the Concert of Europe was not functioning.

The history of international organizations and their success in preventing wars or major incidents is not outstanding, but they have provided the opportunity for nations to discuss differences.

E. European Defense

Another traditional approach to preservation of the peace was the establishment of alliance systems which attempted to balance power. This was evident in the two major alliances of the post-World War II period.

Interdependence

In 1949, twelve nations (U.S., Canada, Great Britain, France, Belgium, the Netherlands, Luxembourg, Italy, Portugal, Norway, Denmark, and Iceland) formed the **North Atlantic Treaty Organization**. They pledged to come to the aid of any member who was attacked with military force, if required. In the years that followed, Greece, Turkey, Spain, and Germany joined **NATO**.

NATO has a unified command and a military force which integrates units from the armies of member nations. The Supreme Allied Commander has traditionally been an American. However, disagreements have damaged the unity of NATO at different times, examples include the Greek-Turkish dispute over Cyprus, and President DeGaulle's withdrawal of French forces from the unified NATO command in the 1960's.

Post World War II Alliances

NATO countries*

Warsaw Pact

Non-aligned

* NATO nations not shown
include Canada and the United States

The question of U.S. strategic weapons in Germany became a problem for NATO. Other nations, such as Switzerland, have sought to obtain security by adopting a position of neutrality. However, as Belgium unfortunately learned in both World Wars, neutrality is not a protection against attack, if your borders are exposed to hostile powers. The mid 1980's saw considerable easing of Cold War tensions. Gorbachev, Reagan, and Bush agreed to missile and troop cuts. In the 1990's, the rise of democratic governments and economic problems in the Soviet Union led to dissolution of the Warsaw Pact. Western nations reorganized and streamlined the NATO alliance in response to the increasing role of the European Community. Critics wondered if NATO was needed due to the collapse of communism and the dissolution of the Soviet Union itself.

Questions

1   Which statement is true of the post-World War II period?
    1   Only the former Soviet Union developed atomic weapons.
    2   Nuclear weapons proliferated among a number of nations.
    3   No attempts were made to stop the spread of nuclear weapons.
    4   Nuclear weapons were placed in outer space.

2   Decisions made at the Teheran, Yalta, and Potsdam led to
    1   the spread of communism.
    2   a democratic government for Poland.
    3   a united Germany.
    4   a Soviet withdrawal from the war against Japan.

3   Which was true of the Soviet suppression of the 1968 Czech revolt?
    1   It was supported by the entire communist world.
    2   It established limits beyond which liberalization could not go.
    3   It led to revolt against the communist leadership in the U.S.S.R.
    4   It led to serious disruption of the Czech economy.

4   In the 20th century, international peace organizations have been most successful in
    1   settling disputes between major powers.
    2   limiting terrorist activities.
    3   preventing localized wars.
    4   solving economic and social problems.

5   In the immediate post-World War II period, the U.S. policy toward communism was called
    1   detente.
    2   containment.
    3   collective security.
    4   peaceful coexistence.

6   The Suez Canal Crisis was unusual post-WW II history because
    1   a U.N. Army was sent in to protect Egypt.
    2   the U.S.S.R. and the U.S. voted together to condemn the attack.
    3   Britain and France refused to obey the U.N. resolution.
    4   the Canal was peacefully internationalized.

7 Benefits of membership in the Commonwealth of Nations include
  1 access to British atomic weapons.
  2 governmental control from London.
  3 economic and trade benefits.
  4 representation in the British Parliament.

8 The organ of the U.N. charged with keeping world peace is the
  1 Security Council.
  2 General Assembly.
  3 Economic and Social Council.
  4 International Court of Justice.

9 The U.N., the League of Nations, and the Concert of Europe all sought to
  1 return pre-war governments to power.
  2 preserve international peace.
  3 use military force to defeat aggression.
  4 establish an international military force.

10 Which was a major reason for the success of Soviet domination in Eastern Europe after World War II?
  1 Eastern Europeans accepted the doctrine of Pan-Slavism.
  2 The democracies of Western Europe needed greater security.
  3 The Soviet Union had military forces in Eastern Europe as a result of World War II.
  4 Western Europeans feared Nazism would be rekindled in Eastern Europe.

Essays

1 The results of World War II have had a lasting impact upon European history and the global power structure. Discuss *three* of the following: [5,5,5]

    • European attempts to coordinate defense
    • The impact of World War II on colonial empires
    • The impact of the atomic age on the postwar world.
    • Changes in the international power structure

2 The "Cold War" was a major determinant of the foreign policies of the United States and the Soviet Union.

  a Explain how decisions made at the wartime conferences helped to produce the "Cold War." [5]

  b Discuss the factors, other than the wartime conferences, which aided the spread of communism in the postwar world. [5]

  c Explain and evaluate the "containment" policy of the U.S. [5]

Unit Seven

Glasnost
Proletariat
Perestroika
Dictatorship
Command Economy

Revolution
Soviet Bloc
Communism
Westernization
Ethnic Populations

500   BC   AD   1000   1500   1700

· Slavic Migrations   · Varangian Bulgar & Magyar Invasions   · Ivan the Terrible

      · Romans in E. Europe   · Kiev City–state   · Peter
                                            the Great

                               · Mongols

                  · Eastern Orthodox Church

Eastern Europe
Russia and
Central Asia

1800		1900		1950		1990	2000

- Duchy of Warsaw
  - Napoleonic Invasion
- Austro–Hungarian Empire

- WW I
- WW II
- USSR Formed
- Bolshevik Revolution
  - Stalin

- Cold War
  - Hungarian Revolt
- Hitler Invades USSR

- *Glasnost*
  - Pro–Democracy ·
    Movement
  - USSR ·
    Collapses

Unit Seven: Eastern Europe, Russia, And Central Asia

I. The Physical/Historical Setting

Geography always plays an important role in the life and development of a region. The mountains, deserts, and climate have protected the people of the area from aggressors. The rivers and plains around the Danube, and the steppes of Central Asia, however, have been invasion routes. The ethnic diversity of the area is enormous. There is a long history of struggles between various groups.

A. Characteristics Of The Region
Diversity
Physical Features

This region is more than 12 million square miles and is more than 2.5 times the size of the United States. It is the largest nation in the world. It is located in the extreme north of the Eurasian land mass and most of it has mid-latitude wet-&-dry cold winter climates (Dw or Df). The northernmost regions have Tundra (ET) or Ice Cap (EF) climates. As a consequence, much of the country has long winters and short summers.

The severity of the climate has also acted as a protection against invaders. However, beginning with the Caspian Sea and moving east, there is a cool desert area (Bw & Bs climates). The vacation area along the north coast of the Black Sea is closer to a temperate Mediterranean (Cs) climate and is able to produce crops such as citrus fruits and grapes.

The tundra region (see map page 299) is a land of long, harsh winters It is an area of short, cool summers. Much of the land is permafrost and not arable. The herding of reindeer is the chief occupation. South of the tundra is a large forested area encompassing nearly 50% of the region. The people earn their living from timber and furs.

Nations of Eastern Europe, Russia, & Central Asia

The steppe, or plains area, is south of the forested region. It stretches 3,000 miles from border to border. It is a vital area for the economy of the region because it is where much of the farming occurs, especially wheat. It is also a major industrial area. Unfortunately, the flat grasslands have proven to be a popular invasion route. The most southerly area is the desert which is very dry and largely inhabited by nomads. However, in recent years, with modern irrigation techniques, crops such as cotton have been produced.

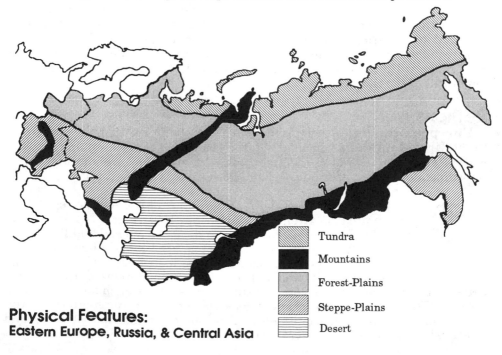

▨	Tundra
■	Mountains
▤	Forest-Plains
▨	Steppe-Plains
▥	Desert

Physical Features:
Eastern Europe, Russia, & Central Asia

Climate: Eastern Europe, Russia, & Central Asia

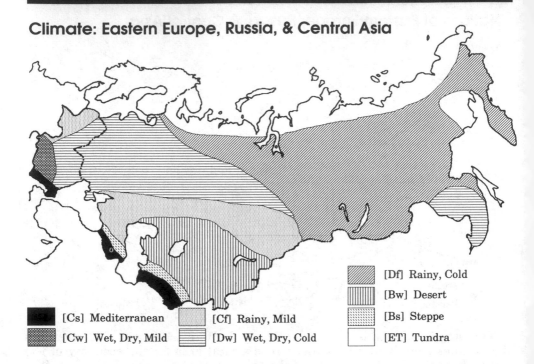

[Df] Rainy, Cold

[Bw] Desert

[Bs] Steppe

[ET] Tundra

[Cs] Mediterranean

[Cw] Wet, Dry, Mild

[Cf] Rainy, Mild

[Dw] Wet, Dry, Cold

The rivers are a vital source of inland transportation and communication. Their importance is accentuated by the fact that the region is largely land-locked. Most of the Pacific and Arctic coasts are frozen year round and the Caspian, Black and Baltic Seas are almost completely landlocked and other nations can control their exits. The **Ob**, **Yenisei**, and **Lena Rivers** flow northward in Siberia toward the Arctic. The **Amur** flows east forming part of the border with China and empties in the Sea of Okhotsk. Farther to the west, the **Dneiper**, **Don**, and **Volga** are vital arteries of trade and commerce. The Volga, with its interlocking system of canals to other rivers, is the most important of the Soviet rivers.

Regions

European Russia extends from its western border with Eastern Europe to the **Ural Mountains** which are considered to be the dividing line between Europe and Asia. However, the mountains are low. They are not much of an impediment to travel, and the people on both sides are very similar.

Environment

Siberia occupies the Northern part of the Asiatic region and is an area of extremes. The far north is tundra. Moving southward is forest area, the grasslands of the steppe, and finally, an area of fertile farmland. Development of Siberia has been slow. From the tsars to the communists, it has been a place of exile for political opponents. It was not until the completion of the **Trans-Siberian Railroad** in the 20th century that real development of Siberia started. The communist government took strong steps to promote the development of the area because of its natural resources, industrial potential, and location that made it less vulnerable to attack.

To the south of Siberia lies **Central Asia**. It is an area comprising mostly fertile steppes with some deserts. It is surrounded by mountains except on the north; they go from Lake Baikal in Siberia to the Caspian Sea on the west. The Caucasus Mountains, running from the Black to the Caspian Sea, form the dividing line between Europe and Asia in the southwest.

The **Transcaucasus** area lies between the Black and Caspian Seas and below the Caucasus Mountains. It is actually a part of Asia, but the population is mixed Asian and European.

Natural Resources

The region has one of the best natural resource bases in the world and is self-sufficient in many important raw materials. It is the world's leading producer of platinum, nickel, and iron. Somewhat surprisingly, it is also the leading producer of oil, much of which it sells to Eastern Europe. Its coal reserves are enormous, and it has 40% of the world's known gas reserves. Its recent construction of a gas pipeline from Siberia to Eastern Europe has enabled it to supply not only its satellites, but also a number of West European nations.

Nuclear power generators supply a considerable amount of the region's electricity. However, after the **Chernobyl Nuclear Power Plant** accident in the Ukraine (1986), questions arose about safety. Hydroelectric power is still the most significant source of electricity.

Physical Features Of Eastern Europe

Eastern Europe makes up nearly 1.3 million square miles of the region. It is located between Western Europe and the interior of Eurasia. It has been a convenient route for invaders.

Eastern Europe

In Eastern Europe, mountains always played an important role. The **Carpathians** are the longest mountain range and cross Romania, Hungary, Poland and Czechoslovakia. Other ranges include the **Balkans**, the **Rhodopes** in southern Bulgaria, the **Bohemian** and **Sudetens** in Czechoslovakia, and the **Julian** and **Dinaric Alps** in parts of Yugoslavia and Albania. These mountains have served as barriers to invaders and provided protection to inhabitants.

Eastern Europe is also an area of vast plains, some of which have been major invasion routes. This is particularly true of the **Northern European Plain** which crosses Poland and the northern part of East Germany. The **Great Hungarian Plain** is in the middle of Eastern Europe and is an agricultural and horse raising region. Other plains are located among the various mountain ranges. There are also a number of scenic lakes located in the mountain areas, such as Lake Balaton in Hungary.

Environment

Rivers play a significant role in the life of the area. By far, the **Danube** is the most important waterway. It winds its way past major cities in Hungary, Yugoslavia, Bulgaria and Romania on its way to the Black Sea. It is used not only for trade and commerce, but also is a source of irrigation water, fish, and hydroelectric power.

Natural Resources Of Eastern Europe

In terms of natural resources, Eastern Europe is not as well endowed as the Soviet Union. **Polish Silesia** has significant amounts of coal and iron ore, which is vital to the country's continuing industrialization. The **Czech Republic** also has important coal and iron deposits which make it an important industrial country. The former republics of **Yugoslavia** have rich mineral resources such as iron ore, lead, copper, and zinc. As a consequence of strong government financial investment, the value of industrial production is three times that of agriculture.

Romania is the only country of Eastern Europe with significant deposits of oil, a resource which made it a target during World War II. However, the country remains underdeveloped industrially. The same is true of **Bulgaria**, **Hungary**, and **Albania**. They lack strong mineral resource bases and remain largely agricultural producers. All three are attempting to develop more industry.

B. Early Peoples

The Slavs

Diversity

Of the many tribal groups that migrated into what is now Russia, the dominant group was the eastern **Slavs**. They originated in what is now eastern Poland, White Russia, and the Ukraine. One Slavic group migrated to the forest areas of Russia, settled along the rivers and became traders developing routes from the Baltic to the Black Sea. The **Poles**, **Czechs**, and **Slovaks** are descendants of another group, and the **Croats**, **Serbs**, and **Slovenes** of Yugoslavia claim a third group as their ancestors.

Kiev and **Novgorod** became important trading centers for the Slavs who settled along the rivers in Russia. These Slavic centers were constantly threatened by invaders from Central Asia. Among them were the **Khazars** who demanded tribute from the Slavic traders. The Slavs were not prepared to fight, and turned for protection to a warrior-merchant group, the **Varangians**. They came from what is now Sweden and established firm control over many of the Slavic routes. **Oleg**, one of their chiefs, took over Kiev in about 862 A.D. The Slavic and Varangian cultures fused, providing the basis for the modern Russian culture.

Non-Slavic Peoples

Although most areas of Eastern Europe were also under Slavic control, Hungary, Bulgaria, Albania, and Romania had additional influences. Hungary was affected by the **Magyars**, a nomadic tribe that established itself in about 900 A.D. Bulgarian civilization is a result of a combination of the Slavs and the **Bulgars**, an invading group from Central Asia. Albanians and Romanians are descendants of peoples who settled the area long before the Slav, Magyar, and Bulgar peoples arrived. As a consequence of this variety, significant cultural differences are still apparent in Eastern Europe and the Soviet Union today.

Diversity

A Mix Of Cultural Legacies

By about 900 A.D., the Russians established a loose confederation of city-states with the **Grand Prince of Kiev** at its head. The local princes were expected to protect their city-states and administer justice and, in return, received part of the town's profit from trade. **Veches** (assemblies) of all adult male citizens dealt with local affairs. The society was divided into several classes: the Grand Prince and nobles; **boyars** (the wealthy merchants and landowners), and peasants (the largest group).

Culture

A prosperous trade developed between the Russians and the Byzantine Empire. After the Muslims gained control of the Mediterranean Sea in the 8th century, the only safe route between the Byzantine Empire and Western Europe was through Russia. As a consequence, the Russians came into contact with the cultures of both areas, but that of the **Byzantines** appealed to them most.

One of the most significant effects of this exposure to the Byzantine culture was the conversion of **Vladimir**, the Grand Prince of Kiev, to the **Eastern Orthodox Catholic** faith. Tremendous cultural diffusion was the result. In 988 A.D., the Orthodox religion became the official religion of Russia. It provided the basis for beginning the establishment of a Russian identity. Church architecture with the onion-shaped domes, the painting of icons, and the **Cyrillic alphabet** were all results of this diffusion. This strengthened Russian ties with the Byzantine Empire and led to greater differences with Western Europe.

Even when the government structure of Russia failed to function, the Orthodox Church continued to act in much the same fashion as the Roman Catholic Church acted during and after the decline of the Roman Empire. However, other areas of Eastern Europe were Christianized from Rome and their culture reflected that of Western Europe. They developed substantial cultural differences from the Russians.

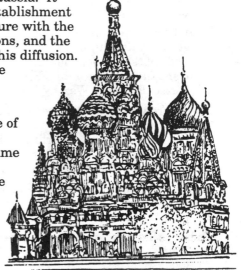

Legacy Of The Mongols

Under **Yaroslav** in the 11th century, Kiev reached its height and had a "golden age." Yaroslav's successors were not able to preserve the peace and civil wars occurred. When the **Mongols** entered Russia in the 13th century, there was no one strong enough to oppose them. Unfortunately, the Mongol conquest denied the Russians access to the changes of the Renaissance then going on in Western Europe. The fall of Constantinople to the Ottoman Turks in 1453 A.D. completed the isolation. As a consequence, Russia was slow to enter modern times.

Initially, the Mongols devastated Russia and burned cities such as Kiev. The peasant population became their **serfs**. Later in the 200-year Mongol rule, the Russians were allowed to practice the Orthodox religion and control local affairs providing that a tribute payment was made to the **Khan** (Mongol leader). Russian princes were allowed to keep their positions if they collected taxes and kept law and order for the Mongols. Thus, systems resembling the **feudalism** and **absolutism** of the West developed in Russia.

Later Russians did join together against the Mongols. This gave them a sense of unity, but their long isolation caused development of a unique culture which would make interaction with others difficult.

Questions

1   Russia has
   1   few natural boundaries that provide protection.
   2   long, hot summers and cool, moist winters.
   3   its chief vacation area along the Pacific Ocean coast.
   4   small rivers of little economic significance.

2   Which of the following climate and vegetation zones is accurately paired with its description?
   1   tundra - long, harsh winters with permafrost
   2   forest - major industrial and farming area
   3   steppe - produces fur and lumber products
   4   desert - dry, arid climate with no crops

3   Real development of Siberia began with the
   1   Russian Revolution of 1917.
   2   exile of tsarist opponents.
   3   completion of the Trans-Siberian Railroad.
   4   Russo-Japanese War.

4   Rivers are vital in Russia because they
   1   all flow south.
   2   are avenues of transportation and communication.
   3   connect Siberia with the west.
   4   form the major route from Moscow to Leningrad.

5   The Soviet Union was the world's leading producer of
   1   gas.   3   oil.
   2   gold.   4   diamonds.

6   The most important river in Eastern Europe is the
   1   Amur.   3   Danube.
   2   Ob.   4   Rhine.

7   Most Eastern European countries have
    1   excellent mineral resources.   3   have major oil reserves.
    2   largely farming economies.   4   no industrial development plans.

8   The Slavs were
    1   the dominant rulers of Russia in medieval times.
    2   members of the Islamic faith.
    3   the major cultural group of Eastern Europe.
    4   chiefly of the boyar class.

9   Which is an example of cultural diffusion from the Byzantine Empire to Russia?
    1   modern technology   3   feudalism
    2   the Latin alphabet   4   the Eastern Orthodox Church

10 Which was a result of the 13th century Mongol invasion of Russia?
    1   Russia was brought into contact with Western Europeans.
    2   Russia was unable to take part in the Renaissance.
    3   Russia was formed into a modern industrial society.
    4   Russia began to establish a democratic government.

11 Which happened under the Mongol's rule of Russia?
    1   No Russians were allowed in the government.
    2   The practice of the Eastern Orthodox religion was denied.
    3   Tribute was paid in exchange for control of local affairs.
    4   The peasant population became free.

12 Early Russian culture reflected the contributions of the
    1   Byzantine Empire, Orthodox Church, and Mongols.
    2   Orthodox Church, Mongols, and Persians.
    3   Germans, Mongols, and Magyars.
    4   Western Roman Empire, Byzantine Empire, and Mongols.

13 Early Russia resembled the West in its
    1   use of Renaissance ideas.   3   adoption of a feudal system.
    2   use of classical architecture.   4   acceptance of Protestantism.

14 Parts of Eastern Europe and Russia developed differently because
    1   rivers were more important in Russia's development.
    2   the Eastern Orthodox branch of Christianity took hold in Russia, and parts of Eastern Europe adopted Roman Catholicism.
    3   the Russians were not subject to invasions, while Eastern Europe was conquered many times.
    4   Eastern Europe was more influenced by the Asian civilization and Russia was more influenced by Western Europe.

Essay

Geography has had a significant impact on the development of Russia and Eastern Europe.

   a   Explain how Russian historical development was influenced by geography. [6]

   b   Discuss the economic role of rivers in Russia and Eastern Europe. [3]

   c   Discuss the extent to which a resource base helps to make the economies of Russia and Eastern Europe interdependent. [6]

II. Dynamics Of Change

A. Rise Of Tsarist Power In Muscovy

Early Tsars

While the Mongols ruled Russia, the princes of Moscow began to increase their power. One of these princes, Ivan I, persuaded the Orthodox Church to move its headquarters to Moscow and convinced the Mongols to name him "grand prince of all Rus." Subsequent rulers further increased the territory under the control of the rulers of Moscow. **Ivan III** (1462-1505) eventually threw off "the Tartar yoke" in 1480, by refusing to pay tribute to the Mongols.

Power

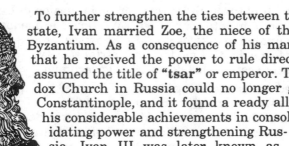

To further strengthen the ties between the church and the state, Ivan married Zoe, the niece of the last emperor of Byzantium. As a consequence of his marriage, he claimed that he received the power to rule directly from God and assumed the title of **"tsar"** or emperor. The Eastern Orthodox Church in Russia could no longer get direction from Constantinople, and it found a ready ally in the tsars. For his considerable achievements in consolidating power and strengthening Russia, Ivan III was later known as Ivan the Great.

Ivan the Great

His grandson, Ivan IV (1533-1584), however, was known as **Ivan the Terrible**. He harshly suppressed noble opposition to his power, encouraged the development of a new class of nobles (who were given land in return for military service), and began a policy of tying the peasants to the soil, thus establishing systems similar to the **feudalism** and **serfdom** of Western Europe. He also established secret police who swiftly acted at the slightest suspicion of disloyalty to the tsar. Ivan even killed his son in a fit of temper.

Ivan the Terrible

Ivan continued the expansion of Russian territory. His attempt to gain territory on the Baltic Sea failed, but he did obtain the middle Volga area, the Caspian Sea, and the steppe area of Siberia. As the borders of Russia were expanded, the tsars followed a policy of **Russification**. Conquered people were forced to adopt the Russian language, culture, and religion in an attempt to increase the degree of unity within the country. In addition, there were increased contacts and communications with the West during Ivan's reign.

After Ivan's death, Russia was ruled by weak tsars and suffered from foreign invasions, natural disasters, peasant revolts, and civil wars. Finally, an assembly of nobles selected **Michael Romanov** to rule Russia in 1613, thus the **Romanov Dynasty** began. During the 17th century, the tsars became increasingly interested in Western Europe and Europeans with specific skills such as merchants, engineers, and doctors began to make their way to Russia. However, most

Technology

Expansion Of The Russian State

Trans-Siberian
Rail Road

Varangian
Kiev-State 1000 AD

Early Tsarist State

18th-19th Century
Expansion

Russians were suspicious of them and they were forced to
live in segregated areas.

Peter The Great

One Russian who was fascinated by the foreigners,
and spent much time with them, was the man who became **Peter the Great** (1682-1725). He learned about
the arts of fighting wars and ship-building from foreigners and was determined to use European technology to
achieve his objective of strengthening Russia. With
this in mind, he undertook a tour of Western
Europe as a private citizen to learn what he
could of western ways. He worked in a ship-
yard in the Netherlands, and visited England,
before a revolt of nobles in Russia forced him to
return. On his return, the revolt was firmly
suppressed and ended with the executions of
those involved.

Peter the Great

Peter then began his program of **westernization**. In order to emphasize
his determination to modify Russian tradition, men were ordered to shave off
their beards, wear short coats, and nobles were to wear western dress at
court. Women were expected to socialize with men. These changes aroused
considerable hostility among conservative Russians. He sent Russians to
study western technology and offered high salaries to western experts to
come to Russia. Schools were started, canals constructed, a navy established,
and the army reformed. Military roads were built between major cities.

In his government, Peter was willing to use men of all different
backgrounds. He developed a civil service system to allow them to
advance into the ranks of the nobility. The Orthodox Church was
placed directly under his control when he established the Holy

Culture

Synod headed by his appointee to replace the **Patriarch** (church leader). All of these reforms were designed to increase Russian power and resemble steps taken by West European rulers of his time.

Peter continued the Russian pressure for access to the sea which later expanded into a desire for warm water ports. He wanted a "window on the west" --a geographic outlet on the Baltic Sea. The Baltic was controlled by Sweden. The **Great Northern War** (1708-21) against Sweden was at first a disaster, but a major victory at Poltava gave Peter the southern shores of the Gulf of Finland. His attempts to duplicate his success against the Persians in the Caspian Sea area failed.

Peter turned his attention to the construction of a new capital on the Baltic coast, the city of **St. Petersburg** (today's Leningrad). This marshy area was not a desirable area for the capital and it proved to be costly in terms of money and lives. Nobles were expected to construct homes in the new city and spend at least part of the year there.

Peter succeeded in strengthening Russia. He established policies that later rulers were to follow, but there are real questions about how far reaching his westernization reforms were. There was industrial progress, but the government remained in the hands of the aristocracy, subject to the tsar's control. The Patriarch was changed, but the church functioned much as it had before. There was deep division that caused controversy between the **Westernizers** (those who favored the adoption of western ways) and the **Slavophils** (those who favored the traditional Russian values).

Catherine The Great

Peter's immediate successors were weak and short-lived. It was not until **Catherine the Great** (1762-1796) assumed the throne that conditions were right for further progress. Catherine assumed the throne under unusual conditions. Her weak husband was assassinated. There is some evidence that the deed was done with her knowledge. She was a former German princess who was well known for her intellectual interests. She corresponded with some of the leaders of the Enlightenment including Voltaire and Diderot.

Initially, she indicated that she intended to introduce some enlightened reforms earning her the title of **enlightened despot** (one who uses autocratic power for the benefit of the people). She carried out some changes in governmental structure, codified the laws, limited the use of torture, and allowed some religious toleration. However, a peasant insurrection in 1773, caused by the deteriorating conditions of the serfs, changed her attitude to one of repression. As a consequence, the power of the noble landlords increased. They were also freed from compulsory military service to the state. Serfdom in Russia began to resemble slavery in the United States.

In foreign affairs, Catherine was determined to expand Russia at the expense of Poland and the Ottoman Empire, both of which were very weak at this time. While she was involved in a war with the Ottoman Empire, Austria proposed that Russia, Prussia and Austria divide Poland. Austria was hoping to distract Russia from the Balkan Peninsula, an area that it hoped to control.

This was the first of three partitions that resulted in the removal of Poland from the map of Europe in 1795. Ultimately, Catherine was also able to gain control of the north coast of the Black Sea when she signed a peace treaty with the Ottoman sultan. Thus, Catherine continued the Russian search for outlets to the sea and expansion, this time in the direction of the west.

Role Of The Orthodox Church

The Russian Orthodox Church has played a major role in the history of Russia and in the daily lives of the people. Peter effectively moved it under tzarist control. The close ties with the state increased the influence of the clergy. Monasteries received gifts of land. This sometimes led to corruption.

The parish priests, however, remained very close to the people and lived in very similar circumstances. Frequently they were not well educated and their religion began to include superstitions. At times, they led revolts against the government, but the hierarchy of the Church usually supported the tsars. Much of the cultural development of Russia has also centered around the Church. The magnificent churches with their onion-shaped domes that dot the landscape are reminders of the pervasive influence of religion.

After the communists assumed control in 1917, there was a period of violent persecution. In 1927, the leader of the Church pledged absolute loyalty to the government and established the basis for the church-state relationship. The support given by the Church during World War II led to an easing of restrictions and improved relations.

B. Development Of Eastern Europe

Eastern Europe received more influence from the West than did Russia. Poland, Czechoslovakia, East Germany, and Hungary followed the Roman Catholic Church, and in some later cases, one of the Protestant sects.

Poland

Poland is probably the country in which Roman Catholicism has played the greatest role. It developed close ties with Polish nationalism that it retains to the present day. During the 17th century, Poland reached its height under the leadership of **King John Sobieski**. The system of nobles electing the king left the country vulnerable to foreign interference.

Interference culminated in the late 18th century, with three partitions imposed by Austria, Prussia, and Russia. Napoleon briefly reconstructed a small Polish state, the **Grand Duchy of Warsaw**. However, the Congress of Vienna placed Poland under the indirect control of the Russian tsar.

After revolts by the Poles the constitution was abolished and the tsar ruled directly. Intense Russification followed. It only increased the Polish sense of nationalism and determination to have an independent nation state, a goal that was finally realized at the end of World War I.

Hungary

The Magyars (Hungarians) invaded the Carpathian basin from south and west of the Ural Mountains and became Christians under King Stephen I

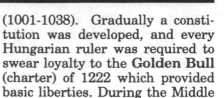

(1001-1038). Gradually a constitution was developed, and every Hungarian ruler was required to swear loyalty to the **Golden Bull** (charter) of 1222 which provided basic liberties. During the Middle Ages, both the Mongols and the Turks threatened Hungary, but it was the **Hapsburg** kings of Austria who defeated the Turks in 1683, and were finally able to gain control of the area.

In the aftermath of the French Revolution and Napoleonic era, there was an increase in Hungarian nationalism. A strong revolt against Austrian control in 1848 was suppressed with Russian assistance. After its defeat in the Austro-Prussian War (1866), Austria was forced to make concessions to the Hungarians. The **Compromise of 1867** established the dual monarchy, Austria-Hungary, and gave Hungary a large degree of self-government.

Ottoman Empire

By the time the **Ottoman Turks** conquered Constantinople in 1453, they had already gained control of Bulgaria and parts of Yugoslavia and Hungary. Later they conquered the rest of the Balkan peninsula. The **Ottoman Empire** reached its height under **Suleiman** (1520-1566), who conquered much of Hungary sending panic throughout Christian Europe. However, he failed to conquer Vienna. Subsequently, the Turkish fleet was defeated by Spain, and Turkish power began to decline. While the Ottomans controlled the Balkan area, the various religious groups were allowed religious toleration and control over local affairs. They were taxed heavily but those who converted to Islam were relieved of this obligation.

Bulgaria

During the 19th century, the Ottoman Empire weakened due to internal problems and European wars. Its hold on the Balkans decreased and gradually the people were able to gain independence. **Bulgaria** received a degree of independence as a result of the **Treaty of San Stefano (1877)** and the **Congress of Berlin** (1878), but full independence was not declared until 1908.

Romania, Yugoslavia, And Albania

Parts of **Romania** were freed from Turkish control in the 17th century, but it was not until the **Congress of Berlin** that Romania received total independence. Sections of modern **Yugoslavia** received independence at various times. The area of **Serbia** received technical independence after the **Russo-Turkish War** of 1877-78. Austria-Hungary received a degree of control that aroused Serbian nationalism to a point of being a major cause of World War I.

"Republics" of Yugoslavia
Violent Disintegration

After the war, Serbia became a part of Yugoslavia. The last state, **Albania**, was created after the Balkan Wars of 1912-1913 at the insistence of Austria, which was determined to deny Serbia access to the sea.

C. Russian Reforms In 19th Century

Napoleon Bonaparte is an important figure in Russian history. In helping to defeat him, Russia emerged as a major power in international affairs and played a significant role at the **Congress of Vienna** (1815). In the Napoleonic era, many Russian soldiers learned of nationalism, democracy, and the ideals of the French Revolution as they marched through Europe. These factors had a substantial impact on 19th century Russia.

Alexander I

Alexander I, tsar at the time of the defeat of Napoleon and the Congress of Vienna, was the grandson of Catherine the Great. On her orders, he was educated in the *philosophe of Enlightenment.* He had absorbed some liberal ideas, but at the same time, he strongly believed in the autocratic power of the tsars.

Change

Prior to the Napoleonic invasion, Alexander had instituted a program of reforms that were abandoned because of the war effort. After the wars, many urged that he return to this program that would have established a constitution, freed the serfs, and placed limits on the tsarist power, but he refused to do so. Instead, the new lands obtained at Vienna were subjected to Russification based on the principle, *"one church, one government, one language."* Freedom of speech and press was limited. Secret societies developed to press for reforms.

Nicholas I

On his accession to the throne Alexander's successor, **Nicholas I** (1825-1855), was faced with the **Decembrist Revolt**, a palace coup d'etat. The revolt was suppressed and Nicholas followed a policy that involved censorship and repressive use of the secret police. It has been said that he refused to allow the importation of sheet music because he feared that the musical symbols were a secret code for communication between revolutionary groups. In terms of foreign policy, he successfully expanded Russian territory in the Balkans at the expense of the Ottoman Turks. However, this increase in power aroused the hostility of Britain, France, and Austria who opposed him in the Crimean War (1854-56).

Alexander II

Nicholas' son, **Alexander II**, assumed the throne during the Crimean War. The defeat in the Crimean War cost Russia much of its previously gained territory in the Balkans. Alexander realized that changes were necessary if Russia was to remain a great power. He signed an **Emancipation** Act in 1861, which freed the serfs.

The government also purchased some land from the noble landowners to provide the former serfs with the means of earning a living. This land was turned over to the **mir** (village community council) which was then responsible for obtaining payments from the peasants. The peasants were not free to leave except with the mir's permission. Many peasants were not happy because there was not enough land. Gradually, some of the peasants became landless farm laborers and others moved to towns to obtain work. A small number were able to purchase land and expand their holdings, increasing class differences.

Political Systems Alexander II also provided for elective assemblies to govern local affairs, reformed the courts to include more western principles of justice, provided public primary schools, and established a banking system. Many people felt that his reforms had not gone far enough and urged the establishment of a national legislative body (**Duma**). Alexander II was killed by a terrorist in 1881 and succeeded by his son. Alexander III blamed his father's liberalism for his assassination and his reign was one of the most repressive in terms of human rights, but he did not abolish his father's reforms.

Economic Change

The 19th century also saw tremendous change in the economy of Russia. The expansion of Russian railroads in the 1870's led to the development of

Change large scale iron and steel industries. The government played a major role in the financing of the industries and its chief objective was to strengthen the military. As a consequence, heavy industry received most of the financial aid and consumer production was largely ignored.

The most spectacular feat, however, was the construction of the **Trans-Siberian Railroad**. Foreign loans, especially from France, were a significant factor in making the railroad possible (see map page 307).

In fact, by 1914, one-third of the national debt was for railroad construction. The construction of the railroad was responsible for opening Siberia to settlers. Approximately five million people moved into the area within ten years, beginning the development of what has become one of the most important industrial areas of Russia.

D. Russian Contributions To The Arts

During the 19th and 20th centuries, Russian musicians and writers made major contributions to European culture. In doing so, they reflected European cultural trends such as nationalism and romanticism. In many instances, they were critical of the government. Composers produced many ballets, symphonies and operas in which their love of the motherland and its people was apparent. Novelists tried to capture the essence of life in Russia in their works.

Musician	Works
Tchaikovsky	*1812 Overture, Nutcracker Suite, Swan Lake*
Rimsky-Korsakov	*Scheherazade, Flight of the Bumblebee*
Mussorgsky	*Boris Godunov*

Writer	Works
Pushkin	*Eugene Onegin, Boris Godunov,*
Tolstoy	*War and Peace, Anna Karenina*
Dostoevsky	*Crime and Punishment, The Brothers Karamazov*

An overview of Russian contributions to the arts would not be complete without an acknowledgment of their contributions to ballet, a field in which they have excelled. The St.Petersburg Ballet Company, now the **Kirov Ballet,** produced some of the greatest dancers of all time including **Anna Pavlova** and **Vaslav Nijinsky.** The dances were choreographed to display the tremendous technical skill of the dancers. Later, the dances, dramatic scenes, and stories were blended together in works such as *The Firebird* and *Prince Igor.* In recent years, the **Bolshoi Ballet** has become the best known of the Russian companies, largely because of its foreign tours.

E. The Russian Revolution Of 1905

Pressures mounted in Russia in the first part of the 20th century. Industrialization, the land hunger of the peasantry, and rising political opposition encouraged Nicholas II to undertake a war against Japan to distract the attention of the people from their grievances. In addition, Nicholas' advisors favored the war to gain much desired warm water ports in Manchuria and Korea. In order to achieve this objective, it was recognized that Russia would have to confront Japan, which also desired these areas.

Russia was defeated in the **Russo-Japanese War** in 1904-05, by what was considered a third rate military

World Issues:
Determination of
Political and
Economic Systems

power. As in the case of the Russian defeat in the Crimean War, opposition to the Tsar increased. In this instance, the opposition culminated in the **Revolution of 1905** and subsequent reforms. There were three main opposition groups in Russia at this time:

- The **Kadets** (Constitutional Democrats) were members of the middle class who favored a constitutional monarch in Russia with a role in the government for the educated.

- The **Social Revolutionaries** were the strongest party. They drew most of their support from the peasantry. Their program called for "land socialism" with the land to be controlled by the local government and given to the peasants based on their ability to cultivate the land.

- A third group, the **Social Democrats**, followed the ideas of Karl Marx. In 1903, this group broke into two parties, the **Mensheviks** and the **Bolsheviks**. The Mensheviks believed that Russia would have to develop an industrial society and have a prolonged period of bourgeois democratic government before the revolution of the proletariat could occur. The Bolsheviks, under the leadership of **Vladimir Ilyich Lenin**, believed that the period of bourgeois democracy could be brief and be followed quickly by the proletarian revolution.

Bloody Sunday, the most well known period of violence during the Revolution of 1905, occurred when a group of demonstrating workers led by **Father Gapon**, a priest of the Orthodox Church, staged a peaceful march to the Winter Palace to present a petition to Tsar Nicholas. Someone ordered the soldiers protecting the Palace to fire on the workers. Hundreds were killed or wounded. This sparked strikes and mutinies throughout the country. Finally, a general strike forced the tsar to act.

Nicholas II issued the **October Manifesto** which promised a national Duma and granted basic civil liberties. This satisfied the Kadets who then supported the government helping to suppress the revolution. The tsar gradually decreased the influence of the Duma by limiting its powers and directed some of the remaining dissatisfaction into a new **pogrom** against the Jews. However, life did become somewhat freer in Russia and a land reform program decreased peasant dissatisfaction.

F. WW I And Russian Revolution Of 1917

A wide variety of factors was responsible for the outbreak of World War I, but one of the key causes was the nationalism of the East European nations. It was a nationalism supported by Russia as part of a **Pan-Slavic** movement that the Russians hoped would decrease the power of Austria-Hungary and the Ottoman Empire in the Balkan Peninsula, and possibly win them warm water ports. Russia actively encouraged this feeling and was a sponsor of the **Balkan League** which attacked the Ottomans in the first Balkan War.

The immediate cause of World War I, the assassination of the Archduke Franz Ferdinand of Austria-Hungary by a Slavic nationalist from Serbia, resulted in Russian support of Serbia in the face of the Austrian ultimatum. This encouraged Serbia to take a firm position which led to the Austrian declaration of war and the chain reaction which brought on the war.

Russian Army Mobilization

Much to the surprise of everyone, the Russian army mobilized speedily and entered the field against Austria-Hungary and Germany before the Germans could complete the conquest of France. The Germans had to withdraw part of their army from the western front to face the Russian army. This led to the stalemate in the West that was to exist for most of the War.

However, neither the government nor the economy were strong enough to sustain the war effort. Soldiers were sent to the front lines without weapons and casualties mounted. In the Battle of Tannenberg, the Russians suffered so many casualties that the Russian commander killed himself.

On the home front, serious shortages of consumer goods and even food could not be made up by increased mechanization, so production declined. Old problems of the 19th century such as the autocratic government, limitations on civil liberties, and land hunger continued to create dissatisfaction. Finally, in March 1917, demonstrations broke out in St. Petersburg. The soldiers refused to fire on the people. The Duma demanded and received the abdication of the tsar.

Provisional Government

The leaders of the Duma formed the **Provisional Government** which was recognized by Russia's wartime allies as the official government. During the same time, the St. Petersburg Soviet was established by the Social Revolutionary and Social Democratic Parties and refused to cooperate with the Provisional Government. The Soviet had the support of many of the people because its program appeared to meet their demands.

Political Systems

During 1917 between January and September, the leftists (socialists) of the St. Petersburg Soviet gained strength in Russia. Bolshevik leader Lenin, who had been in exile, returned to Russia, increasing the party's cohesion and effectiveness. Major war defeats during the summer further disillusioned the Russian people with the war effort.

The people placed the blame on the Provisional Government. An attempt on the part of the conservative military to gain control was defeated by the Provisional Government with the aid of the Bolsheviks. By November 1917, Lenin thought that the right time had come for the **revolution of the proletariat.**

Demands	Provisional Gov't. Program	Bolshevik Program
Peace	Continue the war	Immediate peace
Land	Eventual land reform	Immediate land reform
Bread	No real plan	Proposed rationing

November Revolution

The **November Revolution** was swiftly and most effectively carried out in St. Petersburg with a minimum loss of life. The leader of the Provisional Government fled into exile and other government members were arrested. In a week, the Bolsheviks gained a secure hold on Moscow. From 1917 to 1921, a civil war raged in the south and central regions of the country.

During this period of upheaval, many of the ethnic groups tried to establish their independence. As a consequence of the **Treaty of Brest-Litovsk** which the Bolsheviks signed with the Germans in 1917, the peoples of Finland, Estonia, Latvia, Lithuania, and Poland were able to maintain their independence until World War II. Similar attempts by the peoples of Central Asia and the Caucasus region met with failure.

Vladimir Ilyich Lenin

As the new leader of the **Union of Soviet Socialist Republics**, Vladimir Ilyich Lenin faced the task of adapting the ideas of Karl Marx to a society that did not fit Marx's idea of the one likely to have a proletarian revolution. Lenin believed that the Party should be small and made up of a revolutionary elite which would lead the masses. He also thought that the peasantry, as well as the proletariat, could be a revolutionary class, and that it was possible to move to the stage of the proletarian revolution without a long period of industrialization under a bourgeois, democratic government.

Marx never wrote much about what the society and government would be like after the proletarian revolution because he did not wish to be accused of being a utopian socialist. Therefore, Lenin was able to suggest specifics based on the few general statements made by Marx. Essentially, Lenin was a pragmatist. He took Marx's ideas and modified them to fit the situation that existed in the Soviet Union and then claimed anyone who disputed his approach was a **revisionist**.

Questions

1   Ivan the Great was able to unify and strengthen Russia through his refusal to pay tribute to the Mongols, his marriage to the niece of the last Byzantine emperor, and
   1   his adoption of the divine right theory.
   2   adoption of Western European culture.
   3   the abolition of feudalism.
   4   defeat of German invaders.

2   Peter the Great is known for his policy of
   1   westernization.   3   peace.
   2   religious freedom.   4   traditionalism.

3   The policy of Russification forced the people to
   1   emigrate from Russia if they were Jewish.
   2   adopt the Russian language, culture, and religion.
   3   accept the government's policy of economic control.
   4   allow foreign ownership of industries.

4   Catherine the Great's attempts at reform were ended when
   1   Poland invaded Russia.   3   a peasant insurrection occurred.
   2   she was overthrown.   4   the power of the nobles decreased.

5   Which was the achievement of Catherine the Great?
    1   She conquered France and ended the French Revolution.
    2   She conquered Austria and Prussia.
    3   She helped to divide up Poland.
    4   She took over a large amount of territory from China.

6   Poland is a country which has
    1   a long history of independence.
    2   accepted the Russian Orthodox religion.
    3   never been ruled by foreigners.
    4   struggled to establish itself as a nation.

7   Hungary was able to establish a large degree of self-government
    1   immediately after the Turks were defeated.
    2   during the French Revolution.
    3   after the Austro-Prussian War.
    4   during the time of the Mongol conquest.

8   Under Ottoman control, the people of the Balkan Peninsula were
    1   forcefully converted to Christianity.
    2   allowed religious toleration.
    3   freed of tax obligation.
    4   denied control of local affairs.

9   Which was the achievement of Ivan the Terrible?
    1   He expanded Russian borders to the Volga and Caspian Sea areas.
    2   He made the Orthodox Church move to Moscow.
    3   He freed the serfs from control by noble landlords.
    4   He began the industrialization of Russia.

10   Alexander I of Russia did
    1   consistently follow a reactionary policy.
    2   refuse to enforce Russification.
    3   not wish to increase Russian territory.
    4   not carry out proposed reforms.

11   The Russian Emancipation Act in 1861 established
    1   freedom of speech.   3   freedom for the serfs.
    2   freedom of the press.   4   a national Duma.

12   In which of the following artistic fields are Russian contributions most widely acknowledged?
    1   painting   3   ballet
    2   sculpture   4   opera

13   During the late 19th century, which was true of the Russian economy?
    1   It began to industrialize.
    2   There was no railroad construction.
    3   Agriculture declined as a peasant way of life.
    4   Communist took over the government.

14   The Bolshevik reform group believed Russia
    1   would have proletarian revolution after a brief bourgeois period.
    2   did not need peasant support for revolution.
    3   could eliminate all government control immediately.
    4   was not ready for revolution in 1917.

15 The October Manifesto provided for
  1   pogroms against the Jews.   3   an absolute monarchy.
  2   a Duma and civil liberties.   4   the start of the 1905 Revolution.

16 During the pre-World War I period, Russia opposed
  1   Pan-Slavic movements.   3   Austria's influence in the Balkans.
  2   the Balkan League.   4   East European nationalism.

17 The Bolsheviks were able to establish their control of Russia
  1   without bloodshed.   3   only after a civil war.
  2   with allied help.   4   despite German opposition.

18 World War I helped to cause the Russian Revolution because
  1   the government was incompetent and casualties were high.
  2   Russia was abandoned by its allies.
  3   unemployment among farm laborers was high.
  4   the Russian Army was unable to mobilize.

19 A policy of the Provisional Government was
  1   a rationing plan for bread.
  2   an immediate land reform.
  3   continuation of participation in World War I.
  4   support of the Bolsheviks.

20 Which was Lenin's belief?
  1   Marx's ideas could be adapted to apply to Russia.
  2   only the proletariat could be revolutionary.
  3   Communists should have a large, democratically organized Party.
  4   A long period of bourgeois, democratic government was needed.

Essays

1 Change in Russian history has been caused by many different factors. Select *three* of the following pairs. For *each*, explain how the factor cited first contributed to reform during the reign of the ruler with whom it is paired. [5,5,5]

> • Drive for westernization - Peter the Great
> • The Enlightenment - Catherine the Great
> • Loss of the Crimean War - Alexander II
> • Loss of the Russo-Japanese War - Nicholas II

2 Several factors have significantly affected the development of Russia.

> • Russification   • Autocracy
> • Pan-Slavism   • Search for warm water ports
> • Drive for westernization

Select *three* of the factors listed above and for *each one* selected, discuss one significant impact that it had on Russian history. [5,5,5]

3 The Russian Revolutions of 1917 are among the most significant events that have occurred in modern history. Discuss *all* of the following:

a 19th and 20th century causes of the 1917 revolution. [5]
b Reasons for the increase in support for the Soviet between March and November, 1917. [5]
c Lenin's modifications of Marx's ideas to fit the situation in Russia. [5]

III. Contemporary Nations And Cultures

A. U.S.S.R. Becomes A Totalitarian State

Civil War

During the period of the civil war in Russia (1917-1921), the Bolsheviks effectively used the well trained **Red Army** under the leadership of **Leon Trotsky**. The opponents of the Reds, the **Whites**, included former tsarist army officers, land-owning nobles, members of the middle class, Russia's former World War I allies, and some of the peasantry. However, the White effort was not coordinated and frequently consisted of isolated resistance on the fringes of the country while the Reds controlled the interior. Victims of the civil war were the Tsar and his family, all of whom were shot by the Bolsheviks to keep them from being liberated by an advancing White Army.

Choice

During the civil war, the Bolsheviks followed a policy called **War Communism**. This policy turned control of industries over to the workers, called for peasant ownership of the land, and seizure of farm surpluses for distribution to the cities. By 1921, production was less than 50% of pre-World War I levels. It is also interesting to note that one of the first structures established by the new regime was the **Cheka** (secret police).

Lenin

At the end of the civil war, Lenin made the determination to "take one step backward" in order to revive the economy. He initiated the **New Economic Policy** (NEP). This policy allowed some capitalism in the economy. The government retained ownership of the "commanding heights" of the economy, that is, the major natural resources and industries. Others were turned over to private ownership. Farmers were allowed to sell their surpluses in a free market and to keep the profits. As a consequence, by 1928, production was restored to pre-World War I levels.

Stalin And Trotsky Struggle For Power

Lenin died in 1924 before he had the opportunity to see the full effects of the NEP. His death led to a struggle for power between his followers, Josef Stalin and Leon Trotsky.

Stalin had been in charge of ethnic minorities under Lenin and had later become **First Secretary** of the Communist Party which gave him access to all Party records, intimate knowledge of the background of Party members, and the ability to appoint followers to high positions.

Stalin was known for his machiavellian tendencies and willingness to be ruthless. He believed that it was possible to have a proletarian revolution in one country, build up that country, and eventually export revolution to other areas.

Political Systems

Trotsky had a base of power in the Red Army which was largely his creation. He was a brilliant orator and known for his command of Marxist ideology. He believed in immediate world wide revolution. Stalin emerged as the victor, Trotsky was exiled and later killed in Mexico, perhaps on the orders of Stalin. General Secretary of the Communist Party has become an extremely important position in the Soviet hierarchy, and subsequent rulers have all held this position.

Stalin's Totalitarian Regime

Josef Stalin

Trotsky was not the only one to suffer at Stalin's hands. During the late 1930's, Stalin carried out a **purge** of the Party to eliminate any opposition or suspected opposition. Leftists who were accused of Trotsky leanings were executed as were rightists who were accused of favoring a less severe policy in dealing with peasants.

Very significant, however, in terms of subsequent European history, Stalin also purged the leadership of the Red Army in the period right before the outbreak of World War II. This purge is sometimes cited as one of the reasons for the Nazi-Soviet Non-Aggression Pact of 1939 as Stalin needed time to train new Red Army leaders.

Economically, Stalin decided to abandon the NEP. In 1928, he began the first of the **5-year plans**. He called for government ownership of all the means of production with a government central planning agency to make basic economic decisions, in effect a command economy. However, some capitalistic principles, long denounced as unfair, were included. Most factory workers were paid on a piece-work basis and factory managers were rewarded or punished based on whether their factories met production quotas established by the government.

Stalin was primarily concerned with the development of heavy industry and did little with consumer or light industry. In order to achieve his industrial objectives, changes were made in the agricultural sector of the economy also.

Stalin needed workers for his factories, but he also needed high agricultural productivity to feed the population and to earn foreign currencies to pay for necessary machinery imports. To achieve Choice these objectives, he ordered that the small peasant farms be merged into large **collective farms** to be run by the government and cooperatively farmed by the peasants. He hoped that this would permit increased mechanization, increase production, and free some peasants for factory work.

Collectivization also gave the government more ability to control farm production and plan the economy as a whole. On collective farms, the peasants were to share in the profits. In addition, they were allowed private plots of about one acre in size, which they could farm for their own profit.

There was tremendous opposition from the peasants, especially in Ukraine. Most peasants had supported the communists based on the pledge to give them land. Stalin was ruthless in dealing with the opposition. Many were executed and thousands were sent into Siberian exile. However, the peasants were ingenious in showing their opposition through the slaughter of livestock. It took nearly 20 years to bring the herds back to the levels of the 1930's.

The industrialization of the Soviet Union was very successful. No western country had ever shown as much growth in a period comparable to the first two 5-year plans. Production of iron and steel increased four times, and coal three and a half times between 1928 and 1938.

Technology

By 1939, only Germany and the United States exceeded the Soviet Union in gross industrial output. Much of this development was east of the Ural Mountains in new industrial centers. This proved to be a wise move when Hitler later invaded the older industrial areas of the western U.S.S.R.

Totalitarian Government Changes

In 1922, Russia became the **Union of Soviet Socialist Republics** (U.S.S.R.). There were four republics at first: the Russian Federation, the Ukraine, Byelorussia, and Transcaucasia. By World War II, there were fifteen. The 1922 Constitution gave ethnic groups in the republics certain powers within the union. As time went on, Stalin centralized power in Moscow. He created a new authoritarian constitution in 1936. Ethnic groups in the republics lost powers. Brezhnev changed the constitution slightly in 1977 to give different groups more rights on paper, but not in practice.

Lenin's 1922 Constitution created a national legislature - the **Supreme Soviet**. It was a bicameral body. Representatives of the people served in the Soviet of the Union. Representatives of the republics and territories served in the Soviet of Nationalities. These houses became "rubber stamp" bodies. They merely endorsed decisions of Communist Party leaders.

The Supreme Soviet appointed a **Council of Ministers**. It ran the country's daily operations. The leader of the Council was the **Premier**, the real head of the government. The U.S.S.R. was a one-party totalitarian state. From Lenin

Political Systems

through Gorbachev, party leaders and government leaders were the same people. Real power rested in the party's leadership committee, the **Politboro**. The leader of the Politboro, the First Secretary, usually became the Premier of the government. Periodically, the government held elections. However, there was only one candidate, the Communist Party candidate. As a result, the U.S.S.R. became a totalitarian state ruled by the elite of the Communist Party.

B. Totalitarian Government After Stalin
Khrushchev

Stalin died in 1953. A struggle for power took place in the Politboro. **Nikita S. Khrushchev** won the struggle. He was a strong, clever man, but not as ruthless as Stalin. In fact, Khrushchev shocked the nation by denouncing Stalin. He reviled the long-time dictator for a variety of crimes: personal

Khrushchev

cowardice, foreign policy mistakes, and terrorizing citizens. The attacks on Stalin's reputation boosted Khrushchev's popularity with younger party leaders. Stalin's old line supporters were angered. They avoided open criticism of Khrushchev, but quietly sabotaged his policies.

Khrushchev wanted to improve the Soviet standard of living. He said government spent too much on heavy industry and military production. He tried to increase agricultural production and consumer goods. Khrushchev tried to reduce the power of central economic planners. He also tried to open new lands in Central Asia to settlers. This **"Virgin Lands Program"** failed because the climate was poor for the crops the government ordered the settlers to grow. This failure helped to topple Khrushchev.

Khrushchev's worst blunders came in foreign policy. At heart, he wanted to prove communist societies gave people a better life. To do this, he wanted to diminish the costly arms race with the U.S. and its allies. Khrushchev spoke of **"peaceful coexistence"** with the Western democracies. However, his construction of the Berlin Wall, placement of nuclear missiles in Cuba, and the disputes with Mao's China all hurt the chances for coexistence. His old enemies in the Politboro forced Khrushchev to retire in 1964.

Brezhnev

In the mid 1960's, **Leonid Brezhnev** emerged from another Politboro struggle in the **Kremlin** (central government compound in Moscow). By the 1970's, Brezhnev was First Secretary and Premier. Like Khrushchev, he first tried to cut down central planning to produce more consumer goods. The quality of goods improved, but quantities fell short of needs. By the early 1980's, military and heavy equipment production once again received economic priority.

Brezhnev's foreign policy was uneven. Friction continued with China. In 1968, Brezhnev ordered an invasion of Czechoslovakia to stop democratic reformers from taking power. Relations with the Western democratic nations improved. Brezhnev signed several treaties on arms and human rights (see SALT and Helsinki Accords). There was more cooperation on Middle East problems.

Culture

Diversity

Identity

Cultural Diversity In The U.S.S.R.

Ethnic Groups		Religions
Armenians	Latvians	Armenian Church
Azeris	Lithuanians	Buddhists
Bashkirs	Moldavians	Evangelical Baptists
Byelorussians	Russians	Georgian Orthodox
Chuvash	Tatars	Judaism
Georgians	Tadzhiks	Lutherans
Germans	Turkmen	Roman Catholic
Jews	Ukrainians	Russian Orthodox
Kazakhs	Uzbeks	

Détente, a warmer, more cordial atmosphere, resulted. The Cold War thawed. However, in 1979 it froze again. The Soviets invaded Afghanistan to help communists take over the country. Angered, the U.S. and other Western nations embargoed grain sales to the Soviets and boycotted the 1980 Summer Olympic Games in Moscow.

World Issues: *Determination of Political and Economic Systems*

Brezhnev died in 1982. His two successors continued his policies. Both Konstantin Chernenko and Yuri Andropov died soon after taking control. Neither had much of an impact on domestic or foreign affairs.

C. Life And Culture In A Totalitarian State
The Diversity Of Soviet Peoples

Lenin's U.S.S.R. drew together the many diverse peoples of the Tsars' Russian Empire. The country had over 90 ethnic groups speaking 80 different languages. The Slavs were the largest group. Within it were many subgroups such as Russians, Ukrainians, and Byelorussians.

The mountainous Transcaucasia region was between the Black and Caspian Seas. It contained more than forty ethnic groups, most of whom were of Turkic or Persian origin. East of the Caspian Sea, Central Asians later formed several ethnic republics of their own. The Islamic religion remained a strong cultural force in these regions.

In the early days of the U.S.S.R., some of the major ethnic groups (see chart, pg. 322) controlled their own republics. They designed their own constitutions. They guaranteed preservation of their languages, cultures, and local governments. Moscow gave smaller ethnic minorities similar guarantees. Citizenship

As time went on, the central government in Moscow took more control in the republics. The original ideals of individual rights and local rule faded as the country became more totalitarian. As with the old Tsarist "Russification Policy," Moscow ordered the Russian language taught in all the republics. Communist leaders moved Russians into the different republics to "homogenize the nation" (blend the culture).

The Diversity Of Religion

The communist leadership proclaimed the Soviet Union officially **atheist** (denied the existence of God). However, the national constitution guaranteed freedom of religion. The Russian Orthodox Church retained the largest membership of any organized religion. However, communist leaders were suspicious of any organizations that would undermine their control. The government watched and regulated all religions carefully.

In Transcaucasia and Central Asia, nearly fifty-five million people followed Islam. Again, communist leaders feared the power of any cultural force such as Islam. They knew it could unify people and spur independence movements along the southern borders.

There were also about three million Jews in the U.S.S.R. Anti-semitism was common in Russian history. Under Tsarist rule, Jews were often victims of

pogroms (violent raids and brutal resettlements). The Jewish **pales** (isolated settlements, ghettos) were often overrun and destroyed. Under the totalitarian rule of the communists, Jews found they had few rights. The communists sentenced those who protested to forced labor in **gulags** (remote prison camps). Jews found it nearly impossible to **emigrate** (leave the country).

Urbanization

At the time of the Bolshevik takeover, the country was largely rural. The bulk of the people were peasants, living in small rural villages. Lenin and the communists knew they had to build an industrial society to succeed. Stalin forced industrialization on the country (see pages 321-322). This resulted in extensive urban development. The government spurred urban growth in Siberia and Central Asia with housing and pay incentives. In general, urbanization and resettlement were too rapid and poorly planned. The government built factories, but neglected housing for workers. Even in the 1970's and 1980's poor housing remained a problem in major cities.

The Changing Role Of Women

Social changes under communist rule included new roles for women. Women became equals to men in most respects. They composed over 50% of the Soviet work force. Women outnumbered men in the fields of education and medicine. They also equaled men in technical fields, assembly line work, and manual trades. Women received equal pay for equal work. However, men still outnumbered them in administrative, supervisory, and managerial positions.

Change

A huge loss of lives in World War II (estimates exceed 20 million) left many jobs to fill and widows with families to support. The government actively encouraged women to join the work force. It provided day care centers for their children and guaranteed job security after pregnancy and maternity leaves.

Legally, men and women were equal in Soviet society. Divorce was a simple administrative procedure if there were no children. The procedure divided property equally. Streamlined court proceedings decided custody of children and property division. In reality, women were still primarily responsible for child care, cleaning, and household management. The economy made few modern appliances available. As in the old Russia, husbands were not expected to help around the house.

Totalitarian Censorship Of The Arts And Sciences

Totalitarian governments try to control all social activity. In the Soviet Union, communist leaders blocked free expression in art. They insisted art reflect what they called "social realism." They expected artists to paint themes which glorified work and supported patriotic goals. Some artists fled the country. Ironically, the communists preserved much art and treasure of the Russian past in Tsarist palaces they converted to museums.

Culture

The totalitarian government controlled literary expression also. Under Stalin, official censors blocked publication of any works critical of communism. Authorities censured, exiled, or imprisoned writers frequently. Even after Stalin's death strict censorship remained. **Boris Pasternak** received global recognition for his novel

Dr. Zhivago. Claiming there were ideas critical of the Bolshevik Revolution, the government refused to publish the book. They forced Pasternak to decline the Nobel Prize for Literature in 1958.

In the 1970's, dissident author **Aleksandr Solzhenitzyn** wrote about the forced labor camps of the Stalin Era. His friends published *Gulag Archipelago* outside the U.S.S.R. The communist censors banned all of his works inside the country. Solzhenitzyn left his homeland in protest. In the West, he became a critic of Soviet human rights policies.

Aleksandr Solzhenitsyn
"...punishment for dissidence..."

From Tsarist times, Russians were scientific leaders. After the communists seized control, many scientists and technicians left the country. The government sponsored research programs. However, research was strictly controlled. The renowned Soviet Academy of Sciences became the control agency. Its bureaucrats directed and monitored all major research programs. Western critics felt this limited scientific innovation and free exchange of ideas.

The government funded research projects for military and space research. Significant medical research opened the field of laser eye surgery. However, the U.S.S.R. fell behind in fields such as microelectronics (computers) and automotive technology.

Glasnost - *Openness*
"...perhaps, opening a new window on the world..."

B. Decline Of Totalitarian Rule

Gorbachev Brings Change

Mikhail Gorbachev came to power in 1985. He was a younger leader in the Politboro who began to change the governmental structure. His *glasnost* policy allowed people more freedom to criticize and try to reform the government. He allowed dissidents to leave the country, permitted more Jews to emigrate, and freed some political prisoners.

Under Gorbachev, constitutional reforms gave more power to a new national legislature (**Congress of the Peoples' Deputies**) and created a stronger Presidency. The control of the Communist Party diminished. Reforms allowed rival parties.

Gorbachev was less successful at reforming the command structure of the economy. His *perestroika* policy allowed the people to explore market economy forces such as self interest, competition, credit, and profit. It promoted privately owned small business. It encouraged local plant managers to decide about the quality and quantity of consumer goods.

Gorbachev

In foreign policy, Gorbachev reduced Soviet influence in Eastern Europe. This allowed democratic movements to grow. Mass demonstrations and protests toppled communist rule. Germans tore down the Berlin Wall and the reunified their country in 1989. The Warsaw Pact dissolved in 1991. Summit meetings with Western leaders reduced missiles and military presence in Europe. Some hailed this as an end to the Cold War. Gorbachev received the Nobel Peace Prize in 1990.

While Gorbachev became a hero abroad, his cautiousness toward reform created instability at home. Anti-reform Politboro members launched a coup against him in the summer of 1991. Democratic resistance rallied around the

The Success of Gorbachev
... the world loves me, but will I also be a hero at home?...

Russian Federation President **Boris Yeltsin**. The Red Army refused the coup leaders' orders to fire on civilians. The coup disintegrated, and so did the Soviet Union.

Just before the coup, Gorbachev prepared a new **Treaty of Union** to return real power in local and regional matters to the republics. After the coup, republics began to declare independence. Gorbachev could not hold the country together and resigned as President. The totalitarian state that Lenin created in 1917 faded into history.

Yeltsin Begins A New Era

After the aborted coup against Gorbachev, Boris Yeltsin emerged as a key personality. Yeltsin originally rose through Communist Party ranks with Gorbachev's help. By 1987, he felt Politboro leaders would not permit Gorbachev to reform the U.S.S.R. Yeltsin resigned from the Communist Party. He won the Presidency of the Russian SFSR Parliament as an independent reform candidate. Soon after, he won the first democratic election for President of the Russian SFSR. While the coup leaders held Gorbachev prisoner in the Crimea, Yeltsin led public demonstrations defying the coup.

Boris Yeltsin

The coup fell apart when Red Army commanders and troops refused to fire on their own people. Gorbachev returned and resigned from the Communist Party. However, it was clear he had to share power with Yeltsin.

Gorbachev ended armed confrontations in the Baltic Republics, and Gorbachev recognized the independence of Estonia, Latvia, and Lithuania in 1991. As the Baltic Republics gained independence, the Ukraine and other republics prepared to leave the Soviet Union. Yeltsin took action on his own. He negotiated a loose military and economic alliance (**Commonwealth of Independent States**) of republics. After this, Gorbachev resigned. His policies led to an end of the Soviet Union.

The Soviet "Ship Of State" Sinks, Leaving The Former Republics To Survive On Their Own.

World
Issues:

*Determination of
Political and
Economic Systems*

A New Power Structure

The **Commonwealth of Independent States** (CIS) became a loose alliance of former Soviet republics with little central control. Critics compare it to the weak U.S. government under the Articles of Confederation (1781-1789). CIS members agree on only a few policies.

The U.N. gave Russia the Security Council seat that belonged to the U.S.S.R. Other republics applied for U.N. membership. Yeltsin continued the Gorbachev's pattern of foreign policy. He shares some control of the nuclear arsenal with other CIS members. However, the republics oversee the bases on their soil. Questions about the military, foreign policy, currency, and trade relations remain unanswered.

Change

Like Yeltsin in Russia, new leaders in the Ukraine, Belarus, and Kazakhstan control their new governments. Unresolved civil struggles plague the Transcaucasian and Central Asian regions. In some areas, the Communist Party retains power.

Economic chaos concerns leaders. Market systems work on trial and error. It takes time before consumers and producers achieve price equilibriums. In Russia, the government ended many price controls, but currency is unstable and shortages of most products exist. Russians are fearful and angry. Some have demanded a return to the communist system. Some foreign aid is helping Russia. Yeltsin seeks more. However, private foreign investors lack confidence to risk long term investment in the region's development.

The Force Of Nationalism In The Region

In the western areas of the region, Slavic groups dominate Russia, Belarus, and the Ukraine. They use the Cyrillic alphabet and are mainly Eastern Orthodox Christians. They are strongly nationalistic and guard their independence fiercely.

In the Baltics, the Latvians, Lithuanians, and Estonians differ linguistically and culturally from the Slavic groups. The Baltics share a long history of struggles for their existence. They use the Latin alphabet and are mainly Roman Catholics and Protestants. The Baltic Republics have strong national identities. As coastal nations, their sea links with Poland and Western Europe are vital to survival.

Identity

The Transcaucasian region is in turmoil. Among the more than forty ethnic groups there are many diversities of language, traditions, and religions. Christian Armenians and Muslim Azerbaijanis have been in an armed struggle over territory for years.

The forces of tradition and modernization threaten the Central Asian republics. Islam and Muslim culture predominate. Turkish and Iranian influences are strong. Political possibilities range from a new federation to further fragmentation.

The Force Of Religion In The Region

The *glasnost* policy eased religious restrictions. Resumption of active practice of religion gained strength. Churches reopened. Training of the clergy increased. Many young people are attending services. Baptisms and marriages in the Orthodox Church increase. However, anti-semitism is on the rise. Disturbing news reports say that the Pamyat, a local racist group, frequently attacks Jews.

The Force Of Democracy In The Region

Glasnost awakened a new generation of regional peoples to freedom. The power of the pro-democracy movement astonished the world. Its force surprised the older generation, trained under totalitarian regimentation. Long silent, the people criticized their government and the quality of their lives. They participated passionately. They joined campaigns and ran for office. The new regional parliaments bristled with political and economic reform proposals.

The success of democratic reforms in the region depends on implementation. Success also rests on setting up free economies. *Glasnost* worked far better than *perestroika*. *Glasnost* opened a repressive government to criticism and let people participate. *Perestroika* promised a free economy. People who have almost no skill or experience making economic decisions must enter a risky, insecure world. Democracy depends on establishing a free economic life.

C.Totalitarianism In Eastern Europe
Political Patterns After World War I

At the end of World War I, both the Ottoman and the Austro-Hungarian Empires disappeared. For leaving the war, Russia lost considerable territory in Eastern Europe. The region's many ethnic groups desired national autonomy. The 1919 Paris Peace Conference tried to satisfy those desires. At the Conference, diplomats signed numerous treaties creating new nations from the rubble of the old empires: the three Baltic Republics, Czechoslovakia, Hungary, Poland, and Yugoslavia.

The new national boundaries dissatisfied many of the smaller minorities. Power struggles among opposing groups made the new governments unstable. Most of the new nations began as democracies. The need to solve the land reform problems, ethnic clashes, the inexperience with self government overwhelmed the new nations. In little more than a decade, all except Czechoslovakia fell into some form of totalitarian dictatorship.

Eastern Europe

Soviet Dominance After World War II

During World War II, either the Nazis or Soviets held the Eastern European nations. As the war ended, the Red Army pushed the Germans westward. The Soviets set up communist puppet governments backed by the presence of Soviet occupation forces. After the War, the military remained to make the nations Soviet Satellites (near colonies). The Warsaw Pact and COMECON bound the nations to the U.S.S.R. militarily and economically. (See Sections IV and V for details on these treaties.)

Despite this Soviet control, there was resistance. In 1956, Khrushchev denounced Stalin's brutal rule. This triggered democratic revolutions in Hungary and Poland. Soviet troops crushed the revolts. In 1968, Warsaw Pact nations joined in suppressing a revolt in Czechoslovakia. Afterwards, the **Brezhnev Doctrine** declared the Soviet Union would intervene in any nation where communist rule was threatened.

Pro-Democracy Movements

When Gorbachev unleashed *glasnost* in the U.S.S.R., he allowed it to extend into the Eastern European nations. In some cases, he urged the communist regimes to copy his *glasnost* and *perestroika* reforms. He did not order Soviet troops to help faltering communist regimes. Pro-Democracy movements unseated communists and set up freer governments. Gorbachev played a major role in unifying the two Germanies.

In the early 1980's, the move toward democracy in Poland caused nationwide strikes by labor unions joined under the **Solidarity** organization. Led by **Lech Walesa**, Solidarity received backing from Roman Catholic Church leaders. The government outlawed Solidarity and imprisoned some of the strike leaders. In the mid 1980's, Gorbachev's policies revived the Solidarity movement. In 1989, Poland held free elections. Solidarity candidates won 99 of 100 senate seats. In 1991, Walesa won the presidency. The government replaced the command system with a free market structure. The Walesa government **privatized** (sold to private businesses) former state factories and production facilities. This was not a simple task. Poland has deep economic problems. Difficult negotiations with the West have not stabilized the shaky economy.

Lech Walesa

The influence of pro-democracy movements in Yugoslavia reopened age old ethnic feuds. Ethnic nationalist movements Balkan minorities arose as they had before World War I. President Milosevic's communist regime could not stop bloody outbursts. The pro-democracy movement led to Yugoslavia's disintegration.

Intervention by the European Community and the U.N. led to a truce in the ethnic and religious civil war in 1991. Bosnia, Croatia, Slovenia, and Macedonia became independent. Serbia and Montenegro remained united under the name Yugoslavia. (See map pg. 311.)

In 1992, strong Serbian nationalist groups began fighting Croats and Muslim groups for power in Bosnia. The insurgents received aid from Yugoslavian Serbs. Deaths, destruction and dislocation of people mounted. The E.C., N.A.T.O., and the U.N. negotiated to end the fighting. In June 1993, the U.S. agreed to aid in a U.N. peacekeeping mission, but the "Balkan powder keg" remains volitile.

Former political prisoner and playwright **Vaclav Havel** led Czechoslovakia toward democracy. The country's 1948 constitution recognized two major ethnic regions - the west for Czechs and one in the east for Slovaks. By 1992, the pro-democracy movement led to the two regions separating quietly (the **"Velvet Revolution"**). The Czech Republic emerged as a strong industrial nation , while the agricultural east emerged as Slovakia.

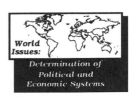

World Issues:
Determination of Political and Economic Systems

The reunited Germany, Poland, the Czech Republic, Slovakia, and Hungary appear to have good chances for democracy. They have more experience with democratic institutions and free market structures. Global concerns with the breakup of the Soviet Union have deflected attention from the struggling Eastern European nations. Political and financial support has diminished. Loss of former Soviet markets presents economic problems for the former satelites

Questions

1   War Communism called for
   1   a revolution of the peasantry.
   2   worker control of industries.
   3   free markets for agricultural produce.
   4   suppression of Lenin and the Bolsheviks.

2   The New Economic Policy (1921-1928) called for
   1   government ownership of all the means of production.
   2   some elements of capitalism in the economy.
   3   forceful sale of agricultural produce to the government.
   4   collectivization of farms.

3   Josef Stalin was
   1   the founder of the Red Army.
   2   a brilliant orator.
   3   General Secretary of the Party.
   4   a believer in immediate worldwide revolution.

4   During the 1930's, Stalin tried to strengthen his hold on the U.S.S.R. by
   1   purging many of his opponents.
   2   increasing the civil rights of the people.
   3   encouraging the development of capitalism.
   4   signing an alliance with the democracies.

5   The first Five Year Plan had as a major goal
1   expansion of consumer industry.
2   establishment of private farms.
3   strengthening of heavy industry.
4   increasing imports.

6   The collectivization of farms
1   failed completely.   3   increased livestock production.
2   was opposed by peasants.   4   increased farm employment.

7   During the 1930's, an industrial development of the Soviet Union might best be described as
1   a slow steady increase.
2   a period of tremendous growth.
3   largely centered west of the Ural Mountains.
4   slowed by insufficient coal and iron.

8   As General Secretary and Premier of the U.S.S.R., Nikita Khrushchev
1   expressed strong support of Stalin's actions.
2   did not expand the farm area.
3   faced no major foreign crises.
4   followed a policy he called "peaceful coexistence."

9   Under General Secretary Leonid Brezhnev, the U.S.S.R.
1   returned to Stalin's foreign policy.
2   decreased attention to consumer industry.
3   began a policy of detente with the West.
4   refused to negotiate on arms reductions.

10 President Gorbachev's policy of glasnost involved
1   increased cultural exchanges.
2   restrictions on Jewish immigration.
3   complete freedom of the press.
4   ending all capitalist activity in the economy.

11 To aid the troubled Soviet economy, Gorbachev
1   increased the role of central planners.
2   created large numbers of collective farms.
3   permitted private ownership of small businesses.
4   decreased production of consumer products.

12 The general pattern for treatment of dissenting groups in the Soviet Union under communist control was one of
1   persecution.   3   protection of civil rights.
2   encouragement of religion.   4   toleration.

13 Today, the Orthodox Church in Russia is
1   experiencing a large increase in the number of priests.
2   opposing the glasnost policy of Gorbachev.
3   having an increase in baptisms and marriages.
4   attracting primarily young people.

14 Before the Soviet Union disintegrated, women were
1   in the highest positions in the country.
2   receiving equal pay for equal worth.
3   encouraged to remain in the home.
4   not allowed to become doctors or teachers.

15 Under the U.S.S.R.'s totalitarian regime, artists were
1 allowed complete freedom of expression.
2 expected to portray themes of "social realism."
3 denied access to the necessary tools of their trade.
4 limited by their lack of an artistic heritage.

16 An area of weakness in Russian technological development is (the)
1 space program.   3 military hardware.
2 development of computers.   4 atomic weapons.

17 During the inter-war period, the countries of Eastern Europe
1 successfully dealt with their minority problems.
2 carried out comprehensive land reform programs.
3 frequently fell victim to dictatorships
4 remained under the loose control of the Austrian Empire.

18 Which of the following happened in the U.S.S.R. after World War II?
1 There was little evidence of dissent between the communist countries.
2 There were several attempts at revolution in Eastern Europe.
3 Soviet leadership of the communist countries was only challenged by Cuba.
4 The Soviet Union never interfered in the affairs of its satellites.

19 During the period of totalitarian rule in the Soviet Union, which group had the most political power?
1 the Supreme Soviet
2 the Russian Orthodox Church
3 the Communist Party
4 the Commonwealth of Independent States

Essays

1 Leaders of the U.S.S.R. (and now Russia) have shown an ability to change policies to fit shifting conditions. Choose *three* of the following pairs. Explain the circumstances surrounding the event mentioned and how it affected the policy of the leader with whom it is paired. [5,5,5]

 a Post civil war economic conditions - Lenin

 b Purge of the Red Army - Stalin

 c World-wide emphasis on human rights - Gorbachev

 d Change to democracy - Yeltsin.

2 Economic dissatisfaction has been a source of many problems in Russian History. Discuss any *three* of the following: [5,5,5]

 a economic problems in 19th century Russian history.

 b the economic causes of the Russian Revolutions of 1917.

 c the problems caused by the implementation of the Five Year Plans.

 d the economic problems faced by Yeltsin.

IV. Economic Development
A. Command Economy

Today, the republics of Eastern Europe, Central Asia, and Russia struggle to change **command economies** (run by central decision making). A **market system** (individual decision making) replaces official agencies such as the old Soviet **Gosplan**. Ideally, personal choice and the profit motive will become the driving force of the economy as it is in the West. It is impossible to drop all government roles. However, a free market works best with **laissez-faire** (minimal government regulation).

After the November 1917 Revolution, a policy of **War Communism** was followed during the Civil War (1917-1921). As a result of the economic scarcities resulting from the chaos of this period, Lenin instituted the **New Economic Policy** (NEP). NEP allowed some capitalist incentives to encourage production while the government maintained ownership of the major means of production.

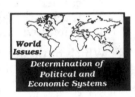

World Issues:

Determination of Political and Economic Systems

Heavy Industry vs. Consumer Goods

In 1928, Stalin instituted the first **Five Year Plan** which placed primary emphasis on the development of heavy industry, but recognized that an increase in agricultural production would be crucial to success in the industrial area. Gosplan made the economic decisions based upon the national goals established by the Party and the estimates of needs sent up the hierarchical ladder from the local factory managers. An enormous amount of paperwork was involved and there were frequent problems with under or overproduction of a particular product. However, spectacular growth was achieved, especially in areas such as coal, iron, and steel production.

Because of the emphasis on heavy industry, little was done initially to improve consumer goods production. Scarcity of consumer goods was the **opportunity cost** (economic "trade-off") of heavy industry. Also, there were frequent complaints of poor quality of goods because of the emphasis on achieving quotas. In effect, people were required to make sacrifices for future generations. There was little sympathy for the human costs in the relentless drive for rapid industrialization.

Choice

Under Brezhnev and Kosygin, some decentralization of planning occurred and there was a brief period when a higher priority was placed on production of consumer goods, but high military production and poor agricultural yields reversed the trend on consumer production.

Gorbachev's *perestroika* tried to increase production of consumer goods. Ownership, management, and profit sharing arrangements changed drastically in factories and farms. *Perestroika* called for **privatization** (placing government facilities under private ownership and reducing government regulation of business). Old government bureaus dragged out conversion to market structures. Some bureaucrats feared loss of power. Some communists resented market reforms. Many workers simply did not understand or trust the

**The Frustrations
of Gorbachev**
*... the world loves
me, so why did
everything fall
apart at home?...*
(Compare to the
cartoon
on page 326.)

new incentives. Confusion mounted. Production dropped. Agricultural production nearly halted. Shortages grew worse. Anger and resentment against Gorbachev mounted as suffering increased.

To balance the nation's finances, Gorbachev reduced the military and foreign aid by: 1) increasing incentives to state farms and factories; 2) enabling the ruble to be valued as an international currency; 3) allowing more foreign investment and businesses to operate in the U.S.S.R. (a MacDonald's Restaurant opened in Moscow in late 1989); 4) allowing more small businesses to be privately owned and operated.

These economic changes encouraged Westerners. However, for more than two generations, the population was educated under a communist system. Many were suspicious. Many did not wish to give up the security of socialist benefits for the risks of competitive capitalism. Others, such as Russian Federation President **Boris Yeltsin**, felt the communist command system failed. He felt that preserving it was useless.

World Issues: World Trade and Finance

These divisions led to the August 1991 coup by those who wished to restore the communist system (see section III). Yeltsin and his followers helped Gorbachev win. Afterwards, Gorbachev remained too cautious for Yeltsin and the market reformers. Yeltsin prodded and finally took the initiatives that led to the end of the U.S.S.R. and Gorbachev's resignation.

Problems In Agriculture

The most troubled part of the economy has traditionally been agriculture. Beginning with the first Five Year Plan, small farms were collectivized against the vigorous and sometimes violent protests of the peasants. As already indicated, many peasants were executed, imprisoned, or exiled to Siberia and about 50% of the existing livestock was slaughtered in protest.

Choice

It was hoped that collectivization would release farm workers for factory jobs, give the government increased control over production, and increase efficiency. Initially, all farm products except those from the private plots were sold to the government which could then set prices and establish allocation priorities.

Farm Type	Size	Method Of Paying Workers
Collective	Varied, but smaller than state farm	Shared in the profits of collective and kept after tax profits from private plots.
State	Average size was 75,000 acres	Paid factory workers with similar benefits.

Private plots on **collective farms** (2-3% of the land) produced nearly one-third of the dairy products, vegetables, and meat in the old Soviet Union. Khrushchev set up most of the **state farms** under his Central Asian "virgin lands policy." The land and climate were unsuitable for this ambitious project. Its failure forced Khrushchev from office.

Scarcity

Khrushchev also tried to decentralize agricultural planning. Local incentives did increase farm production slightly. Also, when Kosygin, Brezhnev, and Gorbachev put more money into farm machinery and transportation, production increased. However, the spending programs were inconsistent and so was production.

Russia still imports food. Market reorganization, and breakdowns in the transportation system caused production to drop in 1991. There were critical food shortages. Humanitarian food supplies flown in from Western nations helped Russians survive.

World Trade

World Issues:
World Trade and Finance

Until recently, Russia's trading partners were the COMECON members in Eastern Europe. Gorbachev's *glasnost* and *perestroika* policies allowed Eastern European nations to turn toward trade with Western Europe. The policies encouraged Western businesses to broaden trade inside the U.S.S.R. Occidental Petroleum, Pepsico, McDonald's and others responded. The August 1991 coup slowed the momentum, but economic ministers are working to encourage foreign investment.

World Issues:
Energy: Resources and Allocations

Russia has tremendous wealth in natural resources and leads the world in the production of such vital resources as coal, iron ore, and oil. It also has a greater variety of mineral resources than any other country in the world. In the past, the government devoted much effort to developing mineral resources. There is a base for exporting these resources. It may be the main hope for the country's survival

Technological Advancement

Russia has been a world leader in technological development. The space program is an outstanding example of its progress. Its "firsts" included: the first space satellite in 1957, first manned space orbit in 1961, the first space-walk, the first space station, and two Venus probes in 1982. However, outside of these programs bureaucrats traditionally discouraged technological innovation. Since 1983, new programs began to provide financial incentives for advances in technology.

Education has long received priority in the country. It begins with state operated kindergartens and nursery schools that also serve as day care centers. Compulsory education begins at age 6 and continues until 17, six days a week. The system is centralized with the same textbooks being used throughout the country. Major emphasis is placed on mathematics, science and foreign languages.

At age 15, students take a state examination that determines whether they prepare for a university or go to a trade school. Those who train for a university take an additional examination at the end of their high school careers to qualify; about one in five students is accepted by a university. University education is free and students are given a special living allowance.

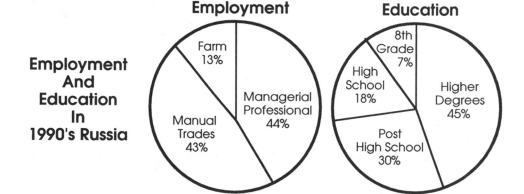

Employment And Education In 1990's Russia

Employment
- Farm 13%
- Managerial Professional 44%
- Manual Trades 43%

Education
- 8th Grade 7%
- High School 18%
- Post High School 30%
- Higher Degrees 45%

Housing

A scarcity of housing or adequate housing, especially in major cities, is a weakness of the economy. In the aftermath of World War II, housing was erected speedily and without much concern for quality. As a consequence, much of what does exist is in poor condition.

For those in lower income brackets, state housing was predominant and the rent was fixed at 4 to 5% of income. The average number of rooms in state housing is 2.3, and 88% had indoor plumbing.

B. Democratic Changes And Economy

Problems continue with the inadequate quantity and poor quality of housing in the region. As the governments reduce the military, even more housing is needed. Germany is sending funds to aid housing development so that Soviet troop withdrawal will continue. The movement toward a market encourages individuals to buy their homes and apartments. The need for housing does create new construction jobs. However, the countries' money problems make it difficult to fund new housing projects.

The move toward democracy eased tensions between east and west. It has Western governments reconsidering trade policies. Some will change bans on exporting new technology to the former Soviet republics. The new countries may have more access to computers and electronics. Concerns still exist about the former Soviet nuclear and space programs, however. Western governments fear that nations such as Libya, Iran, and Iraq may try to purchase technology with military applications, or recruit trained personnel involved in these programs.

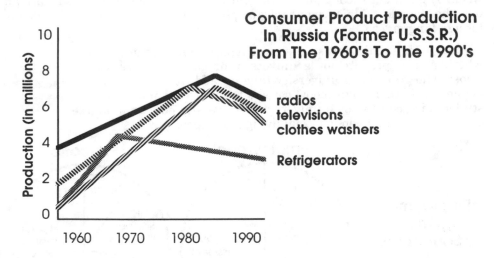

Consumer Product Production In Russia (Former U.S.S.R.) From The 1960's To The 1990's

radios
televisions
clothes washers

Refrigerators

Questions

1 Until Gorbachev, Soviet leaders hoped that collectivization of farms would
   1 establish a market economy.
   2 increase the number of farm laborers.
   3 increase government control over production.
   4 eliminate problems of overproduction.

2 In agriculture, Gorbachev's reforms tried to
   1 eliminate the private plots.
   2 decrease incentives on the collectives.
   3 improve ties between farmers and their markets.
   4 increase the number of farm laborers.

3 Russia recently increased trade with
   1 other communist nations.   3 COMECON allies.
   2 Western nations.   4 less developed countries.

4 In terms of mineral resources, Russia has
   1 the greatest variety of mineral resources of any country.
   2 had to import large quantities of coal and iron ore.
   3 many easily exploited resources.
   4 almost no known oil reserves.

5   Which reflect U.S. government trade policies with former republics of the U.S.S.R.?
1   a free trade approach
2   prohibition on the export of grain
3   support for the oil pipeline construction
4   limits on exports of "hi-tech" products

6   Which is true of education in the former republics of the U.S.S.R.?
1   Primary emphasis is placed on the humanities.
2   Major exams for students have been abolished.
3   It is designed to meet the needs of the government.
4   There are few vocational training centers.

7   People accustomed to state direction through a command economy find it hard to
1   accept the risks of market-oriented economies
2   use natural, human and financial resources efficiently
3   eliminate the use of consumer goods
4   accept central planning by the government

Essay

Discuss *each* statement below, using specific information to prove the validity of each statement. [5,5,5]

a   Communist economic goals ignored the needs of individuals.

b   *Perestroika* used capitalist incentives to solve economic problems.

c   Agriculture presents most critical economic problems for the republics of the former Soviet Union.

V. The Former U.S.S.R. And Eastern Europe In The Global Context

A. Soviet Foreign Policy: 1917-1945

In the aftermath of World War I, the Western European countries and the United States were very concerned about the spread of communism. The communists' attempt to seize power in Germany, and the actual seizure of Hungary, confirmed the fears of the democracies and made them reluctant to establish normal relations with the Soviet Union.

It was not until 1933, in fact, that the United States diplomatically recognized the existence of the Soviet Union. The U.S.S.R. did not join the League of Nations until 1932. However, the increasing power of the Soviet Union forced the Western nations to acknowledge its presence, although they were not prepared to cooperate in a Soviet desired collective security arrangement during the mid-1930's.

By the time that the threat of Nazism was clearly recognized by the democracies, Stalin had grown distrustful of the West and was willing to reach a temporary accommodation with Nazi Germany. The **Nazi-Soviet Non-Aggression Pact** (1939) was the result. This agreement recognized Soviet interests in Finland, the Baltic states, and the Bessarabian region of Romania, and agreed to divide Poland between the Soviet Union and Germany. The Soviet Union promised to stay out of any war between Germany and Poland or Germany and the democratic nations of the West. This agreement was the signal for Germany to attack Poland without fear of a two-front war. It led directly to the outbreak of World War II.

In June 1941, Hitler attacked the U.S.S.R., an attack that was not totally unexpected. Soviet expansion into Eastern Europe concerned the Germans, who were interested in the agricultural area as a compliment to their industrial base. Romania, Bulgaria, Hungary, and Yugoslavia were all occupied by the German Army. Hitler then moved to obtain the grain producing area of the Ukraine and the oil wells of the Caucasus.

By the Fall of 1941, the German Army had advanced to the outskirts of Moscow and Leningrad. The Red Army held its positions. By the summer of 1942, the siege of Stalingrad began, but the German Army was exhausted and the "scorched earth" policy of the Soviets deprived the Germans of any ability to live off the land.

By late summer, the Germans began an all-out assault on Stalingrad which Stalin ordered held at all costs. With the aid of the Russian winter, General Zhukov was able to begin a counteroffensive that was not to end until the War was over.

A contributing factor to the Soviet stand at Stalingrad, and the subsequent offensive, was the arrival of aid from the United States. American war materials and supplies reached the Soviet Union along routes through the Persian Gulf and the Arctic Ocean. Although the Allied help was indispensable to the Soviet war effort, it must be stated that the Soviet Union lost more men at Stalingrad than the U.S. lost in the entire War.

During the War, the leaders of the United States, Great Britain, and the Soviet Union met at a series of wartime conferences to discuss strategy and postwar plans.

Wartime Conferences		
Conference	**Participants**	**Major Decisions**
Teheran	Stalin, Roosevelt, and Churchill	Open a second front on the continent to ease the pressure on the Russian front.
Yalta	Stalin, Roosevelt, and Churchill	Free elections to be held in Russian occupied Eastern Europe; Germany to be divided into four occupation zones; USSR to enter war against Japan in exchange for territories lost in 1905; U.N. to be established with big power veto.
Potsdam	Stalin, Truman, & Churchill (later-Atlee)	Agreements on demilitarization, denazification of Germany; provisions for war crimes trials for Nazis; and reparations in kind with the Soviets to receive the most.

Unfortunately for the Western nations, these wartime agreements laid the basis for much of the Soviet power in the postwar world. By the end of the war, the European nations had lost much of their power and their ability to act as counterweights to the Soviet Union. There were essentially two world superpowers, the U.S. and the U.S.S.R.

B. Communism In Eastern Europe

The postwar exhaustion and economic desolation of Western Europe made the Eastern Europe area vulnerable to the Soviet power. As the Red Army pushed the Germans back across Eastern Europe, communist regimes were established in the countries liberated from Nazi control.

These puppet regimes were aided by the continued presence of the Red Army which indicated the Soviet Union's determination to establish a buffer zone between itself and Western Europe. A series of friendship and economic treaties made the economies of the satellite countries and the Soviet Union interdependent.

Attempts on the part of the satellites to establish full national independence, such as in the cases of Hungary in 1956, Czechoslovakia in 1968, and Poland on numerous occasions, have been met with threats and the outright use of force and denial of human rights (see page 290).

Church Influence

The Roman Catholic Church has often led protests in countries such as Hungary and Poland. In 1949, when the Hungarian government seized Church lands, nationalized Church schools, and dissolved Church organizations, Josef Cardinal Mindszenty encouraged demonstrations. He was sentenced to life imprisonment. He was freed in the 1956 Revolution and given asylum in the U.S. Embassy. Later, Mindszenty was removed from his position of leadership in Hungary by the Vatican. This paved the way for a 1964 accord that led to an improvement in church-state relations.

In the case of Poland, the Church has been a leader in the dissent directed against the communist regime, continuing the centuries old link between religion and nationalism in Poland. In 1978, the election of the first Polish Pope, **John Paul II**, intensified this relationship and called international attention to the position of the Church in Poland.

Human Rights　At times, the Church has tried to act as an intermediary between the people and the state. Some local parish priests defied church hierarchy and were outspoken in their support for the outlawed Solidarity union, defying the Polish Church hierarchy. As the government yielded to popular calls for reform, the Church leaders joined with Solidarity and anti-communist groups to bring about an end to total communist control of the government.

Communists Lose Power

As the decade of the 1980's closed, every Eastern European state was the scene of some open opposition to communist authority. In Poland, East Germany, and Czechoslovakia, democratic movements caused the resignations of Communist Party leaders after accepting constitutional changes allowing coalition governments. Romanians violently overthrew the harsh dictatorship of Nicolae Ceaucescu and executed him. However, in both Romania and Bulgaria, communists remain entrenched as the main political group.

Until recently, the nations of Eastern Europe were tightly controlled by the U.S.S.R. economically, militarily, and diplomatically. The **Council of Mutual Economic Assistance (COMECON)** was established in the aftermath of World War II as the Soviet answer to the Marshall Plan of the United States. COMECON was used to develop an interdependence between the economies of the satellites and the Soviet Union. While Eastern European dependence on the U.S.S.R. for oil and markets for their goods is still strong, there are obvious signs that the economic pattern is being changed as the Eastern European nations move toward modifying their economic structures.

In 1955, the Soviets created the **Warsaw Pact Alliance**. It combined the military forces of the satellite nations under Soviet command. This gave the Soviets control of the armed forces of the Eastern European nations.

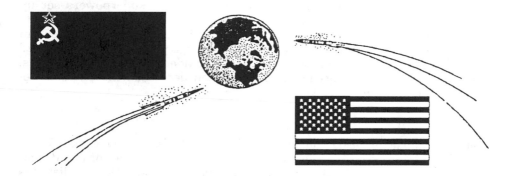

C. Cold War Confrontations

During the past World War II period, the U.S. and the Soviet Union were adversaries in many fields. There was constant military competition, a space race, a struggle for the loyalty of the Third World, and an economic competition designed to prove the worthiness of their respective economic systems. As a consequence, the **Cold War** developed (an intense conflict in which the two superpowers use all means, short of direct military engagement).

Military

Military strategies and technology changed so often, it was difficult to tell which nation had power. In the 1980's tensions relaxed. **SALT** (Strategic Arms Limitation Talks) and **START** (Strategic Arms Reduction Talks) limited nuclear arms, troops, and conventional weapons. After the collapse of communism and the disintegration of the U.S.S.R. in the 1990's, the situation changed completely.

Space Race

Initially, the Soviet Union had the lead in the space race with the first cosmonaut who orbited the earth, but the U.S. was able to accomplish the spectacular feat of landing men on the moon. Both nations continue to deploy military spy satellites as well as communications satellites.

Technology

Third World

Both sides in the Cold War used economic and military aid to gain support in the Third World. Less developed nations quickly learned the art of playing one superpower against the other to get more aid.

Economy

The U.S.S.R. made tremendous economic progress after World War II. It led the world in production of many vital resources. However, the Soviets lagged in industrial output and standard of living.

Cultural Programs

Despite intense Cold War competition, the superpowers set up valuable cultural exchanges. Students, farmers, and cultural groups exchanged visits. The **Bolshoi Ballet** drew large American audiences. American musicians and stage performers often toured the Soviet Union. Technological exchanges included joint space ventures. Diplomatic summit meetings in the 1980's often decreased the tensions between the superpowers.

Foreign Policy Differences

Cold War tensions eased considerably in the 1980's. However, the Soviet still had problems with China. Each considered itself the leader of world communism. Both sought to influence less developed nations. Border disputes continued along the Amur River and in Central Asia.

Problems in Central Asia

In the late 1970's and throughout the 1980's, Soviet leaders became concerned with the growth of Islamic fundamentalism in the southern border regions of Central Asia. The religious movement opposed the atheism of communism. It revitalized Muslim traditionalism. The Soviets invaded Afghanistan in 1979. They claimed this was to support the communist regime. However, it was also to check the spread of Islamic fundamentalism in the southern border republics.

D. Sweeping Change in the 1990's

Gorbachev's *glasnost* policies led to changes in the diplomacy of the Soviet Union. He decreased the Soviet presence in Eastern Europe, allowed the reunification of Germany, and released dissidents such as Sakharov and Sharansky. These moves opened doors to negotiations with the U.S. and the Western Allies. Economic changes under his *perestroika* opened the Soviet Union for foreign investment and trade.

In 1991, Gorbachev was nearly overthrown by reactionaries (see Section III). Yeltsin's assumption of power led to the dissolution of the Soviet Union and Gorbachev's resignation. How the new military and economic confederation called the Commonwealth of Independent States will function is in question. Yeltsin reassured the world that the new arrangement is stable. Many pessimists in the Western World now fear nuclear control is in doubt. All the newly independent republics have leaders with different ambitions. Optimists say the Cold War Era is over. A whole new era of foreign policy is at hand.

Questions

1 After World War I, the Soviet Union was
   1 treated as an ally by the democracies.
   2 spreading communism.
   3 immediately recognized by the U.S.
   4 never in the League of Nations.

2 What was the importance of the Nazi-Soviet Non-Aggression Pact?
   1 Hitler was free to attack Poland.
   2 It made the Germans supreme in the Baltic Sea area.
   3 Stalin promised to help Germany in its war against the democracies.
   4 The Soviet Union declared neutrality in World War II.

3 Hitler attacked the Soviet Union because
   1 it threatened his ally, Italy.
   2 he needed Soviet grain and oil.
   3 he feared Stalin's foreign policy in Asia.
   4 it expanded into Greece.

4 The major battle of Hitler's Russian campaign was
   1 Moscow.   3 Stalingrad.
   2 Leningrad.   4 Kiev.

5 Which was true of the economic status of the Soviet satellite nations of Eastern Europe during the Cold War?
   1 They were self sufficient in agriculture.
   2 They were very dependent on Soviets for vital resources.
   3 They were interdependent with Western European economies.
   4 They were free market systems.

6 Economically, the former satellite countries of Eastern Europe were
   1 agriculturally self-sufficient.
   2 dependent on the Soviets for vital resources.
   3 interdependent with the economies of Western Europe.
   4 free of government control.

7 The Warsaw Pact was the communist equivalent of
   1 NATO.   3 League of Nations.
   2 United Nations.   4 COMECON.

8 In the former communist satellite countries of Eastern Europe, the Roman Catholic Church was
   1 controlled by the government.
   2 treated with complete toleration.
   3 often in the leadership of government opposition.
   4 free from control by the Pope.

9   Which was true of the superpowers' attempts to limit the arms race during the Cold War?
1   They failed.
2   They succeeded from time to time.
3   They destroyed all nuclear weapons.
4   They only agreed to limit conventional arms.

10 What was a result of détente?
1   There was an increase in cultural exchanges.
2   Technological cooperation ended.
3   Both nations refused to participate in summit conferences.
4   Competition between nations ended.

11 The Islamic fundamentalist movement concerned the U.S.S.R. because it
1   needs Iranian oil.
2   fears its impact on its Muslim population.
3   wishes to preserve traditionalist ways.
4   supports freedom of religion for all groups.

12 Under Gorbachev, the Soviet Union pursued a policy of
1   refusing to allow dissidents to emigrate.
2   ignoring Western proposals on arms limitations.
3   increased cooperation and communication.
4   isolation from the West.

Essays

1   Major trends in Russian (and Soviet) foreign policy for centuries have included expansionism and the search for warm water ports.

   a   Briefly develop the pre-20th century historical roots for this statement. [5]

   b   Discuss Stalin's foreign policy in light of this statement. [5]

   c   Describe the policies of Soviet (And Russian) leaders after Stalin in relation to this statement. [5]

2   A major result of World War II was the emergence of the U.S. and the Soviet Union as the two superpowers. Their rivalry extended far beyond their opposing ideologies.

Fields

• Economics   • Technology and space
• Military   • Third World nations

Choose *three* of the above fields and, for *each one* explain their rivalry, and the impact of the rivalry in the fields selected in the global context. [5,5,5]

Unit Eight:
The World Today

One major idea stressed in this Global Studies course is the interdependence of the people of the regions studied. Today, more than at any other time in history, the people and nations have the ability to investigate, analyze, and discuss the issues that will affect the future. Life in the 21st Century will be influenced by international policies that are able to use present and future technology for the improvement of human conditions.

It is impossible to totally predict the future, but as author Alvin Toffler wrote in his sequel to *Future Shock* entitled *The Third Wave*:

"...asking the very largest of questions about our future is not merely a matter of intellectual curiosity. It is a matter of survival..."

The global community must face rapid changes in these areas:

- **population pressures**
- **political power structures**
- **human rights**

- **balance of world trade**
- **environmental issues**
- **technology**

I. Population Pressures

A. Population Growth In Developed And Developing Nations

It is important to realize the dramatic impact that increased population has upon world hunger, urbanization, and the achievement of improved standards of living. Many global issues such as overcrowding, depletion of resources, pollution of the environment, and political unrest are a direct result of overpopulation and the uneven distribution of the world's peoples. This is most evident in the overcrowded conditions in many of the world's urban centers, and more than 80% of these are located in the world's lesser developed nations.

World Issues:
Population

In 1800, only 3 percent of the world's people lived in cities. Today, over 40percent live in urban centers. Most of this increase is attributed to the steady migration of rural villagers seeking better economic opportunities. As this phenomena continues, traditional family patterns are changing from rural, agrarian (farm based), extended family lifestyles to urban, industrial-based, nuclear family lifestyles.

Change

Although slums may be found in any urban area, slums are even more prevalent in the less developed nations because availability of urban housing has not kept up with the rapid population increases and migrations. It is estimated by the United Nations that more than half of the urban population in the Third World nations live in slums, and this creates an ever widening gulf between the "haves" and "have nots."

United Nations and other international efforts help the poor. Volunteer efforts such as the Peace Corps, CARE, religious missions, and Live Aid also help. Inspiration also comes from efforts such as those of **Mother Teresa.** This Albanian Catholic nun founded Missionaries of Charity in the 1940's. The Missionaries treat the sick and starving in the less developed countries such as India. Mother Teresa received the Nobel Peace Prize (1979) for her lifelong efforts to relieve global suffering.

Contributing to this dilemma is the rising birth rate in many of the lesser developed nations due to religious objections to birth control. Large families (to assist in farming and to provide a sense of social support for elders) are also the norm in rural communities.

"Food Production falling behind Population Growth"

B. World Hunger

World Issues:
Hunger and Poverty

Most **demographers** (people who map population movements) agree that the world's population growth must be slowed if the world is to survive famine and hunger. It's a fact that hunger exists in every nation of the World. Many factors have contributed to hunger throughout the world, and some of these are political, environmental, economic, social, and technological. However, President John F. Kennedy may have said it best when he addressed the World Food Congress in Washington, D.C. in June of 1963:

> The war against hunger is truly mankind's war of liberation... There is no battle on Earth or space more important (for) peace and progress cannot be maintained in a world half-fed and half-hungry... We have the capacity to eliminate hunger from the face of the Earth. Victory will not come in the next year... but it must be in our lifetime.

The **United Nations Food and Agricultural Organization** which consists of agronomists, (agricultural economists), nutritionists, and philosophers continues their monumental task of developing strategies to combat world hunger. They stress that the battle can only be won through curbing population growth through the use of science and technology and good will and common sense. Very often hunger has not been the result of a shortage of food, but rather the unequal distribution of wealth and technology.

C. Education - A Growing Gap Between "Haves" And "Have-Nots"

Although global literacy has had a measurable decline in the last twenty years, the gap between those who have access to information and those who do not has continued to grow. For a lesser developed region or nation to modernize, it is most essential that the society have an educated citizenry.

the "Have" nations

the "Have Not" nations

D. Trade In An Interdependent World

Many nations have attempted to establish a balance between traditional values and modernization. This has been a difficult task to accomplish as increased world trade has established cross cultured connections and a growing sense of global interdependence. Very often the developing nations look to the economically advanced industrial western block nations for immediate solutions to their common problems of poverty, hunger, and lack of economic development. In their "revolution of rising expectations," the developing nations are demanding the following changes:

Interdependence

- A more equal balance of payment for natural resources and manufactured goods.
- Capital to finance infrastructure (transportation and communication networks) and to train skilled workers.

But Third World indebtedness has proven to be a threat to global financial stability, and the delicate balance of interdependency is being strained.

II. Economic Development And World Trade

World Issues:
World Trade and Finance

As the economic systems of the world have become more interdependent, decisions in one nation or region have vast implications for all regions. When the OPEC cartel reacted to Western nations aid to Israel in the 1970's, the cost of oil to the average consumer rose greatly. This caused inflation in the industrial nations and hardships for developing countries.

A. Growing Gap: Rich And Poor Nations

Newly independent nations remain highly dependent on the West for trade, foreign aid, and food. This has often led to bitterness and resentment. A comparison of the life expectancy and Gross National Product statistics illustrates the gap between rich and poor nations.

Nation	1988 GNP (billions)	Life Expectancy Male	Female
UNITED STATES	$5,200	71.6	76.3
SOVIET UNION	2,500	64.0	74.0
JAPAN	1,800	73.0	78.0
W. GERMANY	1,208	67.2	73.4
FRANCE	1,000	70.2	78.5
GREAT BRITAIN	843	70.2	76.2
PEOPLES' REP. OF CHINA	393	65.5	69.4
BRAZIL	375	61.6	65.7
INDIA	287	52.0	50.0
EGYPT	32.5	55.9	58.4
IRAN	93	57.1	59.0

B. Resource And Energy Management

Human resources are crucial to the world's future. Many of the developing nations have introduced population planning on a nationwide basis, where it has not conflicted with the dominant religion. Continued population growth has· a negative effect on an economy, urban development, and the general quality of life.

Financial resources are also crucial. Many developing nations are faced with large debts which are increasingly difficult to repay. In 1986, Mexico declared a moratorium on its payments to creditor nations. Economic development for all nations depends on prudent use of globally - scarce natural resources.

World Issues:

Economic Growth and Development

C. Tradition vs. Modernization

The conflict between cultural tradition and the pressure to adopt Western institutions has led to social unrest in some developing regions. Urbanization in Africa and India has lured people from the villages and weakened traditional cultures. Waves of migrants create congestion and breakdown of vital public services. Part of the reason for the Iranian Revolution in the late 1970's was an attempt to restore traditionalism to an underdeveloped nation which was in the process of becoming "Westernized."

World Issues:

Political and Economic Refugees

III. Changing Political Power Structures
A. The Superpowers
And The Cold War

Power

World War II so weakened France, Britain and other major powers that their colonial empires virtually collapsed. Two newer nations filled the power vacuum: the Soviet Union and the United States. These two nations became the poles for a new political competition: democratic government v. communist. Each grouped a bloc of allies around itself (NATO, SEATO, Warsaw Pact, etc.). Neutral nations tried to balance the complex structure. There were many diplomatic, military, economic, and ideologic confrontations. They occurred in every global region. Many times the superpowers were behind the scenes while small allies engaged in open warfare. Occasionally, there were confrontations over Berlin or Cuba. The collapse of the Soviet Union in 1991 and the fading of communist governments leads to speculation that this era is ending.

B. The Third World

As the developing nations gain maturity, they become an increasingly important factor in keeping the balance of peace. Their role and combined voting power in the United Nations is evidence of this.

Interdependence

The fading of Cold War confrontations does not mean the globe is free of threats. Russia and the Commonwealth of Independent States have authority over the former arsenal of the U.S.S.R. Other nations have nuclear weapons. Britain, France, China, India, Israel, and Pakistan are among them. U. N. inspection teams say Saddam Hussein is close to having nuclear capability in Iraq. A host of smaller countries have impressive military forces and often commit acts of aggression. Economic and political competition in less developed countries of the Third World is sometimes fierce. Many have military forces far beyond their needs. Some nations specialize in selling arms. Some encourage terrorists. Some wish to overthrow their neighbors by supplying arms to rebel forces. Keeping the peace in new world arrangement will not be easy.

Third World nations do not often share the same sense of responsibility for keeping the balance of peace, and many critics feel they present greater potential for upsetting the balance in seeking their national interests. Iraq's 1990 invasion of Kuwait is an example.

C. Arms Control
Differing Perceptions

While war is universally condemned as a means of settling international conflict, meaningful arms control measures are difficult to achieve. The

World Issues:
War and Peace

Limited Nuclear Test Ban Treaty (1963) and its counterparts for space and underwater have been relatively successful despite some nonadherence by nations such as France and China. The **Nuclear Non-Proliferation Treaty** (1968) was not signed by a number of countries which have gone on to develop nuclear capability. In fact, the U.S. and other nuclear countries have assisted nations, such as Pakistan, Israel, and Libya in developing peaceful uses of nuclear energy only to find that the aid has led those countries to develop nuclear weapons. As these nations become involved in disputes, the potential of nuclear war increases.

Status Today

Toward the end of the Cold War, the superpowers made several bilateral attempts at arms limitation. The series of treaties in the 1970's known as the **SALT** agreements, (Strategic Arms Limitation Talks) cut certain types of missiles and numbers of warheads. Problems arose over inspection procedures. The security of new weapons and technology always concern nations.

Technology

START (Strategic Arms Reduction Talks) continued limiting nuclear arms. Summit meetings between the superpowers reduced troop levels in Europe. Diplomats spoke of an end to the Cold War by the time Gorbachev resigned and the Soviet Union ceased to be (1991). Leaders of the new republics in Eastern Europe and Central Asia declared that the former Soviet arsenal was under control. Russia's President Yeltsin traveled to Western capitals with assurances that arms reduction would continue.

D. Terrorism As A Political Weapon

Terrorism has seen increasing use since the end of World War II as groups with large military forces struggle to achieve their political and economic goals. Groups such as the **Palestine Liberation Organization** (PLO), the **Irish Republican Army** (IRA), the **Red Brigades** in Italy, and assorted other small groups have resorted to terrorist attacks to bring attention to their demands. Evidence that these groups sometimes work together was seen in the 1973 attack on the Tel-Aviv airport in Israel by Japanese terrorists working with the PLO.

In 1981, investigations into the attempted assassination of Pope John Paul II indicated terrorists travel with great freedom through countries of Eastern Europe.

World Issues: **Terrorism**

Global attempts to stop terrorism have not met with great success. The U.N. has been relatively ineffective, but measures taken by individual countries to protect likely targets, increase travel security, and train anti-terrorist units to free hostages have had some deterrent effect.

IV. Environmental Issues

American biologist Renee Dubos believes that throughout history the Earth's peoples have behaved as if there were infinite amounts of air, soil, water, and other natural resources. The results have often been shocking. The world's environment has been gradually deteriorating into filthy water, foul air, and devastated lands. If humankind's existence depends on the protective **biosphere** (the thin layer of air, water, and soil surrounding the Earth), it is imperative that we establish a favorable balance between developmental growth and environmental concerns.

Environment

A. Pollution Of Earth And Atmosphere
Water And Earth Contamination

Throughout history, people have done little to protect the environment. But, as the Earth's population has increased dramatically in the 20th century, people have used more and more of the Earth's resources and created pollution of the air, water, and soil.

Air pollution has become most severe in the industrialized nations on our globe as millions of tons of waste are released each day into the atmosphere. These are visible in the form of smoke, smog, soot, and ash from factory smokestacks. They also emit carbon monoxide, hydrocarbons, and other toxic wastes.

Our water cycle has been interfered with as sewage and dangerous toxic wastes have been dumped into rivers, lakes, and oceans. Many of these contaminants have also found their way into people's drinking supplies. Some chemical pesticides and fertilizers have increased agricultural production, but have also poisoned the Earth. The difficulty of disposing of chemical **toxic waste** in industrial nations has led them to seek disposal sites in poorer, developing nations. There is now concern that whole regions of the Third World will become uninhabitable.

Acid Rain: International Issue

Acid rain (air pollutants that travel in precipitation) is a global concern. Natural resources like lakes, forests, plant and animal life suffer the adverse effects of acid rain pollution. Even our great landmarks of the past (sculptures and historical buildings) suffer from the corrosion caused by this form of contamination. Acid rain scars marble and corrodes bronze, destroying art as well as life. This has forced cultural as well as environmental groups to join forces and promote legislation to prevent the burning of sulfuric coal which is estimated to cause over 80% of the pollutants in acid rain.

Environment

However, many of the world's political leaders equate environmental protection with economic assaults on industry, and have failed to actively promote protective legislation. Yet, failure to act has caused unnecessary human suffering (lung disease) and billions of dollars in often irreparable damages to natural as well as physical resources.

B. Erosion And Desertification

Maintaining an ecological balance is necessary to prevent disasters like the widespread famine that has recently occurred in the Sahel in Africa. Loss of available land to the spreading desert (**desertification**) is not entirely a natural phenomena. Too many people, too many herds and over-cultivation of the dry areas of our world cause soil erosion.

Another devastating act that contributes significantly to soil erosion is **deforestation** (over-cutting of timber resources). This is occurring in Brazil's Amazon rain forests. When the ecological balance is over-strained, the land often becomes unsuitable for human habitation. More careful environmental planning by national leaders in areas of rural development is essential to prevent unnecessary disasters.

Greenhouse Effect

Yet another environmental issue arising from poor environmental management is the "Greenhouse Effect" (see illustration). Scientists feel it is already changing air quality, rainfall, and climatic patterns worldwide.

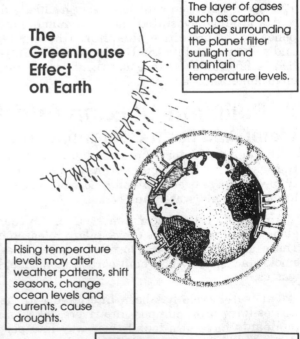

The Greenhouse Effect on Earth

The layer of gases such as carbon dioxide surrounding the planet filter sunlight and maintain temperature levels.

Rising temperature levels may alter weather patterns, shift seasons, change ocean levels and currents, cause droughts.

Deforestation, modern industries and urbanized life produce too many waste gases that have radically altered the composition of the planet's protective atmosphere.

C. Urbanization: Environmental Concern

Massive traffic jams, ugly factories, garbage and sewage problems, and a lack of green space (parks and gardens) characterize many of the world's urban centers. In many of the developing nations, poorly managed urban growth, has caused severe ecological damage in the breakdown of air and water quality and traffic pollution (noise and air).

Rashmi Mayur, a Bombay, India urban planner, wrote in an article, *"Supercities - The Growing Crisis,"* that some cities are becoming so gargantuan that, for most of the people living in them, life has become a nightmare. Large cities are exploding in the developing world as poor people migrate from villages and towns to search for survival in the cities.

World Issues:
Political and Economic Refugees

Very often they are escaping one wretched condition for another as shanty towns and slums continue to grow in alarming numbers. The cities simply do not have enough resources to provide for these millions of people who are seeking survival. How can cities cope and be revitalized? Mayur offers these suggestions for urban planners:

· Available resources must be judiciously and selectively used, and efforts must be made to develop new indigenous resources.

· The benefits of resources must be distributed equitably.

· A fair system of sharing and contributing resources must be assured.

Such role model cities as Zurich, Edinburgh, Leningrad, and Beijing can be used to demonstrate positive alternatives for desirable urban living.

D. Effects Of Development Upon The Seas

Another environmental concern is the threat to fish in our oceans, seas, and bays when garbage and sewage has been disposed in these areas.

Aside from over exploiting our world's major fishing grounds, a new phenomena called **anoxia** (oxygen depletion) has wiped out many shellfish. Environmental groups are closely monitoring the effects of aquatic life that is exposed to anoxic water. As fish are a significant source of protein in many people's diets, it is necessary to preserve these fishing areas from pollution and over exploitation.

Biologist René Dubos indicates it will be expensive to protect and restore our rapidly deteriorating environment. If we are to survive, he says we must accept **Stewardship of the Earth**, protecting it while using it. This will be difficult. For industrial nations it will mean accepting reduced living standards. For underdeveloped countries it may well mean never achieving the living standards of developed ones.

V. Human Rights

Attitudes about human rights differ greatly among nations.

A. Universal Declaration Of Human Rights

The foundation of modern thinking on human rights is found in the U.N. declaration pioneered by the efforts of Eleanor Roosevelt in the opening years of the United Nations. It contains the fundamental statement that all human beings are entitled to dignity and possess natural political, social, and economic rights such as freedom of speech, assembly, and a decent standard of living.

B. Helsinki Accords, 1975

The United States and the Soviet Union joined thirty-three other nations in signing a treaty in Helsinki, Finland, which pledged security and cooperation in Europe. The treaty formalized post-World War II territorial arrangements, but it also stated mutual respect for basic human rights and encouraged travel among the citizens of the signing nations.

C. Recent Violations Of Human Rights

Slavery, a denial of basic human rights, still exists in forced labor camps in totalitarian states and in some underdeveloped areas of the world.

Apartheid: South Africa

The intense efforts of the white majority to deny basic rights to the black majority through the policy of apartheid has recently begun to crumble. Constant protest and defiance of apartheid laws, international trade sanctions, divestiture, and world public opinion have created pressures the government can not stave off.

Dissidents And Forced Labor Camps: U.S.S.R.

During the 20th century, those trying to leave totalitarian nations have been denied human rights. For example, the Soviet Union often denied Jews permission to emigrate. Often, the government condemned **dissidents** (outspoken critics) as disloyal. It denied them work and decent housing. It exiled some dissidents to Siberian work camps or to mental institutions. This happened to the Nobel Prize winning physicist **Andrei Sakharov** in the 1970's.

Genocide: Cambodia And Uganda

Even in our age, mass political executions are carried out around the globe. The communist government in Cambodia under Premier Pol Pot initiated a massive and bloody purge of the country which resulted in nearly four million casualties from 1977 to 1985. In Uganda, under the bloody rule of Colonel Idi Amin (1971-79), an estimated 300 thousand of his political opponents were murdered.

Political Oppression In The Contemporary World

The collapse of Soviet communism cut foreign aid to Cuba. Until then, dictator Fidel Castro furnished troops, military training and supplies to communist rebel groups in Latin American and Africa. One short-lived success was in Nicaragua. Communist Daniel Ortega and his Sandinistas ruled there for a decade until defeated in a free election in 1989.

Across the globe in Sri Lanka, a Tamil minority continues to fight the Sinhalese majority and now resorts to terrorism. Both sides have ignored basic rights of innocent people.

World Issues:
Determination of Political and Economic Systems

In Northern Ireland, Protestant majority groups have denied human rights to Catholics who have often fought back through the radical terrorist attacks of the Provisional Wing of the Irish Republican Army.

VI. Technology

Throughout history, there have occurred certain noteworthy changes that have dramatically altered peoples' lifestyles. In previous centuries, the commercial age and the scientific and industrial revolutions have changed people's daily work and living habits. Today, the world is being transformed in an age of rapid technological development and the computer revolution.

John Naisbitt, author of the book **Megatrends**, is optimistic that our future holds great opportunities. What lies ahead for the World in the 21st century? An optimist would say a technological renaissance could free humankind from much of life's drudgery. The resulting economic boom could promote the highest standards of living in world history.

A. The Silicon Chip

The silicon chip demonstrates how modern technology can be packaged into low cost mass produced intelligence data gatherers that have and will continue to change every aspect of our global society. These single tiny chips made of material that can be easily mass produced for a few cents each have made it possible to open a world market of low cost computers for home, schools, industry, medicine, and government activities.

World Issues:
World Trade and Finance

A computer expert, Jon Roland of Texas, foresees these technological breakthroughs and economic consequences:

- *Instant Information* — a pocket size universal communications data bank network
- *Home Banking* — financial business conducted by tamper proof personal computers
- *Self-Guided Planes and Cars* — computers piloting vehicles safely to their destinations
- *Classroom Computers* — computer assisted instruction which is impartial, and adapts to the individual's needs

---

B. The Green Revolution

World Issues: Population

There is an old Mexican saying, *"a full belly, a happy heart. An empty stomach, be careful."* In order for political stability to exist in the world's developing nations, it is essential to raise enough food to support rapid population growth. By the year 2000, the projected world population will be six billion people. At that rate, our agricultural production must increase two-fold.

Technology

In the late 1960's, **The Green Revolution**, a scientific breakthrough developed wheat and rice seeds with extremely high yields. But, to obtain the best results, a high cost fertilizer made of petrochemicals was essential, but the farmers in the developing nations do not have the extra funds for this fertilizer. Very often, the Green Revolution has only benefited large plantation farmers who can afford both the irrigation and fertilizers.

As agronomist Norman Borlaug, the Nobel-Laureate and founder of the Green Revolution has stated, *"we have the possibility of keeping up with the world food situation. But it's going to mean a reallocation of resources - use of fuel for agriculture instead of the family car."* Humankind must be educated to see the benefits of these new techniques or lurking on the horizon may be large scale global famine in the developing nations of the world.

C. Medical Breakthroughs

Advanced medical knowledge and technology are changing the quality and length of human life. Can the majority of people live to the age of 100 or more and can wonder drugs cure such diseases as cancer, AIDS, and senility?

The current AIDS problem, transmitted through sexual contact and blood contamination, is a frightening example of the limits of medical knowledge. Neither a cure nor a vaccine has been found for the deadly HIV virus. It continues to infect large numbers of people around the globe. Public education aimed at prevention is still the main defense, but in underdeveloped and illiterate societies, educating the public is so difficult that there is fear their populations may be devastated in far worse proportions than even the recent famine in Africa. In the early 1990's, more than two million cases had been diagnosed just in the United States.

World conferences have been called, and concerted international medical effort have been launched by the U.N.

In the next century, the world's peoples can expect to live longer, healthier lives as medical scientists discover new treatments for major disorders. Transplants have created a major breakthrough in surgery, and the use of artificial parts on the human body is common even today. The genetic frontier poses perhaps the most controversial area of medical research as the power to manipulate genes must not be abused. On a positive note, the medical world may be able to cure many diseases by altering genes.

Drug treatments will continue to unlock cures for previous terminal diseases. One item that will not be easily cured is the problem of astronomical health costs, and ethical decisions concerning who will receive expensive medical treatment will create an ever widening gulf between the economic "haves" and "have nots" in the world.

D. Transportation And Communication

Faster, easier, more comfortable travel and a vast communications network controlled by powerful computers and laser beams is the technological scenario for today's infrastructure (transportation and communication network) and that of the future. Although the automobile will still remain the primary means of travel in the developed world, cars have and will become totally electronic and computerized. **Technology** Computerized high speed rail and air transportation is projected to ease the significant demands and the ability to move the Earth's people and products from one location to another.

Despite enormous costs, vast improvements must also be made to mass transit systems within the world's urban centers in order to prevent urban **gridlock** (enormous time consuming traffic congestion). In many corporate communication laboratories throughout the developed world, modern technology has created computers that talk, televisions that with the use of satellites provide hundreds of channels, and telephones that are small enough to be worn on a person's wrist.

As Thomas Emerson, a New York based physicist has stated, *"the limits won't be on technology but on man's imagination."* The challenge for the world's leaders will be finding a positive use for all of this creative knowledge.

E. Space Exploration

As with the Age of Exploration, 20th century technologies have developed a new frontier - space. Many scientists and historians predict that this process will carry Earth from its infancy to adulthood. They feel that space has the ability to create new knowledge, products, and an international cooperation that will help a depleted, and strife-ridden world.

It is hoped that through international cooperation the resources of space may be used to create a new found wealth for all the Earth's peoples without imposing negative effects on the environment in our world. Nevertheless, space exploration has had an effect on global communication and will continue to have an effect on relations between nations.

The people of our globe have a love-hate affair with the technological world in which they are living — they are both fascinated and horrified by the world that modern technology has shaped. But as John Naisbitt advocates in **Megatrends**: *"...if we can only get a clear vision of the road ahead. What a fantastic time to be alive."*

VII. Interaction Of Cultures
A. Linguistic Impact

As the world becomes increasingly global in outlook, various cultures are beginning to have significant impact on others. Nowhere is this more obvious than in language. During the Age of Imperialism, the languages of Europe were taught in the colonial possessions. Knowledge of them was a necessity

Culture

for natives who wished to advance in the colonial society. As a consequence, English is spoken by more Indians than any other language in that diverse country. Many people educated in former French and Portuguese possessions speak those languages.

Since the end of World War II, global communications in the form of radio, movies, and television have accelerated the development of an almost international language. Words or terms such as "Levis" and "rock music" are commonly used throughout the world. Technical language, involving computers

Identity

and electronic equipment of various types, has entered many languages in the mother tongue of the country responsible for development. Just as increased communication in earlier eras led to the establishment of national languages, it would appear that an international language is developing in some fields.

B. Institutions

Governments are often seen by people as a vehicle for achieving progress. People in the Third World countries imitated Western styles of government after their independence, in hope of obtaining rapid economic and political development. Many former colonial areas developed parliamentary systems modeled on those of Britain and France. Later they found that their circumstances did not fit the system adopted.

Political Systems

Many of the nations' parliaments fell under the dictatorial rule of a single person who, with military backing, appeared to give firmer direction against economic problems. In truth, the areas often lacked skilled labor and capital to develop rapidly.

Many such areas drifted into a socialist structure, seeking to have the government join enterprises in managing resources that individuals could not. Kenya, for example, allows a broad degree of individual capitalist activity and investment. Kenya's neighbors, with greater government control of their economies, have not done as well. Foreign investment in hotels, offices, factories, and even U.S. - based fast-food franchises are increasing in socialist countries.

C. Technologies

Many countries are desirous of increasing the level of their technology, but face a dilemma of trying to maintain their traditional culture in the face of rapid change. This was a problem experienced by Tsarist Russia under Peter the Great. Today, modern production techniques copied from the West or Japan mean nations must yield to heavy foreign investment. Countries sometimes try to protect their investments by denying export permits to protect their security.

D. Customs And Beliefs

As a result of improved communications, many customs and beliefs have spread from nation to nation. This has been recognized by the European Common Market. The EEC has established a cultural delegate and is attempting to start a European cultural market. One area that is becoming globalized is clothing style. High fashion designers select their inspiration from all historic periods. For example, the Victorian approach to women's blouses and dresses are popular as well as the fabric designs from early African civilizations.

As more people in a nation come into contact with other cultures, increasing numbers in urban areas adopt western fashions or blend them with their own native styles. Purity of native fashions is usually retained for cultural ceremonies, but otherwise assimilation is evident. Sports are especially internationalized. Baseball is enormously popular in Japan, tennis in Czechoslovakia, gymnastics in Eastern Europe, and soccer in the U.S.A.

Religious beliefs are also spread easily in the modern world. Islamic fundamentalism is a force well beyond revolutionary Iran. It is evident in Saudi Arabia, Egypt, Afghanistan, and parts of Central Asia. Western churches seek to spread their doctrines as they send young missionaries to do humanitarian work in developing nations.

Questions

1   From 1945 into the 1990's, which was primarily responsible for keeping world peace?
   1   the Security Council of the United Nations
   2   many nations
   3   the United States and the Soviet Union
   4   Western Europe

2   Which is true of less developed nations ("the Third World")?
    1   They always follow the policies of the superpowers.
    2   They always vote as a unified bloc in the United Nations.
    3   Self interest guides their loyalties.
    4   They refuse any responsibility for keeping world peace.

3   During the Cold War Era, the superpowers were unable to agree on
    1   questions involving nuclear tests.
    2   limits on long range nuclear missiles.
    3   Strategic Defenses systems for outer space.
    4   the permissible number of warheads.

4   Since the end of World War II, means of communication have
    1   increased the possibility of global war.
    2   increased similarities among people.
    3   decreased internationalism.
    4   decreased the spread of technology.

5   Many global issues such as overcrowding and pollution of the
    environment are a direct result of
    1   high unemployment.
    2   a farm based economy.
    3   overpopulation.
    4   a balance of World Trade.

6   A major factor contributing to the rapid growth of urban centers in the
    20th century is
    1   the search for better economic opportunities.
    2   the influence of village elders.
    3   peoples' love of crowded conditions.
    4   the development of the automobile.

7   A major reason for higher birthrates in the Third World is
    1   promotion of birth control devices.
    2   religious objections to practicing birth control.
    3   a population highly educated in hygiene.
    4   political leaders need large populations for military power.

8   Which of the following is a negative side of using pesticides and chemical
    fertilizers?
    1   They increase crop yields.
    2   They reduce the size of most vegetables.
    3   They may contaminate the soil.
    4   They encourage urban dwellers to move into farm country.

9   A major contributor to the creation of acid rain has been the
    1   underground nuclear testing.
    2   burning of sulfuric coal.
    3   emissions control testing of nations.
    4   wood-burning stoves.

10 Recently, a major world region where desertification has caused widespread famine and death has been
   1   China's Gobi Desert.
   2   Africa's Sahel.
   3   India's Punjab.
   4   the Atacama Desert of South America.

11 People who study the effects of population growth are called
   1   nutritionists.   3   demographers.
   2   futurologists.   4   anthropologists.

12 Aside from over-fishing many of our oceans, seas, and bays, humans have also killed many shellfish through a process called
   1   anoxia.   3   erosion.
   2   pneumonia.   4   deforestation.

13 A major reason for the success of the Silicon Chip in today's computer revolution is
   1   its low cost.
   2   its impressive large size.
   3   its limited ability to store information.
   4   the limited changes it can bring to human life.

14 One of the most significant negative aspects of the Green Revolution has been
   1   the production of too much food.
   2   the high cost of petrochemical fertilizers for high yields.
   3   the achievement of political stability in the developing world.
   4   the buying of time to forestall worldwide famine.

15 A major area of modern medical technology that raises a heated philosophical debate has been
   1   artificial human organs.
   2   genetic tampering.
   3   wonder drugs as cures for terminal diseases.
   4   prolonging old age.

16 The latest frontier in modern technology is space, and the vehicle that presently offers the best hope for space development is
   1   sputnik.   3   the space shuttle.
   2   the space lab.   4   liquid fueled rockets.

Essays

1 Discuss the impact that *three* of the following 20th century events have had on the Earth's environment. [5,5,5]

   - The nuclear accident (1986) at the Chernobyl plant in Ukraine (former U.S.S.R).
   - Desertification in the Sahel
   - British industrial air pollutants causing acid rain
   - Deforestation of the Amazon rain forest of Brazil

2   Discrimination has been a problem faced by many groups of people throughout the world.

a   Identify *two* groups that have experienced discrimination and showhow the group experienced discrimination. (Include the location, time period, and historical events) [9]

b   Describe a specific action taken by one group to overcome the discrimination. [3]

c   Discuss how successful the group was in overcoming discrimination. [3]

3   A definite economic gap exists between the developed and developing nations of our global community. Describe *three* major factors which have contributed to this problem, and give one suggestion that might help narrow the imbalance. [5,5,5]

4   The development of a global perspective has been increasingly apparent since the end of World War II.

> • Arms Control
> • Technology
> • Customs and beliefs

a   Identify one way in which each of the above fields has been affected by the global outlook. [9]

b   Explain how the "globalizing" of these fields will affect the future. [6]

5   In 1948, the United Nations General Assembly unanimously approved the Universal Declaration of Human Rights. The Declaration included the following rights:

> • Every person has the right to leave any country, including his/her own, and to return to that country.
> • No one shall be subjected to torture, or to cruel, inhuman or degrading treatment.
> • Everyone has the right to work and protection against unemployment.
> • No one's basic rights shall be violated on account of sex, race, or religion.
> • No one shall be subjected to arbitrary arrest, detention, or exile.

a   Select *three* of the above human rights. For *each one* discuss a specific example of a nation's violation of that right since 1948. Use a different nation for each right violated. [12]

b   Discuss *one* reason why the United Nations has been unable to protect the rights listed in the Universal Declaration. [3]

6　Many problems can be considered global because they affect people and nations beyond any one nation's borders.

- Scarcity of Energy Sources
- Spread of nuclear arms
- Poverty
- Lack of investment capital
- Terrorism

a　Choose *three* of the problems listed above. For *each one* chosen, show how the problem is global in nature. [9]

b　Discuss an attempt to deal with *each* of the problems analyzed in *a*. [6]

7　Technology has opened up new frontiers for humankind in the 20th century. Select *three* areas listed below and describe a significant benefit that technology can give to the world's peoples. [5,5,5]

- Computer Revolution
- Medical Breakthrough
- Space Exploration
- Green Revolution
- Infrastructure

Global Concepts

Concepts: *Examples*:

Change
Variation or alteration
of an existing situa-
tion...

- Effects of the Crusades [243]
- French Revolution [253]
- Independence for India [70]
- Communes in China [115]

Choice
Determining a
preference for a
particular idea or
system, ususally
applies to economic
decisions...

- U.S.S.R.'s communist system [335]
- Israel's mixed system [219]
- China's economic development under Deng Xiaopong [115]

Citizenship
The duties, rights, and
privileges of a member
of a state or nation...

- Direct democracy under Pericles in Athens [233]
- Forces that have kept political participation from developing in Latin America [169]

Culture
The common concepts,
habits, art, and
institutions of a group
of people...

- Influence of Confucian philosophy on Chinese civilization [96]
- Russian Contributions to the Arts [313]
- Golden Age of Muslim Culture [201]

Diversity
Characterized by many
different groups or
situations...

- Variation of South American landforms leads to a variety of life styles, crops, and separate cultures [155-156]
- Geographic factors have promoted diversity in Western Europe [230]

Empathy
To understand other
people's problems and
points of view ...

- Spanish missionary priests sought to understand and act to alleviate mistreatment of African slaves and Native Am. Indians [165]
- Industrial era reforms for workers [259]

Environment
The conditions and
circumstances
surrounding a group or
event...

- Rainfall shapes South Asian life [56]
- Rapid urban growth in Latin America [173]
- Size of Russia slowed its development [300]

Concepts: Examples:

Human Rights
Just and fair claims to
natural, traditional, or
legal powers and
privileges...

- Treatment of races in South
  Africa [33]
- Jews in Nazi Germany [271]
- Stalin forced collectivization in
  Ukraine [322]

Identity
Feeling being able to
share in the ideas and
experiences of others...

- Islamic Fundamentalism [220]
- Myths and legends in African
  history [17]

Interdependence
Being mutually
influenced or
controlled by similar
forces...

- Economic development of Southeast Asia and Japanese trade
  [84]
- Marshall plan aided post-WW II-
  recovery in Europe [282]

Justice
Fair and reasonable
administration of laws;
equitable behavior...

- Romans' Laws of the Twelve
  Tables [236]
- South Africa's racial problems [33]

Political Systems
Specific structures for
governing society...

- Evolution of British Parliamentary system [275]
- Power of the Communist Party
  in in totalitarian U.S.S.R. [322]
- Communism in Latin America
  [182]

Power
Capability to act
decisively in
situations...

- Japan's pre-World War II expansion [135]
- Rise of the Nazi State [270]

Scarcity
Limits on quantities of
goods and resources
necessitating allocation
and choices...

- Japan's dependence on other
  nations because of lack of critical
  petroleum resources [145]
- Middle East's economic
  development [218]

Technology
Practical application of
scientific principles for
productive uses...

- India's future tied to
  technological development [83]
- Europe's industrialization [258]

World Issues

Issues:	Examples:

War and Peace

Economic and political conflicts and accommodations often have far-reaching consequences because of the intricate network of global relationships.

- Europe and the preludes to WW I [262]
- Japan and the prelude to WW II [136]
- Arab-Israeli Conflicts [209-212]
- Cold War politics in Europe [288]
- Discussion of changing political power structures in today's world [351]

Population

Overpopulation not only has serious implications for the nation or region in which it occurs, but strains resources of others. Conflicts arise as crowded nations seek more territory or as people migrate to more sparsely populated areas.

- India's population problems [72]
- African Problems [44]
- Discussion of world population pressures [348]

Hunger and Poverty

The forces of industrialization, urbanization, and environmental depletion reveal inadequate food and resource distribution.

- Hunger in Africa [45]
- Discussion of world hunger [349]

Political and Economic Refugees

Resettlement of groups uprooted by wars, natural disasters, and industrialization causes stress and conflict throughout the globe.

- Transition & urbanization [351]
- European refugees help Zionists establish Israeli state after WW II [206, 209-212]
- Palestinians [206, 209, 212, 223]

Economic Growth and Development

Technological progress brings increased contact among people. It forces re-evaluation of traditional life-styles. A mixture of systems for making economic decisions has resulted from international contacts.

- India's economic development [81]
- A mixed economy in Israel [219]
- Discussion of economic development in today's world [350]
- Latin American Development [177]
- The British Economy [284]

Issues: Examples:

Environmental Concerns

Devastation of the land and sea by natural and human forces has repercussions beyond a particular region because the scarcity of critical resources intensifies competition for them elsewhere.

- Desertification of Sahel in Africa [46]
- European Efforts [278]
- Discussion of environmental issues [353]

Human Rights

Freedoms enjoyed by some societies are not shared by all. As international contact broadens, common expectations for human decency and justice rise.

- Apartheid in South Africa [33]
- Hungarian Revolution [331]
- Discussion of human rights in today's World [356]

World Trade and Finance

Interaction of economic needs and desires demonstrate the interdependence among nations.

- Divestiture over Apartheid [34]
- Discussion of economic development and world trade [350]

Determination of Political and Economic Systems

Transfer of decision-making power among groups alters internal and external structure.

- Chinese Cultural Revolution [110]
- French Revolution [253]
- Discussion of changing political power structures in today's world [351]

Energy: Resources and Allocations

The competition of industrially developed and developing nations for limited supplies of fossil fuels create global political and economic strains. The danger and limitations of artificially produced fuels create worldwide stresses.

- OPEC [218, 224]
- Discussion of energy resources in today's world [351]

Terrorism

As the use of violence as a political weapon to intimidate others becomes more common, governments and individuals are being drawn into issues that were once only national or regional in scope.

- PLO [212, 223]
- Anti-semitism [277]
- Discussion of human rights in today's world [356]

Glosssary Of Terms
With Page References

Abbasid (8th C. Shi'ite revolt set up separate Muslim region in Persia), 201

Abbasid Caliph (religious ruler of eastern regions of the Muslim empire), 203

Abolitionist movement (19th C. anti-slavery movement in Western Europe & U.S.), 25-26

Abraham (Hebrew prophet), 199

Absolutism (concentration and exercise of ruling power usually by a monarch), 246, 248, 304

Abu Bakr (7th C.; father-in-law of Mohammed; first Caliph, religious leader of Muslims), 200

Acid rain (air pollutants that travel in precipitation), 354

Aconcagua (highest peak in Andes; 22,831ft.), 156

Act of Supremacy (1534; Anglicanism official religion of England), 245

Afghanistan, 121, 189, 223-24

Africa: Agriculture, 28, 42, 45-46; Art 19-20; culture, 21; economics, 42; education, 28; exploitation, 28; life in transition, 38; overpopulation, 44; physical features, 14-16; slave trade, 24-26; role in world affairs, 52; unifying influences, 27

African National Congress (ANC; South African civil rights group), 33

African Kingdoms (Ghana, Mali, Songhai, ancient states had high cultural and economic development), 18-19[chart], 24-26

Afrikaners (Boers original Dutch colonists in South Africa), 26,33

Age of Discovery (period of global exploration and colonization by Europeans in 15th and 16th C.), 163, 250-251

Age of Enlightenment (18th C. European age of scientific and philosophical development), 25, 252

Age of Imperialism (19th C. African and Asian colonization by European industrial nations for raw materials), 361

Agrarian (farm based life-style), 349

Agriculture, subsistence (producing for one's own basic needs), 42

Agronomists, (agricultural economists), 349

AIDS (Acquired Immunodeficiency Syndrome), 358

Akbar (Mughal ruler of India, 1555-1605), 61

Albania, 302, 311

Alexander I (Tsar, Napoleonic Era; d. 1825), 255, 311

Alexander II (Tsar; emancipated serfs, established Duma; d. 1881), 311

Alexander the Great (Hellenistic conquerer & unifier of ancient Middle East, d. 323 B.C.), 59, 235

All-India Muslim League (Bengali independence movement; 1906), 65

Allah (Muslim name for God), 199

Alliance for Progress (U.S. assistance policy for Latin America in 1960's), 182

Alluvial soil (rich in minerals from mountains' drainage), 57,189

Al Mansur (second Caliph, established Islamic capital at Baghdad, 8thC. A.D.), 201

Alps (mt. range in Central Europe), 230, 232

Amazon River (massive basin in the center of South America), 156

American Revolution (as extension of European Enlightenment thinking), 253

Amin, Idi (Ugandan dictator; massacred of thousands of his political opponents from 1966 to 1985), 356

Amritsar Massacre (brutal suppression of a 1919 demonstration in Punjab by British), 66

Amulets and Charms (used in African religions to spiritually protect individuals), 20

Amur River (river in East Asia, forms disputed part of Russian - Chinese border), 300

Analects (Confucius' sayings - guide to correct behavior), 97

Anatolia (central plateau of Turkey), 189

Anatomy of Revolution (Crane Brinton: examines the patterns of modern national revolutions), 254

Ancestor worship (in African religions, forebearers are considered a living part of the tribal community), 19

Andes Mountains (major north-South range of South America), 156

Andropov, Yuri (succeeded Brezhnev; U.S.S.R. leader, 1983-84), 323, 325

Anglican Church (Church of England), 245

Animism (belief that objects contain a spirit), 128

Anoxia (oxygen depletion), 355

Anthropology (study of origins and development of human culture), 17

Anti-imperialism (strong desire for freedom from foreign control), 31

Anti-Semitism (anti-Jewish feeling), 269

Apartheid (South African policy of total racial separation), 33-34, 52

Appeasement (policy of giving in to aggressors to avoid war), 273

Aquino, Benigno, (Philippine leader, assassinated 1983), 77

Aquino, Corazon (deposed Marcos regime; President of Philippine Republic, 1986), 77

Arab-Israeli Conflicts, 210, 222

Arabian Nights (collection of stories told at the Caliph's Court in the 8th and 9th centuries), 202

Arab Nationalism (movement to unify Arab nations), 207

Arab socialism (improvement of the social and economic conditions for all Arabs), 213, 218

Arafat, Yassir (spokesman for Palestine Liberation Organization), 212

Architecture: African, 21; Greek, 234; Modern, 279

Archeology (study of human existence by means of its physical remains), 17

Archipelago (island chain: peaks of undersea mt. ranges), 58, 125

Argentina , 155,157, 171

Ariel (Jose Rodo, modern Latin American literature), 184

Aristocracy (government by a small, privileged class), 235

Aristotle (Greek philosopher, d. 322 BC), 234

Aristophanes (ancient Greek dramatist, d. 380), 234

Armada (Spanish naval fleet), 163

Art: African 21; European,279; Latin American, 183

Aryans (early conquerers of India, c. 1500-500 BC), 59

Ashanti (ancient African kingdom), 24-26,

Ashikaga Shogunate (feudal Japanese rulers,1338-1567), 130

Ashley Report (mine safety in British Industrial Revolution), 259

"Asia for the Asiatics" (desire to rid Asia of European/Amer. influences), 272

Asimov,Isaac (contemporary science fiction writer), 359

Asoka (3rd C. BC Mauryan ruler of India), 59-60

Assimilation (being absorbed into a new culture), 179

Asturias, Miguel Guatemala (writer on Cent. Amer. Indian culture), 184

Aswan High Dam (Egypt controversial project on the Nile River under Nasser), 190, 213

Ataturk, Mustapha Kemel (Turkish WW I hero, established the Republic of Turkey in 1923), 207

Atheistic belief (belief that there is no God), 329

Atlantic Charter (Allies World War I aims became basis for United Nations Charter in 1945), 31

Atlas Mountains (North Africa) 15

Atom Bomb (dropping by U.S. on Japan), 138, 148

Audiencas (crown-appointed advisory to viceroys in colonial Lat. Am.), 164

Autonomy (self-rule), 66

Austria-Hungary, 262-63

Austro-Prussia War (1866, Bismarck used as stepping stone to unification of Germany), 257,310

Athens (center of ancient Greek democracy and culture), 233-234

Axum (ancient African kingdom), 24

Aztec (highly developed AncientIndian civilization in Mexico), 158-159

Babylonians (ancient Middle East civilization), 193

Baghdad (ancient center of civilization in Iraq), 191

Balance of Power (diplomatic arrangement of alliances to keep peace in 19th c. Europe), 205-206, 262

Balfour Declaration (World War I promise of nationhood; attempt to gain Jewish support for the British war effort), 206

Balkans (mountain range in southern Europe; Yugoslavia and group of small countries often torn by nationalist/ethnic strife (Bosnia, Croatia, Macedonia, Serbia, Slovenia), 262, 301, 310, 315

Baltic Sea (northeastern Europe), 300

Bangladesh (East Pakistan declared independent country, 1971), 53, 73, 89

Bao Dai (Japanese installed as Emperor of Vietnam, c. WW II), 74

Bantu (South African people; self-governing "Bantustans"), 16, 34

Baptism (Christian rite), 245

Barrios (Latin American urban slums), 158, 173, 179

Bartolome de las Casas (colonial Latin American priest led protests over the mistreatment of Indians and African slaves), 165

Battle of Britain (Hitler's relentless air attacks on British), 273

Battle of Tours (Franks stopped Muslim invasion, 8th C. A.D.), 238

Battle of Vienna (Ottoman expansion into Europe checked, 1683), 205

Battle of Waterloo (final defeat of Napoleon, 1815), 256

Batista, Fulgencio (Cuban dictator deposed by Castro in 1958), 171

Bavaria (southern province of Germany), 269

Bay of Bengal (southeastern coast of India), 56

Bedouin (formal tribal organization of nomadic Arab tribesmen), 191

Beer Hall Putsch (1923 uprising began Hitler's rise to fame), 269

Belarus (also Byelorussia, White Russia; independent nation (1991) in Eastern Europe between Poland and Russia; formerly one of the 15 republics of the Soviet Union; original member of the Commonwealth of Independent States [CIS]; Minsk is capital and center for CIS.), 299, 330

Belgium, 26, 35, 230

Benin (ancient African kingdom), 21, 24-25

Begin, Menachem (Israeli Prime Minister, Camp David Accord, 1977), 211

Berlin Airlift (Allied attempt to supply German city cut off by Soviets in 1948), 289

Berlin Conference (1884-85; African territorial claims partially worked out by Europeans), 26, 35

Berlin Wall (built by Soviets in 1960's to deter escapes from communist zone of the city), 289

Beveridge Report (British post-World War II plan for expansion of socialist programs), 285

Bill of Rights (limited power of monarchs in England, 1689), 249-50

"Black Ivory" (name for the Africans captured and sold as slaves), 25

Biafra (Republic of), 36, 51

Bible (sacred scriptures of Judeo-Christian religion), 194

Bicameral (two house legislature), 71, 275

Birth Control (see World Issues - Population), 348

Bismarck, Otto von ("Iron Chancellor" unified modern German state in late 19th c.), 257

"Black Market" (economic structure, engages in illegal trade), 335

Black Sea, 298, 300

Blitzkrieg ("lightning war" tactic used by Nazis), 273

Bloody Sunday (period of violence during the Russian Revolution of 1905), 314

Bicameral (two house legislative body), 275

Boers (Dutch settlers of South Africa), 26, 33

Bohemia (mountainous province of Czechoslovakia), 301

Bolivar, Simon (leader of South American independence movement; founder of Gran Colombia), 166, 169

Bolsheviks (Russian Marxist political group leadership of Lenin), 314-17, 320
Bolshoi Ballet (touring dance company of U.S.S.R.), 313
Bonaparte, Napoleon (see Napoleon), 255
Bonsai cultivation (technique of arresting the growth of trees), 130
Borges, Jorge Luis (Argentine author), 184
Borlaug, Norman (Agronomist, founder of the Green Revolution), 358
Bosnia (W. central Balkan nation broke from Yugoslavia 1991), 331
Bourgeoisie (middle class), 254
Boxers (anti-imperialst group led rebellion in China, 1900), 104
Boyars (wealthy merchants and landowners in Medieval Russia), 303
Boycott (economic punishment: customers refuse to purchase goods or services), 43
Brahma (Hindu Deity, the creator), 59
Bramaputra (major river system in India), 56
Brazilian Highlands (south-central region near the Atlantic coast, contains Brazil's
      major population centers), 157
Brezhnev Doctrine (Soviet pledge to intervene in any nation whose actions
      endangered communism), 290, 331
Brezhnev, Leonid (Soviet leader 1965-83), 290, 324-25, 331
British Commonwealth of Nations (assoc of former Brit. colonies), 36, 49, 66
Brinton, Crane (historian: *Anatomy of Revolution*), 254
Buddhism (major religion of east. & cent. Asia, 6th C. BC), 60, 97-98, 119, 128
Buddha (the Enlightened One, founder of Buddhism, 6th C. B.C.), 60
Bhutto, Benazir (Pakistan's first woman President), 73
Bulgaria, 302, 310
Bulgars (an invading group from Central Asia), 302
Bureaucracy (excessive power concentrated in gov't. agencies) 46, 99, 103, 134
Burma, (see Myanmar) 67
Bush, George (President of U.S.), 146, 172, 297
Bushido (fuedal Japanese warriors' code), 129, 137
Bushmen (South-Central African people), 16
Buyid (dynasty which sujugated Persia in 900's), 203
Byzantine Empire (East. Roman Empire reached its peak in 4th & 5th C. AD),
      195-197, 237, 243, 303

Cabinet (of Ministers), 141, 275
Caesar Augustus (first Roman Emperor, c. 27 BC), 236
Caesar, Julius (military dictator of Rome, d. 44 BC), 236
Cairo, Egypt, 191
Caliph (title for successor to Mohammed as leader of Islam), 200
Calvin, John (Swiss theologian, Eur. Protestant Reformation, c. 1560's), 245
Cambodia (Kampuchea), 57, 75-80, 89-90
Camp David Accords (1979 Middle East peace agreements), 211, 213
Campesinos (paid laborers, tenant farmers, or peasants of Lat. America), 177
Cape Colony (Dutch colony of South Africa, 1652-1806), 33
Cape-to-Cairo Railroad (Cecil Rhodes project for linking British territories along
      Africa's east coast), 33
Capetown (capital of South Africa), 33
Capitalist system (private enterprise; market economic structure), 251
Captain-General (colonial governors of Portuguese Brazil), 165
Caribbean, 158
Carpathians (mountain range crosses Eastern Europe), 301
Carranza, Venustiano (early 20th C. Mexican statesman), 171
Cartel (combination of economic units to limit competition), 218
Carter, Jimmy (U.S. Pres.; 1970's Mid-East peace agreements), 172, 211, 213
Catherine the Great (absolutist Russian Tsarina, 1762-1796), 308

Castes (rigid Hindu system of hereditary social groupings dictating one's rank and occupation), 60

Castro, Fidel (Cuban communist leader), 172, 182, 357

Catholic Counter Reformation (church movement in the 16th century offset the Protestant Reformation), 164, 246

Catholic missionary zeal (Christianizing Latin Am. Indian population), 163

Caspian Sea (large lake in central Asia; environmentally impacted), 301

Caucasians (members of the white race), 158

Caudillo (local ruler with dictatorial power in Latin America), 170

Cavaliers (king's supporters, English Puritan Revolution, c. 1650), 249

Central America, 156

Central American Federation (post-independence attempt at unification, c. 1820), 169

Central Intelligence Agency (U.S. espionage network), 172

Central Treaty Organization (CENTO: multi-lateral defense agreement with Middle East and British, c. 1950's), 88

Chad Basin, 15

Chamorro, Violeta (unseated Sandinistas 1990), 172

Chao Phraya (river basin in Thailand), 58

Charlemagne (8th C. A.D. leader of the Franks; Holy Roman Empire), 238

Charles I (British king, dethroned & beheaded in Puritan Revolution, mid-1600's), 249

Charles II (British king, restored to monarchy after Cromwell's death in 1658), 249

Charter companies (private trading enterprises licensed by government; outposts became bases for colonies), 26

Chartist movement (19th C. movement by British workers to demand the suffrage for themselves), 259

Chauvinism (nationalist extremism in 19th & 20th C. Germany), 256

Cheka (Tsarist secret police), 320

Chernenko, Konstantin (succeeded Andropov as U.S.S.R. leader, d.1984), 323,325

Chernobyl (1986 nuclear power accident in Ukraine), 301

Chiang Kai-shek (military leader of Chinese Nationalist government & the Kuomintang party), 105-06, 119-20

Chile, 158

Chin (Qin) Dynasty (221 B. C. - 210 B.C., unified China), 98-99

China: 94-124; Confucian tradition 96,119; goods 102; people 94; Interest in Economic Development 114; Interest in Foreign Trade 102; writing, 119

China, People's Republic of , 106

China's Sorrow (the Yellow or Huang River's constant flooding), 96

Chinese Communist Party (split over tactics of Mao Zedong in 1960's), 109-12, 115-16

"Chinese Essence" (preservation of Chinese social and political order during Western Imperialist period in the 19th C.), 103

Christian Phalangists (political group in Lebanese civil war), 212, 222

Christianity, 194; missionary work in Africa, 21

Churchill, Winston (British Prime Minister during WW II), 31, 288

City-states (Sparta and Athens ancient Greece), 233

Civil War (Russia, Reds v. Whites, 1917-1921), 320

Clan (an association of lineages), 19

Click language (African cultural ties), 16

Climate (Koeppen's classifications), 9; Africa, 15; India, 56; S.E. Asia, 58; China, 96; Japan, 126; Middle East,190; Latin America,155-157; W.Europe, 230; E. Europe and U.S.S.R., 300

Clive, Sir Robert (led military expeditions laid basis for Brit. rule in India), 64

Codified Laws (organized and written), 233

Colbert (mercantilist finance minister and advisor to France's absolutist, King Louis XIV), 248

Cold War (WWII global power clash between democratic and communist centered on superpower relations), 288, 343

Collective farms (large agricultural enterprises run by the Soviet government), 321

Colonization (Latin America by Spain and Portugal), 154, 163-65

"Colossus of the North" (indicates powerful role of the U.S. in Latin American affairs), 181, 183

Columbus, Christopher (explorer in pay of Spanish Crown credited with beginning the Age of Colonization in Latin America), 163, 251

COMECON (Soviet sponsored common market for Eastern European nations), 282, 331, 337, 342-343

Command System (Soviet economic controls), 335

Commando Economy (government agencies do all economic decision-making for the society), 82

Commercial Revolution (economic movement which opened Europe to world wide trade enterprises in the 1400's), 251

Committee of Public Safety (operated the Reign of Terror during the Fr. Rev. which resulted in the execution of 15-45,000 opponents in the 1790's), 254

Common Market (EEC, trade assoc. of West. European nations), 42, 49, 285

Commonwealth Immigrants Act (limited immigration within the British Commonwealth), 277

Commonwealth of Independent States ([CIS]; military and economic confederation of former Soviet republics formed after U.S.S.R. collapsed in 1991), 328, 336

Commonwealth of Nations (a worldwide organization of former British colonies), 49, 286, 291

Communes (socialistic cooperative farms), 110, 115

Communism: Africa 50-51; China 105-06; Cuba, 172; Europe 260-261, 288; Russia, 322

Communist Manifesto (Karl Marx's work: socialist doctrine), 260

Communist Party (U.S.S.R. & Eastern Europe), 105-106, 323

Compromise of 1867 (established the dual monarchy, Austria-Hungary, and gave Hungary a large degree of self-government), 310

Concert of Europe (19th C. intern'l organization established to preserve peace), 292

Concordat of 1801 (established friendly relations with the Catholic Church on Napoleon's terms), 254

Confucianism (basic social philosophy of China from ancient), 96-97, 99, 112

Congo (river basin of cent. Africa; Belgian colony; loc. of Zaire), 15, 26, 35

Congress of Berlin (1878, self-government to parts of Balkans), 311

Congress of the People's Deputies (Soviet Union's national legislative body under Gorbachev; chose President and Supreme Soviet; dissolved nation in 1991), 323

Congress of Vienna (1815, organized the restoration of political power in Europe after the defeat of Napoleon), 256, 311

Conquistadores (Spanish conquerors of Latin American Indian lands, set up colonial rule), 164

Constantine the Great (Roman Emperor; issued the Edict of Milan in 313A.D.), 195

Conservative Party (in Great Britain, currently headed by Margaret Thatcher), 276, 285

Constantinople (cent. city of East. Roman Empire; formerly Byzantium), 195

Constitutional monarchy (Britain's system of limited monarchy and Parliamentary rule), 275

Contadora Group (meeting of leaders of Central American republics to seek solutions to the frequent outbreaks of violence in Central America), 183

Continental System (Napoleonic trade regulations of 1806 to hurt British trade and to help France establish economic supremacy on the Continent), 255

Contras (rebel group seeking to overthrow communist rule in Nicaragua), 172

Control of Pollution Act (British environmental regulations, 1974), 278

Coptic Christianity (Ethiopian branch of Christian church), 20

Cordillera ("backbone" mountain chain, Andes of South America), 156

Cosmopolitan (a wide mixture of cultural traits), 45

Council of Europe (sets policy for the European Community), 279

Council of Ministers (see Soviet government), 322

Council of Mutual Economic Assistance, (COMECON: Soviet-sponsored common market arrangement for Eastern Europe), 282, 337, 343

Council of Trent (16th C. reorganization of the Catholic Church in response to the Protestant Reformation), 246

Counter Reformation (offensive drive by the Roman Catholic Church in the 15th C. against the Protestant Reformation), 164, 246

Coup d'état (military overthrow of the governments), 32, 74, 170, 212, 255

Creditor nations (nations to whom others owe money), 351

Crimean War (c.1854, cost Russia much Balkan territory), 312

Criollos (American-born sons of Spanish nobles), 165

Cromwell, Oliver (Brit. Puritan dictator, declared Lord Protector 1653), 249

Croatia (N.W. Balkan nation broke from Yugoslavia 1991), 331

Crusades (attempts by various Medieval Christian nobles to win back Jerusalem and its surrounding regions from Muslims), 203, 243

Cuba, 171

Cuban advisors in Africa (aid for communist insurgents), 37, 51, 183

Culture (a people's whole way of living: language, traditions, customs, institutions, folkways), 10

Cultural diffusion (cultural patterns spreading from one people to other), 10

Cultural Revolution (power struggle in Maoist China in the mid-1960's), 110-11

Cuneiform (ancient Sumerian system of writing), 192-93

Cyrillic alphabet (modified form of the Greek alphabet basis for Russian and some Slavic languages), 197, 303

Czar (see "tsar"), 306

Czechoslovakia, 279, 290, 302, 331

Czech Republic (separated 1992 from former Czechoslovakia), 331

Da Vinci, Leonardo (central figure of Italian Renaissance), 244

Daimyo ("Great Lords" of Japan's fuedal era, 1300-1600), 130

Dante (Italian Renaissance writer: *Divine Comedy*), 244

Danube River (major European trade route), 232, 302

Dark Ages (Early European Medieval period; 500 to 1000 A.D.), 237

"Dark Continent" (popular 19th C. name for Africa because its vast interior sections were unknown to European colonial powers), 14

Darwin, Charles (19th century British biological theorist on evolution; *Origin of Species*, 1859), 261

Das Kapital (Marx's 1867 elaboration of communist philosophy), 260

"Day of Infamy" (President Franklin Roosevelt's reference to the Japanese attack on U.S. naval forces at Pearl Harbor in 1941), 137

Deccan Plateau (occupies most of Indian peninsula with much mineral wealth), 57

Decembrist Revolt (a palace coup d'état against the Tsar in 1825), 312

Declaration of Independence (U.S. revolutionary document by Thomas Jefferson reflected the ideas of John Locke), 253

Declaration of Principles for Palestinian Self-rule (agreement between Yitzhak Rabin [Israel] and Yassir Arafat [PLO] September 1993 in Washington, DC), 212, 222

Declaration of Rights of Man (French Revolution), 254

Default (cannot make debt payments), 179

Deforestation (over-cutting of timber resources), 46, 354

Deists (European Enlightenment thinkers who embraced the idea that God established the laws governing the universe, and then left it to run according to His established rules), 252

de Klerk, F.W. (Prime Minister of Republic of South Africa, 1989—), 34

Democratic socialism (mixed economic systems in European nations with extensive welfare systems), 285

Democritus (Greek thinker who expounded elementary ideas about the basic composition of matter), 234

Demographers (people who map population movements), 349

Demographic maps, 8

Deng Xiaopong, (reformist Chinese leader after Mao, '76-'87), 112, 115-6

Denmark, 232

De Rosas, Juan Manuel (Argentine dictator, 1829-1852), 171

Desertification (loss of available land to the desert), 46

Desert Shield and Storm, Operation (see Persian Gulf conflict), 215

Deserts (climatic classification having little or no rainfall), 16

Dependent states (colonies), 154

Détente (more cordial diplomatic atmosphere), 324

Dharma (sacred duty one owes to family and caste), 59

Diario, Ruben (Nicaraguan poet), 184

Diaspora (dispersion of the Jews from Palestine into world, c.70 A.D.), 194

Diaz, Porfirio (Mexico dictator, 1876-1911), 171

Dictatorship of the Proletariat (Marxist dogma that indicates working classes will
    eventually rule society for the benefit of all), 260

Dienbienphu (final defeat of French colonialism in Vietnam, 1954), 74, 290

Diet (two-house legislature of Japan), 141

Dinaric Alps (moutain chain in Yugoslavia and Albania), 301

Diocletian (Emperor who divided Roman Empire into 2 parts, 3rd C. AD), 195

Direct democracy (citizens having direct say in the making of decisions rather than
    being represented by officials), 233

Dissidents (those who disagree with governmental policies), 325-27

Divesting (termination of investments in South Africa enterprises as an economic
    protest against apartheid policy), 34, 43, 52

Divine right (absolute power coming from God), 248

Divine Rulers (African chieftans considered lesser gods or priests in charge of
    ceremonies worshiping ancestral deities), 20

Dneiper River (river system in western Russia, Ukraine), 300

"Dollar Diplomacy" (interventionist U.S.- Latin American Policy of early 20th C. based
    on protection of commercial investment), 182

Dome of the Rock Mosque (Muslim shrine in Jerusalem), 201

Domestic system (commercial production done in homes and coordinated by an
    entrepreneur), 252

Dominican Republic, 182

"Domino Theory" (communist victory in one small, weak state would lead to other
    nations falling), 89

Don River (river system in western Russia, Transcaucasia), 300

Doric Columns (Ancient Greece), 234

Dowager Empress (ruler of China in late 19th and early 20th C. under western
    imperialists influence), 103

Drakensberg Mountains (Southern Africa), 15

Dubcek, Alexander (leader of the Communist Party of Czechoslovakia, c.1968), 290

Dubos, Rene (American biologist), 353, 355

Duma (national legislative body under Tsars in 19th & 20th C.), 312

Eastern Europe: Physical Features, 301-02; Natural Resources, 302; Development,
    309-11; Church Influence, 342; Soviet Ties, 342

Easter Rebellion of 1916 (Irish uprising against British, leading to independence), 276

Eastern Orthodox Catholic Church, 196; 237, 243, 303

East India Company (British trading company set up basis for colonial endeavors), 64

Ecology (preserving the natural environment), 145

Economic nationalism (stimulation of internal development using government policies
    to eliminate outside competition), 179

Ecuador, 158

Ecumenism (movement to seek unity among different religions), 273

Edict of Milan (granted freedom of worship to all Christians in Roman Empire, 313
    AD), 195

Edo (center of Japan's Tokugawa government, later called Tokyo), 130

Egypt (called "Gift of the Nile" because of annual flooding which deposits rich alluvial soil in river valley), 189, 192-193, 210-213

Eightfold Path (Buddhism's basic religious concepts), 60-61

El Dorado (Spain's conquistadores explored the New World seeking this mythical city of gold), 164

Elizabeth I (absolute monarch of England in 16th C., established the nation as a power in Europe), 247

Emancipation Act in 1861 (Tsar Alexander II freed Russian serfs), 312

Embargo (refusal to sell or trade), 136

Emerson, Thomas (American physicist), 359

Enclosure Acts (British farm lands fenced for pasture purposes), 252

Encomiendas (vast Latin American plantations), 165, 177

England (colonial interest in Latin America), 165

Engels, Frederick (collaborator with Karl Marx on *Communist Manifesto*, 1848), 260

English Channel (narrow strait separates the British Isles from the European mainland), 230

Enlightened despot (ruler who uses autocratic power for the benefit of the people), 308

Enlightenment (intellectual movement in 17th and 18th centuries began a search for natural laws that governed man's existence.), 252

Environment (the setting in which people live), 7-8

Erasmus (Renaissance writer, *In Praise of Folly*), 244

Estates General (French Parliament), 247

Ethiopia, 26, 51

Ethnocentrism (viewing all cultures as inferior to one's own) 38, 95

Euphrates River, 189-93

European Coal and Steel Community (established in 1951 by 5 western European nations based on plan by Robert Schuman of France), 285

European Economic Community ("Common Market," EC), 49, 279, 285, 361

European Atomic Energy Community (Euratom), 285

European Colonialism (in Latin America), 165

European Russia (extends from the western border to the Ural Mountains which are usually considered to be the dividing line between Europe and Asia), 300

Excommunication (depriving a person of church membership), 240

Explorers (Age of Discovery 15th and 16th C.), 251

Extended Families (three or more generations under one roof), 38

Extraterritoriality (foreignors not subject to a host country's laws), 103

Factory Act (1833, protection for British workers), 259

Family: group associations, 19; nuclear, 38; planning, India, 72

Family Responsibility System (China; began in 1981, allows the peasants some produce to be sold for profit), 115

Faza (8th C. AD Kenyan city-state), 37

Fazendas (Brazilian ranches), 165

Federal Republic of Germany (name for West Germany before reunification in 1989), 289

Federation of Malaya, 77

Fertile Crescent (Middle East region between the Tigris and Euphrates Rivers considered to be the Cradle of Civilization), 189

Feudal Period of Japan (1185-1600), 129

Feudalism (landholding-based lord/vassal economic-political-social system of medieval Europe), 238-239, 304, 306

Fichte (early 19th C. German national theorist), 257

Fief (self-sufficient feudal manor), 238

Finland, 232

First French Empire (Napoleonic Empire, c.1800-15), 255

Five Human Relationships (basic Confucian structure), 97

Five Pillars (basic beliefs and duties of Muslim faith), 61, 200

Five Year Plans: Chinese command economic structures, 110, 114-16; Soviet command economic structures, 321, 335

Food shortage (economic problems of India), 83

"Four Modernizations" (revision of China's economic priorities under Deng Xiaopong), 112, 115-17

Four Noble Truths (basic beliefs of Buddhism), 60

Fourteen Points (WW I peace plan for Europe drawn up by U.S. President Wilson, 1918), 263

Fragmentation (div. by regional culture and geographic barriers), 169

France: 230; & Africa, 50; & S.E. Asia, 67, 74, 84, 247-248, 253-256, 257, 283-285; & Latin America, 165

Franco-Prussian War (1871 conflict used to enhance prestige of new German state under Bismarck), 257

Franks (people of the central and western sections of France in the 8th century A.D.), 238

Franz Ferdinand, Archduke (heir to Austrian throne; 1914 assassination fomented WW I), 263, 315

Free market systems (economy which operates according to the relationship of supply and consumer demand), 82

French Union (also French Community; retained ties with former colonies; similar to British Commonwealth), 291

Fuehrer (German title for leader used by Hitler), 271

Fuji (large Japanese corporation), 144

Fujiwara family (ruled Japan from the 10th through 12th centuries AD), 127

Gandhi,Indira (Indian Prime Minister: 1966-84), 70, 73

Gandhi, Mohandas (non-violent Indian independence movement leader, assassinated1948), 27, 66, 70-71

Gandhi, Rajiv (Indian Prime Minister 1984), 73

Gang of Four (power struggle in China after Mao's death), 111

Ganges(major river system in India), 56-57

Gapon, Father (a priest of the Russian Orthodox Church, staged a peaceful march to the Tsar's Winter Palace which fomented the Bloody Sunday massacre in 1905), 314

Gautama, Siddarta (founder of Buddhist faith, 6th C. B.C.), 60

Gaza Strip (Mediterranean coastal territory taken from Egypt by Israel in the 1967 war), 210-11

Geneva Agreements (after French defeat in1954, provided for an independent and neutral Indochinese states), 290

Genghis Khan (13th C. Asian conquerer est. Mongol Yuan dynasty in China), 99

Genocide (deliberate elimination of a racial or cultural group), 272

Geographers, 15

German Democratic Republic (East Germany), 289

Germanic tribes (overran Europe in the 5th-7th C.), 237

Germany (East and West), 231, 256-257, 262-264

Ghali, Bhutros - (6th U.N. Secretary General, 1992 -)

Ghana (West African empire 7th-11th C. A.D.), 18, 20

Ghana, Republic of (first Sub-Saharan European Colony to achieve independence after World War II), 32

Ghettos (ethnic or cultural area or neighborhood), 269

Ghuru Nanak (founded Sikhism in India in the 15th century), 62

Ghuru Mahavira (founded Jainism in India in the 6th c. A.D.), 62

Gladstone, William (19th C. British Prime Minister), 276

Glasnost ("openness"- Gorbachev's policies), 325, 331, 345

Glorious Revolution (Catholic James II deposed; placed Protestant WilliamIII [of Orange] & Mary II on English throne in 1688), 249

GNP (total value of goods and service produced annually), 83
Goebbels (Hitler's minister of propaganda), 271
Golan Heights (taken from Syria in 1967 Arab-Israeli War), 211
Golden Age of Chinese culture (Tang Dynasty,618 - 907 AD), 99
Golden Age of Muslim culture (Abbasid Dynasty, 750-1258 AD), 201
Golden Bull (Hungarian charter 1222; provided basic liberties), 310
Good Neighbor Policy (F. D. Roosevelt's Latin American policy, c.1933), 182
Gorbachev, Mikhail (reformer became Soviet leader 1985; negotiated end to Soviet
    dominance of Eastern Europe, Cold War; began *glasnost* democratic constitution-
    al reforms and *perestroika* economic reforms; resigned Soviet Presidency in 1991),
    326-345
Gosplan (Soviet Union's central economic decision-making agency for resource
    allocation and production goals), 335
Government of India Act (British Parliament began structure for home rule,1935), 66
Gran Chaco (200,000 square-mile flatland shared by Argentina, Bolivia, and
    Paraguay), 157
Gran Colombia (short lived union of Venezuela, Columbia, Peru, Ecuador, and Bolivia,
    c. 1820), 169
Grand Duchy of Warsaw (a small Polish state briefly constructed by Napoleon, early
    1800's), 310
Great Depression (worldwide economic collapse; cause of social and political upheaval
    in Germany in 1930's laid groundwork for Hitler's Nazi movement), 270
Great Hungarian Plain (an agricultural and horse-raising region in the middle of
    Eastern Europe), 302
Great Leap Forward (Mao's major economic reorganization of the late 1950's in
    China), 110, 115
Great Northern War (Peter the Great v. Sweden, 1708-21), 308
Great Reform Bill (British reform which gave middle classes the right to vote), 259
Great Rift Valley (Eastern Africa), 15
Great Trek (1836;Boer migration from South African coast to interior after British
    took Cape Colony), 26, 33
Great Wall of China (built as an invasion defense on northern borders of China in Qin
    period, c.220 B.C.), 99
Greece, 232, 233-35
Greek tragedies (Aeschylus, Sophocles, and Euripides), 234
Green Revolution 1960's (scientific breakthroughs in agriculture), 45, 83, 358
Green space (parks and gardens), 355
Greenhouse Effect (see environmental pollution and illustration), 354
Greenland, 232
Gridlock (enormous traffic congestion), 359
Grito de Dolores (Mexican independence movement), 166
Gross National Product (sum of goods and services produced in a year), 150, 176, 350
Groups Area Act in 1950 (divided 13% of So. Africa among 10 Bantu homelands), 33
Guild system (medieval syst., centralization of craft production), 252
Gulag Archipelago (officially censured 1968 work critical of Soviet system by exiled
    Aleksandr Solzhenitsyn), 330
Gulf of Aqaba (Israel's vital oil supply depot), 210
Gutenburg Press (invention of the movable type printing), 246

Habeas Corpus Act (17th C., guaranteed arrested Englishmen a statement of
    charges, bail, and a fair and speedy trial), 249
Hagia-Sophia (Byzantine church of "Holy Wisdom", later converted to an Islamic
    mosque), 196
Hague Conferences (pre-World War I, attempted to limit the arms race without
    success), 292
Haiku (Japanese poem of only 3 lines), 142
Han Dynasty (210 B.C. - 220 A.D., expanded China's control over Central Asia), 98-99

Hanoi (North Vietnam capital), 75
Hapsburgs (Austrian dynasty which defeated the Turks in 1683), 310
Harappa (India'searliest civilization), 59
Hausa (West African Islamic city-state of the 14th century), 20, 24
"Have nots" (Third World countries; undeveloped nations), 349
"Haves" (the developed, educated, wealthy, industrial nations), 349
Hebrews Ancient civilization of Middle East), 193-194
Hegira (flight of Mohammed in 622 AD to Medina), 199
Heian Classical Period (Japan,794-1185, lessened Chinese cultural domination), 129
Hellenistic culture (extension of ancient Greek influence by Philip of Macedon and
    Alexander the Great), 196, 233, 235
Helsinki Accord of 1975 (human right agreements), 326, 356
Heng Samrin (Kampuchean leader; a former Khmer Rouge leader), 76
Henry VIII (Tudor king of England, created Anglican church), 245
Herzel, Theodor (19th C. Zionist leader), 206
Hierarchy (ascending order of leaders), 170
Hieroglyphics (ancient Egyptian system of picture writing), 192-3
Hildago, Miguel (Catholic priest began Mexican independence movement, 1810), 166
Himalayas (in Asia, world's highest mountains), 56
Hindenburg, Paul von (German President, 1922-32), 270
Hinduism (major religion of India), 59-61, 72
Hippocrates (Greek father of medicine; studied nat'l causes of disease; originated oath
    physicians take to serve best their patients), 234
Hirohito, Emperor of Japan, 141
Hiroshima (U.S. atom bomb target),138, 273
Hispaniola (Caribbean island contains Haiti, Dominican Republic), 166
Hitler, Adolf (Nazi leader of Germany 1933-45), 269-73, 340
Hittite Empire (North Africa; skilled crafts were widely diffused in Africa after its fall,
    c.1200 BC), 17
HIV virus (known cause of the disease AIDS), 358
Ho Chi Minh (1890-1969, communist Viet Minh leader), 74-75
Hokkaido (Northernmost major Japanese island), 125
Holocaust (Nazi genocide against Jews), 209, 271-72
Holy Land (Israel/Palestine), 203
Holy Roman Emperor (Charlemagne crowned in 800 A.D.), 238
Holy Synod (Russian Orthodox Church placed under direct control of Tsar Peter in
    early 18th C.), 308
Homo Habilis (able man earliest human remains in Africa), 17
Hong Kong, 103, 123, 277
Honshu (largest and most developed island of Japanese group), 125
Hottentots (central African people), 16
Huguenots (French Calvinists), 248
Huks (Post-independence Philippine communist guerrillas), 77
Huitzilpochtli (Aztec god of sun and war), 159
Hungarian Revolution (harshly suppressed by Red Army in 1956), 331
Hungary, 302, 342
Human Rights: Recent Examples of Violations: Apartheid - South Africa, 356;
    Dissidents and forced labor camps - Soviet Union, 356; Genocide - Kampuchea
    and Uganda, 356
Humanism (European Renaissance revival of classical studies and critical spirit), 244
Humanitarianism (promotion of human welfare and social reform), 25
Hussein, Saddam (President of ruling military council of Iraq; launched recent wars in
    Persioan Gulf region), 212, 215, 225, 334

Iberian peninsula in Europe (Spain and Portugal), 154, 232
Ibo people (Biafran secessionists in 1960's Nigerian civil war), 36
Iceland, 232

Ideographs (pictures used for concepts or ideas), 119, 129, 159

Imperialism (extension of political and economic control of a nation over other groups or territories), 26-28, 261-262

Impressionist (school of art popular in Europe in 19th & 20th c.), 279

Inca (highly developed Indian civilization in Peruvian Andes of South America, c.1200-1600 AD), 158, 160

Indian Constitution of 1950 (British Parliamentary base), 71 [chart]

Indian Ocean, 56

Indochina (French colony which became Vietnam, Laos, Cambodia), 74

Indo-Gangetic Plain (north central India, stretches from Pakistan to Bangladesh), 57

Indonesia, Republic of, 78

Indo-Pakistani wars (border disputes over Punjab, Kashmir since 1948), 70

Indus River (India - site of early civilizations), 56, 59

Industrial Revolution (socio-political change occurring when production of basic necessities becomes organized mechanically; began on large scale in England about 1750), 102, 258-60

Inflation (a period of significantly rising prices without a counterbalancing rise in production; demand outweighs supply, causing prices to rise), 286

Infrastructure (a society's total transport and communication system) - 134, 155, 177, 359

Instrument of Government (England under Cromwell's Puritan rule in the 1650's, first modern written constitution), 249

Insular (separateness; Japanese culture due to island geography), 125

Interdependence (mutual dependence of people on each other), 7-8

International Monetary Fund (IMF; U.N. financial agency aidsThird World development), 49

Iran, 88, 190, 214

Iran-Iraq War (1980-1988), 214

Iraq (Persian Gulf nation; site of Ancient Mesopotamia), 190, 214-215, 225

Ireland, 230, 276-277

Irish Free State (Eire; independence from England achieved in WW I period), 276

Irish Republican Army (IRA; militant group seeking independence for Northern Ireland; "Provisional Wing" of IRA engaged in terrorism), 276, 353

Iron Chancellor (see Bismarck), 257

Iron Curtain (After WW II, Churchill coined the phrase to describe the prevention the free flow of ideas between the West and the communist dominated Eastern Europe.), 288

Irrawaddy (major river system in Burma region), 58

Isabella, Queen of Spain (financed the voyage of Christopher Columbus, 1492), 251

Islam (Arabic word meaning "submission to the will of God"; major world religion founded in Middle East by prophet Mohammed, 7th C. A.D. 199-203; see Muslim culture) 20; in S/SE Asia, 60-61, 70, 73; Islamic fundamentalist movement, 213, 220, 344; Islamic Rev. in Iran, 214, 220

Israel (independence - 1948), 209-212, 219

Italy, 232, 256-257

Ivan III (Ivan the Great; 1462-1505; overthrew Tartars in 1480), 306

Ivan IV (Ivan the Terrible; Russian ruler,1533-1584), 306

James II (English king deposed in Glorious Revolution 1688), 249

Jammu, 70

Japan: Constitution of 1947 outlawed war 148; cultural origins, 126-29; dependence on imported petroleum, 145; economy, 144; educational system141; food supply, 145; imbalance in trade relationships, 145, 149; industries & S.E.Asia, 84, 149; population characteristics, 141-42; social conditions, 142; topography, climate and resources, 126; in World War II, 74, 106

Jainism (religious sect founded by Ghru Mahavira in 6th C. A.D.), 62

Jehovah's Witnesses (persecuted by Nazis), 271

Jericho (oldest settlement to be uncovered by archeologists), 191

Jerusalem (center of Muslim-Christian conflict, see Crusades), 211

Jesus Christ (founder Christianity; major world religion), 194

Jews (see Hebrews, Judaism), 194, 209-212, 329

Jewish Star Decree (Nazis required wearing a yellow Star of David on Jews clothing in 1930's), 271

Jihad (Islamic holy war), 20, 61, 200

Jiang Qing (China: led group in power struggle after Mao's death in 1976), 111

Jinnah, Mohammed ali (founder of Pakistani independence movement) 66, 73

John Paul II (Pope in 1978), 278, 342; attempted assassination, 353

Johnson, Lyndon (U.S. President; escalated Vietnam war) 51, 75

Joint stock company (private enterprises used by English to finance exploration and colonization projects, 16th-19th C.), 251

Jordan, 210 [map]

Jose de San Martin (19th C. South American liberator), 166

Judaism (major world religion; c.1400 BC; belief in one God, social justice, and moral law), 194

Juarez, Benito (Mexican reformer of 1850's), 171

Judeo-Christian ethic (primary shaper of the values, ideals, and cultures of the western world), 195, 237

Julian Alps (mountains of Yugoslavia & Albania), 301

Junta (committee of military rulers), 170

Justinian Code (6th C. A.D. collection of civil law, preserving the Roman legal heritage; has had great impact on the concept of human rights), 196

Kaaba Shrine (Muslim holy place in Mecca, Saudi Arabia), 199

Kabuki (traditional Japanese dramatic form originated in the 16th century), 130

Kadar, Janos (aided by Red Army in setting up new government after the 1956 Hungarian Revolution), 331

Kadets (Constitutional Democrats; members of the middle class who favored a constitutional monarch in Russia, c.1917), 314

Kahn, Ayub (Prime Minister of Pakistan), 73, 88

Kaiser Wilhelm iI (German monarch, c.WW I), 261

Kalahari basin (desert wasteland in southern Africa), 15

Kami (in Japanese tradition, the gods who created the islands), 127

Kamikaze (typhoons; winds of the kami or divine ones), 129; WWII pilots, 137

Kampuchea (Cambodia), 57, 75-76, 90, 356

Kanem-Bornu (Islamic state northeast of Lake Chad destroyed by French in 19thC.), 24

Karma (idea that a person's actions carry unavoidable consequences and determine the nature of subsequent reincarnation), 59

Kasavubu, Joseph (Military commander involved in Zaire's early power struggles & civil war, early 1960's), 35

Kashmir (controversial territory in N.W. India), 70, 88

Kellogg-Briand Pact (1928 Pact of Paris proposed a worldwide non-agression structure), 270

Kennedy, John (U.S. President in 1960's: set up Peace Corps, new Latin American policy) 51; quoted on world hunger, 182, 349

Kenya (Republic of), 37-38, 361

Kenyatta, Jomo (nationalist leader; 1st President of Kenya), 32, 37-38

Khan, Ghengis (13th c. A.D. Mongol conquerer), 99, 304

Khazars (invaded Russia from Central Asia, demanded tribute from the Slavic traders, c. 700 A.D.), 302

Khmer Rouge (communist insurgent group in Kampuchean civil war, c. 1960-80), 76

Khomeini, Ruhollah (leader of Iranian Shi'ite Muslims who over threw Shah in 1978), 214, 220

Khrushchev, Nikita S. (First Secretary & Premier, U.S.S.R. 1956-65), 289, 324, 336

Kibbutz (system of Israeli collective farms), 219

Kiev (important trading center for the Slavs; a loose confederation of city- states established under the Grand Prince of Kiev in 900A.D.), 302-03

Kikuyu (Kenya's largest tribal group), 37

Kinshasa (Zaire's capital), 36

Kinship (extended family bonds), 19, 38

Kirov Ballet (produced some of the greatest dancers of all time including Anna Pavlova and Vaslav Nijinsky), 313

Knights (land-holding nobles became fighting men under Europe's medieval feudal system), 239

Koeppen, Wladimir (19th C. Austrian geographer, created a system of classification of climates), 9, 15, 190

Kongo (anciet African kingdom; modern Angola), 18, 24

Koran (Qur'an – Islam's sacred text), 61, 199, 208

Korea: 134-35,314; Korean War (1950-53), 120, 122, 128, 144

Kublai Khan (Mongol emperor of China, launched armadas against Japan in 1274 and 1281), 129

Kuomintang (Nationalist Party in 20th C. Chinese Civil War), 104-06

Kush (ancient African kingdom), 18

Kuwait, 218

Kyoto (served as Japan's capital until 1868), 128

Kyushu (one of the four major islands of Japan), 125

Labor Party (favors socialist programs in Britain), 71, 276, 285

Lagos (capital of Nigeria), 36-37

Landed aristocracy (oligarchy; governing power of elite group in Latin American nations), 169

Lao People's Democratic Republic (Laos), 57, 76

Latin America: 152 -185; agricultural production,176; architecture, 184; communism, 182; colonial period, 163-167; cultural contributions, 183-84; dominance of U.S., 176; encomienda system, 177; industrialism, 176; literature, 184; migration, 179; post - independence era, 176; resources, 157; tourism, 178

Latin-based languages (Spanish and Portuguese [Brazil] led to general description of region as "Latin America"), 154

Latins (European people who founded Rome, c. 1500 B.C.), 235

Leached soil (minerals and nutrients are washed away by constant rainfall), 16

League of Nations (world peace organization established after WWI), 149, 270; condemns Japanese aggression, 136, 272, 290

Leakey, Mary & Richard (Anthropologists uncovered earliest human remains in Africa, 1972), 17

Lebanon, 212, 222-223

Lebensraum (Hitler's expansionist policy of "living space"), 272

Lee Kwan Yew (Singapore's Prime Minister, led the anti-British movement in the late 1950's), 77

Legalism (Chinese philosophy - punishment should be very severe for even minor offenses), 97, 98

Legion of Honor (award established by Napoleon for those who performed important services for France), 255

Lena River (U.S.S.R.), 300

Lenin, Vladimir Ilyich (Marxist leader of Boshevks in 1917 Russian Revolution), 314-17

Leopold, King of Belgium (established Belgian Congo colony in central Africa, began the imperialist "Scramble for Africa", c. 1880's), 35

Levant (a rich agricultural plateau of Syria, Lebanon, and Israel bordering the Mediterranean Sea), 189

Li Peng (Chinese Premier who unleased troops on the Chinese student demonstrators in Beijing's Tiananman Square in 1989), 112

Liberal Democrats (Japanese Political Party),141
Liberia (West Africa), 26
Libya (North Africa), 50, 213
Limited Nuclear Test Ban Treaty (1963; outlawed tests in the atmosphere), 288, 352
Lin Shao-qi (Chinese President in 1960's; later opponent of Mao i), 110
Lineage (tracing of one's ancestry to a common ancestor), 19, 38
Literacy in the World, 349
Llanos (Spanish for plains; region of northern South America), 157
Locarno Pacts (helped establish European boundaries after WW I), 270
Locke, John (English enlightenment), 253
Lok Dal (one of two major parties in India), 71
Lome Convention (economic trade agreements for African nations, 1975), 49
L'Overture, Toussaint (led 1791 insurrection established Dominican Republic), 166
Lon Nol (Cambodian General led coup against Prince Sihanouk in 1963), 75-76
Long March (1934 general retreat of Mao's communist forces), 105-06
Louis XIV of France (17th c. French divine right ruler), 247-8, 253
Lumumba, Patrice (Marxist leader in Congo [Zaire] civil war, c. 1960's), 35
Luther, Martin (German cleric began Protestant Reformation c.1517), 245
Luxembourg, 230
Lydians (ancient civilization of Western Turkey), 193

Macarthur, Douglas (American commander, WW II & Korea; supervised post-war
    occupation of Japan), 120, 138
Macedonia (3rd Cent. B.C. Balkan kingdom of Philip & Alexander the Great;
    independent nation broke from Yugoslavia in 1991), 331
Machismo (exaggerated sense of masculine dominance in Latin American culture),
    174
Machiavelli (wrote The Prince, c.1530; advice on how to increase and hold power), 246
Machu Picchu (Incas' famed fortress city in the Peruvian Andes 6,750 feet above sea
    level), 161
Magna Carta, (guarantee of rights signed in1215 by English King John), 249-50, 275
Magsaysay, Ramon (Philippine President, 1953-57), 77
Magyars (Eastern European nomadic tribe that established itself in the region c. 900
    A.D.), 303
Mahan, Alfred Thayer (Am. Naval Captain coined the term "Middle East"), 188, 222
Mansa Musa (most famous of the Muslim rulers of Mali,14 C. A.D.), 20
Malaysia (federation of Malaya, Singapore, North Borneo, and Sarawak) formed in
    1963), 57, 76-77
Malayan peninsula (S.E.Asia), 58
Mali (West African Islamic kingdom, c.1200 A.D.), 18, 20
Manchu-Ching (Chinese dynasty, 1644 - 1912), 99
Manchuria (territorial conflict: Japan & Russia. c. 1905), 134-35, 149, 314
Mandate (right or command), 97, 206
Mandela, Nelson and Winnie (S. African anti-apartheid leaders), 33-34
Manor house (European feudal system: usually walled in for protection, surrounded
    by a moat, or at least on high ground), 239
Maps, 7
Mao Zedong (Chinese leader, established communist regime, 1949, d. 1976), 105-06,
    109-12, 115, 122
Marco Polo (Italian visitor to the court of Kublai Khan, 13 C.), 99
Marcos, Ferdinand (Philippine dictator,1965-86), 77
Mare nostrum (Mussolini's expansionist program for to restore Italy as a power in
    Mediterranean, c.1930's), 272
Market System (economic decisions based on free interaction of consumers and pro-
    ducers, minimal government regulation; also capitalism), 335

Marlowe (writer in Elizabethan England), 247
Marshall, George (U.S. Sec'y of State, responsible European Recovery Act), 120, 127, 282
Martel, Charles (turned back Muslim invaders at Battle of Tours, 8thC.A.D.), 238
Marx, Karl (19th century author *Communist Manifesto, Das Kapital*), 260-61; see Marxism
Marxism (Economic interpretation of history, Class struggle, Surplus Value Theory, and the Inevitability of Socialism), 105, 115, 260-61
Mate Grasso (extensive plains area of Brazil), 157
Mau Mau (Kenyan terrorist group in 1950's), 37
Mauryas (ancient civilization of India, 3rd C. B.C.), 59
Maximillan (Austrian archduke set up by the French as emperor of Mexico,1863), 171
Maya (Cent. American Indian civilization, 1500 B.C.-1548 A.D.), 158-159
Mazzini (organizer of 19th C. nationalists in Italy), 257
Mecca (Islamic holy city, Saudi Arabia), 199
Medieval period (500 to 1500 A.D. in Europe, also considered the feudal period), 237-240
Mediterranean Sea, 189, 230, 233
Megatrends (1985 work by John Naisbitt), 357, 360
Meiji Restoration (industrial era reorganization of Japan's power structure), 127, 133-34
Mekong (Southeast Asian river system), 58
Mensheviks (conserv. Marxist revolutionary party in Russia, 1900-17), 314
Mercantilism (establishing colonies as government-sponsored private business enterprises to bring wealth to mother country), 163, 252
Mesoamerica (Central America), 159
Mestizos (racial mixture formed when European colonizers of Latin America intermarried with Indians), 158
Mexico, 157, 170-71; oil production, 178
Michelangelo (Italian Renaissance artist: *Sistine Chapel, Pieta*, and *David*), 244
Middle Ages (see medieval), 237-240
Middle East:186-227; climate and natural resources, 190; democratic reforms, 215; impact of Islamic Fundamentalism, 220; impact of Western values, 220; mineral resources, 190; population distribution, 191; population growth, 220; role of religion, 215; role of women, 215; terrorism, 212
"Middle Kingdom" (China's ethnocentric reference to its culture as the center of the universe), 95, 128
Midway, battle of (1942 sea battle considered to be turning point for U.S. in Pacific theater of WW II), 137
Mines Act of 1842 (English worker safety), 259
Ming Dynasty (China, 1368-1644), 98, 99
Mir (Tsarist Russia: village community council), 312
Missi dominici (Charlemagne's traveling investigators), 238
Missionaries (sent to build churches & schools in settlements; taught Iberian languages, culture to Latin Americans), 163
Mitsui (large Japanese corporation), 144
Mitsubishi, Large Japanese corporation, 144
Mixed Economic System (combines elements of market and command), 43, 81-82, 219, 285
Mobutu, Joseph (Mobutu Sese Seko, leader of Zaire), 35
Model Parliament (English legislative prototype, established the concept of the power of the purse in 1295), 248, 275
Mohammed (originator and major prophet of Islamic faith), 61, 199-200
Moi, Pres. Daniel (2nd president of Kenya after 1st president Kenyatta), 38
Mohenjo Daro (India's earliest civilization, c.3000 BC), 59
Moldova (also Moldavia; independent nation [1991] in Eastern Europe between Romania and Ukraine; formerly one of the 15 republics of the Soviet Union), 299, 328
Mombasa (early East African trading state), 37

Mongol Yuan (Chinese dynasty, 1279 - 1368), 99

Mongols (Central Asian nomads, extensive conquests, 1200-1400 A.D.), 99, 204, 304

Monogamy (having one wife), 38

Monroe Doctrine (U.S. 1823 policy warned European nations against re-establishing
colonies in Latin America), 182

Monsoons (prevailing winds in East, South, and Southeast Asia; shift direction in
summer and winter), 56, 58, 96 [map], 126

Montenegro (S.W. Balkan state joined with Serbia in new Yugoslavia in 1991), 331

More, Thomas (statesman & author Renaissance England; *Utopia*), 244

Morley-Minto Reforms (Parliament broadened Indians' participation in colonial
government, 1908-09), 65

Moscow (capital city of U.S.S.R.), 329

Mosque (a house of worship for Muslims), 197

Moses (law-giver, leader of ancient Hebrew civilization), 199

Moshav (Israeli government agricultural organization), 219

Mossadegh, Mohammed(Iranian nationalist leader in 1950's), 214

Mother Teresa (Albanian Catholic nun; founded Missionaries of Charity [1940's] treat-
ing the sick and starving in India; Nobel Peace Prize in 1979), 348

Muawiyah, Caliph (Sunni Muslim leader established the Omayyad Dynasty, 632
A.D.), 201

Mughal (Mongol rulers of India,16th-19th C. A.D.), 59, 61

Mujahidin (Afghani Muslim insurgents who challenged the Soviets with organized
guerrilla raids, 1970's and '80's), 223

Mukden Incident (alleged Chinese attack on Japanese military train in 1937), 136

Mulattoes (Afro-Caucasian intermarriage in Latin America), 165

Multinational corporations (major business enterprises involved in many nations -
Unilever, Mitsubishi, ITT, General Motors, Exxon, Royal/ Dutch Shell,
Philips-Gloeilampenfabrieken), 42, 178, 181

Munich Conference (1938 summit meeting at which Britain and France appeased
Hitler, yielding Czech territory), 273

Music, African 21; Latin American 183; Russian 313

Muslim era, 199-203

Muslim League (agitated for partitioning of India into Hindu and Muslim sectors), 66

Mussolini, Benito (Italian Fascist leader, 1922-40's), 136, 273

Myanmar (Burma changed its name in 1989), 57

Myths and Legends (American culture), 17

Nagasaki (site of 2nd atomic bomb dropped by U.S. in 1945), 138, 273

Nairobi (Kenya's capital), 38

Namib (desert in southern Africa), 16

Namibia (formally Germany's South-West African colony; in 1968, U.N. Resolution
435 named the area Namibia), 34

Napoleon Bonaparte (ruler of France in early 1800's), 255, 311

Napoleonic Code of Laws (legal system for 19th C. French Empire), 255

Nara (Japan's earliest capital city), 128

Nasser, Gamal Abdul (nationalist leader of Egypt in 1950's), 212-213, 218-219

National Congress Party (ruling party in India), 65, 71

National Convention (power group in French Revolution, led by Robespierre, Danton,
and Marat), 254

"National Front" or "National Union" (power groups struggling in Angolan civil war),
51

National Insurance Service and National Health Service (British welfare system), 285

National Party (German right wing group aided Nazis in early 1930's), 270

National Socialist German Workers Party (Nazi Party), 270

Nationalism (a strong feeling of unity for people who desire to control their own
destinies) in Africa, 31; in China, 104; in Mid-East, 207; in Europe, 256-257

Nationalization (gov't. takeover of private enterprises), 84, 179, 213, 219

Native Land Act of 1913 (forbade black South Africans to own land outside reservations), 33

Natural Law (philosopical theories developed out of Sir Isaac Newton's discovery of the universal law of gravitation), 252

Natural Rights of Man (basic human rights theories growing out of Enlightenment era), 25, 252

Nazi Germany (persecution of Jews), 209, 270-272

Nazi-Soviet Non-Aggression Pact (1939), 273, 340

Nehru, Jawaharlal (disciple of Gandhi in the Congress Party, became the first Prime Minister), 71, 81, 83

Neimeyer, Oscar (Latin American architect), 184

Neo-colonialism (a new outside control of African economic life), 42

Neolithic Revolution (life began centering on agriculture), 191

Nepotism (the appointing of family members to control the key positions in government), 32

Neruda, Pablo (Chilean author), 184

Netherlands, 78, 165, 230

New Economic Policy (NEP; Lenin's socialist economic structure for the U.S.S.R.), 320, 335

New Harmony (utopian living experiment by English socialist Robert Owens in Indiana, U.S.A., 19th C.), 260

New Lanark, Scotland (utopian living experiment by English socialist Robert Owens, 19th C.), 260

New Testament (the Gospels of Matthew, Mark, Luke, and John), 194

Newton, Sir Isaac (universal law of gravitation, 18th C.), 252

Ngo Dinh Diem (President of the Rep. of South Vietnam, 1955-62), 74

Nicaragua, 172

Nicholas I (repressive Russian Tsar 1825-1855), 312

Nietzsche, Friedrich (19th C. German philosopher), 269

Niger (major West African river basin), 15

Nigeria (Federal Republic of), 37-38

Nihongi (*Chronicles of Japan*, 8th C. history of the Yamato Clan), 127

Nile River Basin (Egypt), 15, 189-93

Ninty Five (95) Theses (Martin Luther and reformation), 245

Nirvana (Hindu cycle of reincarnation broken when one achieves a perfect state of mind), 60

Nixon, Richard (U.S. involvement in Vietnam), 75, 120

Nkrumah, Kwame (nationalist leader and first President of Ghana), 32

No Confidence (in British gov't policy, the cabinet must either resign (in which case the opposition party forms a cabinet), or "go to the country" (election is held to determine reaction of country to issue involved), 276

Noh (plays of 14th century: Japanese myths and history), 130

Nok culture (ancient African civilization, c. 700 B.C.), 36

Nomadic (life-style of constant moving about, seeking food), 15, 188

Non-alignment (refuse to always be on same side in all issues), 49, 88

Noriega, Manuel (Panamanian dictator deposed 1989), 172

North Atlantic Drift (warm Gulf Stream currents modify Western Europe's climate), 230, 293

North Atlantic Treaty Organization (NATO; Western European and Canadian-American defense agreement), 290, 294

North Sea petroleum drilling (energy source for Western Europe), 230

Norway, 232

November Revolution (see Russian revolution of 1917), 316

Novgorod (important trading center for the Slavs who settled along the rivers in early Russia), 302

Nuclear Family (mother father, children), 38

Nuclear Nonproliferation Treaty (1968; attempted to stop spread of nuclear weapons to countries not already having them), 288, 352

Nuclear Test Ban Treaty (1963), 352
Nuremberg Trials (Nazi leaders tried for war crimes), 272
Nyerere, Julius (nationalist leader and first President of Tanzania), 32

Oasis (tiny fertile spots with water in desert), 15, 188
Ob River (Russian Siberia), 300
Occupation of Japan by U.S. (1945-1952), 138
October Manifesto (issued by Nicholas II, promised more power for the national
    legislature [Duma], and granted basic civil liberties, 1905), 314
O'Higgins, Bernardo (liberated Chile: 1810-1823), 166
Ogaden (region ruled by Ethiopia), 51
Old Testament (Bible; Jewish teachings and law on moral behavior), 194
Olduvai Gorge (Tanzania, East Africa, one of the most famous finds in modern
    anthropology), 17
Oleg (Varangian chief took over Kiev in about 862 A.D.) , 302
Oligarchy (power in the hands of a small group), 134, 169
Olympics (ancient Greek competitive games), 235
Omayyad (Muslim dynasty, 632 A.D.), 200-01
One-crop economies (Latin America: coffee, bananas, or sugar), 177
OPEC (cartel of oil producing states), 50, 218, 224, 350
Opium War (Anglo-Chinese power struggle 1839 - 1842), 102, 123
Opportunity cost (economic cost of making choices: in U.S.S.R., traditional scarcity of
    consumer goods was the economic "trade-off" of emphais on heavy industry), 335
Oral Traditions (myths, legends, anecdotes which provided entertainment and
    education for the young, and preserved traditions), 17
Orange Free State (established by Boer settlers after Dutch South African Cape
    Colony fell to British, c.1830's), 33
Orders in Council (British response to trade restrictions of Napoleonic Continental
    System), 255
Organization for African Unity (settles disputes, promotes causes), 32
Organization of American States (OAS; mutual assistance league for U.S. & Latin
    American nations), 154, 181, 183
Organization of Petroleum Exporting Countries (OPEC), 50, 218, 224, 350
Origin of Species, The (see Charles Darwin), 261
Orinoco River (northern South America), 156
Ortega, Daniel (Nicaraguan President), 172
Ottoman Empire (Major Muslim political structure from 14th to 20th C.), 197, 204-06,
    310
Outer Space Treaty (1967; prohibited spread of nuclear weapons to outer space), 288
Owen, Robert (19th C. English utopian socialist), 260

Pahlavi, Shah Muhammed Reza (overthrown in 1978 Iranian Revolution), 214
Paisley, Rev. Ian (leader of Northern Ireland Protestants), 277
Pakistan, 56, 66, 70, 73, 89
Palestine, 209, 212, 223
Palestinian Liberation Organization (PLO; seeks separate Palestinian Arab state in
    areas occupied by Israel; involved in terrorist activities; headed by Yassir Arafat),
    212, 223, 225, 353
Pampas (cattle and wheat region of Argentina),157
Pan-Africanism (movement to provide for African unity in world political and
    economic issues), 30, 32
Panama, 172
Pan-Americanism (movement to provide for inter-american unity in political and
    economic issues), 182
Pan-Arabism (movement to provide for Arab unity in world political and economic
    issues), 212

Panchayats (village councils in India), 72

Pan-Slavism (movement to provide for Slavic unity in world political and economic issues, pre-WW I), 315

Paris Peace Conference of 1919 (Treaty of Versailles), 264, 273

Parliament (British governmental system), 248, 259

Parthenon (temple erected by ancient Athenians to honor Athena, goddess of the city), 234

Patricians (nobles of ancient Rome), 235

Pass Laws (South African laws stated that all non-whites over 16 must carry passbooks which restricted where they could travel and work; repealed in 1984), 34

Pasternak, Boris (Soviet writer: *Dr. Zhivago*; denied the right to accept the Nobel prize; publication of the book in the Soviet Union was denied because it was critical of communism), 330

Patagonia (cold desert area on the southern tip of the South American continent), 157

Pathet Lao (Laotian communist movement), 76

Patrilinial (male-dominated ancestral/social structure), 174

Pax Romana (200 year domination of ancient Mediterranian world by the Romans), 237

Peace Corps (American volunteers for development of education, agricultural, and industrial programs in Third World nations), 51

Peaceful coexistence (Khrushchev's foreign policy of minimizing confrontations with Western powers), 324

Pearl Harbor (U.S. naval base in Hawaii), 67, 136-37

Peasant Revolution (basis for Mao Zedong's success in Chinese civil war), 106

Pedro I (proclaimed independen Brazilian empire in 1822), 166

Peking (Beijing; China's capital), 136

Peninsularies (Iberian-born nobles who acted as crown appointed rulers in colonial Latin America), 165

People's Republic of China (Communist regime came to power in 1949), 106

People's Republic of Kampuchea (earlier called Cambodia), 75-76

Per capita consumption (total production of nation÷ population), 335

Per capita income (total national income ÷ population = share per person), 82

Perestroika (Gorbachev's proposals for restructuring U.S.S.R.'s economy), 202, 325, 331, 345

Pericles (ancient Greek statesman,461-429 B.C.), 233

Peron, Juan (Argentine ruler, d. 1974), 171

Peron, Eva ("Evita"), 171

Perry, Commodore Matthew (U.S. naval officer negotiated reopening of Japan to international trade, c.1853), 133

Persian Gulf (center of oil production in Middle East), 56, 145, 214, 225

Persian Gulf Conflict (Iraq's invasion of Kuwait), 215

Persians (center of ancient Mid-East civilization, modern-day Iran), 193, 202

Peru, 158

Peter the Great (Tsar,1682-1725, attempted to westernize Russian culture and economy), 307

Peter's Pence (obligatory donations to Pope: Medieval Europe), 240

Petition of Right (1628 act strengthened British Parliament), 249-50

Philip of Macedonia (ruler of Hellenes; father of Alexander the Great; 359-336 B.C.), 235

Philippines (Republic of the), 77

Philip II of Spain (defeated by Elizabeth I of England in famous English Channel battle 1588), 247

Phnom Penh (capital of Kampuchea), 75

Phoenicians (Mediterranean traders; developed an alphabet code in which each letter stood for only one distinct sound), 192-93

Pictographs (pictures used for writing), 119, 129

Pierce, Franklin (U.S. President authorized Perry's mission to open Japanese trade relations, 1854), 133

Plato (philosopher of Ancient Greece, d.347 B.C.), 234

Plebians (common people of ancient Rome), 235

PLO (see Palestinian Liberation Organization), 212, 223, 225, 353

Pogroms (violent purges, often against the Jews), 269, 314

Pol Pot (Kampuchean Premier & violent purges of 1970's), 76

Polish Silesia (significant amounts of coal and iron ore vital to the country's continuing industrialization), 302

Political Philosophers (17th-18th C. European Enlightenment: Locke, Voltaire, Montesquieu, Smith, Paine), 252-53

Politics and Ethics (Aristotle's work advised moderation in life as well as the use of logic and reason), 234

Polygamy (having more than one wife), 38

Polyrhythmic (African music using two or more rhythms at once), 21

Polytheism (belief in a multiplicity of gods)

Pontoon (floating bridge suspensions), 273

Pope Urban II (called for a crusade to regain control of the Holy Land from the Muslim Turks in 1095), 243

Popular Movement (Soviet-backed Angolan civil war group), 51

Population density (number of people per square mile), 94

Population explosion (straining African resources today), 27

Po River valley (Italy), 234

Portugal, 154, 163-167, 232

Portuguese missionary work (Africa), 21

Potsdam Conference of 1945 (post-WW II disagreements among WW II Allies), 289 [chart], 341

Power of the purse (financial control British Parliaments used to decrease the power of kings in need of additional revenues), 248

Pre-Columbian times (before the first voyages of European discovery by Columbus in 1492), 158-61

Presbyterian (Calvinist church organization), 245

Precedents (past actions and decisions that act as models), 275

Pretoria (administrative capital of South Africa), 33

Prime Minister (the nation's chief executive; British Prime Minister is the majority leader of the House of Commons), 141, 275

Prince Henry (15th C. Portuguese ruler encouraged voyages of exploration), 251

Privatization (market economic reforms to turn government operated facilities into private businesses), 335

Protestant Reformation (16th - 18th C. Europe religious reform), 245-246

Puerto Rico (U.S. Caribbean possession), 172

Punjab (troubled Indian province), 70

Purge of the Soviet Communist Party (late 1930's, Stalin brutally eliminated any opposition), 321

Puritan Revolution (1642; overthrow of British monarchy), 249

Puritans (Calvinist Anglican reformers), 248

Pygmy people of African rainforest, 16

Pyramidal social structures (the forerunners of Latin American structures of today), 159, 165 [chart]

Pythagoras (ancient Greek mathematician; principles of geometry, d.500 B.C.), 234

Pyrenees (mts. on French-Spanish border), 230, 232

Qaddafi, Muammar (Libyan leader overthrew monarchy, 1969; used vast oil reserves to promote terrorism and revolutions in Middle East), 213

Que chua (spoken language of Inca), 161

Quipu (Inca civilization; official records), 161

Quotations of Chairman Mao (Mao's communist philosophy), 111

Qur'an (*Koran* – Islam's sacred text), 61, 199, 208

Rabbis (Jewish religious teachers), 194
Rabin, Yitzhak (Prime Minister of Israel - signed *Declaration of Principles for Palestinian Self-rule* in Sept. 1993 with PLO's Yassir Arafat), 212
Radio-Carbon Dating (scientific method of determining the age of dead organic matter by measuring its Carbon 14 emissions), 17
Raphael (Renaissance painter, *Disputa*), 244
Reagan, Ronald (U.S. President 1981-89), 51, 142, 172, 225, 325, 352
Red Army (successful in stabilizing and securing Russia for the Bolsheviks 1917-21, under the leadership of Leon Trotsky), 320
Red Brigades in Italy (leftist terrorist activities), 353
Red Guards (Chinese students mobilized in 1960's Cultural Revolution), 111
Red River (Vietnam), 58
Re-flagging of Kuwaiti oil tankers (as U.S. vessels to insure the safe transportation of vital petroleum supplies to the free world), 225
Refugee camps (Israeli-PLO problems), 212
Regions (areas with common physical, political, economic, and /or cultural traits), 8
Reign of Terror (French Revolution in 1790's; resulted in the execution of between 15-45,000 presumed opponents of the French Rev.), 254
Reich Culture Chambers (Nazi agencies established to control the work of artists, sculptors and all others in the fine arts), 271
Reichstag (lower house of the German parliament), 270
Reincarnation (Hindu belief in rebirth of the soul in another form of life), 59
Renaissance (13th -17th centuries European revival of classical culture), 243-44
Republic (definition of), 236
Republic, The (most famous of Plato's *Dialogues*), 234
Republic of Biafra, 36
Republic of China, 104, 109; (Taiwan gov't: 120-21)
Republic of Indonesia, 78, 84
Republic of South Africa, 33-34, 256
Republic of South Vietnam, 74
Republic of Singapore, 77
Republic of the Philippines, 77
Restoration period (rule of Charles II in 1660's after English Puritan Revolution), 249
Revisionist (one who attempts to change accepted views of Marx), 316
Revolution of the proletariat (uprising and control of society's productive resources by the working classes), 316
Rhine River and its canal system (vital Western European communication-transportation route for centuries), 231
Rhodes, Cecil (British imperialist in Africa), 24, 33
Rhodopes Mountains (southern Bulgaria), 301
Ritual ceremonies (of African tribal religions at birth, puberty, and death), 20
Rio de la Plata (River of Silver in South America), 156
Rocky Mountains of North America (extend into Central America), 156
Roland, Jon (computer expert of Texas predicted technological breakthroughs), 352
Role model cities (Zurich, Edinburgh, Leningrad, and Beijing demonstrate positive alternatives for desirable urban living), 355
Roman Catholic Church, 20, 154, 163-165, 239-240, 243, 303
Roman Empire, 194-95, 235-237
Romanesque and Gothic cathedrals, 240
Romania, 302
Romanov, Michael (ruled Russia in 1613, established the Romanov dynasty), 306-307
Romanticism (19th C. European literary and artistic movement), 279
Rome-Berlin-Tokyo Axis (1939 alliance of three of the aggressor nations of the world), 136, 272
Roosevelt, Eleanor (wife of FDR: U.N. crusade for human rights), 356
Roosevelt, Franklin D. (U.S. President, 1933-45), 31, 137, 182, 288
Roosevelt, Theodore (U.S. President 1901-09), 172, 182

Rosetta Stone (aided in deciphering Egyptian hieroglyphics), 192

Rotten boroughs (in Britain, areas with little or no population and representation in Parliament), 259

Roundheads (see Puritan Revolution in England), 249

Royal Niger Company (private British charter company set up trading enclaves along sea routes to the Orient), 26

Rub al Khali ("empty quarter" huge Saudi desert region), 189

Ruhr Crisis (1923; highlighted Weimar Republic's economic problems), 269

Russia (ancient civilization of easternmost Europe; spread into Central Asia under empire of Tsars; overthrown by Bolshevik revolution in 1917 under Lenin; also see U.S.S.R. and Russian Federation), 302-316

Russian-American Confrontation Since World War II, 343-45

Russian-British Rivalry, 205

Russian Dancers (Anna Pavlova, Vaslav Nijinsky), 313

Russian Federation (independent nation [1991] in E. Europe and Asia; formerly largest of the 15 republics of the Soviet Union and its center; one of the original members of the Commonwealth of Independent States [CIS]; Moscow [cap.]), 322-345.

Russian Music (Tchaikovsky, Rimsky, Korsakov, Mussorgsky), 313

Russian Orthodox Church, 308, 329

Russian People, 327

Russian Religion, 328

Russian Revolution of 1905, 314

Russian Revolutions of 1917, 315

Russian Writers (Pushkin, Tolstoy, Dostoevsky), 313

Russification (conquered people were forced to adopt the Russian language, culture and religion in an attempt to increase the degree of unity within the country), 306

Russo-Japanese War (1904-1905), 134-35, 314

Russo-Turkish War (1877-78), 311

SALT agreements (U.S.-U.S.S.R. arms limtation treaties, 1970's), 325

Sadat, Egyptian President Anwar (signed Camp David Accords with Israel, assassinated 1981), 211, 213

Sadler Report on factories (19th C. British industrialization), 259

Sahara (world's largest desert), 15, 188

Sahel (a drought-stricken area of west central Africa), 43

Saint Peter's Basilica: Rome, (center of Roman Catholic religion), 244

St. Petersburg (Peter the Great's westernized imperial Russian capital on Baltic; also Leningrad under communists), 308

Saigon (Vietnam capital), 75

Salt March (Gandhi's non-violent protest of British tax system), 66

Salween (major river basin in Burma), 58

Samurai (warrior class in feudal Japan), 129

Sandinistas (Nicaraguan communist guerrilla movement named for 1920's rebel, Augusto Sandino; converted country to Marxist state,1979), 172, 182

Sanskrit language (ancient India), 59

Santa Anna, Antonio Lopez de (Mexican dictator after independence in 1821), 170

Satellite (nation dominated by an outside power; Eastern Europe controlled by Soviet Union 1945-1990), 331

Saudi Arabia, 206

Savak (Iranian Shah's hated secret police), 214

Savanna climate (Tropical grassland[Bs]), 16

Savimbi, Jonas (Angolan rebel leader), 51

Scandanavia (Norway, Sweden, Finland, Denmark, Iceland, and Greenland), 232

Schism (split usually in religious matters), 200

Schuman, Robert (French statesman whose plan was to remove barriers and the movement of workers within those industries between Western European nations after WW II), 285

Scientific socialism (see Marxism), 260-61
Scorched-earth policy (retreat and destroy tactics used by Russians to defeat
     Napoleonic invaders), 256, 340
Scramble for Africa (European imperialism in 19th C.), 26-28, 35
S.E.A.T.O. (see Southeast Asia Treaty Organization), 87-88
Seko, Mobutu Sese (also Joseph Mobutu; leader of Zaire), 35
Second Sino-Japanese War (1937-1945), 136
Selassie I, Haile (Ethiopian Emperor, 1930-74), 32, 51
Seljuk Turks, 203-204
Semites (ethnic group made up of the Arab, Assyrian, and Hebrew peoples), 191
Sepoy Rebellion (1858 Hindu and Moslem mutiny against British), 64
Serbia (central Balkan nation now part of Yugoslavia), 311, 331
Serbs (dominant ethnic group in central Balkans), 331
Serfs (peasants legally bound to the land), 239, 304, 312
Seven Years War (Anglo-French colonial struggle, 1757-1763), 251
Shah Jahan (Indian ruler, 1629-58), 61
Shakespeare (Elizabethan era dramatist), 247
Shanghai (major port of the Yangtze, China), 95
Shari'a (Islamic moral rules are incorporated into a code of law), 200
Shikoku (one of the major islands of Japan), 125
Shintoism (Japanese religion), 128
Shi'ites (Muslim fundamentalist sect), 200, 214, 220
Shiva (Hindu deity), 59
Shogun (Japanese feudal military ruler), 129
Shotoku (Japanese regime blended Chinese culture, 592-621 A.D.), 128
Siberia (Northern part of Asiatic region of U.S.S.R.), 300
Sierras (coastal ranges of Central America), 156
Sihanouk, Norodom (Cambodian ruler 1942-63), 75
Sikhism (Hindu sect founded in the 15th century), 60, 62, 70, 73
Silkworm missiles (fired by the Iranians at U.S. vessels in Persian Gulf), 352
Silicon Chip (low-cost electronic computer technology), 357
Sinai Peninsula (conquered by Israel in 1967 war; returned to Egypt by Camp David
     agreement), 211
Singapore, 57-58, 77, 84
Sino-Japanese War (1894-1895; ended Chinese power in E. Asia), 103, 134
Sino-Soviet Relations, 121
Six Day War (1967 Arab-Israeli War), 211
Slavs (dominant E. European tribal group; ancestors of Poles, Slovaks, Czechs,
     Slovenes, Croats, Serbs), 197, 302
Slave Trade (Africa), 24-26
Slavophils (18th C. Russia, favored the traditional Russian values), 308
Slovakia (eastern region of former Czechoslovakia; independent 1992), 331
Slovenia (N.W. Balkan country; broke away from Yugoslavia, 1991), 331
Sobieski, King John (17th C., Poland reached its height under his leadership), 309
Social Darwinism (see Darwin), 261
Social Democrats (early 20th C. Russian Marxist party), 314
Socialism (Marxist influenced economic system: gov't. controls means of production),
     43, 260-61
Socialists (Japanese Political Party), 141
Socialist Republic of Vietnam, 74
Socrates (Greek philosopher, d. 399 B.C.), 234
Soldiers of fortune (mercenaries), 50
Solzhenitsyn, Aleksandr (dissident expelled from U.S.S.R.), 327
Somalia (poor E. African nation; starvation & civil war in 1990's U.S.- Soviet rivalry
     in), 51
Somoza (Nicaraguan dictator overthrown by communists, 1979), 172, 177
Sonar (helped the Allies German U-boats in WW II), 279
Songhai (ancient West African kingdom), 18

South America, 154-185
Souvanna Phouma, Prince (pro-Western Laotian leader in1960's), 76
Souphanouvong, Prince (Laotian communist leader), 76
South and Southeast Asia, 54-91
Southeast Asia Treaty Organization (SEATO; multilateral defense arrangement with
    U.S. in 1954; disbanded in 1975), 87-88
South-West Africa People's Organization (SWAPO; communist guerrilla group in
    Namibia), 34
Soviet Academy of Sciences (past role in discouraging technological innovation), 337
Soviet advisors in Africa (aid insurgents in civil wars), 37, 50-51
Soviet Central Asian Muslim Republics (government has some fear of fundamentalism
    causing rebellion), 223-24
Soviet Union (see U.S.S.R.), 89, 322
Space Race (U.S.-U.S.S.R. Cold War struggle), 343
Spain, 154, 163-67, 232
Spanish-American War in 1898 (made U.S. colonial power in Western Hemisphere),
    77
Sparta (ancient Greek city-state, ruled as military oligarchy), 233
Spenser (Elizabethan literary figure), 247
Spheres of influence (imperialist sectioning off of China trade), 103, 205
Sri Lanka (currently involved in a civil war in which basic rights violations and
    terrorism are frequent), 56, 357
SS (Nazi secret police violated human rights, and discouraged the opposition), 271
Stalin, Josef (Soviet dictator,1925-53), 273, 320
Stanley, Henry (American news correspondent, explored central Africa in late 19th
    C.), 35
Status quo (current situation), 170
Stephen I (King of Hungary, 1001-1038), 310
Steppe (open grassy plains; also type Bs climate), 16
Strait of Gibraltar (Western entrance to the Mediterranean), 232
Strait of Hormuz (narrow area of Persian Gulf sees frequent attacks on oil tankers),
    215
Strategic Arms Limitation Treaty (SALTI placed limits on certain types of missiles.
    SALTII placed limits on delivery vehicles, warheads, but U.S. Senate did not
    ratify the agreement because of its concerns over Soviet activities in Cuba and
    Afghanistan), 343, 352
Strategic Defense Initiative (SDI; also referred to as "Star Wars;" proposed U.S.
    space-based missile defense system; a stumbling block to U.S.-Soviet arms
    reduction negotiations), 352
Stuart rulers (Scottish house succeeded Tudors in England), 247
Substitution policy (Latin American economic policies which restricted imports and
    encouraged local manufacturers to produce similar consumer goods), 176
Subsistence agriculture (producing barely for one's own needs), 42, 45
Sudeten Mountain Range (Czechoslovakia), 301
Suez Canal (crisis occured when nationalized in 1956 move by Nasser), 210, 218, 291
Suharto (military ruler of Indonesia), 78, 84
Sukarno (first President of Indonesian republic), 78, 84
Sulieman the Magnificent (ruled over golden age of Ottoman Empire, 1520-1566), 204,
    310
Sultan- (title used by Arabian imperial rulers), 203
Sumerians (ancient civilization in Mid East's fertile crecent, c. 3000 B.C.), 191-193
Sun King (reference to France's Louis XIV's absolute power; monarch as center of all
    existence), 247
Sun Yat-sen (early 20th C. Chinese nationalist leader established the Republic of
    China), 104
Sunnis (orthodox Islamic sect), 200
Supercities - The Growing Crisis (concern on unchecked urban growth), 355
Superpowers (powerful political states - U.S. and U.S.S.R.), 222, 274, 351

Supreme Allied Commander (NATO), 294
SWAPO (South West Africa - guerrillas), 34
Sweden, 232

Talmud (holy book of Judaic faith, knowledge, and ethics), 194
Taiwan (Republic of China; stronghold of Chinese nationalists), 106, 121, 134
Taj Mahal (magnificent Indian building of Shah Jahn's reign), 61
Tang dynasty (China; revived Confucianism, 618-907 A.D.), 98
Taoism (ancient Chinese philosophy; revered nature, self-knowledge, simplicity), 97
Tara Singh (nationalist leader, demanded special status for India's Punjab state as a
    semi-autonomous Sikh homeland), 70
Teheran Conference of 1943 (WW II Allied meeting - Stalin/FDR/Churchill), 289, 341
Tel Aviv airport (site of 1973 attack in Israel by Japanese terrorists working with the
    PLO), 353
Ten Hours Act (1847 British law limits work: women, children), 259
Tenochtitlan (Aztec city-state; present site of Mexico City), 159-60
Terrorism (systematic use of violence to force a group to do something), 212, 215, 223
Thailand, 57, 76, 90
Thames River (Great Britain), 230
Thatcher, Margaret (British Prime Minister, 1979-), 71, 276
Theocratic (governmental rule by religious officials), 20
Theory of Natural Selection (see Darwinism), 261
Three Principles of the People (basic political philosophy of Chinese Republic's
    founder, Sun Yat-sen, c. 1912), 104
Third World (underdeveloped nations, usually unaligned in world politics), 52, 81,
    122, 182, 184, 348, 351
Thirty Eighth Parallel (38°N; division between N. & S. Korea), 120
Tiananman Square Massacre (Beijing, 1989), 112
Tigris River (in South West Asia, empties into Persian Gulf; site of ancient
    civilizations of Middle East), 189-93
Tikal (major city of Mayan civilization in Central America), 159
Timbuktu (ancient Islamic trading city of West Africa), 20
Tithe ("a tenth"; in Medieval Europe, 10% of earnings were to be donated to church),
    165, 240
Toffler, Alvin (contemporary writer on future, works: *Future Shock*, *The Third Wave*),
    347
Tokugawa Seclusion Policy (isolation for Japan,17th-19th C. A.D.), 130
Tokugawa Shogunate (1603-1868; feudal rule in Japan), 127, 130
Tokyo (capital city of Japan), 130
Tomb Period (tribal rule in Japan, 300- 650 A.D.), 127
Topographical maps, 8
Torah (Hebrew holy scripture; books of the Old Testament), 194
Totalitarian government (absolutist government exercising total control over all
    aspects of the lives of the people), 271, 320-322
Toxic waste (dangerous poisons, chemicals, and materials), 353
Transvaal (one of the inland colonies established by Dutch Boers in South Africa, c.
    1830), 33
Transcaucasus (unstable mountainous area in extreme southeastern Eurasia between
    Black and Caspian Seas; many contending ethnic / religious groups; Georgia, Ar-
    menia, Azerbaijan),322, 326
Trans-Siberian Railroad (opens U.S.S.R.'s Siberian region to development, in 20th C.),
    300, 312
Treaty of Brest-Litovsk (Bolsheviks signed peace with the Germans in 1917, removing
    Russia from WW I), 316
Treaty of Kanagawa (Japan-U.S. agreement, opened trade, 1854), 133
Treaty of Nanking (China ceded the island of Hong Kong to Britain and opened five
    treaty ports to foreigners,1842), 103

Treaty of Portsmouth (ended Russo-Japanese war, 1905), 135

Treaty of San Stefano (1877, granted Bulgarian autonomy), 311

Treaty of Shimonoseki (1895; ended Sino-Japanese War; granted Japan the island of Formosa [Taiwan]), 134

Treaty of Tordesillias (set up by Pope in1494 to divide colonial regions of Spain and Portugal), 163

Treaty of Versailles (ended WW I in 1919; noted for harsh treatment of Germany and establishment of League of Nations), 264

Tributary system (Chinese dynasties required conquered regions to send tribute [gifts] to the Manchu overlords), 100, 102

Tripartite Pact (1940: Germany, Italy, Japan in Axis Alliance), 137

Triple Alliance (pre-WW I: Germany, Austria-Hungary, and Italy) , 262

Triple Entente (pre-WW I understanding of France, Russia, and Britain), 262

Tropical rainy (wet) climate (rainforest [Af]), 15

Tropical dry climate (usually desert [Bw]) 16

Tropical Wet-and-dry climate [Aw], 16

Trotsky, Leon (major figure of Boshevik Revolution; organized Red Army; exiled by Stalin;assassinated in Mexico, 1940), 320

Truman, Harry S (U.S. President; set up Marshall Plan and other aid programs for underdeveloped nations to insulate against communist insurgency after WW II; see Truman Doctrine), 88, 120, 138, 288

Truman Doctrine (1947; designed by U.S. to help Greece and Turkey resist the threats of communism), 290

Tsar (Russian Emperor, also spelled as czar and tzar), 306

Tsetse fly (carries the "sleeping sickness," destroys the effectiveness of the horse, oxen, and manpower in sub-Saharan Africa), 18

Tshombe, Moise (leader in brutal power struggle in Congo [Zaire] after independence), 35

Tutu, Bishop Desmond (S. African anti-apartheid leader; awarded 1984 Nobel Peace Prize), 33, 356

Tuareg (nomadic people of N. African desert), 15

Tudors (Englilsh dynasty, 1485-1603), 247

Tundra (type ET climate; subarctic treeless plain), 298

Turkey, 88, 195, 209 [map]

Turks (nomadic people of southwest Asia; rose as dominant Mid East group 1450-1915 A.D.; see Ottoman Empire), 202-06, 243, 250

Twenty-One Demands (Japanese attempt to sujugate China in the Pre-WW I period), 135

Twelve Tables (codified laws of the ancient Romas), 236

Uhuru (rallying cry for African independence movement), 31

Ukraine (independent nation [1991] in Eastern Europe bordered by Belarus, Poland, Czechoslovakia, Hungary, Moldova, Romania and Russia; formerly one of the 15 republics of the Soviet Union; one of the original members of the Commonwealth of Independent States [CIS]; Kiev [cap.]), 299

Union of South Africa (joined Cape Colony, Transvaal, and Orange Free State into semi-autonomous state in British Empire c.1910; became independent Republic of South Africa in 1961), 33

Union of Soviet Socialist Republics (U.S.S.R. or Soviet Union; formed after 1917 revolution) 298-345; 351

UNITA (party in Angolan civil war; also the National Union), 51

United Kingdom (see Great Britain), 230

United Nations 32, 49, 122, 182, 210-11, 291-93, 348; Court of Justice, 293; Economic and Social Council, 293; Food and Agricultural Organization, 349; General Assembly, 90, 293; Resolution #242 - 211; Resolution #435 - 34; Secretariat, 292; Secretary General, 292; Security Council, 292; Trusteeship Council, 292; Univ. Decl. of Human Rights, 356

United States: & Africa 50-51; & U.S.S.R., 343; & Europe, 293; & India, 89; & People's Republic of China, 119-21; & Japan, 138, 144-48; & Philippines, 77, 90; & Latin America, 181; & Middle East; 222; U. S. Constitution, 169, 253; U.S. Immigration and Naturalization Service (INS), 179; U.S.-Japanese Mutual Security Pact (1951), 148
Ural Mountains (dividing line between Europe and Asia), 300
Urengoi (natural gas pipeline from Siberia to W, Europe), 337
Usury (lending money at interest), 240
Utopian socialist (Robert Owen), 260

V-1 and V-2 (jet-propelled bombs developed by Nazis in WW II), 273
Varangians (Slavic warrior group protected Kiev state in Russia), 302
Vasco da Gama (15th C. Portuguese explorer; reached India via Cape Horn in Africa in 1498), 251
Vassals (knights swearing oaths of loyalty to the more powerful nobles in Medieval European feudal system), 239
Veches (in early Russian society, citizen assemblies dealt with local affairs), 303
Velvet Revolution (quiet, voluntary 1992 separation of Czechoslovakia into the Czech Republic and Slovakia), 331
Versailles, 247. 264, 269, 270
Viceroys (Spanish crown-appointed colonial governors in Lat. Am.), 164
Viceroyalties (Spain's New World administrative regions: New Spain, Peru, New Grenada, and LaPlata), 164-165
Vietnam, 74-75, 88
Vietnam War, 57, 74-75, 120, 122, 290
Vietnamese "boat people," 77
Vikings (Norsemen; 8th and 9th C. invading groups overran Europe), 238
Virgin Lands Plan (1960's U.S.S.R. plan by Khrushchev for vast new state farms), 336
Vishnu (Hindu deity), 59
Vladimir (Grand Prince of Kiev; effected conversion to the Eastern Orthodox Catholic Church), 303
Volga River (Russia), 300

Walesa, Lech (led Polish Solidarity Labor Movement; worked for democratic reforms to end communist regime; elected President of free Poland 1991), 330
War Communism (Bolsheviks' initial command economic policy after U.S.S.R. was established), 320, 335
Warlord (Chinese military dictators of each province after Republic founded in 1912), 104
Wars of Liberation (communist insurgent movements in Third World aided by China), 122
Warsaw Pact (Soviet alliance of Eastern European nations; gave Soviet commanders control over the satellites' armies), 290, 331, 343
Washington Naval Arms Conference (1922, limited Japanese naval power in comparison to that of Britain, France, and the U.S.), 136
Weimar Republic (weak German government, 1919-33), 269
West Bank of Jordan (Israeli-controlled Palestinian area), 210 [map], 211-212
West (XI) River (China; area of earliest civilizations), 94
Westernization (Peter the Great's attempts to emulate Europe and modernize 17th C. Russian society), 307
Whites (after 1917 opposition group of Bolshevik Revolution), 320
William III (of Orange) and Mary II (17th C. English monarchs installed after Glorious Revolution, after Stuart King James II), 249
Wilson, Woodrow (U.S. President, WW I), 182, 263
Women (Africa, 39; Japan, 142; Latin Am., 174; Mid-East, 215; U.S.S.R., 239
World Bank and IMF, 42, 50

World Food Congress in Washington, D.C. (1963), 349

World Today (issues and problems): arms control, 352; cultural conflict, 351; customs & beliefs, 361; economic systems, 350; developing nations, 348; education, 349; environmental issues, 353; erosion & desertification, 354; "Haves" and "Have-Nots", 349; human rights, 356; hunger, 349; institutions, 360; linguistic impact, 360; population pressures, 348; resources and energy, 351; space, 359; superpowers, 351; technology, 357, 361; terrorism, 353; trade, 350; transportation and communication advances, 359; water and earth contamination, 353

World War I (1914-1918) 31, 135, 206, 262-65, 315

World War II (1939-45) 31-2, 66, 106, 119, 137, 182, 209, 272-74

Xavier, Francis (Christian missionary: China & Japan in 16th C.), 130

Yalta Conference (1945: WW II Allied meeting; Stalin/FDR/Churchill planned end of war), 289, 341

Yamato Clan Leaders (first emperors of Japan, c. 220 A.D.), 127

Yaroslav (11th century ruler; Kiev city-state federation reached its height and had"golden age"), 304

Yayoi Culture (300 B.C.; early Asiatic conquerers of Japan), 127

Yellow (Huang) & Yangtze (Chang Jiang) River Valleys (sites of early Chinese civilizations), 94

Yeltsin, Boris (Russian Federation President; tried to accelerate Gorbachev's reforms; held reform government together during August 1991 coup in U.S.S.R.; presided over dissolution of Soviet Union),327-345

Yenisei River (Siberian region, U.S.S.R.), 300

Yom Kippur War (1973 attack on Israel by Egypt & Syria on the Jewish Day of Atonement), 211

Yorba (Ancient West African trading state), 24, 25

Yoritomo (first military ruler to take the title Shogun, 1155 A.D.), 129

Yuan Shih-kai (first President of Chinese Republic, 1912), 104

Yugoslavia, 302, 311

Zaibatsu (large, powerful Japanese corporations), 144

Zaire River basin (central Africa, once called the Congo), 15

Zaire (Republic of), 35-36

Zen Buddhism (popular among samurai; required meditation called for much self-discipline), 129

Zimbabwe, 18, 21, 24

Zionism (movement for a Jewish homeland founded1897 by Theodor Herzel), 206, 209

Zulu people (Southern Africa), 26, 33

Examination Strategies

How you approach the final exam and how you use your time can often affect your success.

- **Take the full amount of time:** You've spent a great deal of time and effort getting ready for the exam. A few minutes taken at the end can help you spot errors and make appropriate adjustment.

- **First Reading:** Skim over the whole examination quickly. Answer only those Part I questions of which you are absolutely sure. Skip the rest. When you get to Part II, read the questions and jot down on scrap paper any pieces of factual data you think you might use to answer the question. Do this for *each* question on Part II. It will help you decide which questions to choose to write.

- **Second Reading:** Read Part I again, but more slowly this time. Answer as many questions as you can, but don't be afraid to leave an answer blank for now. As you go through Part I this time, be alert for ideas which you might use in your Part II answers. Jot them down on scrap paper as they come to mind.

- **Write a Part II Answer:** Choose the Part II question about which you feel most confident and write the answer. Be brief. Let the point values guide you on how much to write. Written answers should not be more than two pages. Be sure to label the parts of the answer exactly as they are on the examination.

- **The Global Studies Exam lists these instructions for Part II:**

1)   include specific factual information wherever possible.
2)   keep to the questions asked; do not go off on a tangent.
3)   avoid over-generalizations and sweeping statements which are difficult to prove.
4)   keep these general definitions in mind:
       a.   <u>discuss</u> means "to make observations about something using facts, reasoning, and arguments; to present in some detail"
       b.   <u>describe</u> means "to illustrate something in words or tell about it"
       c.   <u>show</u> means "to point out; to set forth clearly a position or idea by stating it and giving data which support it"
       d.   <u>explain</u> means "to make plain or understandable; to give reasons for or causes of; to show the logical development or relationships of"

- **Third Reading:** Go back to Part I and work briefly on the remaining questions, then write out the remaining two Part II answers using the same guidelines as above.

- **Fourth Reading:** Finish Part I. Take your best guess on any questions of which you are unsure. *Do not leave any answer spaces blank.* Re-read all your answers on Part II carefully, and make corrections and alterations neatly. *Make sure all parts of each answer are properly and distinctly labeled.*

Practice Exam 1 — *June 1992*

Part I (55 credits)
Answer all 48 questions in this part.

Directions (1-48): For each statement or question, write on the separate answer sheet the *number* of the word or expression that, of those given, best completes the statement or answers the question.

1   The early civilizations of the Nile River Valley, Mesopotamia, and the Yellow River Valley were similar because they were
1   industrialized societies
2   monotheistic
3   dependent on fertile land
4   dependent on each other for trade

2   The Russian steppe is most similar in topography to the
1   mountains in Switzerland   3   rain forests in South America
2   deserts in the Middle East   4   savannas in Africa

3   Which quotation best reflects a feeling of nationalism?
1   "An eye for an eye and a tooth for a tooth."
2   "A person's greatest social obligation is loyalty to the family."
3   "For God, King, and Country."
4   "Opposition to evil is as much a duty as is cooperation with good."

4   In most societies, urbanization has
1   weakened traditional values and life patterns
2   strengthened the influence of the extended family system
3   discouraged economic growth
4   promoted population growth

5   Geographic diversity in the Middle East has contributed to
1   unequal standards of living
2   a common economic system
3   similar political systems
4   military alliances with Japan

6   Which factor has contributed most to the social and cultural identity of the Middle East?
1   political stability of the region
2   ability of the region to export oil
3   lack of foreign involvement in the region
4   strong influence of Islam on the region

7   Israel is a country that has
1   an abundance of oil
2   a democratically elected government
3   Islam as its official religion
4   friendly ties to Jordan

8   In 1979, the signing of the Camp David accords by Egypt and Israel indicated that
    1   nationalism was no longer a force in Middle Eastern politics
    2   the differences between Shi'ite and Sunni Moslems had been settled
    3   former enemies were able to negotiate
    4   the Soviet Union dominated Middle Eastern affairs

9   During the 1980's, the economic development of Iran and Iraq was disrupted because of
    1   increased emphasis on agricultural production for export
    2   the war fought between these nations
    3   Communist revolutionary movements in these nations
    4   severe drought and famine in the area

10   A major factor that continues to contribute to terrorist activities in the Middle East is
    1   a decrease in crude oil prices on the world market
    2   the Palestinian effort to establish a homeland
    3   the presence of United Nations forces in Syria
    4   the worldwide rejection of violence as a means to end conflict

Base your answer to question 11 on the table below and on your knowledge of social studies.

STATISTICS FOR SELECTED NATIONS OF SOUTH ASIA

Nations	Population Density (per sq. mi.)	Gross National Product (billion dollars)	Per Capita Income (dollars)	Percent of Labor Force in Agriculture	Literacy Rate (%)
Bangladesh	1,843	15.0	113	74	25
Burma	147	6.5	179	66	66
India	612	190.0	150	70	36
Pakistan	344	35.0	360	53	26
Vietnam	478	9.8	180	70	78

Source: *World Factbook,* 1988

11   Which is a valid statement based on the information in the table?
    1   Bangladesh has the highest percentage of children enrolled in school.
    2   Vietnam has the smallest number of workers involved in agriculture.
    3   India produces the most goods and services.
    4   Factory work is the main occupation in South Asian nations.

12   The primary goal of the Indian National Congress (1885-1947) was to
    1   reform the Hindu religion
    2   partition India between Muslims and Hindus
    3   create a socialist economy
    4   gain independence from Great Britain

13   India has developed a mixed economy that
    1   guarantees government control over the economy
    2   provides open competition without government interference
    3   blends free enterprise with socialism
    4   relies on the traditional barter system

14 "When I go to the office, I put on my shirt and I take off my caste; when I come home, I take off my shirt and I put on my caste."
What is the main idea of this quotation?
1 The caste system continues to influence Indian society.
2 The caste system has been rejected by most Indians.
3 Successful urban workers in India belong to the same caste.
4 The Indian Government officially supports the caste system.

15 In ancient China, one effect on government of the teachings of Confucius was the high status of
1 soldiers
2 merchants
3 farmers
4 scholars

16 During the centuries of dynastic rule, the Chinese rejected other cultures as inferior to their own. This situation illustrates the concept of
1 ethnocentrism
2 imperialism
3 social mobility
4 cultural diffusion

17 After World War II, the Chinese Communists were successful in their revolution mainly because the
1 United States refused to support the Nationalists
2 Communists had the support of the peasants
3 Communists had more technologically advanced weapons
4 Nationalists had been defeated by Japan

18 Which fact about China has been the cause of the other three?
1 The economy of China has trouble providing for all the needs of the people.
2 The Chinese Government has set limits on the number of children families may have.
3 Chinese cities have a severe shortage of housing.
4 China's population exceeds one billion.

19 Which reform took place in Japan after World War II?
1 Japan's industrial capability was greatly reduced.
2 The emperor's position was abolished.
3 Japan became a representative democracy.
4 Labor unions were declared illegal.

20 Which statement best describes Japan since the end of World War II?
1 Japan has become a major force in the world economy.
2 Japan has adopted a policy of imperialism toward other nations.
3 Japan has rejected the influence of foreign nations on its institutions.
4 Japan has returned to a policy of isolation to protect itself from its neighbors.

21　Which statement concerning modern Japan is most accurate?
1　Japan has modernized while maintaining some elements of its traditional culture.
2　Japan has become a leader in global peacekeeping efforts.
3　Japan has shown little concern for its natural environment.
4　Japan has severed all traditional ties in favor of Western values.

22　Traditional African art has had the greatest influence on
1　classical Roman mosaics and pottery
2　Renaissance painting
3　20th-century sculpture and painting
4　medieval European architecture

23　Which is an accurate statement about the partitioning of Africa by European imperialist nations during the 1800's?
1　New nations were based on old tribal boundaries.
2　The cultural and ethnic diversity of the African people was disregarded.
3　The continent was divided equally among the colonial powers.
4　African unity was encouraged.

24　"If we are to remain free, if we are to enjoy the full benefits of Africa's enormous wealth, we must unite to plan for the full exploitation of our human and material resources in the interest of all our people."

-Kwame Nkrumah　(1950's)

This quotation best expresses the major goal of
1　colonialism　　　　　　3　imperialism
2　Pan-Africanism　　　　4　urbanization

25　In the 1980's, global concern for blacks in the Republic of South Africa led many nations to
1　impose economic sanctions on South Africa
2　demand that whites return to their European homelands
3　send troops to South Africa
4　support policies of apartheid

26　The influence of African culture on some areas of Latin America was largely a result of the
1　American Revolution
2　building of the Panama Canal
3　success of Communist revolutions
4　Atlantic slave trade

27　In Latin America, the Maya and the Aztec civilizations were similar in that they
1　showed little evidence of urbanization
2　lacked a strong central government
3　developed complex mathematical and calendar systems
4　used military weapons superior to those of Europeans

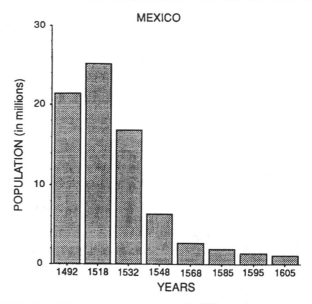

Base your answer to question 28 on the graph at the right and on your knowledge of social studies.

28 Which statement best explains a major reason for the trend illustrated by the graph?
1   The population adopted the European custom of smaller families.
2   The population was exposed to diseases from Europe.
3   Frequent tribal wars throughout the period decreased the population.
4   Much of the population moved to coastal areas.

29 Which major economic problem has been faced by many Latin American nations throughout their histories?
1   lack of capital for industrial development
2   declining birthrate
3   widespread acceptance of Marxist economic policies
4   lack of labor for factories

30 During the 20th century, a major cause of political problems in Latin America has been
1   a decrease in population
2   the declining importance of international trade
3   widespread poverty
4   increasing social mobility

31 "Western Europe owed a debt of gratitude to the Empire that for almost a thousand years ensured the survival of Christianity during a time when Europe was too weak to accomplish the task."
Which empire is referred to in this quotation?
1   Hellenistic
2   Mongol
3   Byzantine
4   Ottoman

32 In Europe, a major characteristic of humanism was
    1   a belief in the supremacy of the state in relation to individual rights
    2   a rejection of ancient civilizations and their cultures
    3   an emphasis on social control and obedience to national rulers
    4   an appreciation for the basic worth of individual achievement

33 Which was an immediate result of the European Age of Exploration?
    1   Islamic culture spread across Africa and Asia.
    2   European influence spread to the Western Hemisphere.
    3   Independence movements developed in Asia and Africa.
    4   Military dictatorships were established throughout Europe.

34 Which principle was established by the Nuremberg Trials after World War II?
    1   Individuals can be punished for their part in state-sponsored crimes.
    2   War-crimes trials can only be held in neutral nations.
    3   War crimes are sometimes justified.
    4   Democracy can be promoted in formerly totalitarian nations.

35 Which statement is valid conclusion about economic cooperation among Western European nations since World War II?
    1   Attempts at cooperative economic ventures have failed.
    2   Efforts to achieve an economically unified Western Europe have generally met with success.
    3   The voters of Western European nations have strongly opposed attempts at international cooperation.
    4   Economic success has resulted in political instability.

36 The religious diversity in Western Europe is mainly the result of
    1   the Congress of Vienna
    2   World War II
    3   the French Revolution
    4   the Protestant Reformation

37 Which term best describes the position of Jews in Czarist Russia?
    1   political elite   3   landed gentry
    2   persecuted minority   4   military leaders

38 "...The organizations of the revolutionaries must consist first, foremost, and mainly of people who make revolutionary activity their profession....Such an organization must of necessity be not too extensive and as secret as possible..."   -V.I. Lenin, 1917

This quotation refers to Lenin's plan to
    1   defeat Germany in World War I
    2   establish democracy in Russia
    3   maintain Communist power in Western Europe
    4   overthrow the Russian Government

39 In the 30 years after World War II, which area was most influenced by the Soviet Union?
    1   Southeast Asia   3   Eastern Europe
    2   North Africa   4   Central America

40 Prior to the 1980's, the emphasis of the Five-Year Plans in the Soviet
    Union was on heavy industry. One result was the
    1   scarcity of consumer goods
    2   abundance of manufactured goods
    3   rejection of agricultural planning
    4   decline in military spending

41 Events in both eastern Europe in the early 1900's and in the Soviet
    Union in the late 1980's were mainly the result of
    1   movements toward the repression of individual rights
    2   declines in the use of advanced technology
    3   the influence of religion on government
    4   challenges by ethnic groups desiring independence

42 Since World War II, people in both Africa and Latin America have
    moved from rural to urban areas. The major cause of this movement has
    been the
    1   rejection of traditional customs
    2   expectation of improved economic opportunities
    3   guarantee of better housing
    4   fear of civil war

Base your answer to question 43 on the cartoon below and on your knowledge
of social studies.

43 What is the main idea of the cartoon?
    1   The Soviet Union's military exercises destroyed large areas of
        farmland.
    2   The central planners of the Soviet Union did not promote industrial
        development.
    3   The economy of the Soviet Union was dominated by the agricultural
        production of small landowners.
    4   In the Soviet Union, modernization efforts focused primarily on the
        military.

44   A major environmental problem affecting Latin America, sub-Saharan Africa, and Southeast Asia has been
    1   air pollution   3   disposal of nuclear waste
    2   deforestation   4   acid rain

45   Which was a characteristic of feudalism?
    1   Land was exchanged for military service and obligations.
    2   Government was provided by a bureaucracy of civil servants.
    3   Power rested in the hands of a strong central government.
    4   Unified national court systems were developed.

46   The rise of independent states in Asia and Africa after World War II demonstrates the
    1   failure of nationalist movements
    2   influence of socialism
    3   success of United Nations peacekeeping forces
    4   decline of European colonial empires

47   The Suez Canal, the Panama Canal, and the Straits of the Dardanelles are similar because they
    1   are strategic waterways that have been the center of conflicts
    2   were part of the French colonial empire
    3   are located in regions that are rich in natural resources
    4   were built during the time of the Roman Empire

Base your answer to question 48 on the cartoon at the right and on your knowledge of social studies.

48   Which is a valid conclusion that can be drawn from this 1989 cartoon?
    1   Marxist economic theories continue to dominate Eastern European Communist nations.
    2   Communist nations have cooperated to resolve common economic problems.
    3   Marxist economic principles have failed to resolve serious economic problems in Communist nations.
    4   Marxist theories have stimulated industrial growth in Communist nations.

Students Please note :
In developing your answers to Part II, be sure to
    (1) include specific factual information and evidence whenever possible
    (2) keep to the questions asked; do not go off on tangents
    (3) avoid overgeneralizations or sweeping statements without sufficient proof; do not overstate your case
    (4) keep these general definitions in mind:
        (a) <u>discuss</u> means "to make observations about something using facts, reasoning, and argument; to present in some detail"
        (b) <u>describe</u> means "to illustrate something in words or tell about it"
        (c) <u>show</u> means "to point out; to set forth clearly a position or idea by stating it and giving data which support it"
        (d) <u>explain</u> means "to make plain or understandable; to give reasons for or causes of; to show the logical development or relationships of"

Part II
ANSWER THREE QUESTIONS FROM THIS PART. [45]

1 Throughout history, bodies of water have had an influence on the economic, social, and political development of nations.

> *Bodies of Water - Nations*
> Amazon River — Brazil
> Black Sea — Russia
> English Channel — Great Britain
> Mediterranean Sea — Greece
> Nile River — Egypt
> Persian Gulf — Saudi Arabia
> Yangtze River — China

Choose *three* of the bodies of water listed. For *each* one chosen, discuss *one* specific way that this body of water has had an influence on the economic, social, *or* political developments of the nation with which it is paired. [You must discuss a different specific way that each body of water you chose influenced the economic, social, or political development of each nation.]   [5,5,5,]

2 Groups of people have often influenced events within a nation or region.

> *Groups - Nations/Regions*
> Afrikaners — Republic of South Africa
> Arab Palestinians — Middle East
> Bolsheviks — Russia
> Jacobins — France
> Nationalists — China
> Samurai — Japan
> Sandinistas — Nicaragua

Choose *three* of the groups listed above and for *each* group chosen:
*   Identify the group and describe how the group influenced events within the nation or region with which it is paired
*   Discuss *one* effect the group had on the nation or region   [5,5,5]

3 During the 20th century, women have influenced the changes taking place in developing nations.

> *Areas in Which Women Have Influenced Change*
> Agricultural development
> Education and training
> Business and employment opportunities
> Health and medicine
> Politics and government
> Social status and social conditions

From the list above, select *three* of the areas in which women have influenced change. For *each* one selected, discuss how women have influenced specific changes that have taken place in that area during the 20th century in developing nations.   [5,5,5]

4 Religions have had a major impact on the lives of people in specific nations or regions.

> *Religions — Nations / Regions*
> Animism — Africa
> Buddhism — Southeast Asia
> Hinduism — India
> Islam — Middle East
> Protestantism — Western Europe
> Roman Catholicism — Latin America
> Shintoism — Japan

Select *three* of the religions from the list. For *each* one selected:
* Describe *one* major belief or practice of the religion
* Discuss how this belief or practice has affected the social, economic, or political life of the people of the nation or region with which the religion is paired   [5,5,5]

5 Throughout the world, developments in technology during the 20th century have contributed to global interdependence and have affected many areas of people's lives.

> *Areas Affected by Technology*

Banking	Communication media
Energy	Entertainment
Employment	Medicine
Travel	Weapons

Choose *three* of the areas affected by technology from the list. For *each* one chosen:
* Describe a specific 20th-century technological development in that area
* Discuss *one* positive effect and *one* negative effect of this technological development on the lives of people throughout the world [Do *not* use examples from the United States in your answer.] [5,5,5]

6   Social, economic, and political changes have often been brought about by specific events and movements in a given place.

Events/Movements - Nations/Regions
Neolithic Revolution - Middle East
Rise of ancient kingdoms - West Africa
Renaissance - Europe
Meiji Restoration - Japan
Independence movements - Latin America
Opium War - China
Green Revolution - India
Development of glasnost - Soviet Union

Select *three* of the events and/or movements listed and for *each* one selected:
•   Discuss *one* major social, economic, *or* political cause of the event or movement
•   Explain *one* major social, economic, *or* political effect of the event or movement   [5,5,5]

7   The exercise of power has sometimes resulted in the violation of human rights.

Power Groups
Conquistadores and the Spanish colonial rulers in Latin America
Stalinist government in the Soviet Union
Adolf Hitler and the Nazi Party in Germany
Communist government in China
Pol Pot and the Khmer Rouge in Kampuchea (Cambodia)
Saddam Hussein and the Ba'ath Party in Iraq

Choose *three* power groups from the list and for *each* one chosen:

•   Explain whose human rights were violated by the power group
•   Describe *two* specific examples of how human rights were violated in this situation
•   Discuss an action that was taken to overcome these human rights violations   [5,5,5]

Answers, Explanations, and Page References
Part I

(Students should note the variety of instances in which material from Part I questions can be useful in answering Part II questions and vice versa. Also, it is useful to compare these questions to those on the other exam in this book.)

1 (ans. 3) A comparative analysis question on the dependence of early river valley civilizations on rich soil and water for farming. (pgs. 94-96, 189-193)

2 (ans. 4) A geographic vocabulary question focusing on similarities between steppes and savannas. Both terms refer to land forms consisting of grassy plains and plateaus. (pgs. 15, 16, 299)

3 (ans. 3) Nationalism reflects strong feelings for country based on unity through common history, religion, language, etc. (pgs. 256-257, 390)

4 (ans. 1) Urbanization often creates a cosmopolitan lifestyle and cultural mixing. This causes a breakdown or assimilation of traditional values. (pgs. 45, 173)

5 (ans. 1) The varied resource availability of the Middle East has created uneven distributions of wealth. (pgs. 188-191, 218-220)

6 (ans. 4) The most powerful social force shaping the culture of the Middle East has been Muslim beliefs and practices. (pgs. 199-202)

7 (ans. 2) Israel is a democratic republic. Answers 1,3,4 contain fallacies. (pg. 220)

8 (ans. 3) The Camp David Accords contained the first peace agreement between Israel and an Arab nation. (pgs. 211, 213)

9 (ans. 2) The Iran-Iraq War strained each nation's economy. It especially cut petroleum production and export. (pgs. 214-215)

10 (ans. 2) Various wings of the Palestine Liberation Organization see terrorism as a political weapon to gain nationhood for their people. (pgs. 214-215)

11 (ans. 3) The validity of each statement has to coincide with the data given. Students would have to know the significance of Gross National Product. Here, the GNP column clearly shows that India produces the most goods and services. (pgs. 81-84)

12 (ans. 4) The Indian National Congress Party's was formed to co-ordinate the drive for its independence. (pgs. 65-66)

13 (ans. 3) A mixed economy blends the free enterprise structure (market) of the private sector with government's socialist control (commmand) of portions of the infrastructure. (pg. 81)

14 (ans. 1) The quotation concerns a continuing role of caste in a changing society. (pgs. 60, 73)

15 (ans. 4) Confucian philosophy of ancient China taught that society would be orderly if everyone knew their proper place. Scholars had the highest status. (pg. 97)

16 (ans. 1) In rejecting other cultures as inferior to their own, the dynasties of China practiced the closed thinking of ethnocentrism. (pg. 95)

17 (ans. 2) The communists' success rested on their convincing peasants they would bring the long-sought land reform the Nationalists did not deliver. (pg. 106)

18 (ans. 2) China's population exceeds one billion. This puts such a severe strain on its housing and economy that the government has created a program to limit the birth rate. (pg. 111)

19 (ans. 3) Following WW II, the U.S. helped Japanese reorganize their oligarchy into a parliamentary democracy. (pg. 141)

20 (ans. 1) After the surrender ending WW II, Japan demilitarized and the U.S. helped it recover and build into a global economic power. (pgs. 144-146)

21 (ans. 1) There has been much modernization and cultural diffusion in Japan since WW II. However, the people manage to maintain various elements of their traditional culture. This can be seen by the preservation of their art and literary forms. (pgs. 141-142)

22 (ans. 3) Traditional African art forms were largely unknown outside the continent, but modern mass media and communications made the world aware of it. (pg. 21)

23 (ans. 2) European imperialists largely ignored the Africans' cultural and ethnic traditions when they created colonial boundaries. (pgs. 27-28)

24 (ans. 2) Ghana's first president hints at a universal dimension in Africa's resources. This reflects the post WW II concept of Pan-Africanism, a movement to strengthen and unify political and economic forces of the entire continent. (pgs. 30, 32)

25 (ans. 1) In a reaction against South African racial policies toward Blacks (Apartheid) during the 1980's, many nations boycotted trade and commercial ventures with the troubled country. (pgs. 34, 52)

26 (ans. 4) African culture gave much to the development of Latin America. African slaves were used on many encomiendas and fazendas. Intermarriages (mulattos) often blurred class lines and diffused cultures. (pg. 165)

27 (ans. 3) The ancient Maya and Aztec civilizations exhibited similar mathematics and astronomical systems. (pgs. 159-160)

28 (ans. 2) Graph reading skills alone are inadequate here. Knowledge of the European conquest of the region is needed. The cause of the decline of population was the exposure of Native Americans to deadly communicable diseases brought by the Spanish conquistadors. (pgs. 160, 163-164)

29 (ans. 1) Finding foreign investments to develop Latin American industries, rather than just exporting raw materials, has been a continual problem for nations in this region. (pg. 178)

30 (ans. 3) In the 20th century, most Latin American nations have experienced a rapid population growth and unchecked urban growth. This led to an increase of severe poverty in the region. (pg. 123)

31 (ans. 3) The quotation on the survival of Christianity in Western Europe refers to the period after the fall of Rome (5th -15th centuries). The Byzantine Empire of Eastern Europe was the only contemporary Christian entity among the answer choices offered. (pgs. 195-196)

32 (ans. 4) European humanism is a philosophy associated with the appreciation of the basic worth of individual achievement. (pg. 244)

33 (ans. 2) A cause and effect question about the European Age of Exploration. A logical result of cultures meeting is diffusion. (pgs. 163-165, 251)

34 (ans. 1) A human rights question reflecting a major principle of the post World War II Nuremberg trials. Individuals (Nazis) are responsible for their participation in state-sponsored crimes. (related data pg. 272)

35 (ans. 2) Observation of Western European nations' cooperation since WW II shows the "Common Market" or the European Economic Community broke long-standing trade barriers. However, a recent Danish plebiscite on the Maastrict Treaty casts some doubt on chances for formal unity. (The latter also lends some credibility to ans. 3.) (pg. 285)

36 (ans. 4) Rise of many Protestant sects during the Reformation contributed to the wide religious diversity in Western Europe. (pgs. 245-246)

37 (ans. 2) Jews in Tsarist Russia were persecuted in violent pogroms. They were often scapegoats for government leaders' problems. (pg. 323)

38 (ans. 4) Simple recall question requires students to connect the exiled Lenin secretly preparing the Bolsheviks for revolutionary activities before the Russian Revolution. (pgs. 314-316)

39 (ans. 3) For most of the Cold War period, Soviet leaders tried to aid communist insurgency on a global basis, but did not have the resources to dominate globally. After 1949, there was competition from China to be the leading Marxist power (eliminates ans. 1,2,4). The Soviets concentrated attention on the buffer zone of Eastern European "satellite nations." created by Stalin. The zone protected the U.S.S.R. from the threat he perceived in the West. The Soviets forced the satellites military and trade alliances. Communists chosen by the Kremlin leaders controlled satellite governments. (pgs. 341-343)

40 (ans. 1) The Five-Year Plans begun in the Stalin Era focused on heavy industry to increase military production (eliminates ans. 4). Agricultural planning was largely unsuccessful, but did receivehigh priority (eliminates ans. 3). Ans. 1 is preferable because production of consumer goods received low priority. The standard of living declined. (There is a misleading ambiguity in the term "manufactured goods" in ans. 2. It is being used as a synonym for consumer goods. However it is unacceptable because steel, capital machinery, and military goods were manufactured goods produced in large quantities under the Five-Year Plans.) (pg. 335)

41 (ans. 4) A comparison of the breakup of the old Austro-Hungarian and Ottoman Empires in the first quarter of the 20th century with that of the Soviet Union. Nationalistic cravings of ethnic groups contributed both upheavals. (pgs. 327, 329)

42 (ans. 2) Expectations for improved economic opportunity caused mass migrations from rural to urban areas in Latin American and African nations since World War II. Such migrations altered the demographics and traditional culture in these global regions. (pgs. 39, 44, 173, 179)

43 (ans. 4) Explanation of question 40 (above) contains a rationale for cartoon interpretation. The former Soviet government's major emphasis on heavy industry and defense (military tank), ignored agricultural productivity and consumer desires (subsistence level peasant). (pg. 334)

44 (ans. 2) Human destruction of the rain forests has disrupted the ecosystems in all three less developed global regions. Answers 1,3,4 incorrect because these factors characterize developed, industrial regions. (pgs. 43, 354)

45 (ans. 1) Definitions of feudalism involve a decentralized landholding system. Use of overlords' land was exchanged for vassals' military service and obligations. Peasants exchanged freedom and labor for the manors' security in a dangerous, lawless societies. (pg. 238-239, 304, 306)

46 (ans. 4) Latent nationalist movements gained power following WW II because Britain, France, the Netherlands, Belgium, Germany and Italy were either defeated and/or economically and militarily exhausted. (pgs. 31, 70-78)

47 (ans. 1) A comparison of similarities existing among these water passages. All have been central to conflicts because of their strategic locations. (pg. 172, 210)

48 (ans. 3) Controversial interpretation because cartoon lacks an overall caption. The "Bankruptcy Court" label over the door relates characters' dejected looks to economic problems in ans. 3. Except for Castro (back row), recognizable caricatures are deceased leaders, making 1989 date in the stem confusing. Ans. 1 is arguable because Marxist principles were still prevalent among socialist leaders in E. Europe in 1989. Ans. 2 is misleading, COMECON resolved some problems. Ans. 4 is misleading because in selected industries growth did take place in some nations. (ques. 40). (pgs. 111, 115, 171-177, 335-336)

Part II

(Students: Note the variety of instances in which Part I material can be useful in answering Part II questions and vice versa.)

1 *Writing Strategy:* Choose this essay if you have a good understanding of the geography's influence on society. Divide your answer into *three* paragraphs, one for each body of water chosen. In *each* paragraph explain a very specific economic or social or political way the water affected life in that country.

- *Amazon River - Brazil:* The river drains the vast basin occupying the northern half of the country. Economically, the heavy rains and leached soil of the rain forests make the basin a poor agricultural area. However, the precious hardwoods, and natural rubber of the rain forest are a source of wealth. (Details on pg. 156)

- *Black Sea - Russia:* The presence of the Black Sea on Russia's southern border influenced its political development. The sea is nearly landlocked, and the Ottoman Empire controlled its exit to the Mediterranean from medieval times into the early 20th century. In the 18th century, Russia's Tsarina Catherine the Great succeeded in conquering the north coast (Crimea). Tsars continued this expansion until the Ottoman Empire disintegrated in WW I. (Details on pgs.189, 230, 247, 255)

- *English Channel - Great Britain:* Politically, the English Channel has helped Britain remain independent. Traditionally, it separated the British Isles from European enemies such as France. It provides a protective barrier against invasion. It causes Britain to develop a naval defense and to rise as an imperial power because of its sea power. (Details on pgs. 230, 255, 273)

- *Mediterranean Sea - Greece:* Numerous fine harbors on the Mediterranean influenced the Greeks to turn to seafaring for their livelihood. The near central location on the Mediterranean promoted trade and travel, spreading Greek culture and goods throughout the ancient world. (Details on pg. 230)

- *Nile River - Egypt:* Economically, Egypt became known as the "Gift of the Nile." This fertile river valley with its water supply became an cradle of early civilization. Its confluence with the Mediterranean meant the civilization of Egypt diffused throughout the ancient world. (Details on pgs. 189, 191)

- *Persian Gulf - Saudi Arabia:* Economically, the Persian Gulf carries the huge tankers from Saudi oil fields into the oceans of the world. Saudi Arabia's coastline led the nation to become the involved in economic and political affairs of other Gulf nations. (Details on pgs. 215, 225)

- *Yangtze River - China:* The river is the traditional heart of China's agricultural economy. For centuries, its port of Shanghai enabled produce to be sold to the Pacific region. (Details on pg. 94)

2 *Writing Strategy*: Choose this essay if you can show how group actions influence societies. Divide your answer into *three* paragraphs, one for each group you choose. In *each* paragraph: *a)* identify the group and the time period; *b)* discuss its actions; *c)* discuss the actions' effects on the society.

- *Afrikaners - Republic of South Africa: a)* <u>identity</u>: Afrikaners or Boers were the Dutch settlers who colonized the Cape of Good Hope, South Africa in 1652. *b)* <u>group's actions:</u> After the British captured the Cape Colony in 1806, the Boers migrated inland to preserve their culture.

c) effects: The strong Dutch cultural influence and desire to remain separate from the Africans led to the development of apartheid (legal racial segregation) which plagues the Republic of South Africa today. (Details on pg. 33)

- ***Arab Palestinians - Middle East***: *a)* identity: Arab inhabitants of the area to designated by the U.N. for Jewish resettlement(Israel) in 1948. *b)* group's actions: Palestinian Arabs remained as displaced refugees, claiming rights to a homeland in Israel. *c)* effects: Refugee camps house Arab nationalist groups (Palestinian Liberation Organization). The use of terrorism and military raids to force some recognition and actions for their cause have kept the Middle East in constant political turmoil. (Details on pgs. 212)

- ***Bolsheviks - Russia***: *a)* identity: Bolsheviks were a radical, violence-prone wing of Marxists seeking socialist reforms in Russia. *b)* group's actions: Kerensky's moderate provisional government which took over Russia and forced the abdication of Tsar Nicholas II during WW I. In November 1917, the Bolsheviks used local workers' councils (soviets) to disrupt and unseat the moderates. *c)* effects: Under leaders such as Lenin, and Trotsky, the Bolsheviks won the Civil War and set up a totalitarian Marxist state in the 1920's. (Details on pgs. 315-316)

- ***Jacobins - France***: *a)* identity: The Jacobins were radical extremists who seized leadership of the French Revolution in 1792. *b)* group's actions: Led by Robespierre, the Jacobins launched economic, and educational reforms. However, their violence-prone leaders overthrew the constitutional monarchy, and launched a bloody purge called the Reign of Terror. Their Committee of Public Safety executed thousands of nobles and others deemed enemies of the Revolution. *c)* effects: The carrying of the Revolution to such a destructive extreme paved the way for coup by Napoleon. (Details on pgs. 253-254)

- ***Nationalists - China***:*a)* identity: The Nationalists were the followers of Sun Yat-sen, founder of the modern Chinese Republic. In 1912, they overthrew the imperial structure and redistributed large landed estates to the peasantry. *b)* group's actions: Under Chiang Kai-shek (Sun's successor), the Nationalist Party became corrupt and failed to control the Chinese warlords. They also failed to achieve needed land reform. *c)* effects: The Nationalists' failures drove many to support the more radical programs of Mao Zedong's communist movement. (Details on pgs. 105-106; also see ques. 17 on PART I.)

- ***Samurai - Japan***: *a)* identity: Warrior class in feudal Japan. They were the dominant political group. *b)* group's actions: The Shogun - the dominant Samurai knight controlled Japan for 700 years. *c)* effects: The Samurai discipline and code of behavior (Bushido) shaped Japan's culture of strong sociopolitical loyalties and disciplined service to the official authority. (Details on pg. 129)

- ***Sandinistas - Nicaragua***: *a)* identity: Sandinistas were Nicaraguan Marxists who seized power in the 1970's. *b)* group's actions: Acceptance of

Soviet-Cuban aid allowed the Sandinistas to overthrow the military power of the Samoza dictatorship. *c)* effects: Harsh Sandinista communist rule under Daniel Ortega led to the formation of a "contra" (opposition) force which received aid from the U.S. Constant fighting in the 1980's disrupted the nation. Withdrawal of aid by the Soviets forced Ortega to agree to popular elections in 1990 which he lost. (Details on pgs. 172)

3 *Writing Strategy:* This essay tests your knowledge of how specific actions by women have changed life in today's nations. (*Caution: This is an area not greatly emphasized in the NYS syllabus. Note also that the instructions refer to women in general. It is not necessary to name specific individuals, although it helps to do so.*) Divide your answer into *three* paragraphs, one for each area of activity. In *each* paragraph: *a)* name an LDC and a situation; *b)* describe an action women took; *c)* discuss the effect of the action on the LDC.

- *Agricultural development:* *a)* LDC/situation: Rural poverty is a severe problem in Nicaragua. Most farmers are low paid tenants (campesinos). Land reform and redistribution would result in ownership and greater incentive. *b)* action: Violeta Chamorro's government is seeking to break up the huge encomiendas (commercial plantation) *c)* effects: More food production, but lack of resources has hurt efforts to educate and equip peasants with means to expand production. (See pg. 172)

- *Education and training:* *a)* LDC/situation: Since WW II, Middle Eastern women changed their life patterns because of urbanization, economic modernization, and Western cultural influences. *b)* action: Contrary to traditional Islamic practice, women are admitted to secondary schools, technical schools and colleges. *c)* effects: Strong opposition to this trend from Islamic fundamentalists led to social and political strife in Iran and Egypt. For the most part, the advances life better for women, and societies became more productive. (Details on pgs. 215, 220)

- *Business and employment opportunities:* *a)* LDC/situation: In Sub Saharan African urban centers such as Lagos (Nigeria), Freetown (Sierra Leone), and Nairobi (Kenya), African women pursue careers in medicine, education, business, law, and technological research. *b)* action: Migrations to the cities from rural tribal villages enabled women to break out of a variety of traditionally demeaning roles. *c)* effects: Women now make greater contributions to development in African cities and nations. (Details on pg. 142)

- *Health and medicine:* *a) country/ situation: b) action: c) effects:* *a)* LDC/situation: Substandard health and sanitation practices among the poor in the slums of Calcutta, India led to the spread of disease. *b)* action: The Missionaries of Charity, a Catholic nursing order founded by Mother Teresa, work to educate the poor of Calcutta. *c)* effects: Visiting nurses trained and educated in the Missionaries' hospitals provide greater sanitary training and reduce the incidence of diseases among the poor. (Details on pg. 329)

- *Politics and government*: a) <u>LDC/situation</u>: Women in LDCs of South and Southeast Asia such as India, Pakistan, and the Philippines play influential roles in in government. Increasing numbers of women enjoy suffrage rights and office holding. b) <u>action</u>: India's Indira Gandhi, Pakistan's Benazir Bhutto, and the Philippine Republic's Corazon Aquino are examples of women who have risen to lead their nations. c) <u>effects</u>: Democratic participation has been broadened in the region, encouraging more women to become involved in public life. (Details on pgs. 73, 77)

- *Social status and social conditions*: a) <u>LDC/situation</u>: In India, the caste system once decided all women's associations. b) <u>action</u>: Service in W W II and legislation since independence allowed women to tear down many caste restrictions. c) <u>effects</u>: Especially in urban areas, women are seen frequently in modern situations on television and in movies where the restrictions of caste and tradition are of no consequence. These media images spread to rural area, encouraging others to break down traditional barriers. A broader concept of social equality has resulted. (Details on pg. 142; see also question 14 on Part I.)

4 *Writing Strategy*: Choose this essay if you understand how ideas can move people and change nations/regions. Divide your answer into *three* paragraphs. In *each* paragraph: a) explain a belief of the religion; b) describe how the action influenced the nation/region.

- *Animism - Africa*: a) <u>belief</u>: Animism involves a belief that inanimate objects contain a spirit. Traditional African religions have sacred masks, charms, and statues identified with nature. Believers feel these have supernatural powers. b) <u>influence on nation/region</u>: Ritual ceremonies at birth and death encourage Africans to treat the natural environment with great respect and sometimes cause conflict with economic endeavors which endanger the ecosystem. (Ideas on pgs. 19-20)

- *Buddhism - Southeast Asia*: a) <u>belief</u>: Buddhism involves following the Eightfold Path directing humans toward spiritual perfection (Nirvana). b) <u>influence on nation/region</u>: Buddhist priests affected political life in Vietnam in the 1960's. Undemocratic governmental practices created an elitism contrary to the equality fostered in Buddhist practice. The monks' protests caused widespread demonstrations against the Diem regime, and led to a coup in 1963. (Details on pgs. 60, 74)

- *Hinduism - India*: a) <u>belief</u>: Hinduism involves a belief in reincarnation - rebirth of the soul in another form of life. Adherence to the duty (dharma) one owes to family or caste results in reward in the next reincarnation. b) <u>influence on nation/region</u>: Strict confines of caste resulted in rigid social structures and acceptance of fate (karma) made conquest and dominance easy for British Raj. (Details on pg. 59)

- *Islam - Middle East*: a) <u>belief</u>: Islamic beliefs include the practice of *jihad*, or crusades to bring the religion to infidels. Early *jihads* became holy wars which sent Muslim armies throughout the Middle East, North Africa, and Persia. b) <u>influence on nation/region</u>: In the 20th century, resurgent Islamic fundamentalism has led Shi'ite groups to agitate for power in Iran, Iraq, Lebanon, and Egypt. These modern *jihads* led to violence and revolution in the Middle East, compounding the already volatile nature of politics there. (Details on pgs. 199-200, 214)

- *Protestantism - Western Europe*: a) belief: Protestantism was an attempt to reform the Christian Church in the 16th century. Leaders such Luther and Calvin emphasized self-interpretation of scripture and theology. b) influence on nation/region: The independence of mind fostered by Protestantism affected life in Western Europe. With growth of movable type presses to publish books and tracts, self-interpretation reading became widespread. Literacy rose. Communication and education improved life and led to more participation in political affairs. (Details on pgs. 245-246)

- *Roman Catholicism - Latin America*: a) belief: Roman Catholicism involves a belief that the primary marriage obligation is procreation. The Church opposes all artificial means of birth control except natural methods. It strongly opposes abortion. b) influence on nation/region: As in other less developed regions, declining infant mortality rates, have led to serious overcrowding, especially in cities. The dominant position of the Church in Latin America makes governmental attempts to deal with overpopulation difficult. Birth control methods advocated in India, Africa and China are vehemently opposed by powerful Church leaders. (Details on pgs. 163-164, 170, 173-174)

- *Shintoism - Japan*: a) belief: Shinto beliefs include the idea that the land itself is sacred. b) influence on nation/region: This affected political decisions in Japan at the end of WW II. Shinto beliefs held leaders from surrendering their homeland when confronted with an awesome Allied invasion. President Truman's advisors indicated the Japanese would fight to the death. This influenced Truman's decision to drop the atomic bomb on Hiroshima. Even in the face of the awesome destruction of the new weapon, Japanese leaders would not surrender until a second bomb proved the futility of holding out. (Details on pgs. 128)

5 *Writing Strategy:* The World Today (Unit VIII) is the basis for this essay. Choose it if you can clearly identify modern technological advances and show why they affect all people. (Note that examples from U.S. cannot be used.) Divide your answer into *three* paragraphs. In *each* paragraph: a) describe a 20th century invention or technological process; b) state a positive global effect, and c) state a negative global effect of the technological advancement.

- *Banking*: a) 20th century invention/technological process: Global computer linkups. b) *positive* global effect: Facilitates international business transactions. Helps travelers get funds needed quickly. c) *negative* global effect: Makes it easier for international drug cartels to "launder funds"making law enforcement and prosecution difficult. (Details on pg. 357)

- ***Communication media****: a)* 20th century invention/technological process: Satellites orbiting in space make it possible to transmit phone conversations and televisions programs globally. *b) positive* global effect: Cost of international communication has decreased considerably. The concept of the "global village" has emerged. Information transmission and response to problems (starvation, earthquakes) can take place much more rapidly. *c) negative* global effect: Monitoring, spying and censorship (rights violations) can also become more frequent. (Details on pg. 359)

- ***Energy****: a)* 20th century invention/technological process: Nuclear power now generates electricity in many areas of the world. *b) positive* global effect: Dependence polluting fossil fuels (coal, oil) has been reduced. Benefits of cheap electric power can be brought to LDCs, raising the quality of life. *c) negative* global effect: The accident at Chernobyl cause widespread illness in Ukraine, Eastern Europe and Scandinavia. Disposal of dangerous nuclear waste is also a problem. (Details on pgs. 218, 224)

- ***Entertainment****: a)* 20th century invention/technological process: The development of television and VCR's revolutionized entertainment. *b) positive* global effect: Cultural diffusion is occurring at a rapid rate. Awareness of other people's ideas and a sensitizing to others' values increases international understanding *c) negative* global effect: Decreased amount of time spent in reading, especially among students has had negative effects on educational achievement. (Details on pg. 361)

- ***Employment****: a)* 20th century invention or technological process: Use of computers and robotics have changed the nature of work. Industries are no longer labor intensive, but capital intensive. *b) positive* global effect: Dangerous and unhealthy assembly-line employment has been eliminated in developed nations and production more consistent. Jobs are safer and less physically demanding.*c) negative* global effect: Technological skills needed for modern jobs, even in agriculture, are difficult to obtain. Prospects of job displacement and prolonged unemployment are greater in technological industries. People in LDCs are also disadvantaged because the opportunity to get sophisticated training is limited. (Details on pgs. 144-146, 361)

- ***Medicine****: a)* 20th century invention/technological process: New vaccines to prevent life-threatening diseases such as polio, measles, diphtheria. Laser micro-surgery enables procedures previously impossible. *b) positive* global effect: Many lives are being saved. Infant mortality has been reduced and life expectancy has increased in most societies. *c) negative* global effect: Such medical breakthroughs increase longevity, which increases already difficult population problems in LDCs. (Details on pg. 358)

- ***Travel****: a)* 20th century invention/technological process: The development of the airplane made it possible for people to travel thousands of miles in short periods of time. *b) positive* global effect: Foreign leaders can visit other nations and negotiate agreements in face-to-face personal diplomacy. *c) negative* global effect: Airplane safety is becoming a problem. Overcrowded municipal airports and air corridors increase accident occurrence. (Details on pg. 359)

- ***Weapons***: *a)* 20th century invention/technological process: The airplane, tanks, poison gas, rockets, and nuclear ICBMs are examples of modern weapons. *b)* *positive* global effect: Weapon technology can often be converted to peacetime uses (commercial air transport, chemical fertilizers) *c)* *negative* global effect: Modern weapons, such as the Agent Orange defoliant used in Vietnam, cause permanent genetic injuries and other disabilities to the troops using them and neighboring civilian populations. (Details on pg. 352)

6 *Writing Strategy*: This essay is on the power of events to bring about change. Choose it if you know how the event brought about a significant change its own region. Divide your answer into *three* paragraphs. In *each* paragraph: *a)* explain why the event/movement took place; *b)* explain a result of the event/movement.

- ***Neolithic Revolution - Middle East***: *a)* cause: Large numbers of people accepted the more stable lifestyle of raising crops (wheat, rice, millet) and animals in fixed places as opposed to hunting and gathering. *b)* result: Small, stable, defensible farming communities emerged. This enabled specialization of labor moving humans toward higher productivity and a safer, better quality of life. (Details on pg. 191)

- ***Rise of ancient kingdoms - West Africa***: *a)* cause: Politically, the West African empires such as Songhai, Ghana, and Mali developed to control cross African trade. *b)* result: Gold went from Sub Saharan Africa to the civilizations of the north in exchange for salt. Considerable cultural diffusion took place (including the spread of Islamic culture). Ancient African cities expanded and preserved regional culture. (Details on pg. 24)

- ***Renaissance - Europe***: *a)* cause: Socially, the Crusades (11th-13th centuries) brought people of Western Europe into contact with Byzantine, Persian, and Islamic cultures. *b)* result: A new cosmopolitan spirit led to questioning of narrow beliefs and cultural values. This renewal of interest in global knowledge became known as the Renaissance in Europe. Figures such as DaVinci revolutionized the fine and technological arts. Machiavelli opened new approaches to social and political behavior. The Renaissance began an entire renovation of every aspect of European culture. (Details on pg. 243)

- ***Meiji Restoration - Japan***: *a)* cause: In the mid-19th century, Japan began modernizing rapidly. A centralized government replaced the local rule of feudal barons. It made the Emperor a supreme figurehead for a industrial-military oligarchy which held the real power. *b)* result: The Restoration set the scene for industrial development and imperialism. In the 1890's, military leaders began a series of wars which brought resource rich islands and portions of the Asian mainland under Japan's control. Japan's imperialism contributed to causing WW II. (Details on pgs. 133-134)

- *Independence movements- Latin America: a)* <u>cause</u>: The inspiration of the American and French Revolutions, led many in Latin America to seek independence from Spain. Revolts were usually led by politically emasculated criollos (decedents of earlier European settlers) such as San Martín and Bolivar. *b)* <u>result</u>: New Nations and confederations (Gran Colombia) emerged in Latin America which were eventually dominated by local criollo dictators (caudillos). (Details on pgs. 169-170)

- *Opium War - China: a)* <u>cause</u>: The British desire for a favorable balance of trade led them to sell opium to obtain tea and porcelains. Chinese government objections to the unfavorable balance of trade led them to destroy opium shipments. This brought military retaliation by the British. *b)* <u>result</u>: The British forced the Chinese to accept unequal treaties (Treaty of Nanking, 1842) giving marked trade advantages to the British. Eventually, the episode led to foreign dominance of China and division into spheres of trade influence. (Details on pgs. 102-103)

- *Green Revolution - India: a)* <u>cause</u>: As a new nation, India was unable to feed its vast population. Widespread starvation made the government and tradition-bound peasant farmers more willing to accept U.N. offers of technologically advanced agricultural programs. *b)* <u>result</u>: Indian farmers became more productive as a result of Norman Borlaug's "Green Revolution" techniques. The country began to come close to self-sufficiency in food production by the 1970's. (Details on pg. 83)

- *Development of glasnost- Soviet Union: a)* <u>cause</u>: In 1985, Soviet leader Mikhail Gorbachev took steps to grant greater freedom. Under what he termed *glasnost* (openness), he released political prisoners, allowed dissidents to emigrate, and reformed the constitution. *b)* <u>result</u>: Political reforms upheavals inside the Soviet Union led to constitutional changes, freer elections, Gorbachev's own resignation, and finally, the breakup of the U.S.S.R. into a loose confederation of independent republics. (Details on pg. 325)

7 *Writing Strategy:* This essay is about power in society conflicting with and individual rights. Choose it if you can specify how the individuals were hurt by power groups. Divide your answer into *three* paragraphs. In *each* paragraph: *a)* Identify the victims hurt by the power groups: *b)* show two (2) rights violated: *c)* show how people (victims or outsiders) overcame the violations.

- *Conquistadores and Spanish colonial rulers in Latin America:* *a)* <u>victims</u>: Native Americans. *b)* <u>rights violated</u>: Spanish settlers forced Native Americans to work as slaves on encomiendas. Their culture (arts, buildings, religious symbols) was also destroyed. *c)* <u>reaction to</u> <u>violations</u>: Catholic missionaries such as Father Bartelome de las Casas attempted to defend Native American culture, but harsh Viceroys and Church hierarchy ignored such outbursts. (Details on pgs. 163-164)

- *Stalinist government in the Soviet Union: a)* <u>victims</u>: Russian kulaks (wealthy farmers) and Ukrainian farmers. *b)* <u>rights violated</u>: Stalin's Five

Year Plans deprived these people of land and possessions without due process as agriculture was collectivized. Thousands of protesters were murdered for resisting. *c)* <u>reaction to</u> <u>violations</u>: Kulaks and Ukrainian farmers slaughtered nearly 50% of their own livestock or burned their crops in protest in the early 1930's. (Details on pgs. 320-322)

- ***Adolf Hitler and the Nazi Party in Germany****: a)* <u>victims</u>: Jews, gypsies, Jehovah's Witnesses, and homosexuals. *b)* <u>rights violated</u>: Nazis declared these groups inferior. The Nazi Nuremberg Decrees deprived them of basic rights and suffrage and declared them second-class citizens and forced to live in isolated ghettos. Many of these groups were placed in concentration camps and eventually executed. *c)* <u>reaction to</u> <u>violations</u>: Allied forces liberated the camps at the end of WW II. (Details on pgs. 270-271)

- ***Communist government in China****: a)* <u>victims</u>: Students demonstrators and intellectuals protesting harsh undemocratic government rules under Deng Xiaoping. *b)* <u>rights violated</u>: Some were given summary trials and denied legal defense. Many were executed or imprisoned for their protest activities. Many are doing forced labor in prison camps. *c)* <u>reaction to</u> <u>violations</u>: The international community protested the Tiananmen Square Massacre and isolated China with economic sanctions for a short period. (Details on pgs. 109-112, 120-123)

- ***Pol Pot and the Khmer Rouge in Cambodia****: a)* <u>victims</u>: Intellectuals and foreign educated opponents of the Khmer Rouge. *b)* <u>rights violated</u>: Thousands of opponents were imprisoned and/or executed. Thousands more were uprooted from the cities and sent to forced labor in the countryside. Those not sufficiently repentant for decadent urban lifestyles were execute in the rural "killing fields." *c)* <u>reactions to</u> <u>violations</u>: neighboring Vietnam invaded Cambodia to aid opposition groups led to a prolonged civil war in the 1980's. A strong international protest led to a fragile U.N. truce in 1992. (Details on pgs. 75, 356)

- ***Saddam Hussein and the Ba'ath Party in Iraq****: a)* <u>victims</u>: the Kurds, an ethnic group of northern Iraq wishing to form an independent state with other Kurds living in Iran and Turkey. *b)* <u>rights violated</u>: the Ba'ath junta conducted open warfare against the Kurds for almost two decades. Armed attacks, summary arrests, forced imprisonments, and cutting off supply lines into the Caucasus Mountain homelands of the Kurds have been frequent. *c)* <u>reactions to</u> <u>violations</u>: The Kurds use primitive guerrilla tactics against the sophisticated modern weapons of Saddam. Some international aid was provided and pressure was placed on Saddam after the Persian Gulf defeat, but these efforts faded in the past year.

Practice Exam 2 — *June 1993*

Part I (55 credits)
Answer all 48 questions in this part.

Directions (1-48): For each statement or question, write on the separate answer sheet the *number* of the word or expression that, of those given, best completes the statement or answers the question.

1 Nationalism is best defined as
   1 the achievement of world peace and global understanding
   2 the desire to take over other societies by force
   3 a method of solving basic economic problems of the society
   4 the loyalty of a people to their values, traditions, and a geographic region

2 In France, a person drinks coffee imported from Brazil, works at a computer made in Japan, and uses gasoline from Saudi Arabia in a German automobile. This situation illustrates the concept of
   1 empathy   3 interdependence
   2 scarcity   4 world citizenship

3 The Incas, the Romans, and the Mongols were similar in that each
   1 developed systems of writing
   2 extended control over neighboring peoples
   3 established industrial economies
   4 adopted democratic political systems

4 In Africa, an effect of topography and climate has been to
   1 encourage rapid industrialization of the interior
   2 prevent the development of kingdoms
   3 promote large-scale trade between Africa and Asia
   4 promote the growth of diverse societies

5 Which statement best describes the political situation in Africa after World War II?
   1 Increased nationalism led to independence for many African nations.
   2 France and West Germany sought to establish colonies in Africa.
   3 European nations increased their control over their African colonies.
   4 The United Nations opposed the idea of self-determination for African nations.

6 The economic systems of most newly independent African nations have been characterized by
   1 private ownership with a minimum of government involvement
   2 a Communist model of government ownership of agriculture
   3 self-sufficiency with few exports or imports
   4 a mixture of government and private ownership

Base your answer to question 7 on the cartoon at the right and on your knowledge of social studies.

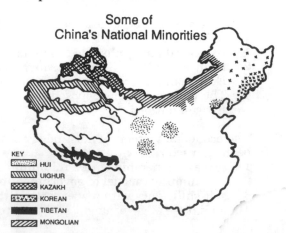

7   What does the cartoon illustrate about the Republic of South Africa?
1   The white minority continues to gain power.
2   Racial equality in employment and education has been achieved.
3   The black majority is forcing concessions from the white minority.
4   The British Government still has control over internal affairs.

8   In India today, the continued discrimination based on caste illustrates
1   a commitment to a capitalist economic system
2   the gap between law and tradition
3   the influence of the cold war on India
4   the declining role of religion in modern society

9   Which is a valid statement about the history of South Asia?
1   Religious beliefs have both unified and divided the people of the region.
2   Little cultural diffusion has occurred in this region.
3   Urbanization has strengthened the traditional beliefs and lifestyles of the people of the region.
4   Superpower involvement has brought peace and economic prosperity to the region.

10   During the 19th century, Europeans were able to divide China into spheres of influence mainly because the
1   Chinese were eager to adopt Western culture
2   Europeans had technologically superior military forces
3   Europeans were willing to adopt Chinese customs
4   Chinese lacked raw materials and resources

Some of China's National Minorities

Base your answer to question 11 on the map at the right and on your knowledge of social studies.

11   This map reflects the concept of
1   cultural uniformity
3   topographic variety
2   balance of power
4   ethnic diversity

KEY
HUI
UIGHUR
KAZAKH
KOREAN
TIBETAN
MONGOLIAN

12　A major goal of the Cultural Revolution in China during the 1960's was
　　to
　　1　restore China to the glory of the Han dynasty
　　2　reemphasize Confucian traditional values
　　3　weaken Communist ideas
　　4　eliminate opposition to Mao Zedong

13　In the People's Republic of China, which factor best reflects Marxism?
　　1　communal work teams on farms
　　2　ownership of small farms by individuals
　　3　small family-owned businesses in villages
　　4　foreign influence on the economy

Base your answer to question 14 on the
cartoon at the right and on your
knowledge of social studies.

14　What is the main idea of the
　　cartoon?
　　1　Chinese students have succeeded
　　　　in achieving their demands for
　　　　democratic reform.
　　2　The government of China has
　　　　encouraged dissent in the hope
　　　　that criticism will quickly fade
　　　　away.
　　3　The Chinese Army has opposed
　　　　student pro-democracy
　　　　demonstrations.
　　4　Human rights have not been
　　　　repressed by the government of
　　　　China.

BREAKING AWAY

Source: *The Finger Lakes Times*, May 27, 1989

15　Until the 1500's, China and Japan
　　were similar in that both
　　1　were invaded by the Mongols
　　2　welcomed Christian missionaries
　　3　had little contact with western European nations
　　4　were developing democratic traditions

16　Which is an accurate statement about Japan's natural resources?
　　1　Japan has extensively used the seas for fishing.
　　2　Large reserves of petroleum are located in the northern part of
　　　　Japan.
　　3　Japan has large fertile plains suitable for growing grain.
　　4　Large coal and iron-ore deposits are located in the mountain regions.

17　In Japan, the samurai code of Bushido helped bring about
　　1　equality among Japanese citizens
　　2　a culture that accepted militarism
　　3　peaceful relations with other nations
　　4　an increased interest in science and technology

18   Which situation has contributed most to recent Japanese economic growth?
1   The Japanese Government has placed limits on Japanese exports.
2   Japanese industries spend very little on the research and development of new products.
3   The Japanese Government and Japanese businesses have cooperated with each other.
4   Japanese citizens save less of their incomes than the citizens of other industrialized nations do.

19   Who were David Ben-Gurion, Golda Meir, and Menachem Begin?
1   leaders of the modern State of Israel
2   scientists who developed better methods of discovering oil
3   clergy who supported Islamic fundamentalism
4   Egyptian Presidents who encouraged peace with Israel

20   Which condition is a major obstacle to economic development in the Middle East and northern Africa?
1   use of strip mining to obtain minerals
2   reliance on capitalist economic systems
3   lack of access to world markets
4   scarcity of water resources

21   During the late 1980's and early 1990's, the greatest threat to the stability of the nations of Egypt, Algeria, and Morocco was the
1   rising standard of living of their citizens
2   economic reforms taking place in Eastern Europe
3   rise of Islamic fundamentalism
4   lack of financial aid from the United States

22   Which was a characteristic of the policy of mercantilism followed by Spanish colonial rulers in Latin America?
1   The colonies were forced to develop local industries to support themselves.
2   Spain sought trade agreements between its colonies and the English colonies in North America.
3   The colonies were required to provide raw materials to Spain and to purchase Spanish manufactured goods.
4   Spain encouraged the colonies to develop new political systems to meet colonial needs.

23   Which statement best describes a result of the scarcity of native Indian labor in Latin America during the colonial period?
1   Unskilled laborers were imported from Asia.
2   Many people from Spain and Portugal immigrated to the region.
3   Native American Indians from the British colonies went south to work.
4   Large numbers of African slaves were imported.

24   In many Latin American nations, which group has most resisted social and economic changes since the end of World War II?
1   poor farmers   3   union leaders
2   the military   4   the middle class

25   Which is a valid statement about land distribution in many Central American nation?
1   The Spanish distributed land equally among the people.
2   The largest amount of land is owned by the smallest number of families.
3   The largest amount of land is owned by the largest number of families.
4   The government owns most of the land in the name of the people.

26   Which is a major reason Cuban and Nicaraguan revolutionary movements were attracted to communism?
1   Communist groups promised economic reform and better living standards.
2   Business owners and the military were supported by Communist groups.
3   The goal of communism was to encourage religion.
4   Communist leaders promised to reduce Spanish colonialism in the Western Hemisphere.

27   At the present time, which is a major economic problem for many Latin American governments?
1   increased settlement in rural areas
2   low rates of inflation
3   inability to pay foreign debts
4   lack of a chief executive

28   The main purpose of the Organization of American States (OAS) is to
1   integrate the economies of Latin American nations
2   encourage United States military involvement in the region
3   destroy the power of Colombian drug lords
4   provide a way to resolve regional problems peacefully

29   Which statement describes a direct effect of the Renaissance on western Europe?
1   The philosophy of humanism brought about a decrease in the power of the Roman Catholic Church.
2   Art began to reflect an increased emphasis on religious themes.
3   Nationalistic movements among the minority ethnic groups in the region declined.
4   The feudal system was developed to provide stability in a decentralized political structure.

30   An important result of the Industrial Revolution in 19th-century western Europe was that
1   the gap between the wealthy and the poor decreased
2   urbanization increased rapidly
3   the supply of unskilled labor decreased
4   migration to rural areas increased

Base your answers to questions 31 and 32 on the speakers' statements below and on your knowledge of social studies.

Speaker A: By nature, men are free, equal, and independent. No one can be put out of this estate and subjected to the political power of another without his own consent.

Speaker B: The question arises about whether it is better to be loved more than feared or feared more than loved. The reply is that one ought to be both feared and loved, but it is much safer to be feared than loved.

Speaker C: Society's interests are best served by open and free competition. The laws of nature dictate that the struggle of the marketplace produces the best results.

Speaker D: Does anyone believe that the progress of this world springs from the mind of majorities and not from the brain of individuals?

31 Which speaker supports the ideals of democracy?
 (1) *A*   (3) *C*
 (2) *B*   (4) *D*

32 The ideas of the capitalist system are best supported by Speaker
 (1) *A*   (3) *C*
 (2) *B*   (4) *D*

33 The Holocaust in Europe and the actions of the Khmer Rouge in Kampuchea (Cambodia) were similar in that they were examples of
 1 interdependence   3 genocide
 2 segregation   4 empathy

Base your answer to question 34 on the map at the right and on your knowledge of social studies.

34 The map illustrates a division of Europe that led to the creation of the
 1 Axis and the Allied powers
 2 North Atlantic Treaty Organization (NATO) and the Warsaw Pact
 3 Triple Alliance and the Triple Entente
 4 United Nations and the League of Nations

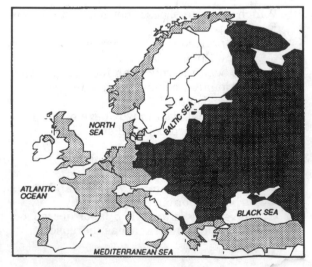

35 Which is a valid statement about the reunification of East and West Germany in 1990?
1 East German prosperity made reunification desirable for West Germany.
2 Reunification was linked to the withdrawal of United States forces from Western Europe.
3 Reunification occurred despite concerns by other European nations over the power of a united Germany.
4 A reunified Germany promised to withdraw from the North Atlantic Treaty Organization (NATO).

36 **"Warsaw Pact Tanks Invade Budapest"**
"Wall Divides Berlin"
"Liberal Czechoslovak Government Replaced"

These historical newspaper headlines were related to
1 Mikhail Gorbachev's introduction of the policy of glasnost
2 Adolf Hitler's efforts to promote national socialism
3 the Soviet Union's acceptance of capitalism
4 attempts by the Soviet Union to strengthen Communist control

37 During the Presidency of Mikhail Gorbachev, which problem faced the Soviet Union?
1 Ethnic minorities demanded the right of self-determination.
2 Agricultural production grew faster than food consumption.
3 The nations of Eastern Europe insisted that the Soviet Union keep troops in Eastern Europe.
4 Western European nations refused to trade with the Soviet Union.

38 After World War II, the rise of independent nations in Asia demonstrated the
1 decline of European global influence
2 influence of the Shinto religion on their cultures
3 success of the peacekeeping forces of the United Nations
4 failure of nationalistic movements

39 The main concern regarding the destruction of the rain forests in areas of Brazil and sub-Saharan Africa is that
1 cities will become seriously overcrowded
2 the temperature of the Earth's surface may increase
3 the per capita income in economically developing nations may increase
4 water supplies in these areas will increase

40 In Mexico and India, the Green Revolution has been successful because it has
1 promoted democratic reform
2 increased agricultural productivity
3 introduced Western culture and values
4 established economic equality among the people

41   During the Cold War Era, many Asian and African nations followed a
     policy of nonalignment because they
     1   had the same goals and needs as the Soviet Union
     2   needed the natural resources of Western European nations
     3   wished to receive aid from the Soviet Union and the United States
     4   were afraid of losing their vote in the United Nations

Base your answer to
question 42 on the circle
graph at the right and
on your knowledge of
social studies.

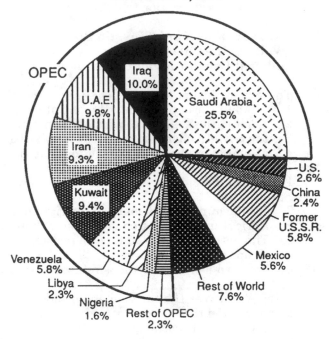

**WORLD'S ESTIMATED OIL RESERVES
JANUARY 1,1990**

OPEC

Iraq 10.0%

U.A.E. 9.8%

Saudi Arabia 25.5%

Iran 9.3%

U.S. 2.6%

Kuwait 9.4%

China 2.4%

Former U.S.S.R. 5.8%

Venezuela 5.8%

Mexico 5.6%

Libya 2.3%

Rest of World 7.6%

Nigeria 1.6%   Rest of OPEC 2.3%

42   Which is a valid
     conclusion based on
     the information in
     the graph?
     1   Only Middle Eastern nations are members of OPEC.
     2   Events in the Middle East have little effect on world oil prices.
     3   No major oil reserves exist in Latin America.
     4   Members of OPEC control approximately 75% of the world's oil
         reserves.

43   Changes in Russia under Peter the Great were most similar to changes
     that occurred in
     1   China before the Opium war
     2   Japan during the Meiji Restoration
     3   Iran after the fall of Shah Pahlevi
     4   France during the feudal period

44   One similarity between Mao Zedong and Fidel Castro is that they
     1   achieved their goals through the use of peaceful resistance
     2   worked to protect citizens' rights to freedom of expression
     3   considered capitalism to be the best economic system
     4   led revolutionary movements that established Communist
         governments

Base your answer to question 45 on the passage below and on your knowledge of social studies.

"I believe that the civilization India has evolved is not to be beaten in the world. Nothing can equal the seeds sown by our ancestors. Rome went, Greece shared the same fate; the might of the Pharaohs was broken;...but India is still, somehow or other, sound....What we have tested and found true on the anvil of experience, we dare not change."
- Mohandas Gandhi, 1946

45 What is the main idea of the passage?
1 Life in modern India must be based on past Indian achievements.
2 Rome and Greece had the most advanced ancient civilizations.
3 Modern societies have little to learn from ancient societies.
4 All ancient civilizations have collapsed.

46 One similarity between Axum, Kush, and Nubia was that they were
1 military leaders in the Neolithic Age
2 rivers along which early trade developed
3 writers of epic poems about Greek cities
4 early civilizations in Africa

47 Notre Dame Cathedral in Paris, the Dome of the Rock in Jerusalem, and the Great Pyramid in Egypt are examples of
1 architectural accomplishments that reflect religious beliefs
2 the influence of Buddhist architecture on conquered nations
3 ancient architectural monuments no longer in use
4 the influence of cultural diffusion on contemporary architecture

48 The Suez Canal, the Strait of Hormuz, and the Strait of Gibraltar are important because they
1 prevent attacks on bordering nations
2 control access to vital trade routes
3 limit Russian access to warm-water ports
4 prohibit the movement of ships carrying nuclear weapons

Students Please note :
In developing your answers to Part II, be sure to
(1) include specific factual information and evidence whenever possible
(2) keep to the questions asked; do not go off on tangents
(3) avoid overgeneralizations or sweeping statements without sufficient proof; do not overstate your case
(4) keep these general definitions in mind:
    (a) <u>discuss</u> means "to make observations about something using facts, reasoning, and argument; to present in some detail"
    (b) <u>describe</u> means "to illustrate something in words or tell about it"
    (c) <u>show</u> means "to point out; to set forth clearly a position or idea by stating it and giving data which support it"
    (d) <u>explain</u> means "to make plain or understandable; to give reasons for or causes of; to show the logical development or relationships of"

Part II
ANSWER THREE QUESTIONS FROM THIS PART. [45]

1   Throughout history, groups of people have taken actions to oppose those in power.

Groups
   Arab Palestinians in the Israeli-occupied territories
   Philosophers of the Enlightenment in France
   Solidarity in Communist Poland
   Sikhs in India
   Boxers in China
   Contras in Nicaragua
   African National Congress (ANC) in the Republic of South Africa

Select *three* of the groups listed and for *each* one selected:
* State a major goal of the group
* Discuss how the group tried to achieve this goal   [5,5,5]

2   Nationalism and imperialism have often been the cause of military conflicts.

Conflicts
   Hundred Years' War
   19th-century revolutions in Latin America
   Napoleonic wars
   Sepoy Mutiny
   World War I
   Vietnam War
   Persian Gulf War

Choose *three* of the conflicts listed. For *each* conflict chosen, discuss how nationalism *or* imperialism led to the conflict. In your discussion of each conflict chosen:

* Include the historical background of the conflict
* Explain the specific role of nationalism *or* imperialism as a cause of the conflict [You must state whether you are discussing nationalism *or* imperialism.]   [5,5,5]

3   Throughout history, the ideas of leaders have affected their nations. The statements below express the ideas of the leader with whom they are paired.

I am the State. - Louis XIV, France
Promote the upright and banish the crooked, then the people will be submissive. - Confucius, China
Here I stand. I cannot do otherwise. - Martin Luther, a German state
Peace, Bread, Land. - Nikolai Lenin, Russia
The Three Principles: the people's livelihood, the people's democracy, the people's nationalism. - Sun Yat-sen, China
The best way of gaining our freedom is not through violence. - Mohandas Gandhi, India

(Question Part II, #3 continued)
Select *three* of the statements and for *each* one selected:
• Explain the idea of the leader as expressed in the statement
• Describe how the leader's ideas were carried out in his nation
   [5,5,5]

4   The nations and regions of the world face various types of problems that
     affect economic development.

             Problems Affecting Economic Development
     Shortage of investment capital - Eastern Europe
     Desertification - African Sahel
     Overpopulation - China
     Shortage of natural resources - Japan
     Pollution - Western Europe
     Dependence on one-product economy - Latin America

     Choose *three* of the problems from the list and for *each* one chosen:
     • Explain how the problem has affected the economic development of
       the nation or region with which it is paired
     • Discuss *one* specific attempt that has been made by that nation or
       region to overcome the problem   [5,5,5]

5   Geographic factors affect the development of nations throughout the
    world.

             Geographic Factors - Nations
     Mineral resources - Great Britain *or* Zaire
     River systems - Egypt *or* China
     Mountains - Chile *or* Greece
     Location - Italy *or* Korea
     Climate - Russia *or* India
     Strategic waterways - Panama *or* Turkey

    Select *three* of the geographic factors listed. For *each* one selected, discuss
    how the geographic factor affected the political *or* economic development
    of *one* of the nations with which it is paired.   [5,5,5]

6   Throughout history, the basic political, social, and economic rights of some
    groups have been violated.

             Groups of People
     Serfs on European medieval manors
     Untouchables (harijans) in India
     Jews in Europe during World War II
     Peasant farmers (campesinos) in Latin America
     Women and children during the early Industrial Revolution
     Kurds during the 20th century
     Dissidents in the Soviet Union under Stalin

    Select *three* groups from the list. For *each* one selected, use specific
    historical information to explain how the group's basic political, social, *or*
    economic rights were violated.   [5,5,5]

7   Certain events or occurrences in history have brought about significant changes.

Events / Occurrences

Voyages of Columbus
Glorious Revolution in England
Failure of the Weimar Republic in Germany
Defeat of Japan in World War II
Westernization of Iran by Shah Pahlevi
Signing of the Camp David accords by Egypt and Israel
Adoption of glasnost in the Soviet Union

Select *three* of the events or occurrences listed. For *each* one selected:
* Describe the event or occurrence
* Explain how the event or occurrence led to significant changes in a specific nation or region   [5,5,5]

Answers, Explanations, and Page References
Part I

(Students should note the variety of instances in which material from Part I questions can be useful in answering Part II questions and vice versa. Also, it is useful to compare these questions to those on the other exam in this book.)

1 (ans. 4) Nationalism reflects strong feelings for country based on unity through common history and values. (Details on pgs. 256-257, 387)

2 (ans. 3) Shows trade interaction of nations = interdependence involving goods and services provided in our global economy. (Details on pgs. 7, 10)

3 (ans. 2) The ancient Inca, Roman, and Mongol empires were similar in that they all extended control over their neighbors. (Details on pgs. 158, 160, 194-95, 204, 235-237, 304)

4 (ans. 4) A geographic interpretation question on the concept of diversity. Africa's varied topography and climate leads to the development of many different societies. (Details on pgs. 14-16)

5 (ans. 1) In Africa, as colonial rule weakened following WW II, independence movements spread throughout the continent. (Details on pg. 32)

6 (ans. 4) Conflicting ideological and economic goals in many African nations resulted in mixed economic systems. (Details on pgs. 43, 52)

7 (ans. 3) Proportion of black chess pieces to white suggests the government has been forced to make concessions in modern South Africa. (Details on pg. 34; also see *N&N G-S Ten Day Review*, Lesson 8.2)

8 (ans. 2) Despite efforts to legally abolish caste in India, traditional villages still maintain this socially discriminating system. (Details on pg. 72)

9 (ans. 1)　South Asia's history shows a wide variety of religious beliefs have both positive and negative effects on people. The alternative answers are all factually incorrect. (Details on pgs. 59-62)

10 (ans. 2)　19th Century European involvement in China required the use of advanced weaponry and communications to maintain spheres of influence for trade. (Details on pg. 103)

11 (ans. 4)　The map's title refers to minorities, which is synonymous with the term "ethnic diversity."
(Details on pgs. 98-100)

12 (ans. 4)　"Cultural Revolution" was a euphemism for the power struggle between Mao's hard-line communists and more pragmatic groups in the 1960's. (Details on pgs. 110-111)

13 (ans. 1)　Signs of Marxist communism usually involve communal activities as opposed to individual indicative. In Mao's China, the government's imposition of an agricultural commune system was the most obvious sign of Marxism. (Details on pg. 115)

14 (ans. 3)　The tank represents the Chinese government's suppression of the young students' pro-democracy movement (bicyclist) in the Spring of 1989. (Details on pg. 112; also see *N&N G-S Ten Day Review*, Lesson 7.3)

15 (ans. 3)　A basic historical recall question involving awareness that both civilizations chose isolation from the rest of the world until the modern era. (Details on pgs. 94-95, 125-127)

16 (ans. 1)　Being a small archipelago nation, Japan lacks major natural resources but has one of the world's largest fishing industries. (Details on pg. 126; also see *N&N G-S Ten Day Review*, Lesson 9)

17 (ans. 2)　Key is awareness that the samurai were the dominant knight-warrior class. Bushido was the warrior's code of chivalry and loyalty which means the tradition of the ruling class evolved from militarism. (Details on pg. 129)

18 (ans. 3)　Recent growth in the Japanese economy may best be attributed to the government's benevolent industrial policy strengthens large corporations (zaibatsu) with tax breaks, low cost loans, and high tariffs on foreign goods. (Details on pg. 146)

19 (ans. 1)　Requires recall that these were three influential Israeli Prime Ministers since 1948. (Details on pg. 211)

20 (ans. 4)　The Middle East and northern Africa face a major obstacle in economic advancement because of scarce water resources. (Details on pgs. 190-191, 218; also see *N&N G-S Ten Day Review*, Lesson 9)

21 (ans. 3)　The recent revival of Islamic fundamentalism has been a major threat to political and social stability in the north African nations of Egypt, Algeria, and Morocco. (Details on pgs. 213, 216, 220)

22 (ans. 3) The economic concept of mercantilism involves colonies to enhance markets for merchants of the mother country. American colonies became suppliers of raw materials to Spain, but more importantly, they bought Spanish manufactured products. (Details on pgs. 163-164)

23 (ans. 4) Because the Indian population resisted work on the large landed estates and plantations of colonial Latin America, many African slaves were brought to the colonies as laborers. (Details on pgs. 158, 165)

24 (ans. 2) In Latin America, the most resistance to social and economic changes since WW II has come from the military which wants to maintain its traditional oligarchy control over people. Unions, campesinos, and middle class groups have tried to unseat the upper class/military alliance. (Details on pg. 169).

25 (ans. 2) Land reform is traditionally one of the most controversial issues in Latin America. From the days of the colonial encomienda system, land has been owned by only a few, concentrating power in agricultural societies in the hands of a landed aristocracy. (Details on pgs. 165, 177)

26 (ans. 1) Communist revolutions succeeded in Cuba and Nicaragua because they promised the people land reform and better living standards. (Details on pgs. 171-172, 182-183)

27 (ans. 3) Sagging markets and global competition for agricultural products and minerals led to difficulties in repaying the high debt to world banks and foreign investment groups. (Details on pgs. 178-179)

28 (ans. 4) A recall question on the purpose of OAS. This Western Hemisphere organization's purpose is to promote peace and cooperation in Latin American nations. (Details on pg. 181)

29 (ans. 1) A cause and effect question. The broad effects of European Renaissance included more than a change in artistic expression. Movement away from narrow religious themes led to questioning of authority and a decrease in the power of the Roman Catholic Church and even helped to cause the Protestant Reformation. (Details on pgs. 244-245)

30 (ans. 2) Urban centers grew naturally with industrialization since cities supplied necessary resources such as labor, transportation,communication, and financial institutions. Answer 1 is incorrect because, while industrialization raises the general standard of living, it leads to economic class stratification. Wealth becomes concentrated with certain groups. Ans. 3 is incorrect because mechanization called for less skilled labor. Ans. 4 is the opposite of what occurred. People were drawn to the opportunity of cities. (Details on pgs. 258-259; also see *N&N G-S Ten Day Review*, Lesson 5.2)

N.B. On "Speaker A-B-C" questions, students should learn to take two preliminary steps: 1) identify the common thread among the statements (here it is power in society); 2) label the speakers (e.g., A = Enlightenment; B = Machiavellian; C = Laissez-faire/Darwinian, D = Individualist).

31 (ans. 1 or A) Analysis of four different speakers' statements would show that speaker A's views of men being free, equal, and independent most closely supports the ideals of democracy put forth by Rousseau and Locke. (Details on pgs. 252-253)

32 (ans. 3 or C) Analysis of four different speakers statement would show that Speaker C views of open and free competition in the marketplace most closely supports the ideals of a capitalist system. (Details on pgs. 251-252)

33 (ans. 3) A comparison of the two events indicates deliberate state-sponsored mass killings is the common denominator and recognizing this as the definition of genocide. (Details on pgs. 76, 272, 356; also see *N&N G-S Ten Day Review*, Lesson 7.1)

34 (ans. 2) Since there are no labeling hints, student has to recognize this as the east-west division of Europe which followed WW II. In the late 1940's, communist eastern bloc (Warsaw Pact) and anti-communist western (NATO) alliances divided the continent. (Details on pgs. 293-294)

35 (ans. 3) This traditional U.S.S.R. concern regarding German reunification was dropped by Gorbachev as a result of western disarmament negotiations concessions. (Details on pg. 290)

36 (ans. 4) Three separate historic news headlines reflect on Cold War Era behavior of the Soviets in controlling Eastern European satellites. (Details on pgs. 341-343; also see *N&N G-S Ten Day Review*, Lesson 1.3)

37 (ans. 1) As Gorbachev unleashed the forces of self determination with his glasnost policy, the pro-democracy movement grew. Facts negate situations described in answers 2,3,4. (Details on pgs. 326-327; cf. ques. 7 on Part II of this exam.)

38 (ans. 1) Many nationalist movements occurred in Asia following WW II, and this brought to an end the former European colonial empires. (Details on pgs. 70-78; cf. similar idea on Africa in ques. 5 above)

39 (ans. 2) Deforestation in the rain forests of Brazil and sub-Saharan Africa cause scientists to believe that our climate will suffer from global warming (the "greenhouse effect"). (Details on pgs. 46, 354; also see *N&N G-S Ten Day Review*, Lesson 6.2)

40 (ans. 2) A concept question based on knowledge of the Green Revolution's success story of increased agricultural productivity in Mexico and India during the last 20 years. (Details on pgs. 45, 83, 358; also see *N&N G-S Ten Day Review*, Lesson 3.4)

41 (ans. 3) Following WW II, many developing Asian and African nations sought financial aid from both the United States and the Soviet Union, and therefore pursued a policy of non-alignment which allowed them to politically choose either side depending on the issues. (Details on pgs. 49, 88)

42 (ans. 4)   A skill question on reading a pie graph on estimated global oil reserves. From the information provided, the arc representing the portion OPEC nations control = 3/4th of the circumference of the circle, thus 75 % of the supply. (Details on pgs. 218, 224; also see *N&N G-S Ten Day Review*, Lesson 6.4)

43 (ans. 2)   A time comparison focusing on the concept of change. The only answer that fits a sharp westernization cultural change similar to that of Peter the Great's Russia is that of the 19th C. industrial conversion of Japan under Emperor Meiji. (Details on pgs. 307, 133-134)

44 (ans. 4)   A comparison of the two 20th Century world leaders Mao Zedong and Fidel Castro shows that each led communist revolutions in their nations. (Details on pgs. 105-106, 172)

45 (ans. 1)   Answer rests on direct reading of Gandhi's statement. Main idea is that India's survival is linked to the past traditions. (Details on pg. 66)

46 (ans. 4)   Key is recognizing these as former N.E. African trading empires. (Details on pg. 24)

47 (ans. 1)   Key to this comparison of three of the world's architectural wonders is awareness that they are each connected to one of the world's great religions. (Details on pgs. 192-193, 201, 240)

48 (ans. 2)   Key to this comparison of three of the world's strategic water passages is access to trade routes and naval defenses. (Details on pgs. 210, 215, 218, 232)

Part II

(Students should note the variety of instances in which material from Part I can be useful in answering Part II questions and vice versa.)

1 *Writing Strategy*: This essay examines the role opposition groups play in affecting change. Select *three* groups from those given. Set up *three* paragraphs. In *each* paragraph: A) state the goal of the group; B) describe a method the group used to achieve the goal you stated.

* ***Arab Palestinians in the Israeli-occupied territories***: A) <u>Goal</u>: Set up a homeland for Arab Palestinians on the West Bank of the Jordan, the Gaza Strip, and in other territories now controlled by Israel. B) <u>Method of change</u> - violent protests, riots, diplomatic negotiations by Palestinian Liberation Organization, along with global terrorist acts by groups claiming association with the PLO. (Details on pgs. 212, 223, 225, 353)

* ***Philosophers of the Enlightenment in France***: A) <u>Goal</u>: Encourage people to use their powers of reason. B) <u>Method</u>: writers such as Voltaire, Rousseau, and Montesquieu encouraged examination of society and seek government structures reflecting natural law. These suggestions included direct democracy, enlightened despotism, and separation of powers. (Details on pg. 252)

- ***Solidarity in communist Poland***: A) <u>Goal</u>: End oppressive dictatorial communist oligarchy. B) <u>Method</u>: Under the leadership of Lech Walesa, the Solidarity Trade Union Movement began a series of crippling strikes against the government in the 1980's. In 1989, solidarity won a general election and pushed democratic reforms. Poland became the first Iron Curtain country to overthrow communism. (Details on pgs. 330-331)

- ***Sikhs in India***: A) <u>Goal</u>: Sikhs sought more local decision-making power in their Punjab homeland. B) <u>Method</u>: Sikh radicals employ symbolic terrorist tactics against the Indian government. In 1984, India's Prime Minister Indira Gandhi sent troops to suppress demonstrations in the Sikh holy temple at Amritsar. The incident turned violent and resulted in several deaths. In retaliation, Sikh guards assassinated Mrs. Gandhi later that year. However, the government has resisted and reforms in leading to home rule for the Punjab. (Details on pgs. 60, 62, 70, 73)

- ***Boxers in China***: A) <u>Goal</u>: Boxers sought to rid their country of foreign exploitation in 1900. B) <u>Method</u>: An armed uprising in Peking (Beijing) attacked Western colonial trade and diplomatic enclaves with passive cooperation from the government. A combined force from Europe and the U.S. freed the city. The general nationalist unrest eventually led to Sun Yat-sen's revolution against the weak Manchu Dynasty in 1911. (Details on pg. 104)

- ***Contras in Nicaragua***: A) <u>Goal</u>: Contras sought to overthrow the communist Sandinista regime of Daniel Ortega in the 1980's. B) <u>Method</u>: Legal and illegal aid from the Reagan Administration in the U.S. helped the contras to force an internationally supervised election in 1990. Ortega lost to democratic coalition candidate Violeta Chamorro. (Details on pg. 172)

- ***African National Congress (ANC) in the Republic of South Africa***: A) <u>Goal</u>: The ANC seeks abolition of legal separation of races and Black majority rule. B) <u>Method</u>: ANC leaders such as Nelson Mandela and Bishop Tutu organize mass demonstrations which often turn violent. However, they have drawn world attention and cooperation in economic boycotts. The White government dropped the Pass Laws and started constitutional changes. More moderate White leaders emerged who continue to negotiate to reduce tensions and break down social, political, and economic barriers. (Details on pgs. 33-34; also see *N&N's Ten Day Review*, Lesson 7.2)

2 *Writing Strategy*: This essay examines your knowledge of nationalism and imperialism. Select *three* conflicts from those given. Set up *three* paragraphs. In *each* paragraph: state the historical background of the conflict and explain how nationalism or imperialism caused conflict.

- ***Hundred Years War***: <u>Background (Nationalism as Cause)</u>: National identity emerged from this conflict as English and French monarchs fought over English-owned lands in France and over the textile trade. In addition, English King Edward III claimed the right to the French throne. The use of peasants rather than nobles and mercenaries to fight for their rulers' lands, and the appeal of national leaders such as France's Joan of Arc heightened nationalist consciousness on both sides.

- ***19th century revolutions in Latin America***: <u>Background</u> (<u>Nationalism as Cause</u>): The American and French Revolutions inspired nationalist desires in the Spanish and Portuguese colonies of the New World in the early 19th C. Liberators such as Bolivar, Miranda, and San Martin led successful independence movements in the Americas while the colonial mother countries fought the Napoleonic Wars in Europe. (Details on pgs. 166-167)

- ***Napoleonic Wars***: <u>Background</u> (<u>Imperialism as Cause</u>): From the wars of the French Revolution into the early 19th C., France sought to expand its territory and influence. Fearing a spread of revolution, European monarchs fought Napoleon or appeased him temporarily. A monarchist alliance eventually defeated the imperialism of the French in 1815. (Details on pgs. 255, 311; also see *N&N's Ten Day Review*, Lesson 1.1)

- ***Sepoy Mutiny***: <u>Background</u> (<u>Nationalism as Cause</u>): Native Indian troops working for the British East India Co. revolted after against a perception that the foreign company was forcing violation of their national religious rituals. British government sent troops to pacify the region and established firm colonial control in India. (Details on pgs. 64-65)

- ***World War I***: <u>Background</u> (<u>Nationalism as Cause</u>): Slavic groups in the Balkans agitated for national self-rule. Radical Black Hand Serbs carried out terrorist attacks on Turks and Austro-Hungarian authority. In 1914 they assassinated the heir to the A-H imperial throne, triggering war among the rival alliances of Europe. (Details on pgs. 262-263)

- ***Vietnam War***: <u>Background</u> (<u>Nationalism as Cause</u>): Nationalism motivated communist insurgents under Ho Chi Minh during and after WW II to overthrow French colonial dominance in 1954. U.S. aid to South Vietnam's anti-communist despots led to continued fighting by Viet Cong insurgents. The U.S. escalated military presence in the 1960's. This led to full scale war and eventual defeat of the Americans in 1973. The communists unified the country in 1975. (Details on pgs. 74-75)

- ***Persian Gulf War***: <u>Background</u> (<u>Imperialism as Cause</u>): In 1992, Iraqi leader Saddam Hussein invaded and subjugated oil-rich Kuwait. He then threatened Israel and Saudi Arabia. A U.N. sponsored coalition of 26 nations liberated Kuwait and invaded Iraq in 1993. Iraq withdrew and agreed to a truce. However, Saddam's imperial desires remain a threat to Mid-East peace. (Details on pg. 215)

3 *Writing Strategy*: This essay examines leaders' ideas in changing their nations. Select *three* statements from those given. Set up *three* paragraphs. In *each* paragraph: A) explain what the leader meant by the statement; B) explain how the leader put this idea to work.

- ***I am the State – Louis XIV, France***: A) <u>Meaning</u>: Louis' statement reflects his belief he had absolute power by divine right B) <u>Leader's Action</u>: To avoid any sharing of power, Louis never called the Estates General. He gave all the orders on military and financial affairs. Louis had his Finance Minister Colbert institute mercantilist policies to control and extract wealth from the economy. Louis constructed the lavish Versailles Palace and controlled nobles he ordered to live there. (Details on pgs. 247-248, 253; also see *N&N's Ten Day Review*, Lesson 8.1)

- ***Promote the upright and banish the crooked, then the people will be submissive – Confucius, China***: A) <u>Meaning</u>: To maintain an ordered society, emphasis had to placed on codes of responsibility and proper behavior; B) <u>Leader's Action</u>: Followers of Confucian philosophy placed emphasis on individuals' loyalty and obligations to family and community. (Details on pgs. 96-97, 99, 112)

- ***Here I stand. I cannot do otherwise. – Martin Luther, a German state***: A) <u>Meaning</u>: Cleric Martin Luther would not budge from controversial beliefs that the Bible and conscience were the individual's basic guides to truth and salvation. B) <u>Leader's Action</u>: Luther defied the Roman Catholic Church's power to make rules for its members. His translation of the Bible into the German vernacular allowed ordinary people to read and interpret scripture for themselves, undermining the Church's interpretive authority. Luther's defiance led to the Protestant Reformation. (Details on pg. 245)

- ***Peace, Bread, Land – Nikolai Lenin, Russia***: A) <u>Meaning</u>: Revolutionary Lenin wanted Tsarist Russia to withdraw from WW I, provide food for its people, and allow peasants to own their own land. B) <u>Leader's Action</u>: In the early stages of Russia's revolution, Kerensky's Provisional Government withdrew from the war. However, Lenin's Bolsheviks wrested control of the government. They seized rural food supplies for starving supporters in the cities and encouraged peasants to rise up and seize land from landlords. However, in the 1920's the new Marxist state took the land from the peasants and collectivized it. (Details on pgs. 314-317)

- ***The Three Principles: the people's livelihood, the people's democracy, the people's nationalism. – Sun Yat-sen, China***: A) <u>Meaning</u>: In Dr. Sun's revolutionary thought, land reform would enhance people's well being, free elections would ensure democracy, and a new government would diminish foreign interference in the Chinese nation. B) <u>Leader's Action</u>: Instability and corrupt militarism resulted from Dr. Sun's overthrow of the Manchu Dynasty in 1911. Local warlords seized the land, and the new national government was so weak that a civil war raged in China for nearly 38 years. (Details on pgs. 104-106)

- ***The best way of gaining our freedom is not through violence. – Mohandas Gandhi, India***: A) <u>Meaning</u>: Nonviolent, direct action and passive resistance would be the key to India's nationhood. B) <u>Leader's Action</u>: Gandhi used marches, boycotts, hunger strikes, and primitive domestic production to undermine British economic and political power, leading to independence in 1947. (Details on pgs. 70-71)

4 Writing Strategy: This essay test your understanding economic development (advancement). Select *three* problems from those given. Set up *three* paragraphs. In *each* paragraph: A) state how the problem affects the region or nation; B) describe an attempt in that nation to overcome the problem.

*   ***Shortage of investment capital – Eastern Europe***: A) <u>Problem Affects Region</u>: Lack of investment capital has made it difficult for the Eastern European countries to modernize their industries to compete in the global market. B) <u>Attempt to Overcome</u>: E. European nations have sought loans from foreign investors and grants in aid from richer nations. International organizations such as the World Bank and the IMF have helped to stabilize their economies and make lending less risky. These organizations also provide "see money" in the form of grants to aid entrepreneurs. (Details on pgs. 337-338)

*   ***Desertification – African Sahel***: A) <u>Problem Affects Region</u>: West Africa has suffered from famine and as the formerly nomadic population seeks refuge in the cities. B) <u>Attempt to Overcome</u>: African governments have taken steps to limit grazing and cutting the remaining forested areas. Also, dry season farming techniques borrowed from Israel are beginning to increase crop yields. (Details on pgs. 46, 354; also see *N&N's Ten Day Review*, Lessons 2.1 & 6.1)

*   ***Overpopulation – China***: A) <u>Problem Affected Nation</u>: High birth rates and medically enhanced longevity increase population faster than new technologies can increase food supplies and living conditions. B) <u>Attempt to Overcome</u>: From the 1950's on, Mao adopted a one couple = two children policy. Recently, Deng reduced it to one couple = one child. Serious social and economic penalties accompanied violation. (Details on pgs. 111, 114, 348; also see *N&N's Ten Day Review*, Lesson 2)

*   ***Shortage of natural resources – Japan***: A) <u>Problem Affected Nation</u>: Insufficient coal, iron, petroleum and other critical minerals hindered modern economic development in the Meiji Period. B) <u>Attempt to Overcome</u>: Japan's leaders embarked on imperialistic policies (Sino-Japanese War and the Manchurian Crisis) which led to military control of northern China, Korea and Taiwan in the early 20th C. and eventually fomented World War II in the Pacific. (Details on pgs. 74, 84, 106, 126, 144-145, 149; also see *N&N's Ten Day Review*, Lesson 9.2)

*   ***Pollution – Western Europe***: A) <u>Problem Affects Region</u>: Water pollution and acid rain affects major waterways such as the Thames and the Rhine. Aquatic life declines and potable water supplies become endangered. B) <u>Attempt to Overcome</u>: Germany's Ruhr Association tries to police environmental situations. The European Community set up standards. The European Court of Justice enforces sanctions for countries found ignoring them. (Details on pgs. 278, 353-345; also see *N&N's Ten Day Review*, Lesson 6.3)

*   ***Dependence on a one-product economy – Latin America***: A) <u>Problem Affects Region</u>: Countries such as Brazil (Coffee) or Venezuela

(petroleum) find themselves at the mercy of global markets and natural disasters such as droughts, storms, and infestations. Under- and over-production results in price instability and economic difficulties.
B) Attempt to Overcome: Most Latin American countries try to diversify their industrial bases and expand tourism. (Details on pgs. 177-177; also see *N&N's Ten Day Review*, Lesson 5.4)

5 *Writing Strategy*: This essay examines how geography affects historic developments in areas. Select *three* factor/nation combinations from those given. Set up *three* paragraphs. In *each* paragraph: describe how the factor affected the *political* or *economic* life of *one* of the two nations given.

- *Mineral resources - Great Britain* : Economic Effect: Rich iron and coal deposits helped Britain to emerge as the world's first major industrial nation by the early 19th C. Britain's need for additional markets for its manufactured goods led to the imperialism as the century progressed. (Details on pg. 230; Zaire, 35-36)

- *River systems - Egypt* : Economic Effect: The Nile River Delta is one of the world's most fertile agricultural regions. Historians call Egypt the "gift of the Nile. " The river's alluvial soils led to early settlement and the rise of Egyptian Civilization about 4,000 years ago. The river also provided a transportation and communication system for economic expansion. (Egypt details on pg. 188; China, 94-96)

- *Mountains - Greece*: Political Effect: The Balkan Peninsula is very mountainous which makes transportation and communication extremely difficult even today. In early times, small city-states (Athens, Sparta, Thebes) emerged as isolated political units, rather than large empires such as Egypt or Babylon. Each was fiercely independent, and developed its own political and cultural patterns. They often fought among themselves (Peloponnesian War - mid 400's BC). There were alliances, but they often found it difficult to unite when faced with outside conquerors such as Macedonians and Romans. (Greece details on pg. 233; Chile/ South America, 154-158)

- *Location - Korea*: Political Effect: Because of its location, 19th C. Japanese imperialists described Korea as "a dagger aimed at the heart of Japan." Traditionally, it was a cultural bridge between China and Japan and never posed military threat to any nation in the East Asian region. The Japanese leaders used Korea as a stepping stone on the Asian continent to build their empire and conquer Manchuria. (Korea details on pgs. 134-135; Italy, 232-233)

- *Climate - Russia*: Political Effect: The northern tundra is a permafrost region with long, harsh winters. Immediately to the south is the taiga, a forested zone encompassing 5)% of Russia's land mass. The region is huge with little seacoast. While these factors provided some protection, it isolated Russia politically and culturally. These factors moved tsars such as Peter and Catherine to war with neighboring regions (17th-18th C.) to gain outlets to the seas. (Russia details on pgs. 298, 303; India, 56-57)

- *Strategic Waterways - Turkey*: <u>Political Effect</u>: For much of its history, Turkey dealt with challenges by Russia for a water outlet from the Black Sea to the Mediterranean through the Dardanelles & Bosporus Straights. In the 18th and 19th Century, the tsars pressured the Ottoman Empire (Turkey) and its allies for control of the straights. Most significant was the Crimean War of 1854. (Details on pgs. 205, 309, 312; Panama, 172-173)

6 Writing Strategy: This essay tests your knowledge of groups having their basic rights violated. Select *three* groups from those given. Set up *three* paragraphs. In *each* paragraph: use historic facts to describe as clearly as possible violations of the group's rights (mention which rights).

- *Serfs on European medieval manors*: (Economic rights) The feudal system considered serfs to be property of the manor's lord. The feudal rules bound serfs to labor for the lord, receiving food shelter and protection. Serfs could not leave the land or change their way of making a living without the lord's permission. Under feudal law, they were chattel passed on at death to the lord's heirs. (Details on pg. 239; also see *N&N's Ten Day Review*, Lesson 5.1)

- *Untouchables (harijans) in India*: (Social rights) Although the government abolished the Hindu caste system in the 1950's, traditional class structures roles remain strong in rural regions. Harijans are still outcasts prohibited culturally from contact with other groups, and remain in poverty. (Details on pg. 60)

- *Jews in Europe during WW II*: (Socio-political rights) Jews were victims of Nazi Anti-semitism before and during WW II. The Nazis removed their rights as citizens. The government ostracized, isolated, persecuted, detained them. It subjected them to forced labor, tortured and executed them in growing numbers. (Details on pgs. 269-270; also see *N&N's Ten Day Review*, Lesson 5.1)

- *Peasant farmers (campesinos) in Latin America*: (Economic rights) Campesinos are landless agricultural laborers. They work on large estates run in fashion similar to the feudal encomienda system of the Spanish colonial era. Lacking land and education, there is little incentive and their economic lives stagnate. (Details on pg. 177)

- *Women and children in the early Industrial Revolution*: (Economic rights) Children as young as 5 worked 14-16 hour days for only pennies. There were no safety protections, and the mills and mines were dirty and unventilated. Lung diseases, spinal deformities, and miscarriages were common. Governments did not become seriously involved until the later in the 19th C. (Details on pg. 239)

- *Kurds during the 20th Century*: (Political rights) The traditional area occupied by this Muslim ethnic community includes territories in Iran, Iraq, Syria, and Turkey in the southern Caucasus. They agitate for a defined homeland and self-determination. In Iraq, Saddam Hussein's government has subjected them to military raids and gas attacks. Other governments harass them and deny their rights. Governments destroy their villages in Iraq, Syria, and Turkey. The U.S. and U.N. have become involved in guarding their safety, but none of the nations involved wishes to give them territory.

- ***Dissidents in the Soviet Union under Stalin***: (Political rights) Stalin's brutal brand of totalitarianism allowed no dissent, especially from inside the Communist Party. No one could criticize the government. Stalin's NKVD agents (later KGB) rounded up even secret dissenters, and tortured them, subjected them to mock trials and executed or exiled them to gulags for long periods. (Details on pgs. 320, 324)

7 *Writing Strategy*: This essay examines your awareness of how events change regions and people. Select *three* events from those given. Set up *three* paragraphs. In *each* paragraph: A) use facts to describe the event as clearly as you can; B) explain how the event led to significant change for the nation/region.

- ***Voyages of Columbus***: A) <u>Event's Description</u>: Columbus was an Italian explorer working for Spain. He sought an all water passage to the Orient in the late 15th C. B) <u>Regional change in Latin America</u>: Began European conquest and settlement of the Americas. Native American civilizations were destroyed by conquistadors and disease. Iberian civilization absorbed these cultures and the blend shaped modern Latin American culture. (Details on pgs. 163-164)

- ***Glorious Revolution in England***: A) <u>Event's Description</u>: In 1688, Parliament exerted its power by deposing despot James II, and inviting William and Mary to share the English throne. B) <u>National change</u>: Parliament established its supremacy over the monarchy. Events such as this helped England evolve into a constitutional monarchy. Real power flows from the elected Parliament, which broadened from the Glorious Rev. into an indirect form of democracy. (Details on pg. 249)

- ***Failure of the Weimar Republic in Germany***: A) <u>Event's Description</u>: Following Germany's WW I defeat, the abdication of the Kaiser, left a weak central government. Used to autocracy, Germans lacked respect for the inefficiency of a multi-party coalition government. B) <u>National change</u>: Lack of confidence in the government structure led to economic difficulties as Germany tried to finance its post war reconstruction. It defaulted on foreign loans and the burdensome reparations leveled by the 1919 Paris Peace Treaty. These weaknesses, and the devastation of the Great Depression, led the rise of the Nazi dictatorship under Hitler. (Details on pgs. 269-270)

- ***Defeat of Japan in WW II***: A) <u>Event's Description</u>: After Japan's surrender, the American occupation under Gen. MacArthur rebuilt Japan's government and economy. B) <u>National change</u>: The Americans set up a constitutional monarchy, with a democratically elected Diet. The new government let women vote and have more economic rights. Labor unions were established. The constitution abolished war as an instrument of national policy. Unburdened of costly militarism, Japan grew to the second largest global economic power within a generation. (Details on pgs. 138, 144, 148)

- ***Westernization of Iran by Shah Pahlavi***: A) <u>Event's Description</u>: Beginning in the 1950's, the Shah spent huge amounts of Iran's oil income on infrastructure, industries, and schools. B) <u>National change</u>: The shah allowed women to vote, own property, and work outside the home. Often he forced traditional Muslim culture to blend with Western culture by decree. His secret police dealt with Islamic fundamentalist dissent and resistance harshly. By the 1970's, a Shi'ite Muslim Fundamentalist Movement gained enough momentum to force the Shah's exile and set up a traditional Islamic Republic. (Details on pg. 214)

- ***Signing of Camp David Accords by Egypt and Israel***: A) <u>Event's Description</u>: In 1979, Israel's Prime Minister Begin and Egypt's President Sadat signed a peace agreement under the guidance of U.S. President Carter. B) <u>Regional change</u>: The agreement led to withdrawal of Israeli troops from territory taken from Egypt in 1967 and 1973. It was also the first official recognition of Israeli nationhood by a neighboring Arab country. (Details on pg. 211)

- ***Adoption of glasnost in the Soviet Union***: A) <u>Event's Description</u>: In the late 1980's, Mikhail Gorbachev promoted a political policy of *glasnost* (openness & democratic action) to lay the groundwork for restructuring the Soviet economy. He desired to raise productivity and end frequent shortages and famines in his troubled nation. B) <u>National change</u>: The people of the U.S.S.R. experienced more democratic freedom. Gorbachev allowed new political parties, released political prisoners, and increased freedom to criticize the government. *Glasnost* diminished repression. However, the process destroyed the communist system and caused the Soviet Union to disintegrate into many separate nations. (Details on pgs. 290, 326-331)